The impact of the Troubles on the Republic of Ireland, 1968–79

MANCHESTER
1824

Manchester University Press

The impact of the Troubles on the Republic of Ireland, 1968–79

Brian Hanley

Manchester University Press

Published by Manchester University Press
Altrincham Street, Manchester M1 7JA, UK
www.manchesteruniversitypress.co.uk

British Library Cataloguing-in-Publication Data is available

ISBN 978 0 7190 9113 1 hardback
ISBN 978 1 5261 4363 1 paperback

First published by Manchester University Press in hardback 2018

This edition first published 2019

Typeset by Toppan Best-set Premedia Limited

For Cahir

Contents

Acknowledgements

This book has been longer in the writing than I planned, and the list of those who have assisted me in various ways (not all related directly to this work) is also long. I would like to thank (in no particular order):

Kelly Fitzgerald, Conor McCabe, Carole Holohan, John Dorney, Niamh Puirséil, Finbar Cullen, Paul Shannon, Scott Millar, Donal Fallon, Las Fallon, Sarah-Anne Buckley, Conor McNamara, Roisín Higgins, Sean Donnacha Lucey, Dave Browne, Brian Casey, Sam McGrath, Gavin Foster, Peter Rigney, Kevin O'Sullivan, Ida Milne, Tommy Graham, John Gibney, Georgina Laragy, Anne Dolan, Seán O'Hare, Martin Maguire, Richard McMahon, Charles Duggan, Ian Kenneally, Niall Carson, Ged Nash, John Horgan, Mícheál Ó Fathartaigh, Kate O'Malley, Diane Urquhart, Kevin Bean, Liam Weeks, Ciarán Swan, Emmet O'Connor, John Borgonovo, Francis Devine, Jimmy Kelly, Marc Gregan, Frank Keoghan, Vincent Browne, Niall Meehan, John Horne, Liz Gillis, Kevin Brannigan, Steven O'Connor, John Samuelsen, Padraig Yeates, Catherine Cox, Lindsey Earner-Byrne, Paul Rouse, Diarmaid Ferriter, Donal Ó Drisceoil, Niall Whelehan, Enda Delaney, Joe Mooney, Mags Glennon, Ado Perry, Cieran Perry, Fearghal McGarry, Gillian O'Brien, Brendan Donohue, Eddie Lawlor and Will Murphy.

As always the staff of libraries and archives deserve particular thanks.

At UCD Archives I was lucky enough to work with Kate Manning, Orna Somerville, Sarah Poutch and Meadhbh Murphy.

At the National Library I have been greatly assisted by Gerry Kavanagh, Fran Carroll, Glen Dunne, Lidia Laube, Lucy De Courcy and Bernie Metcalfe.

Thanks also to Máire Kennedy, Enda Leaney, Tara Doyle and Ellen Murphy at Dublin City Library and Archives.

Thanks to Anthony Hyland and Emma Lyons at UCD Department of History and especially to Tadhg Ó Hannrachain and Kate Breslin of UCD for their support at a difficult time.

I am exceptionally grateful to Paddy Mulroe for generously sharing his research and also to Dónal McAnallen, Rob Savage, John Johnston Kehoe, Gerard Madden and Alan Power for allowing me to use material of theirs.

The book would not have been completed at all without the support of my family; thanks to Paddy and Kay, Dara, Úna and Patricia.

Most of all I am indebted to Órla for her support while writing this book and especially to Cahir, for making life so enjoyable and putting academia in perspective.

A note on government, society and terminology

In October 1968, the Republic was governed by Fianna Fáil, who had been in power since 1957. The Taoiseach was Jack Lynch. In the election of June 1969, Fianna Fáil were returned with a majority. This administration was faced with the crisis of August 1969 and the resulting Arms Trial which brought the North centre stage for a period, as did Bloody Sunday in early 1972. In February 1973, a Fine Gael/Labour coalition, with Liam Cosgrave as Taoiseach, took power. Cosgrave's cabinet included Conor Cruise O'Brien, Paddy Donegan and Patrick Cooney, all implacable opponents of the IRA. The Coalition was associated in the public mind with a hard line against republicanism.

In 1977, Fianna Fáil won a shock overall majority, with over one million votes and 84 Dáil seats. In 1979, Jack Lynch resigned and was replaced as Taoiseach by Charles J. Haughey, who was popularly associated with a republican stance on the North.

The population of the Republic was 3,192,000 in 1977 and was growing and becoming younger. That year's election was the first time all those over 18 years of age could vote. Over 96% of the state's people were Catholic. Around 30% of the population lived in Dublin and its environs, while the number of people living in towns outnumbered that in rural areas for the first time during the 1970s. Over a quarter of the workforce were employed in agriculture, forestry or fishing at the beginning of the 1970s, while 30% worked in manufacturing and 43.5% in services. In 1973, over half of the Republic's imports and exports were with the United Kingdom.[1]

Terminology

Northern Ireland was often referred to as 'the North' or (by nationalists) as the 'Six Counties'. While the term 'Northern Ireland' itself implied recognition of that state and was therefore eschewed by republicans, by the 1970s it had become part of official discourse in the Republic of Ireland. The Republic was sometimes described by supporters of the IRA (and those from the North more generally) as the 'Free State' and by many people as the '26 Counties', or the south.

The republican movement had split between 1969 and 1970 into Official and Provisional organizations ('Stickies' and 'Provos'). In May 1972, the Official IRA declared a ceasefire (though it did not cease armed activity) and by the mid 1970s the main political focus, north and south, was on the Provisionals. For the sake of brevity in the text, where the Officials are concerned I signal that, but on other occasions 'Sinn Féin' and 'IRA' refer to the Provisionals.[2]

Notes

1 Basil Chubb, 'Society and the Political System' in Penniman, H. (Ed.) *Ireland at the Polls: the 1977 Dáil Elections* (Washington D.C., 1978) pp. 1–20.
2 For a fuller discussion of the Officials, see B. Hanley and S. Millar, *The Lost Revolution: The Story of the Official IRA and the Workers' Party* (Dublin, 2010).

Introduction

On Christmas Day 1971, Cardinal William Conway, the head of Ireland's Catholic Church, addressed Raidió Teleifís Éireann (RTE) television viewers. In sombre tones he told them that

> there is only one subject I can speak about, because it is in the forefront of my mind and, I've no doubt, many of yours. I refer to the tragic situation in the North which is already having repurcussions throughout the whole of Ireland ... I sometimes wonder if you realise how serious this situation could be – even for you. You know, time and again over the past three years when I have been in the Republic, the same thought has kept coming back to my mind again and again. I have been walking down O'Connell Street perhaps, colourful and crowded with people, the cars and the buses moving slowly along – 'life flowing by' – and time and again the thought has occurred to me: I wonder if these good people going in and out of the shops realise that all this busy normal life, which looks so natural and ordinary, is resting only on a crust and that underneath that crust there is a boiling volcano of potential violence: I wonder if they realise how thin that crust is and that when it breaks, and the lava of violence begins to flow on the streets, it's almost impossible to stop.[1]

Conway was not alone in his fears. Warnings of civil war were voiced regularly by trade unionists, journalists and politicians throughout the winter of 1971.[2] These worries were aroused in response to events north of the border. Ultimately, of course, war did not come, but the Northern conflict remained a central part of southern Irish life for the next 25 years.

During the early 1970s, my family lived in Laytown, near Drogheda. My father, along with his workmates, contributed weekly from their wages to the families of those interned in the North. My parents went to see groups like

The Barleycorn, whose hit 'The Men Behind The Wire', was hugely popular during the winter of 1971. But a few years later, living in Limerick, the North was not just more physically distant, but no longer worthy of as much sympathy. The violence there remained a constant feature of television and radio news, but often seemed inexplicable. I heard terms like 'Herrema', 'the Miami' and 'Heavy Gang' but did not understand what they meant. When the IRA were mentioned it was invariably stressed that they were not connected to the 'old IRA' of the War of Independence. But one morning I found a copy of *An Phoblacht/Republican News* on our kitchen table. Its headline 'IRA: Make Britain Pay' was shocking, referring as it did to the recent killing of Lord Mountbatten and 18 British soldiers, events which had brought the conflict back to the centre of everyday discussion. My mother had bought the paper the previous night from a local republican. So the IRA, whom I had only thought of in terms of the North, were obviously also somewhere closer to home. In general, however, my parents, like most of their contemporaries, only mentioned these events in the North in terms of exasperation or sadness. Nevertheless, to me it seemed the conflict was there, all the time.

Basing a book on distant childhood impressions is obviously problematic, especially since many Irish historians stress how *little* impact there was. Joseph Lee has claimed that what he tellingly refers to as 'the Northern virus' inevitably 'infected the Southern body politic' but the 'wonder is that it infected it so little for so long'.[3] John A. Murphy asserted as early as 1975 that 'the Northern troubles had amazingly little impact on the South' and that 'by and large, there was no popular involvement, if we except the emotional outburst and the burning of the British Embassy in Dublin after Bloody Sunday in Derry'.[4] Almost a decade later, Ronan Fanning wrote that it was remarkable 'not how much but how little the high drama of events in Northern Ireland since 1968 have impinged upon politics and society in the Republic'.[5] I have tried to examine the numerous occasions when the war produced popular mobilization across the southern state, when thousands of people were motivated to march, strike or protest at events in Northern Ireland. The conflict divided trade union branches, county council meetings, sporting events and religious congregations. Rival views produced intense and long-lasting fissures. Most dramatically, almost 100 people were killed and hundreds more injured as a result of the violence. Millions were spent on state security and armed soldiers became a common sight in towns across the country. For those living in border areas, the conflict was part of daily life. Politicians blamed the violence for encouraging crime, scaring off tourists, causing unemployment and damaging the economy. But it was also possible to live, as one Garda stationed in Galway recalled, where the atmosphere 'was so far removed from the troubles that … it was though the troubles didn't exist, other than what you heard on the radio or television'.[6] Everyday responses could be influenced by class and regional identity or by religion. Proximity to the border, experience of life in Northern Ireland or

Britain and memories of the War of Independence and Civil War could all affect attitudes.

In attempting to understand these views, it is as well to recognize that there are huge difficulties in reconstructing what people felt or thought. Eamonn McCann has argued that

> great issues don't loom large in our minds most of the time. The events and concerns which dominate public discourse – war and peace, poverty and plenty, cruel oppressions and contending moralities – we crowd these things into a corner of our consciousness. They may be the standard stuff of public pronouncements but they don't define us at all in the way we get through life. Most of our pleasure and almost all our pain has its source in our personal relationships. Nothing that happens in the headlines can send a shard of agony so deep into our being as the loss of someone that's loved or given us the holiday in our hearts that comes from the co-mingling of unrestrained affection. The papers don't provide a snapshot of life as we live and feel it.[7]

Any study dependent on state archives, newspaper reports and memoirs will be limited. It will inevitably, given the balance of society at the time, contain more men's voices than women's, more of those of elites and the middle class than the working class, and more of the politically active than those less involved.

Unlike political activists, most people have no problem holding contradictory opinions. They could march in solidarity with the victims of Bloody Sunday in early 1972 and be appalled by the Aldershot bombing a few weeks later. It might often have seemed, as one republican activist claimed about Dublin in the 1970s, that 'not too many gave a fuck ... nobody cared', but that would be too simplistic an analysis.[8] People who expressed little day-to-day interest in the North would still respond emotionally to events that connected with them. That is why, for example, the Miami Showband massacre could have a bigger impact than dozens of other incidents north of the border and indeed more than some of the killings in the Republic itself. I have tried to gauge attitudes from sources that have been relatively underused by scholars: the best-selling *Sunday World* (probably the most anti-establishment voice in the media), the local press (read by thousands in the 1970s), Sinn Féin's *An Phoblacht* and private letters to politicians.[9] The British Embassy were also perceptive, if sometimes patronizing, observers of southern Irish attitudes to the North, while the *Irish Press* vocalized popular republican views. But, unfortunately, the picture cannot be more than partial.

Any study of the Republic during the 1970s must reflect the fact that it was a period of uncertainty following the optimism of the 1960s. That decade was widely regarded as the 'most successful' in the 'recorded economic history of Ireland'.[10] But in early 1972, unemployment stood at 76,454 – the worst figure for 12 years.[11] Five years later, British diplomats noted that 'in terms of inflation, unemployment, investment and public debt, Ireland is worse off than any country in Western Europe'.[12] Along with economic trauma and industrial strife, the rise of all types of crime produced a sense of fear. Though the Northern conflict always lagged behind these issues in terms of electoral concern, there was a prevailing sense that it had interrupted an otherwise inevitable rise to prosperity. Indeed, many feared that it was the North and its troubles that was dragging the Republic backwards.[13]

Divisions between north and south were not new. In 1922, the Sinn Féin TD Seán Milroy complained that 'there is as little appreciation in Dublin and the South of the state of mind, and habit of thinking, and the point of view of the people in the North, as there is in the North of the people of the South'.[14] Similar views were heard on both sides of the Treaty split. Yet, until the 1970s, nobody in public life in the Republic of Ireland argued that partition was justified.[15] It was routinely denounced both as a crime against the nation's territorial integrity *and* 'our people' in the Six Counties. Sympathy with northern Catholics and hostility to Ulster Unionists was a given. Emotionally and politically the south claimed to want a united Ireland. Yet, faced with the reality of war, the Republic seemed to recoil. This further alienated Northern nationalists, who already felt they had been abandoned for the previous 50 years. These responses continue to inspire controversy today, even if some of the partisans in these debates have jettisoned their former positions. I hope to provide a context for some of these arguments as well as illustrating what was being said at the time.

In contrast to the historians quoted earlier, scholars are increasingly acknowledging the conflict's impact. Tom Dunne has admitted that the war 'was to overshadow all our lives, and to influence profoundly the kind of history my generation would write'.[16] John M. Regan has argued persuasively that the conflict deeply influenced Irish history writing.[17] Recent books by Eamonn Sweeney and Diarmaid Ferriter have included substantial appraisals of how the 'Troubles' affected the Republic.[18] Indeed, Ferriter suggests that the conflict 'defined the island of Ireland in the 1970s'.[19] I have tried to convey a sense of this, though I am conscious of many gaps in the narrative. I would hope that in-depth studies of how the trade unions, movements such as Irish feminism, organizations like the Gaelic Athletic Association (GAA) and institutions such as RTE were affected will emerge.[20]

Chapters 1 and 2 trace the reaction to events after October 1968 until the autumn of 1972, examining the impact of August 1969, the aftermath of internment and the response to Bloody Sunday. Chapter 3 looks at violence south of the border, particularly bombings and shootings and their human cost. Chapters 4 and 5 examine state security, censorship and the popular protests associated with these issues. Chapter 6 looks at changing attitudes to refugees and northern nationalists more generally. Chapter 7 describes the impact of the conflict on southern Protestants. Chapter 8 outlines the controversies concerning the IRA and their activities. In Chapter 9 I look at the question of revisionism and how debates about history were played out not just in academia but also at a popular level. Chapter 10 is a examination of a variety of social and cultural responses to the conflict, including attitudes to Britain and northern Unionists. The book begins with the aftermath of the civil rights march in Derry in October 1968 and concludes in 1979 when the prospect of an end to the conflict seemed dim. While there had been a euphoric reception in the south for Pope John Paul II, there was disappointment that his calls for peace were rejected. The election of Margaret Thatcher in Britain and the appointment of Charles Haughey as Taoiseach seemed to signal a new and more hostile phase in the relationship between the Republic and the United Kingdom.

While researching this book I have greatly benefitted from reading the work of Patrick Mulroe, Gerard Madden, Padraig McGuill, Dan Finn and Olan Long.[21] The analysis, conclusions (and mistakes) in this book, however, are all my own.

Notes

1 *Irish Times*, 25 Dec. 1971.
2 See Chapter 1.
3 J.J. Lee, *Modern Ireland, 1912–1985: Politics and Society* (Cambridge, 1989) p. 458.
4 J.A. Murphy, *Ireland in the Twentieth Century* (Dublin, 1975) p. 171.
5 R. Fanning, *Independent Ireland* (Dublin, 1983) p. 212.
6 Joe Lynch transcript, INCORE, www.green-and-blue.org.
7 *Hot Press*, 20 Oct. 1987.
8 J. Noonan, *What Do I Do Now?* (Dublin, 2005) p. 103.
9 Sixty-one percent of those who bought a national daily also read at least one local paper. C. Morash, *A History of the Media in Ireland* (Cambridge, 2010) p. 185.
10 T.J. Baker and J. Durkan, Quarterly Economic Commentary (ESRI, Dec. 1969). Quoted in C. McCarthy, *The Decade of Upheaval: Irish Trade Unions in the Nineteen Sixties* (Dublin, 1973) p. 25.
11 *Sunday Press*, 9 Jan. 1972.
12 Republic of Ireland Annual Review, 1 Jan. 1977, Foreign and Commonwealth Office (FCO) 87/603 National Archives United Kingdom (NAUK).
13 R. Perry, *Revisionist Scholarship and Modern Irish Politics* (London, 2013) p. 2.
14 M. Hopkinson, *Green against Green: The Irish Civil War* (Dublin, 1988) p. 88.
15 M. Daly, *Sixties Ireland: Reshaping the Economy, State and Society, 1957–63* (Cambridge, 2016) p. 376.
16 T. Dunne, *Rebellions: Memoir, Memory and 1798* (Dublin, 2004) p. 55.
17 J.M. Regan, *Myth and the Irish State* (Dublin, 2013).
18 D. Ferriter, *Ambiguous Republic: Ireland in the 1970s* (London, 2012). E. Sweeney, *Down, Down, Deeper and Down: Ireland in the 70s and 80s* (Dublin, 2010).
19 Ferriter, *Ambiguous*, p. 2.
20 For the Women's movement, see L. Connolly and T. O'Toole, *Documenting Irish Feminisms: The Second Wave* (Dublin, 2005) pp. 25–45. For the GAA, see M. Reynolds, 'The Gaelic Athletic Association and the 1981 H-Block hunger strike', *The International Journal of the History of Sport* 34 (June, 2017) pp. 1–20.

21 O. Long, 'The Land That Made Them Refugees: North-South Population Movements at the Outset of the Political Troubles, 1969–72' (MA: UCC, 2008). D. Finn, 'Challengers to Provisional Republicanism: The Official Republican Movement, People's Democracy and the Irish Republican Socialist Party, 1968–1998' (PhD: UCC, 2013). G. Madden, 'Political Change in Northern Ireland and its Impact on the West of Ireland, 1968–1982' (MA: NUI Galway, 2013). P. McGuill, 'Political Violence in the Republic of Ireland 1969–1997' (MA: UCD, 1998). P. Mulroe, 'The Gardaí, Violence and the Border: Irish Border Security Policy 1969–1978' (PhD: UU, 2015).

1

'Something deep was stirring'

Missiles, including petrol bombs, rained down on the British Embassy as protesters tried to force their way past Garda lines. But it was the crowd who were driven back and away from Merrion Square, some of them breaking windows in the Shelbourne Hotel as they went.[1] The violence took place on the night of Saturday 12 October 1968 and was the third such Dublin protest in the week following the batoning of civil rights marchers in Derry on 5 October.[2] The marchers had come from a rally at College Green, where 500 people had listened to republican and socialist speakers, including Eamonn McCann and Seamus Costello. Costello's party, Sinn Féin, had held their own meeting earlier in the week, and republicans had also organized a 600-strong march in Cork city.[3] A Labour party meeting, at which Belfast MP Gerry Fitt had given an emotional account of the Derry events, attracted the largest crowd of about 1,000. Fitt warned the Unionist government that if future protests were suppressed 'the people of Dublin, young men and women, will cross over the Border'. Dublin's Labour Lord Mayor Frank Cluskey promised 'the people of the North' that their 'days of abandonment are very near an end'.[4]

The focus for many protests over the next three years would be the Embassy at 39 Merrion Square, a four-storey building with the British Passport office located just a few doors away at No. 30. Securing it 'was always a head-ache as far as Gardai were concerned' as the public could walk up just five steps to the Embassy front door, which despite double-glazed windows with reinforced shutters was quite vulnerable, as future protests would show.[5]

'Rough and ruthless men'

The violence in Derry on 5 October, broadcast that evening on RTE news, dominated headlines in the Republic. Visiting the Fianna Fáil Taoiseach Jack

Lynch that week, Nationalist Party leader Eddie McAteer MP had called on the citizens of the 'deep south' to show their support for the people of Derry.[6] Several county councils passed motions pledging solidarity with northern nationalists.[7] The opposition Fine Gael party, 'shocked at the violence against a peaceful demonstration', sent its two Donegal TDs to Derry to gather first-hand accounts.[8] Derry had focused attention on civil rights just as the Republic was preoccupied with an attempt by the government to replace the proportional representation (PR) voting system. A referendum to endorse that change was due to take place on 16 October. Critics noted that without PR, Fianna Fáil would be guaranteed electoral dominance. Campaigners also stressed that the *introduction* of PR was one of the demands of civil rights protesters in the North. Labour's Barry Desmond asserted that 'if P.R. is abolished ... the cities of our Republic will be carved up in the same manner as the notorious ward system of Derry'. Tom O'Higgins of Fine Gael compared Fianna Fáil to the Ulster Unionist party, both run by 'rough and ruthless men ... determined to maintain themselves in office for as long as possible'.[9] Embarrassingly, the government was humiliated in the referendum.[10] To make matters worse, their republican credentials were also called into question. Lynch's administration had followed that of Sean Lemass in seeking cooperation with the Northern government.[11]

Now, Labour leader Brendan Corish alleged that the government's failure to defend nationalists revealed as 'fiction' the 'Fianna Fáil claim that they in some way represent the Republican tradition'. Patrick Lindsay of Fine Gael asked 'what has the Fianna Fáil Party done about partition since 1932? Nothing.' Labour TD Michael Mullen, a senior figure in the Irish Transport and Workers Union, complained that 'we seem to have stalled in this part of Ireland on the important matter of abolishing partition'.[12] Soon, leading Fianna Fáil figures, such as Neil Blaney and Kevin Boland, began to take a more militantly anti-partitionist line.[13] In Letterkenny during November, Blaney reiterated the 'right of the Irish people in their homeland to be united and free' a message that evidently struck a chord with many Fianna Fáil activists.[14]

'The struggle is the same'

For radicals, the referendum result and the growing crisis in the North seemed to confirm the belief of *Irish Times* political correspondent Michael McInerney that 'something deep was stirring in the whole of Ireland'.[15] At Sinn Féin's Ard Fheis in December, party president Tomas Mac Giolla claimed that the 'slumbering and despairing Irish nation has suddenly awakened' and was 'witnessing what we hope is the beginning of the disintegration of two old and corrupt parties in Belfast and Dublin'.[16] Activists would continue to liken Fianna Fáil's administration to that at Stormont. In January 1969, Labour's Noel Browne compared a new Criminal Justice Bill to Northern Ireland's Special Powers legislation.[17] His colleague, Conor Cruise O'Brien, described the same bill as an 'encouragement to the Unionist Party in its continuing denial of civil rights in the Six Counties'.[18] As housing protesters took to the streets of Dublin, their counterparts occupying Derry's Guildhall asserted that 'the struggle is the same: North and South'. Civil rights committees sprang up concerned with the Gaeltacht, local democracy and itinerant rights as well as the North.[19]

The attack on the People's Democracy march at Burntollet and the subsequent rioting in Derry produced another wave of indignation. There were minor scuffles when hundreds of housing marchers joined a demonstration at the British Embassy to support a civil rights demonstration in Newry.[20] Again bringing first-hand accounts of the events, this time to the Labour party conference, Gerry Fitt asserted that 'any Labour leader who is intimidated by the sight of a baton, whether it be wielded by an RUC man or a member of the Garda is unworthy of the name of Labour'.[21] During April, over 4,000 attended a rally at the GPO organized to welcome a People's Democracy march from Belfast. Later, 800 marched to the British Embassy, which had some of its windows damaged by stones. While the march was welcomed by a variety of far-left groups, the reaction of onlookers in Dublin's inner-city was described as 'at best friendly and at worst uncomprehending'. Indeed, some of the marchers themselves expressed confusion over the march's primary objective; support for civil rights or opposition to both states.[22] In the same month, student activists occupied the British Passport Office in solidarity with people in Derry, where clashes had erupted again. They were removed by a large force of Gardaí.[23]

'Total lack of interest'

But outside of the relatively small ranks of republicans and leftists, how important was the North to the average southerner? According to the first Gallup survey of Irish attitudes in 1968, 41% of southern respondents had visited Northern Ireland in the previous two years and one in five had been there more than once; 81% of respondents desired a united Ireland, but belief in the use of force to achieve it was 'confined to a very small minority' of only 2%.[24] Despite the upheavals of the previous five months, another poll in April 1969 found that there was an almost 'total lack of interest in Northern Ireland as a national problem'. Only 1% of respondents identified 'Northern Ireland/Border/Partition' as the most important issue facing the country, while 'Cost of Living' (28%), 'Labour Relations/Unions/Strikes' (24%) and 'Unemployment' (20%) rated far higher; 70% believed Northern Ireland should be allowed solve its own problems, though 19% desired greater intervention by the Irish Government. There were only tiny differences in responses according to social background. Small farmers were more inclined to want intervention, as were Fianna Fáil voters, while Dublin respondents tended to be the most 'non-interventionist'.[25]

The lack of popular interest was reflected in the minor role that the North played in the Republic's general election in June. One senior Fianna Fáil figure remembered that the issue 'scarcely figured in public debates'.[26] The most emotive rhetoric of that campaign was the widespread use of 'red scare' tactics by the government against a Labour party that was depicted as being composed of 'extreme left-wing socialists preaching class warfare'.[27] Despite the hopes of the previous winter, Fianna Fáil won a comfortable majority while Labour's leftist rhetoric was thought to have lost its support.[28]

'No longer stand by'

At this stage, republicanism impinged on the public consciousness mainly through the IRA's activities in the Republic. A spate of attacks on foreign-owned properties brought strong responses from the Fianna Fáil-supporting *Irish Press*. Describing them as a 'Warsaw Pact minded onslaught', it warned that IRA activity would 'land us in the red, both politically and in terms of the shedding of Irish blood and reputations'.[29] But soon the North was back centre stage and drew numbers far beyond republican ranks onto the streets. In Derry, the Battle of the Bogside raged from Tuesday 12 to Thursday 14 August. At 9pm on the night of Wednesday 13, Lynch gave a special address on RTE. His message that the government could 'no longer stand by and see innocent people injured or worse' and the news that army field hospitals were being established near the border seemed to promise intervention. That evening, 2,500 people attended a Sinn Féin rally at Dublin's General Post Office (GPO), which heard demands that the 'Government use all resources at their disposal, including military force ... to defend the people of the Six Counties'.[30] The crowd swelled to about 4,000 as it marched on the British Embassy. Though some stones were thrown at that building, stewards guided the protesters away to Leinster House.

'We want guns'

The situation in Derry seemed to have calmed by Thursday 14, but Belfast had exploded, with reports suggesting that Catholics were being massacred. Television screens showed 'street after street of houses on fire – people streaming out of their homes carrying bundles of clothes ... women and children crying – men trying to put out the fires and gunfire in the background'.[31] At lunchtime on Friday 15, 400 people gathered outside the Embassy, including dockers who had stopped work in protest. Labour TD Michael O'Leary complained to Embassy staff about the 'provocative' display of a Union Flag in celebration of Princess Anne's birthday. The flag was torn down and burnt, while a tricolour was hoisted on a nearby lampost and Embassy windows broken by stones. That evening, 3,000 joined another Sinn Féin protest at the GPO. Tomas Mac Giolla claimed that the IRA had been in action in Belfast, but they needed arms, and that if the Irish Army would not use their weapons to defend the people, then they should 'give them to us'. After the rally, most of the crowd marched down the quays to Collin's barracks and demanded weapons. There were clashes with Gardai before they dispersed. The rally had also heard a call for volunteers to go north, with the promise of transport in Parnell Square.[32] Over 150 people, many of them teenagers, boarded buses, which arrived in Dundalk in the early hours of the morning. The town had earlier seen a march of 2,000, but was now quiet. Amid scenes of confusion, some of the group went to Dundalk barracks, while others boarded a truck and headed for the border.[33]

By Saturday 16, at least seven people had died in Northern violence and hundreds had been forced from their homes. That day saw 'almost continous demonstrations' in Dublin city centre. By the evening, crowds filled 'two-thirds of O'Connell Street' where they were addressed by, among others, three Northern MPs.[34] Paddy Devlin told protesters that the 'only way we can defend ourselves is with guns ... we need them'.[35] Chants of 'we want guns' interrupted several of the speeches, and at one point a man produced a pistol and waved it in the air. After 8pm, some 2,000 people marched to Merrion Square, where they made a determined effort to reach the Embassy. Petrol bombs and stones were thrown at Gardai and a garage was damaged in a quest for ammunition. The United Dominions Trust offices were invaded by protesters and furniture removed for barricades. Gardai baton-charged the crowd and forced them back towards the city centre, but clashes continued as teenagers and people leaving pubs and cinemas joined in the fighting. Gardai were taunted as 'Gestapo, B Special bastards' and pelted with missiles. Over 50 people, including 16 Gardai, were injured and 60 shop windows smashed as trouble continued until 3am.[36]

'Gurriers'

On Sunday 17, the tricolour flew at half-mast over Croke Park where the All-Ireland football semi-final was taking place. GAA president Séamus Ó Riain addressed the crowd, expressing support for 'our people in the Six-County area' and 'their struggle against oppression'. There was a minute's silence for those who had been killed.[37] Meanwhile, 1,000 people attended a rally at the GPO where speakers warned against further trouble. University College Dublin (UCD) lecturer Liam de Paor described those involved in the previous nights violence as 'gurriers', while a statement from the visiting Northern MPs condemned 'squalid incidents of flag-burning, rioting and public incitment in Dublin'. Despite this, several hundred people tried to hold a sit-down in

O'Connell Street. When Gardai attempted to disperse them, they were joined by large numbers of teenagers who began smashing windows. Litter bins were used as impromtu barricades, cars pelted with stones and several shops looted. Observers claimed that people were batoned indiscriminately. A priest described Gardai engaging in an 'uncontrolled and half-frenzied race down the street ... flattening anyone who happened to be slow of pace'. In response, one Garda explained that 'we have been out for three nights and our men are very fatigued. This crowd is just looking for trouble and people are deliberately provoking us.'[38]

'Give everything needed'

Sinn Féin disclaimed involvement in the clashes, and the newly formed National Solidarity Committee cancelled a rally planned for Monday night to avoid more trouble. By then, the arrival of British troops seemed to have brought an end to the violence in Belfast. But across the country protest meetings, generally organized by republicans (sometimes in cooperation with the left), continued. The president of the Union of Students in Ireland, Ciaran McKeown, called for Irish troops to occupy one of the border counties in order to create an international incident and force United Nations intervention.[39] Men boarded a British vessel at Burtonport and burned its ensign.[40] Dock workers in Galway struck and joined Irish Transport and General Workers Union (ITGWU) members in marching to a protest rally in Eyre Square. Dockers and meat factory workers in Sligo also took unofficial action demanding that the Irish Army intervene.[41] At a special meeting of the Dublin Council of Trade Unions, Matt Merrigan of the Amalgamated Transport and General Workers Union (ATGWU) called for military intervention to force the UN to take action. George O'Malley of the ITGWU asked that Dublin trade unionists 'dig into their pockets and give everything needed, perhaps even arms'.[42] The arrival of refugees provided a new focus.[43] In several areas relief committees were formed and a National Relief Fund Coordination Committee was set up with lawyer and former Fine Gael TD Declan Costello as chairman. The committee included Michael Mullen, as well as Labour party general secretary Brendan Halligan and Fine Gael TD T.F. O'Higgins. It was supported by Muintir na Tíre, the National Association of Tenants Organisations, student groups and Catholic, Protestant and Jewish clergy.[44] Mullen had already visited ITGWU branches in Belfast and Derry, but he returned again with Costello in late August to oversee plans for distributing funds. Dublin businessman Dermot Ryan, with the support of former Taoiseach Sean Lemass, established a Northern Ireland Interdenominational Association for 'stricken families' and raised £3,000 within a few days.[45] The government urged that money be channelled through the Red Cross which had collected £1,263 in 48 hours. The Dublin Council of Trade Unions, the Limerick Archconfraternity, the GAA and the republican movement were all collecting money, medical supplies and provisions.[46]

'A step backwards'

While there was widespread recognition that many nationalists had welcomed British troops, ITGWU president Fintan Kennedy made clear that his union could never 'accept that part of our country be occupied'.[47] Fine Gael leader Liam Cosgrave bemoaned the arrival of the 'largest British Army in this country since they surrendered Dublin Castle to Michael Collins in 1922' and asserted that this was 'a step backwards that can never be welcomed'.[48] Not surprisingly, many drew the conclusion that a final reckoning over partition was near. *The Kerryman* newspaper contended that 'any attack on Unionist privilege is an attack on the Border *per se* and at least the Unionists are clever enough to see this'. The paper asserted that it was 'time that the pussyfooting ceased … Ireland was one country, one people even down to the Paisleyites'.[49]

'A notoriously emotional people'

In mid-August, several Labour TDs and senators visited Belfast, Armagh and Derry. Cruise O'Brien noted how 'the courage, determination and tactical skill of the Bogsiders' had succeeded in creating an area in which Stormont's writ no longer ran.[50] Monaghan Fine Gael TDs Billy Fox and John Conlon had also gone to the Bogside and the Falls during August. Young radicals from the south were drawn to the barricades, particularly in Free Derry. In late August, a 'Liberation Fleadh' was held there featuring The Dubliners and Tommy Makem, while RTE's Shay Healy and the popular children's show 'Wanderly Wagon' also performed.[51] Away from most people's attention, the republican movement was recruiting and continuing to re-arm, while a political crisis was brewing at cabinet level. Dublin and Belfast buzzed with rumours of arms shipments and promises of funding for the IRA. The British Ambassador Andrew Gilchrist had worried during August what the events would provoke among 'a notoriously emotional people' like the Irish, speculating that if he 'were a fire insurance company I would not like to have the British Embassy on my books'.[52] But by late September street activity had declined, and the numbers engaging in militant politics, as opposed to relief efforts, were still small. For many of those who had responded in August, however, those events were obscured. John Noonan, a 16-year-old from Finglas, had attended several rallies during August. He volunteered for work with Sinn Féin, who established their own relief centre in Parnell Square. With others he 'made sandwiches, soup and tea, and generally whatever was asked of me'. By September, however, he found that 'things appeared to settle down (and) I drifted back to normal life – back with all the lads playing football on the street'.[53] Nevertheless, he was one of many people who had been radicalized.[54]

'Wild men in the South'

The clashes in Dublin had shown that there were some, particularly the young, who had little compunction about fighting the Gardai. The *Irish Press* warned about 'wild men in the South' who had shown 'their influence in acts of hooliganism around the streets of Dublin'.[55] Sligo Fianna Fáil TD Ray McSharry asserted that 'wild-cat displays' such as strike action were of 'no benefit to the people in the North'. Instead, people should 'fall in line' with the government.[56] Some were expressing worries about escalation. During November, Margaret Tynan, the Fine Gael Mayor of Kilkenny, asked 'do we want the North? Can we afford the North? Does the North want to come in? Clearly we could not afford subsidies to the North of the magnitude of British subsidies.'[57] The attitude of some northern radicals was also causing concern. During the winter, republicans organized a whistle-stop tour of the south-west for Bernadette Devlin, the charismatic young MP for Mid-Ulster. Speaking to 2,000 people in Limerick, Devlin explained that 'the things that had brought the people of the North onto the streets were in existence in the South … if Mr. Lynch had sent one soldier across the Border he would not have been welcome because the things that people in the North were fighting against were in existence in the South'.[58] Many of Devlin's audience may have been confused by this assertion. Sending troops across the border was exactly what most of those who had taken to the streets in August were demanding. The *Limerick Leader* was also upset by the MP's comparison of Gardai to the B-Specials and warned that 'the sooner Miss Devlin realises the seriousness of the damage she is doing then the better for everyone in this country'.[59] But the language of politics in the Republic was being transformed by the northern events. During a dispute over the closure of a village school on the Limerick/Clare border, protesters claimed that while there was 'Civil Rights in the North' they faced 'dictatorship in the South'. When confronted by the same campaigners, Limerick Fianna Fáil TD Desmond O'Malley pointedly asked them 'are you the Paisleyites?'[60]

'Massive support for Lynch'

By the spring of 1970, the IRA had split into Official and Provisional wings, and the crisis over political involvement in gun-running was public knowledge. During May, Lynch dismissed two government ministers, Charles Haughey and Neil Blaney, who were suspected of channelling funds for arms. Blaney, in particular, became a focus for nationalist sentiment. He returned to his native

Donegal to 'a welcome for a hero' after travelling in a 100-car cavalcade from Monaghan through Northern Ireland and into Letterkenny. Blaney told the 7,000-strong crowd that 'we will not rest until ... the reunification of this country'.[61] Despite this enthusiasm, an Irish Marketing Surveys poll of 1,000 adults for *This Week* magazine found 'massive support for Lynch': 82% of respondents favoured him as Taoiseach compared to just 3% for Blaney and 3% for Haughey, while 75% agreed that Lynch was right to sack Blaney. Asked if there were a repeat of the August violence should Irish troops intervene, a substantial minority of 17% were in favour, but a very large majority of 77% against; 83% were opposed to arms being supplied to nationalists, with only 11% in favour. Had the poll been conducted in the autumn of 1969 the results would no doubt have been different, but feelings were no longer running as high.[62] Attitudes towards violence may also have been influenced by the killing of Garda Richard Fallon in a robbery in Dublin during April. Described by the *Irish Press* as 'an act of murderous anarchy' it was the first such incident since the 1940s and caused widespread outrage.[63]

Escalation

Feelings were clearly influenced by the tempo of events in the North. On the ground, republicans and a variety of left-wing groups continued agitation. The British Embassy was the target of protests throughout the spring. One hundred had taken part in an Official Sinn Féin protest during February, while supporters occupied the nearby passport office on two occasions to raise the issue of IRA prisoners in Britain.[64] By the summer of 1970, renewed inter-communal violence and the first major confrontations between nationalists and the British army produced another wave of street activity. In late June, 1,200 gathered in Merrion Square demanding the release of the recently jailed Bernadette Devlin. At this meeting, Seamus Costello appealed for recruits to the IRA.[65] Within a week the British army had shot dead four civilians and wrecked hundreds of homes during the Falls Road curfew, a key moment in the alienation of nationalists from the state. Hundreds of refugees again arrived across the border.

Over the next 12 months, violence escalated. By July 1971, 26 people had been killed and bombings were a daily occurrence, especially in Belfast. Many of those who died were civilians shot by the British army and regular television footage of soldiers in riot gear confronting nationalists produced visceral responses in the south. Republicans stepped up activity, both public and covert. Protests against visiting British dignitaries or aimed at targets associated with Britain continued on a regular basis. British Rail offices in Cork were occupied during a demonstration against the visit of the Lord Mayor of London to the city. A few days later, the office's windows were smashed. In Limerick, four people were injured during scuffles as 150 demonstrators protested outside a reception for London's Mayor.[66] There was also a series of bomb and arson attacks on British targets.[67] During the spring of 1971, disaffected Fianna Fáil activists left that party claiming that it had 'reneged on its Republican principles'.[68] They increasingly rallied around Kevin Boland, who had resigned from the cabinet in protest at the sacking of Blaney and Haughey.[69]

'Up the UVF'

There was a taste of the reality of inter-communal strife as Belfast's Linfield FC played south of the border in the Blaxnit trophy during May. At Lourdes stadium in Drogheda, fans invaded the terrace where Linfield's support were gathered and seized and burned a Union Jack. The two groups exchanged stones until Gardai brought the situation under control, while the Drogheda fans sang 'Amhrán na bhFiann'.[70] Linfield played Cork Hibernians a week later at Dublin's Dalymount Park and more serious trouble ensued. Linfield supporters waved Union Jacks and chanted 'Up the UVF' (Ulster Volunteer Force) at their rivals. The Cork fans replied with chants of 'IRA' and republican songs. Bottles and stones were thrown and Gardai baton-charged supporters inside and outside the ground.[71]

'If you are prepared to take up arms there is a place for you'[72]

These incidents were dwarfed by the popular reaction to the introduction of internment during the early hours of Monday 9 August. Just as in 1969, a huge effort was put into providing aid for the 5,000 refugees who crossed the border, many bringing stories of British brutality and loyalist violence.[73] News soon emerged of the ill-treatment of detainees. Despite the historic use of internment by the southern state, reaction to its introduction by Stormont was universally hostile, local newspapers comparing it to British colonial policy and even to Nazi Germany.[74] The evening of 9 August saw 400 join an Official Sinn Féin protest at the British Embassy. Mac Giolla told the crowd that they had not come to burn the building but 'if we had done … we would have come prepared and there would be no trouble at all doing it'. A rival meeting at the GPO heard calls to join the Provisionals.[75] The following three nights saw crowds of up to 2,000 gather at the GPO carrying placards asserting 'military camps open for refugees – open the arsenals too'. Provisional Sinn Féin's Ruairí Ó Brádaigh told crowds that 'the fight by our blood brothers in the North is our fight'.[76] One thousand attended a protest in Cork city where Jack Lynch of the Official IRA asked that 'anyone that wants to help … give us guns'. A thousand marched in Galway led by the university Republican Club. There were dozens of protest meetings organized by republicans in Tralee, Kilkenny, Cavan, Monaghan and Donegal.[77] Belfast Provisional John

Kelly told 1,000 people in Navan that 'if you are prepared to take up arms there is a place for you'.[78]

'Financial, moral and all other necessary support'

The Union of Students in Ireland (USI) called for the government to suspend diplomatic relations with Britain, and the Ballymun Tenants Association was one of several bodies calling for a boycott of British goods.[79] There were pickets on British banks and calls for protest strikes from, among others, the Lifford Labour party and several union branches.[80] Dozens of local councils unanimously passed motions condemning internment and demanding action by the government.[81] After passing a Provisional Sinn Féin motion demanding British withdrawal, Galway County Council heard Fine Gael's Paddy Collins warn that 'the same tactics that were used from 1916 to 1922 are being used again in the North. I lived and suffered during that period. The British preach liberty for small nations, but they don't practice it here. There is no security for our people in the North ... '[82] Addressing 35,000 people at the All-Ireland semi-final, GAA general secretary Seán O Síocháin promised 'financial, moral and all other necessary support' for the minority population in the Six Counties.[83] Four and a half thousand pounds was raised from raffles at Croke Park alone. The GAA designated the first Sunday of October 'Northern Relief Day' and county boards were instructed to organize as many fundraising games as possible, while blanket permission was granted by Gardai for church gate collections.[84] Every part of the state saw fundraising dances, parish walks and house-to-house collections.[85] Both IRAs were holding their own street and pub collections, sometimes openly asking for money for arms.[86] A broad-based Association of Committees for Aiding Internees Dependents was also established.[87]

'The Men Behind The Wire'

The trade unions were among the most active in responding. The ITGWU estimated that at least 34 of its members had been interned.[88] It supported an appeal by the Dublin Trades Council for workers to donate one hour's pay weekly to a Six County Internees Dependents Fund.[89] By winter, thousands were contributing.[90] In late August, 2,000 joined a march organized by the Committee of Trade Unionists Opposed to Internment, representing 200 Dublin shop stewards from various industries. When the march reached the Embassy, there were scuffles with Gardai, the Union Jack was burned and bottles thrown.[91] A few days later, Dublin Corporation workers marched to the Embassy to hand in an anti-internment petition and a call for the release of republican prisoners held in Britain. Trades councils in other areas also organized public protests.[92] Demonstrations at the Embassy continued throughout the winter. During August, 50 deaf people marched to protest at the shooting dead by British soldiers of Eamon McDevitt, a deaf man, in Strabane.[93] Maynooth clerical students held a 48-hour fast at the Embassy in November.[94] Three hundred students from St. Mary's and St. Joseph's teacher training colleges in Belfast marched to the Embassy after holding a 'freedom concert' at the GPO where they were joined by trainee teachers from Dublin's St. Patrick's College and UCD.[95] More overtly republican protests also took place, with 500 Provisional supporters rallying at the GPO during their Ard Fheis in October.[96] Early that month the anti-internment song 'Free The People' by the Dubliners had reached No. 7 in the charts.[97] But it was the Barleycorn's 'The Men Behind The Wire', released in December, that became the anthem of protest. It reached No. 1 in the Republic's charts in January 1972 and had sold 100,000 copies within months.[98]

'The risen people'

In September, over 1,000 attended the launch of Aontacht Éireann in Dublin. Led by Kevin Boland, the 'new and truly Republican party' asserted that it would support in 'every possible way the risen people of the Six Counties'.[99] The Provisionals were also displaying growing confidence. In the midst of protests after internment, one Cork Provo swore that 'we are determined to go out next Easter and put an epitaph on the grave of Robert Emmett'.[100] Over 5,000 people were present at a rally in that city during October, at which the Provisional IRA Chief of Staff Seán Mac Stíofáin spoke. With him was veteran republican Tomas MacCurtain, son of the martyred Lord Mayor of 1920. MacCurtain asserted the Irish were facing 'the same enemy that our fathers and uncles fought here 50 years ago – and, please God, we'll beat them again'.[101] In late October, a group of political, business and academic figures wrote to British officials warning them that their government's policies

> have had a profound and deeply disturbing impact in the Republic. The strength of support for and tolerance of IRA activities in Northern Ireland – and indeed in the Republic itself – has grown enormously, stimulated first by internment and then by reports of torture and ill-treatment of internees and detainees, of shooting by the British Army of people who have not been IRA activists, and the blowing up of Border roads … the situation in the Republic will, it is believed, deteriorate further and the ability of democratic leaders to control this situation will be seriously weakened. Time is now running against the moderates in the Republic as it has run against the moderates in Northern Ireland.[102]

In Dublin for Christmas 1971, historian Leland Lyons 'got … the feeling' that 'constitutional government itself might be in danger in the Republic'.[103] Though the British Ambassador John Peck reflected that 'Dublin remains for the English a friendly, civilised and orderly city' he could not tell 'whether this will be true in a year's time'. He also believed that many 'Irishmen of property and substance' were increasingly worried, not least because 'throughout the centuries, in times of economic and social unrest, the disgruntled and envious have tended to have a box of matches handy'.[104] That view was echoed by *Hibernia* magazine, which claimed that 'the spirit of revolt in the North has deeply infected the South and the constant T.V. reportage of resistance to forces of "law and order" has not been lost upon the disenchanted, south of the Border.'[105] A class of Garda recruits at Templemore were told that they were either 'very brave men or very stupid' because, according to the officer lecturing them, it looked likely 'there could be a civil war in this country'.[106]

'Slide down the hill to civil war'

The hardening of attitudes was apparent in a *Kerryman* editorial which stated that

> whatever our individual views about the methods, the sympathy of the people of the Twenty-Six Counties generally is with the minority who, in certain areas, are taking a terrific scourging and are paying as far as they can back in kind ... The British forces and their friends in the Six Counties are fighting not only people of native stock but history and geography as well (and) while these six counties are cut off from the rest of Ireland ... there can be no lasting peace.[107]

Others, however, were less sure about whether the price was one worth paying. By the year's end, 180 people were dead. The indiscriminate nature of some of the bombings in Belfast were particuarly shocking.[108] In the south there was also increasing violent activity, with bombs and arson aimed at British targets. Armed robberies, assumed to be carried out by paramilitaries, were becoming frequent and there had been several killings. During November, Derry nationalist MP Ivan Cooper warned a Mayo audience that the conflict 'would not stop at Newry nor Derry, but would spill over all Ireland and leave death and destruction in its wake'.[109] The ITGWU's vice-president John Carroll told trade unionists that 'Ireland today hovers on the brink of civil war'.[110] Journalist John Healy suggested that 'little by little the pus from the running wound of the Northern crisis seeps into our affairs ... this is the way a nation starts to slide down the hill to civil war'.[111] Many others, including Fine Gael's Paddy Cooney and Joe Brennan of Fianna Fáil, used this emotive term during the winter.[112] There were also those, however, who appeared less worried at the prospect, Tuam Fianna Fáil Councillor PM Stapleton telling a meeting that 'if it takes a civil war to solve this, lets have it and get over with it'.[113]

'An act of treachery'

The year ended with the 'first serious clash' between Gardai and republicans since 1969. The *Irish Press* described events in Ballyshannon, Co. Donegal as 'a warning of how very easily the Northern troubles can spill over into the South'. Three men were arrested on suspicion of IRA activities. On 22 December, up to 500 people, including some who arrived from Longford and Derry, besieged the town's Garda station. In order to prevent the men being transferred to Dublin, barricades were erected, a bus commandeered, the Erne bridge blocked and, it was alleged, shopkeepers ordered to close their premises. Gardai clashed violently with the protesters and during baton charges shop windows were smashed. Troops from the nearby Finner camp were called in as back up and soldiers removed the barricades and set up their own checkpoints around the town.[114] This was the first time since the 1930s that the Irish Army had been used to maintain public order. The Provisionals described the troops' role as an 'act of treachery', while local opinion divided sharply on the events.[115] The clashes were a portent of the coming year.

Notes

1 *Irish Times*, 14 Oct. 1968.
2 *United Irishman*, Nov. 1968.
3 *Irish Times*, 9 Oct. 1968.
4 *Irish Press*, 10 Oct. 1968.
5 Superintendent B. Clinton, 6 April 1972, in Department of Justice (D/J) 2003/26/6 National Archives of Ireland (NAI).
6 *Irish Times*, 9 Oct. 1968.
7 Ibid., 8 Oct. 1968.
8 Ibid.
9 *Irish Times*, 10 Oct. 1968.
10 *Irish Press*, 18 Oct. 1968.
11 S. Kelly, *Fianna Fáil, Partition and Northern Ireland, 1926–1971* (Dublin, 2013) p. 297.
12 *Irish Times*, 8 Oct. 1968.
13 Kelly, *Fianna Fáil*, pp. 297–301.
14 *Irish Press*, 9 Nov. 1968.
15 *Nusight*, Jan. 1969.
16 *United Irishman*, Dec. 1968.
17 *Irish Times*, 9 Jan. 1969.
18 Ibid., 8 Jan. 1969.
19 Ibid., 28 Jan. 1969. G. Madden, 'Political Change', pp. 21–22.
20 *Irish Times*, 13 Jan. 1969.
21 Ibid., 27 Jan. 1969.
22 Ibid., 8 April 1969.
23 Ibid., 22 April 1969.
24 *Irish Press*, 26 April 1968.
25 *Nusight*, April 1970.
26 P. Faulkner, *As I Saw It: Reviewing Over 30 Years of Fianna Fáil & Irish Politics* (Dublin, 2005) p. 85.
27 N. Puirséil, *The Irish Labour Party, 1922–73* (Dublin, 2007) pp. 264–269.
28 D. Keogh, *Jack Lynch: A Biography* (Dublin, 2008) pp. 155–158. J. O'Brien, *The Arms Trial* (Dublin, 2000) pp. 29–30.
29 *Irish Press*, 12 June 1969.

30 *Irish Times*, 14 Aug. 1969.
31 Noonan, *What,* p. 29.
32 Hanley and Millar, *Revolution,* pp. 131–132.
33 *Irish Times*, 16 Aug. 1969.
34 The MPs were Paddy Kennedy, Paddy O'Hanlon and Paddy Devlin.
35 *Sunday Independent*, 17 Aug. 1969.
36 *Irish Press*, 18 Aug. 1969. *Irish Independent* 19 Aug. 1969.
37 Ibid., 18 Aug. 1969.
38 *Irish Times*, 18 Aug. 1969.
39 *Trinity News*, 23 Oct. 1969.
40 *Irish Press*, 19 Aug. 1969.
41 G. Madden, 'Political Change', p. 28.
42 *Irish Times*, 18 Aug. 1969.
43 Ibid., 21 Aug. 1969.
44 *Irish Press*, 23 Aug. 1969.
45 *Irish Times*, 19 Aug. 1969.
46 Ibid., 20 Aug. 1969.
47 *Liberty*, Sept. 1969.
48 *Irish Times*, 20 Aug. 1969.
49 *The Kerryman*, 13 Sept. 1969.
50 *Sunday Independent*, 17 Aug. 1969. Report, 26 Aug. 1969, Conor Cruise O'Brien Papers, P82/219 University College Dublin Archives (UCDA).
51 *Irish Press*, 30 Aug. 1969.
52 Kelly, *Fianna Fáil,* p. 303.
53 Noonan, *What,* pp. 30–32.
54 K. Conway, *Southside Provisional: From Freedom Fighter to the Four Courts* (Dublin, 2014) p. 11.
55 *Irish Press*, 21 Aug. 1969.
56 *Western People*, 23 Aug. 1969.
57 *Irish Times*, 3 Nov. 1969.
58 Ibid., 1 Dec. 1969.
59 *Limerick Leader*, 17 Jan. 1969.
60 *Nusight*, Nov. 1969.
61 *Donegal News*, 16 May 1970.
62 *This Week*, 5 and 19 June 1970.
63 *Irish Press*, 4 April 1970.
64 *Irish Times*, 3 and 26 Feb. 1970.
65 Ibid., 29 June 1970.
66 *Irish Independent*, 19 May 1971. *Irish Press*, 20 May 1971.
67 See Chapter 3.
68 *Hibernia*, 27 April 1971; *Irish Times* 8, 14 and 27 May 1971.
69 *Irish Press*, 22 Feb. 1971.
70 *Irish Independent*, 15 May 1971.
71 *Irish Press*, 22 May 1971.
72 *Meath Chronicle*, 21 Aug. 1971.
73 *Leitrim Observer*, 21 Aug. 1971.
74 *Sligo Champion*, 13 Aug. 1971.
75 *Irish Times*, 10 Aug. 1971.
76 Ibid., 13 Aug. 1971.
77 *The Kerryman*, 14 Aug. 1971; *Munster Express*, 13 Aug. 1971; *Anglo-Celt*, 27 Aug 1971.
78 *Meath Chronicle*, 21 Aug. 1971.

79 *Irish Times*, 12 Aug. 1971.
80 *Anglo-Celt*, 10 Sept. 1971.
81 *The Kerryman*, 14 Aug. 1971; *Anglo-Celt*, 13 Aug. and 1 Oct. 1971; *Donegal News*, 14 Aug. 1971; *Connaught Tribune*, 20 Aug. 1971; *Leitrim Observer*, 11 Sept. 1971; *Southern Star*, 2 Oct. 1971.
82 *Connacht Tribune*, 27 Aug. 1971.
83 *Irish Independent*, 23 Aug. 1971.
84 Ibid., 29 Sept. 1971.
85 *The Kerryman*, 27 Nov. 1971.
86 *Irish Times*, 14 Aug. 1971.
87 Donal Gilligan to Sighle Humphries, 19 Dec. 1971, Sighle Humphries Papers, P106/1585 (1–2) UCDA.
88 *Liberty*, Sept. 1971.
89 *Irish Times*, 12 Aug. 1971; S. Cody, J. O'Dowd and P. Rigney, *The Parliament of Labour: 100 Years of the Dublin Council of Trade Unions* (Dublin, 1986) p. 228.
90 Though the DCTU opposed calls for protest strike action as having 'little or no useful effect'. *Irish Times*, 27 Aug. 1971.
91 *Irish Times*, 23 Aug. 1971.
92 *Connacht Tribune*, 10 Sept. 1971.
93 *Irish Times*, 30 Aug. 1971.
94 Ibid., 27 Nov. 1971.
95 Ibid., 9 Dec. 1971.
96 Ibid., 25 Oct. 1971.
97 L. Gogan, *Larry Gogan's Pop File* (Dublin, 1979) p. 47.
98 *Irish Press*, 7 Jan. and 8 April 1972.
99 *Irish Times*, 20 Sept. 1971.
100 Ibid., 14 Aug. 1971.
101 Ibid., 18 Oct. 1971.
102 Note on the Situation in Northern Ireland, 29 Oct. 1971, Garret FitzGerald Papers, P215/5 UCDA. The letter was signed by, among others, Garret FitzGerald and Declan Costello of Fine Gael, Senator Eoin Ryan of Fianna Fáil, Michael McInerney of the *Irish Times* and Nicholas Simms of RTE.
103 L. Lyons to G. FitzGerald, 17 Feb.1972, FitzGerald Papers, P215/4 UCDA.
104 Republic of Ireland: Annual Review for 1971, 10 Jan. 1972, FCO 87/7 NAUK.
105 *Hibernia*, 17 Dec. 1971.
106 Liam Ryan testimony, INCORE, www.green-and-blue.org.
107 *The Kerryman*, 1 Jan. 1972.
108 *Anglo-Celt*, 1 Oct. 1971.
109 *Connacht Telegraph*, 11 Nov. 1971.
110 *Irish Press*, 3 Nov. 1971.
111 *Irish Times*, 10 Dec. 1971.
112 See editorial *Irish Press*, 2 Oct. 1971. Ibid., 3 Nov. 1971. *Irish Independent*, 17 Dec. 1971.
113 *Tuam Herald*, 31 Aug. 1971.
114 *Irish Press*, 23 Dec. 1971.
115 *Donegal News*, 25 Dec. 1971.

2

'The nation on the march'

At around 10.30pm on the night of Sunday 30 January 1972, 50 people gathered at the British Embassy. Their protest was peaceful and they left after midnight. At 1.45am two young women arrived and held their own vigil until 5.50am.[1] These were initial responses to the news that earlier that day British troops had shot dead 13 people in Derry. A Killarney man's reaction on seeing the TV footage – 'The British are murderous bastards' – was doubtlessly replicated across the state.[2] By night, there were few in the Republic who disagreed with Social Democratic and Labour party (SDLP) MP John Hume, that the Parachute Regiment had carried out 'cold-blooded mass murder; another Sharpeville; another Bloody Sunday'. Some news outlets reported Derry's James Connolly Republican Club's call for an 'immediate general strike (to) bring the country to a standstill'.[3]

Monday 31 January

On Monday morning, walkouts began from factories in the Shannon Industrial Estate. An estimated 2,000 workers marched to the airport terminal and demanded the tricolour be lowered to half-mast. By 9am Cork dockers had struck, boarding a British ship and forcing it to fly a black flag. By noon thousands of workers in the city, at Ford, Pfizer, Dunlop, C.I.E. and on various building sites had walked out. They converged on Cork city centre where 'so many marches were taking place that at times columns of protesting workers passed each other in the streets going in opposite directions'. Hundreds of young women from the Sunbeam textile factory, Gouldings chemicals and O'Brien's Plastic plant joined the procession despite cold rain. The promise by the city's Lord Mayor, T.J. O'Sullivan (of Labour), that 'if they want murder they'll have murder –one of theirs will go for each of ours' was met with cheers outside City Hall. There, the Provisional leader Dáithí Ó Conaill was joined by War of Independence veteran Tom Barry for an impromptu rally. In Dundalk at least 5,000 walked out, led by shoe factory workers. Addressing the marchers, local republican Peter Duffy called for a national strike on the day of the Derry funerals. In Galway, dockers boarded a British ship and daubed slogans on it, forcing the crew to replace its ensign with a black flag. University College Galway was shut down and 2,000 marched to Eyre Square, where a British-owned bank was occupied. Members of the Official IRA fired a number of shots in the air at the protest rally. There were also walkouts and strikes in Sligo, Waterford, Limerick, Carrickmacross and Clonmel. Telephone operators refused to handle British calls, airport ground crew stopped servicing British aircraft and shops took British newspapers off their shelves.[4]

Merrion Square

In Dublin there were strikes at the Jeyes factory in Finglas, a Ringsend construction site and Royal Irish Ltd in Glasnevin. From morning, 'small and large groups of people from various firms' arrived at the British Embassy. Many carried black flags or mock coffins painted with the number '13' while their representatives handed in letters of protest. Though 'vociferous', the demonstrators 'nevertheless obeyed the directions of the Gardai'. By lunchtime, over 1,000 Volkswagen, Fiat and Blackhodge assembly plant workers arrived. Then a few stones and bottles were thrown at the Embassy. The protest was joined by ESB workers and students from the Royal College of Surgeons. By 2pm around 6,000 more students – from UCD, Trinity, Bolton Street and Kevin Street – had gathered in the Square, along with pupils from various schools and workers from Gallagher's Tobacco in Tallaght. USI's vice-president Paul Tansey called for strikes on the day of the victims' funerals. During the afternoon protesters threw 'bottles, stones, coins, bolts (and) an occasional petrol bomb' at the Embassy and there were calls on Gardai to stand aside and let them into the building. But despite some minor damage, by 6pm Gardai considered that the Merrion Square area was fairly calm.[5]

'Finish the job that was started in '16'

On Monday evening there were numerous emergency council meetings. Representatives from across the political spectrum urged an aggressive response. Motions were passed demanding a national day of mourning, United Nations intervention, boycotts of British goods or British withdrawal. Veteran Cork Fianna Fáil Councillor Martin Corry demanded the government 'take every step now to see that this country is united in the final fight for freedom. If we were let finish our job in '22 … this would not be our job now (but) we have enough old and young lads in this country, thank God, to finish the job that was started in '16.'[6] On Westmeath county council, a Labour councillor looked forward to the day when they would get rid of the British 'once and for all … He was sure that the young people of today if put to the test would not be found wanting.'[7] At Carrickmacross, Official Sinn Féin's Francie O'Donoghue produced a revolver and announced that 'the only way to talk to the British Army is through the barrel of a gun'. Even those who had traditionally shunned republican sentiment, such as Fine Gael's Paddy Donegan, called on the British Prime Minister to 'withdraw immediately his army from Northern Ireland'. Donegan also promised Louth County Council that he would travel to the funerals in Derry and to a civil rights march in Newry the following Sunday.[8]

'Dignity and discipline'

That night, Jack Lynch appeared in a special broadcast on RTE (watched by 79% of households) and announced that the Irish ambassador was being withdrawn from London and that Wednesday, 2 February would be a Day of Mourning.[9] All schools would be closed and businesses and workplaces were asked to mark the day in a 'suitable' manner. Lynch hoped that 'in (this) time of grave national danger Irish men and women will show the world their patriotism by their dignity and discipline'. He had been receiving telegrams all day from trade unions and community groups demanding a period of mourning. Many also called on Lynch and President Eamon de Valera to attend the funerals in Derry.[10]

'Notice to quit'

Meanwhile, the protests in Dublin had intensified. After 7pm several thousand people gathered at an Official republican rally in Merrion Square. Protesters asked Gardai to 'give us a couple of minutes to burn the bastards out'. Seamus Costello announced that 'notice to quit' was being served on the Embassy and petrol bombs, flares and rockets were used in a sustained attack on the building. Gardai baton-charged the rioters, who scattered, attacking a squad car and fire bombing the British Passport Office in the process.[11] By 9.30pm another march, this time from a Provisional republican meeting at the GPO, arrived in a 'violent mood'. On their way to the Embassy, some of the marchers had petrol bombed British airline offices in Grafton Street. There were now 20,000 people in Merrion Square and a 'continuous see-saw struggle' between protesters and police went on for an hour. Gardai noted that there were a 'large number of genuine demonstrators, especially women (and) a body of persons whose sympathies lay with the Gardai' watching but not taking part in the clashes. At 10.30pm, after using a loud speaker to ask 'all law-abiding citizens' to leave the area, they carried out a baton charge. A combination of heavy rain and Gardai sweeps saw the crowd dwindle, though several hundred people remained until the early hours of Tuesday morning, when clerical students from St. Columban's College in Navan arrived to begin a vigil.[12] Joe Cahill of the Provisionals said that they had 'asked the Gardai to stand aside and let (us) wreck the place' but 'appealed to the people not to attack the Gardai ... our policy is not to provoke direct confrontation with the authorities'. Tony Heffernan of the Officials explained that 'the Gardai were asked to stand back from the embassy, but did not do so until the missiles started flying ... they then formed up on the road for a baton charge and batoned people very badly. These people defended themselves as best they could.'[13]

Tuesday 1 February

Protests continued the following day. In Cork, members of the National Busmen's Union struck for an hour and announced an all-day stoppage for Wednesday. Brewery workers, schoolboys, teachers and ESB employees all joined protests in the city.[14] Sligo saw the 'biggest protest march ever held in the town' with 10,000 joining a trades council demonstration. In Tralee 8,000 took part in a two-hour stoppage, protesters reciting a decade of the Rosary in Denny Street. In Ballyshannon 1,000 people, including large numbers of school students, took to the streets. Four hundred workers at Tipperary's Silvermines began a two-day strike. Dock, ferry and airport staff continued to refuse to deal with British craft. Navan pubs and off-licenses began a boycott of Scotch whiskey.[15] Classes at St. Patrick's College Maynooth were suspended and 1,000 students and staff marched the 15 miles to Dublin to join protests at the Embassy.[16] One hundred and fifty 'Foxrock housewives' picketed the British Ambassador's residence in Sandyford, with placards denouncing the 'new Black and Tans'.[17]

'Whipped into frenzied excitement'

Throughout the day 'thousands of people ... in large and small groups from various industrial and commercial concerns' continued to gather at the Embassy. Gardai described some of these as 'dignified, others boisterous' and 'quite a few ... violent to the extent that they indulged in missile throwing and chanting anti-British slogans'. By 10pm that night there were around 10,000 people at the Embassy, many arriving from a republican meeting in O'Connell Street 'whipped into frenzied excitement (and) wildly shouting that the Embassy should be burned down'. Gardai claimed that 'many North of Ireland people were present in the crowd (and) encouraged the more militant demonstrators to charge the Garda cordon'. A lorry was driven at Garda lines, but its driver was dragged from the cab and the vehicle disabled. At least 70 petrol bombs were thrown and the Fire Brigade doused the front hallway of the Embassy with foam to prevent fire spreading. At 11.30 a gelignite bomb exploded, blowing in the Embassy front door and injuring two Gardai. They thought that this presaged an effort to rush the building, but the crowds started to disperse and by early morning calm was restored. The last of the Embassy's staff left after the bomb attack and Gardai took control of the building. Since no firm could be found to replace the Embassy door, 'old pieces of wood' were used to block the entrance. Early Wednesday morning, British officials informed the Department of Justice that it 'seemed clear that the Gardai could not successfully resist the expected further attempts to burn down the Embassy if they were not supported by the Defence Forces'. Irish diplomats in London were also informed that the Embassy would 'require military support'. Gardai stated that 'consideration was ... given at this stage to seeking the assistance of the Defence Forces ... but it was decided that their presence would only exacerbate the position if arms were displayed'.[18]

Throughout the day there were numerous bomb scares and phone threats aimed at 'British' targets. There were also at least seven arson or bomb attacks. The Royal Liver Society offices in Dun Laoghaire, the Royal Air Force Club in Earlsfort Terrace and Austin Reed Outfitters in Grafton St were all petrol bombed. The Waterford Docks office of Bellferry Ltd was also blown up. The news, linked to a long running dispute, was 'greeted with jubilation' by dockworkers and meant the port was shut.[19]

'The Nation closes down today'

A day of unparalleled protest was expected on Wednesday. The *Irish Independent* announced that 'The Nation closes down today' while the *Cork Examiner* asserted that 'not since the funerals of the Niemba Congo ambush victims, or the great public mournings which accompanied the deaths of Michael Collins and Arthur Griffith will such a day of sympathy have been seen'.[20] Radio Éireann broadcast the funeral mass live from Derry, with commentary by Donnacha Ó Dúlaing and Kevin O'Kelly. In the evening, RTE television featured a live mass from Donnybrook officiated by Belfast priest Fr. Des Wilson, followed by the 1969 documentary 'John Humes's Derry'. A performance of the cantata 'A Terrible Beauty', composed by Brian Boydell for the 50th anniversary of the Easter Rising, would be shown before discussion of the day's events.[21] RTE technicians had made it clear they would refuse to work on any programmes not connected with the Day of Mourning. Trade unions and employer groups had also been issuing instructions in preparation. Most unions called for a two-hour stoppage, for their members to support local demonstrations and donate to relief funds. Workers in Dublin were asked to join the Trades Council march from Parnell Square at 3pm. The Federated Union of Employers recommended that 'member companies ... facilitate and co-operate with employees and trade unions in making arrangements for employees to have some hours leave of absence to attend religious services on this National Day of Mourning'. The Quinnsworth and Pennys stores announced that they would shut for the entire day. The Retail Grocery Diary & Allied Trades Association (RGDATA), called for shops and pubs to restrict their opening hours. The Irish Farmers Association asked members to suspend farm business for at least an hour and to join local protests. Many firms announced half-day or two-hour closures. A number of businesses announced they would open as normal but would donate to relief funds.[22]

Wednesday 2 February

Despite the 'exceptionally high wind and driving rain' that affected most of the country on Wednesday, from early morning crowds gathered in towns and villages. Twenty thousand took part in Waterford's 'biggest demonstration for almost 60 years'. Union contingents carried banners mourning their 'brothers murdered' along with black flags and wooden coffins. Despite some 'shouting, notably from the younger element' the protest was 'very orderly'.[23] Cork's Shandon Bells rang for half an hour and special services took place in the city's churches and its synagogue. Crowds gathered on the Grand Parade, joining protests 'so disorganised that over a dozen parades took place', while the rival republican organizations held separate rallies.[24] In Limerick 10,000 marched, in Mallow 2,000, Ennis 5,000, Skibereen 3,000, Castlebar 5,000, Carlow 7,000, Newbridge 1,500, Wexford 6,000, Kilkenny 6,000, Dundalk 10,000, Dungarvan 3,000, Tullamore 6,000, Tuam 2,000 and Thurles 4,000. Most taking part were identified by their workplaces; Albatross in New Ross, the chipboard companies in Scariff, GEC in Dunleer, ESB workers in Tarbert, bacon factory workers in Claremorris, mine workers in Tynagh, hospital staff in Ballinasloe, CIE workers in Longford, Liebherr factory workers in Killarney.[25] Union contingents were followed by school students, teachers, Macra na Feirme members, GAA clubs, farmers, Old IRA, Organisation of Ex-Servicemen and community groups. In Ardee, Co. Louth marchers included

> one Garda in plain-clothes, another on duty eyeing up the crowd, his collar turned up against the rain … duffle coated, rain soaked clergy, nuns in black headscarves, youths wearing black berets, Ardee ITGWU, Ardee Order of Malta, Ardee Band, Ardee Bread Co., businessmen, men in green berets, children in duffles and little girls wearing plastic rainhats and bewildered looks, old men, old women moving their lips slowly. [26]

The majority of parades went to, or from, a requiem mass. In Mullingar marchers converged on the Cathedral of Christ the King (where) 'Requiem Mass was offered for Derry's dead by Rev. J. Conway':

> Thousands of people packed the Cathedral … The first lessson was read in Irish by Mr. Sean O'Riordan (National Teacher). The second Lesson was read by Garda

Sgt. B.K. Colvert ... Afterwards the parade reformed and marched away. A black coffin was carried in the parade. Tricolours were at half-mast. Many mourning flags were displayed from houses and business premises ... [27]

The majority of the events were peaceful, though militant rhetoric and the burning of British flags was commonplace. Employers, trade unionists and clergy were represented on most platforms, along with all the main parties. Many areas also saw Church of Ireland, Methodist and Presbyterian services of remembrance. In some places republicans were prominent among the protesters, and in Waterford a combined party from both Official and Provisional IRAs fired volleys of shots at the conclusion of the rally.[28]

Derry and Dublin

The funeral mass in Creggan, said by Cardinal Conway, was attended by dozens of politicians from the republic. Five government ministers and over 40 TDs and Senators, along with nine Lord Mayors, travelled to Derry. They included Brian Lenihan, Bobby Molloy, Charles Haughey, John O'Leary and Niall Andrews of Fianna Fáil; Richie Ryan, Garret FitzGerald, T.F. O'Higgins and Paddy Donegan of Fine Gael; and Brendan Corish and Michael O'Leary of Labour. T.J. Maher, president of the Irish Farmers Association, and the GAA president Pat Fanning were also present.[29] Thousands of ordinary citizens also made their way to the city. An estimated 100 cars left Donegal town for the funerals, while others travelled from Mayo, Sligo, Galway, Dublin and Limerick. Meanwhile, in Dublin Jack Lynch, President de Valera and Liam Cosgrave attended mass officiated by Archbishop Charles McQuaid in the Pro-Cathedral. Tánaiste Erskine Childers attended a special service in St. Patrick's Cathedral and there were memorial services in Dublin's Presbyterian and Methodist churches and the city's synagogues.[30] There were also dozens of local services requested by workplaces, union branches or associations. In the Great Hall of University College Dublin, 1,000 staff and students attended the college's first interdenominational service, addressed by historian Robin Dudley Edwards.[31]

'A hint of anarchy'

On Wednesday morning, Dublin was a city of 'closed shops, bars, resturants, theatres and hotels ... boarded over frontage of British firms (with) a hint of anarchy in the air'. A black banner bearing the number 13 hung over the front arch of Trinity College, while the college's tricolour flew at half-mast.[32] From 9.30am onwards, 'thousands of protesting people in marching formation ... en route to and from Church' began to pass the Embassy. Hundreds of schoolchildren and students milled around Merrion Square 'waiting for something to happen'. By lunchtime, dockers, ESB workers, 'neat and orderly civil servants', bus workers and post office staff arrived. Female telephonists knelt and said the rosary while 'most people, including the Gardai, joined in'.[33] Then, to the muffled drums of the ITGWU band, the main body of marchers appeared, including 'many women, some with babes in arms'. Merrion Square soon became 'a mass of thronged people'. There were 500 Gardai present, including most of the senior officers in Dublin. They estimated that 'Merrion Square, East and North as well as a portion of Holles Street and Lower Mount Street were choc a bloc and, judging by the official allowance of four persons per square yard, the density of the crowd was estimated at 50,000'. There was a 'mighty crush' with people climbing trees and lampposts and protesters pushed right on top of Gardai lines. Railings were torn up to allow the crowd to spill into the adjacent park.[34]

'Burn, burn, burn'

From 3pm missiles were thrown as the crowd 'became excited and began (calling) for the destruction of the Embassy'. Petrol bombs exploded to cheers, 'as if … at Croke Park'. Some of the missiles fell short and hit protesters who included Dublin teenagers, trade unionists and students.[35] Some Trinity students, who had been at the Embassy for a party hosted by the ambassador's son – himself studying at the college – a few weeks earlier, were among those chanting 'if you hate the British Army clap your hands'.[36] Gardai claimed that those leading the attacks were 'North of Ireland people, Sinn Féin and Connolly Youth elements'. But there were also huge numbers of 'elderly people, women and children' present and senior Gardai claimed that they felt that 'any drastic action … in view of the density of the crowd could have fatal consequences … preservation of life was much more important than the preservation of property'.[37] By 4pm the makeshift Embassy door was on fire, but there was no sign of the flames spreading to the rest of the building. Believing that the protesters had run out of ammunition, Garda control issued instructions for garages not to sell petrol in containers. However, at least three men climbed onto the balconies on Merrion Square and managed to make their way from balcony to balcony. One, with the 'deftness of a cat burglar', raised a tricolour to half-mast on the Embassy flagpole. Then he used a hatchet to smash some of the upper windows. To cheers and the singing of 'For He's a Jolly Good Fellow' a can of petrol was poured in through the broken window and more petrol bombs then thrown from the crowd. The flames grew fiercer to chants of 'burn, burn, burn' and 'more, more, more'.[38] The Fire Brigade were deployed at the rear of Embassy. At first, they refused to come into Merrion Square and, when they eventually arrived, were subject to obstruction from the crowd. According to Gardai, the Brigade 'declined to fight the fire … (stating) that they would preserve the adjoining buildings if necessary'.[39] The fires took hold and by evening the building was ablaze.

'The burning of the Embassy could not have been prevented'

Thousands stayed to watch the Embassy burn. Then, over 1,000 joined a march to Mountjoy prison to demand the release of Provisional IRA prisoners. The Officials held their own rally and led crowds back to Merrion Square, including a 'strong element of hooligans' who unleashed an 'intense barrage of missiles' at the Gardai.[40] The British Passport Office was fire bombed and a petrol bomb was thrown at the maternity hospital in Holles Street with 'some lunatics suggesting it was a British hospital and should be burned down'.[41] Cars were overturned, shop windows smashed and the British Leyland office in Percy Place was set on fire. The Gardai, reinforced by units from outside Dublin, charged the crowds and took revenge for their earlier humiliations. There were over 30 arrests and 60 injuries reported, but by 12.30am the area was quiet.[42] Privately, Gardai admitted that

> the burning of the Embassy could not have been prevented on this occasion. It was not anticipated that such a vast throng of people would participate in the Assembly outside the Embassy, but the fact that Wednesday ... was officially proclaimed a day of National mourning seemed to incense all otherwise moderate persons and whipped them into acts of remorse and oppression against the Embassy building.

Gardai claimed that 'many of the demonstrators did not approve' of the attacks on them, but believed that all the protesters 'had a grievance against the Embassy building over, inter alia, the shooting of the thirteen persons in Derry'. They asserted that their own officers (24 of whom were hospitalized) 'stood up well to the ferocious attacks made on them' as 'for many ... especially the younger members, it was a frightening experience'.[43]

'Hardly bothered'?

In Britain it was widely believed that the authorities in Dublin had allowed the Embassy to be burned. In Irish popular memory many have echoed Bertie Ahern's assertion that 'the Gardai hardly bothered' to try and prevent the destruction of the building.[44] Provisional IRA leader Joe Cahill later claimed that the Gardai told him that 'we don't want to have to arrest anyone tonight' and that 'quite a number' of them cheered as the Embassy burned.[45] The British Ambassador felt differently, writing to the Garda Commissioner to thank him 'for the work done by the gardai and Special Branch officers (who) behaved with great gallantry in the face of a situation which could not have been expected'.[46] Peck dismissed as 'totally erroneous' the impression that 'the Dublin police had stood and done nothing', claiming that they 'fought on as long as they could'.[47] Many tended to agree with the *Cork Examiner* which saw the burning as the 'lesser of two evils. Had Gardai gone all out to prevent the demonstrators from getting to within a 100 yards of the Embassy there is little doubt that a substantial number of people would have been injured.'[48]

Newry

On Thursday morning the sun shone and the burnt-out shell of the Embassy became an attraction for sightseers.[49] In Cork a march by 1,000 mainly young protesters ended in running battles with Gardai at the British Rail office in Patrick Street.[50] Attention now turned to Sunday, with a civil rights march planned for Newry. The march had been banned and speculation mounted about violence. Ivan Cooper MP called for Irish troops to be mobilized and ready to intervene if the demonstration was attacked. The organizers, the Northern Ireland Civil Rights Association, asked southerners not to travel and instead to attend solidarity protests in the Republic. But on Sunday 6 February 50,000 people, 10–15,000 of them from the south, marched in what was the last great civil rights protest. Thousands travelled by bus or train to Dundalk, while others left their cars south of the border and walked to Newry. They included workers from the cement factory in Mungret, Co. Limerick; Labour party activists from Naas, Co. Kildare; and GAA members from Moate, Co. Westmeath. Several TDs, including Labour's Michael O'Leary, John O'Connell and Noel Browne – along with Kevin Boland and Sean Sherwin of Aontacht Éireann – also attended. Three thousand demonstrated in solidarity in Dublin, 1,000 in Cork, 1,000 in Athenry and 2,000 in Limerick. In Dun Laoghaire, 700 marched to the British Legion offices, while Castlebar saw the 'greatest show of unity in the county town since the days of the Land League' with 10,000 people taking part in the march there.[51] On the same day, 3,000 attended a special fundraising game between Derry and Antrim at Croke Park, while minute silences were observed at all GAA and League of Ireland matches.[52]

'The point of no return?'

Bloody Sunday, the president of the GAA Pat Fanning asserted, had 'drawn the Irish people together. The point of no return has been reached and passed.'[53] Local newspapers reflected that tone, many of them referencing Cromwell, 1798 and the Black and Tans.[54] The *Sligo Champion* claimed that 'the South is in the mood for violence … there is a growing feeling that the only language Britain understands is through a gun barrel … how many more Irishmen must die before Edward Heath realises there is no longer a place for British Imperialism in this country?' *The Kerryman* warned that 'there can be no more talk about the six counties, "Ulster" or Northern Ireland … The British forces must be got out of Ireland at all costs.'[55] By late February 'The Men Behind The Wire' was replaced at No. 1 by Paul McCartney and Wing's 'Give Ireland Back To The Irish'.[56] *Hibernia* magazine detected a 'completely new atmosphere' in the

Republic, 'the emotions of the South have at last spilt over'. The magazine suggested that 'the most significant characteristic' of the events was their 'total spontaniety'. The protest movement was 'completely independent of any political leadership ... the country and the streets dictated the pace (and) politicians are trying to keep up with it'.[57] A Portlaoise schoolboy recalled those days of 'arguments everywhere, on the street, in school among the older lads, about the IRA, about bombs, about guns ... graffiti in the bicycle shed, whoever it was meant for: "Fuck the Queen"'.[58]

'We are going to win this fight'

On Sunday 13 February, the Provisionals held a national rally at Dublin's GPO. Fifteen thousand people attended, many travelling by special buses and trains from across Ireland. Seán Mac Stíofáin told the crowd that 'not since 1916 have the people of Ireland been so roused and determined to reunify this country'. *An Phoblacht* claimed that 'for the first time in possibly 800 years the whole Irish Nation is on the march for full freedom ... the Irish Nation is now on the march and we are going to win this fight'.[59] Other revolutionaries also sensed possibilities, Michael Farrell of People's Democracy asserting that the burning of the Embassy was 'the best thing that happened since the struggle in the North began, and the only pity is that Leinster House did not go up as well'.[60]

Peace and reconciliation?

There was no doubting the rage that followed Derry's massacre, nor the huge level of popular protest in the days afterwards.[61] But the mood differed significantly depending on location and those involved. While many demonstrations had seen militant expressions of anger, others, especially outside the cities, had also been notable for their orderliness and religiosity. The most widespread initial response had been unofficial industrial action, and unionized workplaces formed the backbone of most of the demonstrations. Reflecting on the movement six years later, far-left activists noted how this 'General strike' had occurred 'spontaneously, outside the trade union structures, and independently of the trade union militants'.[62] Union leaderships had in fact counselled caution from an early stage, Irish Congress of Trade Unions (ICTU) president James Cox warning on 31 January that 'it was their view that a strike or a general stoppage of work would endanger rather than assist towards reconciliation and create hardship for workers and people least able to bear it'.[63] That there were no power cuts, that newspapers were published and that radio and television operated cautions against the belief that there was a complete shutdown. Many shops and pubs did open, though with restricted hours, and skeleton transport systems operated.[64] Some, of course, did not attend any marches, but 'in suburban living rooms people stared at those thirteen coffins on the television screens and were silent. In pubs men wrapped in their own thoughts. There was little talk.'[65] By any standards the sheer breadth of protests were extraordinary. But national unity had some limits. Twenty-eight Dublin women were suspended with two days loss of pay by the owner of Irish Waterproof Ltd for missing work in order to attend the funeral mass in Derry.[66]

'A civil war was casting its shadow'

The destruction of the Embassy featured heavily in Dáil debates on Thursday 3 February. Refusing to condemn those who threw petrol bombs, Labour's David Thornley felt that the British Government should have been told that 'while they continued to send their uniformed assassins to Ireland, by keeping an embassy in Dublin they were running a risk'.[67] Neither did Fianna Fáil's James Tunney 'lose any sleep' over the burning of the Embassy, but he did 'reprimand people who would avail of any opportunity to discredit the name of Ireland'.[68] Neil Blaney 'shed no tears' at the loss of the Embassy but felt that 'the Gardai had acted in an exemplary way'. Minister for Justice Desmond O'Malley asserted that the building 'could have been saved only at great risk to innocent lives and this country and its security forces have more respect for innocent human life than another Government in this part of the world'.[69] But Jack Lynch condemned the 'men who, under the cloak of patriotism, sought to overthrow the institutions of this state' and who had 'infiltrated what was a peaceful demonstration (and) fomented violence'. The destruction of the Embassy was 'an action of people who were dangerous, who were, above all, a danger to our freedom and our democracy and to our institutions of freedom and democracy'. Ominously, Labour's Michael O'Leary warned that 'a civil war was casting its shadow over us that could be more calamitous than the civil war of 50 years ago'.[70]

'Mafia-like methods'

Soon, cracks began to appear in what had seemed to be unanimity. Council meetings heard recriminations about intimidation, threats and bomb scares.[71] There were reports of attacks on British citizens living in the Republic and allegations that 'mafia-like methods' were used to force people to close their businesses.[72] During February, at least ten British firms cancelled planned conferences, English drivers withdrew from a motor rally and British Rail closed its offices in the Republic. Bord Fáilte estimated that 2,000 jobs could be lost because of the impact of the violence.[73] One commentator suggested that 'it is all very well for Aer Lingus workers to refuse to handle English newspapers and magazines. They still get their wages at the end of the week. But what about the unfortunate newspaper seller on the corner of the street?

Why should he suffer?'[74] Tralee Trades Council, which had organized the protests in that town, 'cautioned against a total boycott of British goods' because this 'could have a retaliatory action from England and which would affect the employment of Irish workers'.[75] *Business and Finance* magazine argued that the burning of the Embassy

> showed how ill-equipped our security forces are to deal with gelignite and petrol bombing and how determined those who use them are when they feel the occasion justifies it … the failure of the Garda to protect the building can be seen as lending weight to the veracity of those extremists who deliver threats to companies with British associations and demand of Irish retailers that they should cease stocking British goods … the links between Ireland and Britain are extremely important and no extremist action should be allowed destroy them.[76]

'Torturing a kitten'

Soon, political figures took up this refrain. Erskine Childers denounced those who were 'threatening Protestants and British people living in Ireland' as 'pathetically inept and destructive, like a child torturing a kitten'.[77] There were increasing calls for stability. Bishop Browne of Galway had warned during requiem mass on the Day of Mourning that 'we must take care that our unity is not disrupted by minority groups who have no mandate from the people'. The *Irish Press* opined that while

> the burning (of the Embassy) was serious enough; what followed was appalling … gardai on duty there were attacked (and) … one Official IRA spokesman addressed the crowd, virtually inciting them to attack. What do these men imagine they are doing? Do they think that by provoking a war situation here they can resolve the existing one in the North, or that this is the way to launch social revolution … this is not the time to fritter away our energies in internal savagery and disorder. Derry brought a new solidarity into national life … those who challenge that unity, still less the authority of the Oireachtas, for whatever purpose, distract us from our major national purpose…[78]

'Nearly everybody agreed with it'

The burning of the Embassy remains the outstanding popular memory of the south's reaction to Bloody Sunday. Reporting in the immediate aftermath, British journalist Denis Taylor found 'little public shedding of tears … The destruction of one building was reckoned a small price for 13 Irish lives.'[79] One man, angered by the Taoiseach's condemnations, wrote to him, suggesting that while Lynch 'may not have been there, I was, and nearly everybody agreed with it. I have met few to disagree with it.' He then asserted that 'I am not going to lay myself open to a criminal charge by saying *I* burned it but I can assure (you) that I was there as were many others, like myself, neither hooligans nor subversives and I resent bitterly your charge … I thought about my actions beforehand and I considered it necessary to burn the embassy as a gesture.' Furthermore, he was 'quite prepared to pay for the damage … by way of taxes'.[80]

'A safety-valve'

A Rathmines-based rugby supporter explained to the London *Times* that the burning 'was a safety-valve by which the pent-up emotions of a great many Dubliners following the Derry events were released. If you had been, as I was, within earshot of the happenings that day you would have recognized the cheers as the good humoured cheers of a football crowd not the angry roars of a mob.' Complaining about the decision of the Welsh and Scottish rugby teams not to play in Dublin, he asserted that while 'it seems that the impression abroad … is that this city is alive with Republican activists … nothing could be further from the truth'.[81] The British Ambassador would accept that the burning of the Embassy 'was probably inevitable given the surge of cold fury that engulfed the nation after the killings'. However, he found that 'mental attitudes to this event, in retrospect, are interesting' because 'the remorse and shame that immediately visited very many Irishmen were deep and genuine'.[82] While it is unlikely that Peck's social circle reflected majority opinion, there is evidence that some felt troubled by the events. One mother of 'small children' from middle-class Foxrock explained how she and her friends did 'not march or protest and our voices do not get heard'. For her

> our families are our first concern and it is to them our first loyalty lies. While we sympathize with the families of Derry's 13 dead, we cannot but feel fear at the reaction their deaths had here. We do not feel what the newspapers yesterday called 'the nations anger', only sorrow. We fear for our families and wonder what sort of Ireland our children will grow up in. We fear so much for them that we sometimes feel the North should be left alone to get on with its own destruction …[83]

In other instances, however, those who had protested felt that burning the Embassy had been a 'natural symbolic reaction'.[84] A few, more cynically, suggested that the whole affair had been a 'little diversion for the peasants'.[85]

'This trend of affairs cannot be allowed to continue unchecked'

Over the next few months, violence escalated to ever greater levels. On 22 February the Official IRA bombed the Parachute Regiment base at Aldershot, killing seven, including five women cleaners.[86] The response of *The Kerryman* was typical: 'Aldershot and Derry will be forever linked in outrage …This act of terror has advanced no cause, has brought no nearer the solution to the

Irish problem, has given comfort to none except the brutal and depraved. Aldershot was a disaster.'[87] Just a few months later, *Hibernia* would assert that militants were 'losing public support North and South of the border. Indeed their isolation was almost complete ... the IRA had never been more cut off from public support.'[88] The Fianna Fáil and Labour party conferences, which took place in February, had been expected to see bitter rows about the North. But both events ended with expressions of support for the respective party leaderships and calls for stability.[89] In May, the government introduced new powers to deal with paramilitary suspects, including a non-jury Special Criminal Court.[90] Dismissing objections, the *Irish Press* noted that 'we have the appalling spectacle of unchecked bank robberies, we have witnessed the incredible spectacle of the British Embassy being burned down (and) we know that this trend of affairs cannot be allowed to continue unchecked'.[91] The same month, voters decided by a majority of over 80% to support joining the European Economic Community. This was seen as a vote of confidence in the government and also, given vocal republican opposition to the measure, 'widely and correctly interpreted as one in the eye for the IRA'.[92]

'Exceptional national importance'

Violence intensfied again during the summer of 1972, July being the bloodiest month so far. The following month saw a significant by-election in Mid Cork. The government's republican critics believed the poll was of 'exceptional national importance' and was an opportunity to reject Lynch's policy on the North.[93] Aontacht Éireann Kevin Boland made it clear that they believed that

> Armed resistance is justified ... the enemy of the Irish people is still the same enemy that was successfully engaged in places like Crossbarry and Kilmichael – and co-operation with that enemy at present operating in the Six Counties means the same thing now as it did then.[94]

But with a turnout of over 80%, Fianna Fáil triumphed easily, taking 50% of the vote.[95] Boland's party won 1,172 votes, less than 3%.[96] The result seemed to suggest that militancy had limited attraction for southerners, Cork Labour TD Barry Desmond claiming that it illustrated the 'overwhelming desire of the electorate in the Republic not to become involved in the Northern strife'.[97]

'The tide of violence'

But street protest and disorder were increasingly commonplace. In early 1972, *Hibernia* noted how 'the tide of violence (was) lapping along the border', with serious incidents including gunbattles in Donegal, Monaghan and Louth.[98] In

October 1971, British troops began blocking or cratering minor border roads, much to the anger of locals.[99] Protests often led to clashes and there were numerous complaints that British soldiers fired CS gas and rubber bullets into the Republic, hitting both civilians and Gardai.[100] On 19 March, there was a riot in Monaghan town following the arrest of three republicans during one such protest. One thousand five hundred people gathered outside the town's Garda station. Stones were thrown and the Gardai called for army assistance. Fifty soldiers in riot gear arrived and the Gardai charged the crowd and dispersed it, though some petrol bombs were thrown. The Gardai believed that the presence of soldiers 'had a sobering effect' on many of the demonstrators and that it was 'also evident, that a large number, probably the majority, were opposed to any confrontation with the Gardai'. Embarrassingly, however, during the fighting two rifles and a radio were stolen from an Army landrover.[101]

'We'll bring down Leinster House'

Troops were now called out regularly, even being deployed to assist Gardai during clashes with young Travellers in Athlone.[102] Soldiers were again present during May when Mountjoy prison saw a serious riot led by republican prisoners. Part of the jail was wrecked and in the aftermath over 40 republican prisoners were moved to the Curragh military camp. During July, a small left-wing demonstration at the Curragh was met by troops with fixed bayonets.[103] A week later, a republican march of 5,000 to the camp saw clashes with hundreds of Gardai and troops. Some of the marchers cut their way through a wire fence and tried to rush towards the military prison. Though Sinn Féin leaders had called for the rioters to desist, stones and petrol bombs were thrown at troops and a hut was set on fire. Soldiers sprayed demonstrators with fire hoses and finally baton charges forced the marchers out of the base. While asking demonstrators not to throw stones, republican Máire Drumm also promised them that 'we have fought the British Army, we have brought down Stormont and we'll bring down Leinster House'.[104] Troops were also called out to back up Gardai during sectarian rioting in St. Johnston later that month.[105]

'We are in bad trouble here'

During August, at Courtbane, Co. Louth, the Army used tear gas against protesters for the first time since the 1930s. A few weeks later it was used again during a major riot in Dundalk. The trouble began after a protest over the arrest of a local Provisional, during which several hundred people 'many of whom were from across the Border … ran amok'.[106] The town's Garda station was surrounded, its windows smashed, efforts made to break down its doors and 20 vehicles in its carpark burnt out. A journalist who phoned the station was told 'we are in bad trouble here, I can't talk to you we are under siege'. Though it was not admitted at the time, a Garda fired shots over the heads of those trying to break into the building.[107] The Fire Brigade were attacked as they attempted to douse the blazing cars. As well as Gardai reinforcements from Dublin, soldiers were also dispatched to the town. The troops 'in full riot gear with shields and batons … came under constant fire from the stone-throwers'. The army then discharged canisters of CS gas and made baton charges with Gardai.[108] Suspects were 'pulled from cars and searched and roadblocks were set up at the entrance of the town'.[109] The next day, bombs were defused at a local tax office and cinema.[110] Journalists described the 'air of bewilderment' among townspeople

> as they saw their premises attacked. They were shocked as they saw the crowd breaking in the windows of Dunne's Stores, of Woolworth's, of the Post Office, of the banks … the people of the town seemed truly terrified.[111]

During September, there were more clashes outside Mountjoy jail where republicans were on hunger-strike. [112] Tension continued to mount throughout the winter with mysterious fire bombings in Louth, an escape by seven prisoners from the Curragh and another hunger-strike.[113] In December, troops were mobilized again alongside Gardai at Leinster House while the Dáil debated new special powers.[114] If the nation had been 'on the march' in February, by the winter its pace had slowed and its final destination was no longer so clear.

Notes

1 Garda Report by Superintendent B. Clinton, 6 April 1972, in D/J 2003/26/6 NAI.

2 F. O'Donoghue to G. FitzGerald, 30 Jan. 1972, in FitzGerald Papers, P215/4 UCDA.

3 Irish Press, 31 Jan. 1972.

4 Reports from Evening Press, 31 Jan. 1972. Cork Examiner, Irish Independent, Irish Press and Irish Times 1 Feb. 1972. Anglo Celt, Connacht Tribune, Munster Express, Sligo Champion, 4 Feb. 1972. Clare Champion, Dundalk Democrat, Limerick Leader, Western People, 5 Feb. 1972.

5 Garda report, D/J 2006/36/6 NAI.

6 Southern Star, 5 Feb. 1972.

7 Westmeath-Offaly Independent, 4 Feb. 1972.

8 Northern Standard, 4 Feb. 1972. Dundalk Democrat, 5 Feb. 1972.

9 G. Ivory, 'RTE and the coverage of Northern Ireland on the news bulletins in the early years of the Troubles', Irish Communications Review 13 (2012) pp. 31–51.

10 Correspondence 31 Jan. 1972, in D/T, 2003/16/503 NAI. The previous evening, Lynch had expressed his worry over what was likely to be the 'very serious reaction' to the massacre in the south in a phone call to the British Prime Minister. Guardian, 19 Sept. 1999.

11 Evening Press, 1 Feb. 1972.

12 Garda report, D/J 2003/26/6 NAI.

13 *Evening Press*, 1 Feb. 1972. B. Kenny, *Tony Heffernan: From Merrion Square to Merrion Street* (Dublin, 2013) p. 29.
14 *Irish Times*, 2 Feb. 1972.
15 *Donegal Democrat*, 4 Feb. 1972. *The Kerryman*, 5 Feb. 1972. *Meath Chronicle*, 12 Feb. 1972. *Sligo Champion*, 4 Feb. 1972. *Tipperary Star*, 5 Feb. 1972.
16 *Derry Journal*, 8 Feb. 1972.
17 *Evening Herald*, 2 Feb. 1972.
18 Garda report, D/J 2003/26/6 NAI. In fact, troops in riot equipment had been mobilized at Cathal Brugha barracks. Personal information.
19 *Irish Independent, Irish Press, Irish Times, Cork Examiner*, 2 Feb. 1972.
20 *Irish Independent, Cork Examiner*, 2 Feb. 1972.
21 *Irish Times*, 2 Feb. 1972.
22 *Evening Herald*, 1 Feb. 1972. *Cork Examiner*, 1 Feb. 1972.
23 *Munster Express*, 4 Feb. 1972.
24 *Irish Times*, 2 Feb. 1972. *Cork Examiner*, 3 Feb. 1972.
25 *Anglo-Celt, Drogheda Independent, Donegal Democrat, Kilkenny People, Nationalist and Leinster Times, New Ross Standard, Northern Standard, Longford Leader, Roscommon Herald, Sligo Champion, Westmeath-Offaly Independent, Wicklow People*, 4 Feb. 1972. *Dundalk Democrat, Drogheda Independent, Kerryman, Kerryman* (North Cork edition), *Leinster Leader, Leitrim Observer, Limerick Leader, Nenagh Guardian, Mayo News, Meath Chronicle, Tipperary Star*, 5 Feb. 1972.
26 *Drogheda Independent*, 4 Feb. 1972.
27 *Westmeath Examiner*, 5 Feb. 1972.
28 *Munster Express*, 4 Feb. 1972.
29 *Irish Press*, 3 Feb. 1972.
30 *Irish Times*, 3 Feb. 1972.
31 *Irish Press*, 3 Feb. 1972.
32 *Cork Examiner*, 3 Feb. 1972.
33 *Irish Times*, 3 Feb. 1972.
34 Garda report, D/J 2006/36/6 NAI.
35 Noonan, *What*, pp. 33–34.
36 Lucy O'Sullivan, quoted in K. Gillfillan (Ed.) *Trinity Tales: Trinity College in the Seventies* (Dublin, 2011) p. 136.
37 Garda report, D/J 2006/26/6 NAI.
38 *Irish Times*, 3 Feb. 1972.
39 Garda report, D/J 2006/26/6 NAI.
40 Ibid.
41 Noonan, *What*, pp. 33–35.
42 There were charges and jailings over these incidents. *Anglo-Celt*, 24 Nov. 1972.
43 Gardai were not issued with riot helmets or shields. Garda report, D/J 2003/26/6 NAI.
44 B. Ahern, *The Autobiography* (London, 2009) p. 31. See also T.P. Coogan, *The Irish: A Personal View* (London, 1975) p. 225.
45 B. Anderson, *Joe Cahill: A Life in the IRA* (Dublin, 2002) pp. 239–241.
46 J. Peck to M.J. Wymes, 9 Feb. 1972 in D/J 2003/26/6 NAI.
47 J. Peck, *Dublin from Downing Street* (Dublin, 1978) p. 11.
48 *Cork Examiner*, 3 Feb. 1972.
49 *The Times*, 7 Feb. 1972.
50 *Cork Examiner*, 4 Feb. 1972.
51 *Irish Independent*, 7 Feb. 1972.
52 *Irish Press*, 7 Feb. 1972.
53 *Irish Times*, 1 Feb. 1972.

54 *Herald and Western Advertiser, Connaught Telegraph, Limerick Leader, Tipperary Star,* 5 Feb. 1972.
55 *Sligo Champion,* 4 Feb. 1972. *The Kerryman,* 5 Feb. 1972.
56 Gogan, *Pop,* p. 91.
57 *Hibernia,* 4 Feb. 1972.
58 P. Boran, *The Invisible Prison: Scenes from an Irish Childhood* (Dublin, 2009) p. 157.
59 *An Phoblacht,* March 1972.
60 *Irish Independent,* 23 March 1972.
61 E. McCann, *Bloody Sunday in Derry: What Really Happened* (Dingle, 1992) p. 169.
62 People's Democracy, 1978 conference document, Sean O'Mahony Papers, NLI.
63 *Evening Herald,* 1 Feb. 1972.
64 *Evening Press,* 3 Feb. 1972. Some journalists retired to their usual haunt of Mulligans in Poolbeg Street in the aftermath of the burning. A. Madden, *Fear and Loathing in Dublin* (Dublin, 2009) pp. 10–11.
65 *Evening Herald,* 3 Feb. 1972.
66 J.J. O'Keeffe to Lynch, 2 Feb. 1972, in D/T 2003/16/504 NAI.
67 *Irish Times,* 4 Feb. 1972.
68 Ibid., 5 Feb. 1972.
69 Ibid.
70 *Sunday Independent,* 6 Feb. 1972.
71 *Roscommon Herald,* 11 Feb. 1972.
72 *Anglo-Celt,* 11 Feb. 1972.
73 *Sunday Independent,* 13 Feb. 1972.
74 Ibid., 6 Feb. 1972.
75 *The Kerryman,* 19 Feb. 1972.
76 *Business and Finance,* 10 Feb. 1972.
77 *This Week,* 2 March 1972.
78 *Irish Press,* 3 Feb. 1972.
79 *The Times,* 7 Feb. 1972.
80 Name abstracted to J. Lynch, 9 Feb. 1972, in D/Taoiseach 2003/16/189 NAI.
81 *The Times,* 24 Feb. 1972.
82 J. Peck to Secretary of State, 18 September 1972, in FCO 87/11 NAUK.
83 A. Howlett to G. FitzGerald, 3 Feb. 1972, in FitzGerald Papers, P215/4 UCDA.
84 'Ted Smyth' in Gillfillan (Ed.), *Trinity Tales,* pp. 90–91.
85 Tony Meade, *The Kerryman,* 5 Feb. 1972.
86 *Clare Champion,* 26 Feb. 1972.
87 *The Kerryman,* 26 Feb. 1972.
88 *Hibernia,* 9 June 1972.
89 Puirséil, *The Irish Labour Party,* p. 294.
90 *Irish Times,* 27 May 1972.
91 *Irish Press,* 21 Feb. 1972.
92 John Peck, 27 June 1972, FCO 87/11 NAUK.
93 *Irish Times,* 29 July 1972.
94 *Irish Times,* 24 July 1972.
95 *Hibernia,* 25 Aug. 1972.
96 M. Gallagher (Ed.) *Irish Elections, 1948–77: Results and Analysis* (Oxford, 2009) p. 272.
97 *Irish Times,* 8 Aug. 1972.
98 *Hibernia,* 7 Jan. 1972.
99 Ibid., 18 Feb. 1972.
100 *Northern Standard,* 4 Feb. 1972. *Leitrim Observer,* 4 March 1972.
101 Garda Report, 20 March 1972, D/T 2003/17/346 NAI.

102 *Hibernia*, 26 Feb. 1972.
103 *Irish Times*, 3 July 1972.
104 Ibid., 10 July 1972.
105 See Chapter 6.
106 *Dundalk Democrat*, 23 Sept. 1972.
107 V. Conway, *Policing Twentieth Century Ireland: A History of the Garda Síochána* (Oxford, 2013) p. 129.
108 *Dundalk Democrat*, 23 Sept. 1972.
109 *Irish Times*, 22 Sept. 1972.
110 Ibid., 25 Sept. 1972.
111 Ibid., 23 Sept. 1972.
112 *Guardian*, 24 Sept. 1972.
113 *Irish Press*, 30 Oct. 1972.
114 *Irish Times*, 1 Dec. 1972.

3

'It's all going to start down here'[1]

In 1979, after a man was shot dead during a bank robbery in Co. Waterford, the *Irish Press* suggested that the killing 'should shock us all into a realisation of what is happening in our society; the Northern troubles ... have spilled over with a vengence'.[2] By 1980, nearly 100 people in the Republic had died as a result of the conflict and hundreds more had been injured.

Loyalist activities

The first bombs

The first fatality in the Republic was a loyalist. In October 1969, Thomas McDowell of the Ulster Volunteer Force (UVF) was killed while planting a bomb at a power station near Ballyshannon. Over the next two years, loyalists would attack symbolic and infrastructural targets in the South. Wolfe Tone's grave at Bodenstown was bombed in 1969, as was the tomb of Daniel O'Connell at Glasnevin in January 1971.[3] The O'Connell monument in Dublin's main street was blasted in December 1969 and the Wolfe Tone statue in Stephen's Green bombed in February 1971.[4] The UVF also bombed a TV relay station at Raphoe in February 1970 and an electricity sub-station in Tallaght in March that year. They were blamed for an explosion on the Dublin–Belfast railway line during July 1970, the attempted bombing of a Catholic school in the Donegal village of St. Johnston and the destruction of a customs post at Lifford.[5] The bombing of RTE's Donnybrook headquarters in early August 1969 and the Garda Central Detective Bureau at Dublin Castle later that year were also attributed to loyalists.[6] In March 1971, unidentified bombers struck again when several large Dublin department stores, including Arnotts and Clerys, were damaged by incendiary devices.[7] Most of these early attacks occurred at nighttime causing damage to property rather than injuries to people.

Escalation

But with violence intensifying in the North, loyalists began to carry out more deadly actions. An arson attack on a factory in Emyvale, Co. Monaghan during February 1972 was believed to be retaliation for the shooting of Unionist MP John Taylor.[8] In March, letter bombs were sent to the homes of southern-based Provisional and Official IRA leaders.[9] There was another series of incendiary attacks on Dublin department stores in May 1972.[10] In October, a man was injured after a bomb exploded beside a hotel in Clones, Co. Monaghan.[11] The Ulster Defence Association (UDA) claimed responsibility for the bombing of two factories in Donegal during the same month.[12] In late October, as the Provisional Sinn Féin Ard Fheis met in Dublin, fire bombs exploded at several city hotels and a time bomb was found at Connolly Station.[13] The UDA carried out more bomb attacks on businesses in Donegal during November.[14] But far worse was to come in early December.

Sackville Place

In the midst of an IRA hunger-strike and government attempts to introduce new security measures, bombs claimed their first fatalities in Dublin. During the early hours of 26 November there was an explosion at the Irish Film Centre near O'Connell Bridge. Forty people were hurt, several seriously.[15] Less than a week later, at 8pm on Friday 1 December, a car bomb exploded near Liberty Hall. Fifteen minutes later there was another explosion at Sackville Place, killing George Bradshaw and Thomas Duffy. Bradshaw, 30 years old, was a bus driver, while Duffy, aged 23, was a conductor. Both men had left the CIE canteen on Marlborough Street just moments before. A witness described the aftermath:

> there was a large pall of smoke hanging over the area of the blast. At least six cars were on fire ... there were people strewn all over the street. One man was lying unconscious in a pool of blood from his legs ... everywhere there was sobbing and screaming ... people were running in all directions.[16]

Over 130 people were injured in the two incidents. In the following days 'tension, bomb scares and rumours .... rocked and terrifed (Dublin), leaving it deserted and morose'.[17]

Belturbet

A few weeks later, on 28 December, car bombs exploded within an hour of each other in three border towns. In Clones, Co. Monaghan two people were seriously hurt, while in Pettigo, Co. Donegal the explosion destroyed a pub but caused no casualties. In Belturbet, Co. Cavan, however, two teenagers – 14-year-old Geraldine O'Reilly and Patrick Stanley, aged 16 – were killed.[18] O'Reilly, a trainee hairdresser, was queuing for food in a chip shop, while Stanley, a lorry helper, was in a phone box when the explosion took place.[19] As with the Dublin bombs, there were no claims of responsibility. A few days afterwards the bodies of Oliver Boyce and Briege Porter were found near Burnfoot, Co. Donegal. They had been stabbed and shot. Twenty-five-year-old Boyce, a carpenter, and Porter, a 21-year-old factory worker, had been attending a New Year's Eve dance. They were killed by the UDA.[20]

1973

In January 1973, a bus worker, Thomas Douglas, was killed and 17 people injured when another car bomb exploded in Dublin, in 'almost the same spot' as the December attack. Loyalists continued to carry out arson attacks in Donegal over the New Year.[21] In March, Lindsey Mooney, a UDA member, died in a premature explosion outside a pub crowded with St. Patrick's Day revellers in Cloughfin. Fifteen were injured in the blast.[22] In Kiltyclogher, Co. Leitrim, during June 1973, the local vocational school was blown up.[23] Two people were injured by a car bomb in Pettigo during late September and fire bombs were found in Dundalk shops a month later.[24] A bomb near Swanlinbar, Co. Cavan destroyed a Córas Iompair Éireann (CIE) bus in November.[25] During the same month, Noel Thornberry, a Lurgan republican, was shot near Clones. Thornberry managed to escape but his house was blown up by the raiders.[26] In December, a bomb destroyed a pub close to the border in Donegal.[27] Just before Christmas letter bombs were sent from the North to Dublin businesses.[28]

1974

In January 1974, there was an explosion at a bacon factory outside Clones.[29] Gardaí believed the bomb had been intended for the town centre but was abandoned because of a checkpoint.[30] In February 1974, Jack Brogan, a leading Donegal-based republican, was shot in Ballybofey. Though critically injured, he survived. During March a group of loyalists were arrested in Monaghan on their way to kidnap an Armagh republican living in the county.[31] In April there were more fire bombs in Dublin department stores.[32]

'Our Bloody Friday'

Despite several years of such attacks, nobody was prepared for the scale of the horror unleashed on Friday 17 May. Over five minutes around 5.30pm three car bombs exploded in Dublin city centre. The first explosion in Parnell Street killed ten people. A teenage St. John's Ambulance volunteer described how she

> called to a man covered by a plank. When I lifted it up one of his legs was missing and lying nearby … a child aged about 12 lay nearby … there were bodies all over the place: many people were in deep shock and there were terrible injuries.

Among the dead were the young couple John and Anna O'Brien and their two infant daughters, Jacqueline and Anne Marie. Edward O'Neill was killed as he left a barber's shop and his two sons, aged 4 and 6, seriously injured. Eighty-year-old John Dargle, a former British soldier living in Ballybough, was among the dead. Ninety seconds later a bomb in Talbot Street killed 14 people. Belfast doctor John Cooper

> ran back to see a woman on the pavement decapitated; another woman lay dead with a piece of a car engine embedded in her back … there were injured people lying all around … it appeared to me that several of those who had lost limbs were unlikely to survive.

Thirteen of the dead in Talbot Street were women, including Colette Doherty from nearby Sheriff Street who was nine months pregnant, 57-year-old Dorothy Morris who worked at Cadburys and Anne Marren, a clerical worker from Sligo. The last bomb exploded outside Trinity College on Nassau Street. Terence Browne was studying in the National Library when 'a reverberant boom sounded' and hurrying outside he 'watched as human remains were carried away in an ambulance'.[33] The blast killed Anna Massey and Christina O'Loughlin and injured dozens of people.[34]

Just before 7pm another car bomb exploded outside Greacen's pub in the centre of Monaghan. It killed six people and fatally injured another. Among the dead were 72-year-old farmer George Williamson, 40-year-old Peggy White, who worked in the bar, and Archie Harper, an elderly farmer and publican.[35]

The *Irish Independent* described 'Our Bloody Friday' as the 'blackest day in Ireland this century'.[36] Dublin city centre was deserted, with cinemas, shops and restaurants closed. Tourist groups cancelled trips to the city, while the government ordered 500 troops back from United Nations duty.[37] Over a hundred people had been injured, many seriously, while over a dozen of those killed in Dublin came from outside the city, bringing the tragedy to communities across Ireland. Immediately after the bombings, Sammy Smyth of the UDA professed to be 'very happy … There is a war with the Free State and now we are laughing at them.'[38]

Smaller scale attacks continued. During June, a man was forced to drive a car bomb into Clones. The Provisional IRA claimed to have defused the device.[39] In July, an off-duty Garda was held up by armed men on the Cavan–Fermanagh border and forced to drive a car bomb to a Catholic-owned pub in the village of Magheraveely.[40] In September, the village of Blacklion in Cavan was evacuated after another proxy bomb attack.[41] In December, St. Mary's Catholic Church in Swanlinbar was wrecked by a bomb.[42]

1975

In January 1975, John Francis Green, a Provisional IRA member, was shot dead at a farmhouse near Castleblayney.[43] During March, the UDA bombed fishing trawlers at Greencastle, Co. Donegal.[44] On 22 June, an explosion occurred on the main Dublin railway line outside Straffan, Co. Kildare. When CIE staff investigated they found the body of local man Christopher Phelan, who had been beaten and stabbed to death. Phelan had come upon a UVF gang as they placed a bomb on the line, aimed at republicans travelling to Bodenstown.[45]

At the end of July, three members of the Miami Showband were murdered by the UVF in Co. Down. Fran O'Toole from Bray, Anthony Geraghty from Dublin and Brian McCoy from Tyrone were killed while other band members were wounded but survived.[46] In late November, a UDA bomb at Dublin Airport killed John Hayes and injured five others. A worker at the airport, Hayes was 38 and from Balbriggan.[47] A few weeks later a car bomb destroyed Kay's Tavern in Dundalk's Crowe Street, killing two men, 62-year-old lorry driver Jack Rooney and 60-year-old Hugh Watters, a tailor.[48]

1976

In February 1976, there was an explosion in the Shelbourne Hotel and incendiary devices caused damage to eight Dublin department stores and shops.[49] The following month, 56-year-old farmer Patrick Mohan was killed and 26 others injured by a car bomb outside a pub in Castleblayney.[50] In early May, loyalists abducted and murdered forestry worker Seamus Ludlow outside Dundalk. Ludlow, who was 47 and living with his elderly mother, was last seen thumbing a lift.[51] During July, several people were hurt when bombs exploded in hotels in Dublin, Limerick, Galway, Rosslare and Killarney.[52] The UDA also claimed responsibility for burning a pub in Castlefin, Co. Donegal after holding up and robbing its customers, during September 1976.[53]

'We can't afford to take any chances'

In April 1977, a UDA man was arrested after an explosion in Boyers department store in Dublin. Nearly 50 unexploded devices were found in several city-centre shops.[54] This was the last major incident for some years.

The cost of bomb damage ran into millions of pounds. Even small explosions caused disruption and increased feelings of vulnerability. Maev-Ann Wren, then a young student, remembered how in 1974 'few Dublin freshers celebrated their Leaving Certificate results with a night on the town. No one wanted to be in Dublin City Centre … not after the bombs and carnage of that May.'[55] By then 'bombs and bomb scares (had) became a way of life for Dubliners who became accustomed to leaving public places … in a hurry'.[56] These fears extended to the relatives of those working in the capital.[57] Hoax calls seemed to 'be the inevitable consequence of a car bomb tragedy'. But as all threats had to be taken seriously, one warning call could bring chaos to a town, a Garda explaining that 'we can't afford to take any chances: every one of them has to be checked out'.[58] Shops were evacuated, streets cleared and traffic curtailed on a regular basis. Bombs in border areas led to restrictions on parking, interference in social life and demands for a more visible security presence.[59]

'A haven for the IRA'[60]

Loyalists claimed their actions were aimed at reminding the 'people of the Republic of their vulnerability to acts of terrorism and their ambivalence towards it'.[61] In 1972, Unionist MP John Taylor asserted that loyalist bombings in border areas were 'an advantage to Northern Ireland security'.[62] Fellow Unionist John Laird claimed in May 1974 that the victims of the Dublin bombs were 'people who have quietly condoned a terrorist campaign'. Indeed, Irish government ministers complained that British allegations about southern support for the IRA encouraged the bombers.[63] Some of the attacks disrupted the south's tourist trade while others were targeted at republican activists.[64] The bombs also contributed to political confusion, often occurring during periods of crisis. Most, however, were designed to cause death and injury to unsuspecting civilians.

Many of the deadliest attacks were initially blamed on republicans. (The UVF did not claim involvement in the 1974 Dublin/Monaghan bombings until 1993.)[65] The killing of Christopher Phelan was at first thought to be part of a republican feud, while the family of Seamus Ludlow were led to believe that the IRA were behind his killing.[66] The Ballyshannon bombing in 1969 was the subject of much speculation until it transpired that Thomas McDowell was a member of Ian Paisley's Free Presbyterian Church. The impact of the December 1972 bombings, which effectively changed the course of a Dáil vote on special powers, led many to conclude that British intelligence was directing the bombers.[67] The role of Ulster Defence Regiment (UDR) members in the Miami Showband massacre encouraged suspicion about collusion.[68]

'The cancer that is the IRA'

However, many observers noted how the attacks produced a sense of disengagement rather than desire for revenge. In December 1972, the *Guardian* claimed that 'for years people here have had a vague and guilty feeling that they have had it easy and amid the distress and fear a few optimistic souls believe the bombs might in the long run save more lives than they took'.[69] The majority of the worst attacks occurred during the years of the 1973–77 Coalition Government. That administration set the tone in blaming the IRA for provoking loyalists. After the Dublin/Monaghan bombs, Taoiseach Liam Cosgrave asserted that 'everyone who has practised or preached violence or condoned violence must bear a share of responsibility for (these) outrages'. [70] Minister for Justice Patrick Cooney claimed after the Dublin Airport attack in 1975 that 'as long as the cancer that is the IRA continues to flourish' then their actions would bring 'the terror of counter-violence into our midst from those who are opposed to the IRA'.[71]

Many noted how, even in 1974, there was little desire for revenge. *Hibernia* suggested that

> it is a sad but true fact that not until last Friday's bomb outrage ... did the people
> of the South come near to appreciating the full extent of the suffering, terror and
> bloodshed which has been an integral part of everyday life for both communities
> in Northern Ireland for the past four years.[73]

British journalist Gillian Linscott found that while 'few people in Dublin doubt
that the bombings were the work of loyalists' there was 'no sign of sectarian
bitterness ... for most people (the deaths) are seen as personal and family
tragedies not as political martyrdom'.[74]

'Healthy and helpful'

In 1974, the British Ambassador Arthur Galsworthy reported that the bombs
had produced no 'general anti-Northern Protestant reaction' and claims that
British agents were involved seemed to have 'made no headway at all'. Instead
'indignation is directed more against the IRA than the Protestant extremists'.
The Irish Minister for Foreign Affairs, Garret FitzGerald, told Galsworthy that
'popular hostility appeared to be directed more against the IRA, on the basis
that "its their bloody fault for starting it all"'. In the ambassador's view, 'the
reactions of both Government and public have been, from our point of view,
healthy and helpful'.[75] A few weeks later, Northern Irish civil servant Maurice
Hayes found that

> the general public attitude in Dublin to the Northern Ireland situation ranges from
> apathy to ambivalence. Most people are fed up with the Northern Ireland issue
> and wish it would go away – preferably not in their direction ... the car bombs
> had a profound effect and people are very afraid of the spread of violence to the
> South.[76]

'Many people seem to have forgotten'

The most astounding feature of the May 1974 bombings was how quickly
they vanished from public discussion. An *Irish Times* report on the first anniversary
of the massacre found that 'many people seem to have forgotten that the
bombings ever took place'. Though there were 'hundreds of people directly
affected' who had 'lost husbands, wives, friends (and) other relatives' and
survivors had seen 'business, their ability to work effectively (or) to converse
with their neighbours' destroyed, there was little public discussion of the events.
Some survivors were 'shocked at the public's facility for forgetting that the
bombings happened', and while grateful for the 'initial backing, warmth and
support of everyone' they were 'upset that it lasted such a short time'. Moreover,
they could not understand why after the bombings 'cordon after cordon was

evaded by the perpetrators'.[77] Significantly, unlike after Bloody Sunday there was no national day of mourning. Neither was there a response such as the burning of the Embassy that might have lingered as an iconic memory. While many pointed the finger at covert British involvement, this was not reflected in public campaigning for some years.[78]

'Personally known to many thousands'

The popular reaction to the Miami Showband massacre was more emotional than in many other cases. This reflected their familiarity. The *Donegal News* noted how 'the slaying of the Miami bandsmen makes a special impact. The poor victims were personally known to many thousands of dance patrons.'[79] Reports from across the 26 Counties noted the shock expressed by 'hundreds of young dancers' when they heard news of the massacre.[80] That the band's repertoire was non-political, that they had a mixed religious membership and were popular north and south were also factors.[81] UDA leader Glen Barr even claimed that many loyalists were 'hanging our heads in shame that this terrible murder was carried out in the name of Protestantism'.[82] In an unusual move, the British Ambassador was summoned to the Department of Foreign Affairs to explain how the killings could have occurred.[83] Benefit concerts for the Miami victims were held across the Republic.

Republican activities

Over 40 fatalities in the south were caused by republican organizations. In theory, the IRA was forbidden by its General Order No. 8 from military operations in the 26 Counties. From 1968 onwards, however, the organization had carried out armed actions in support of various political campaigns. After 1970, the Official IRA continued these activities, intervening with arms during strikes and land disputes.[84] Though these actions were really a continuation of their pre-1969 policy, most now viewed them through the lens of violence in the North. This was especially the case after Cork Official IRA (OIRA) member Martin O'Leary was fatally injured while planting a bomb during a strike at the Silvermines in Tipperary in July 1971. O'Leary's funeral saw a show of strength by the OIRA and a provocative speech by its leader Cathal Goulding.[85] Goulding's organization also bombed a British naval motor launch and blew up the British Ministry of Pensions Office in Cork during 1971.[86]

In contrast, the Provisional IRA claimed that action in the 'Free State' was forbidden 'even under the most trying circumstances'.[87] However, unclaimed attacks – like the fire bombing of the British Rail offices and British Legion social club in Cork during June 1970 – increased as the conflict intensified.[88] Indeed, 'unofficial' actions by members of republican organizations would also be a feature of the 1970s. There was a blast near Special Branch HQ at Dublin

Castle in July and two attempts to blow up the King George IV monument in Dun Laoghaire during late 1970.[89] During July 1971, there were bombs placed at the offices of the British airline BOAC and a British Rail depot in Dublin.[90] During the same month, Dublin British Legion offices in Hatch Street were burned out while a British Legion Hall in Charleville, Co. Cork was destroyed in an arson attack.[91] Following Bloody Sunday there was a wave of attacks, and between January and November 1972 there were 77 fires or explosions caused by incendiary devices in Dublin alone.[92]

Arms raids

Republicans were also involved in raids for arms. During early 1970, weapons and ammunition were taken from FCA (Army Reserve) halls in Waterford and Cork.[93] Bomb making material was also sought. In January 1972, Gardai foiled a raid for gelignite at Irish Industrial Metal Stores in Galway.[94] However, 2,400 lbs of explosives was stolen from the Cement Ltd magazine, near Drogheda in the same month.[95] The Minister for Justice informed the Dáil that there had been ten 'substantial' raids on explosive stores since January 1971.[96] As a result, all gelignite held by small quarry owners and farmers was brought to central depots guarded by the Army and strict control exercised over its supply and use. As commercial explosives became harder to acquire, the IRA sourced fertilizer and various chemicals.[97] Bord na Mona plants were targeted for large amounts.[98] Paramilitaries also stole legally held firearms or were given them by sympathetic owners. During 1971, there were a series of raids for arms on the homes of ex-British military officers.[99]

Robberies

The most visible sign of increased activity was armed robberies. The IRA had not carried such actions since the 1940s, but in February 1967 a group of disaffected members raided a bank in Dublin. This group, who eventually adopted the title Saor Éire, carried out several robberies over the next two years.[100] In May 1969, the IRA itself robbed a security van at Dublin Airport of £25,500.[101] After 1969, the need for supplies of cash to buy arms became critical and the number of armed robberies increased dramatically. Between 1969 and 1970 there were 17, then 30 during 1971, and in 1972 the number rose to 132. The Garda commissioner was in no doubt that this was 'in great measure ... due to the conditions obtaining in the Six County area and their influence on criminal behaviour here'.[102] On occasion, raiders even told staff and customers that the funds were intended 'for the North'.[103] However, neither the Official nor Provisional IRA publicly admitted robbing banks.[104] Indeed, in 1971 Provisional leader Ruairí Ó Brádaigh claimed that these activities were 'completely contrary to the national interest ... this is not the time and the 26 counties is not the place'.[105]

Saor Éire

In contrast, Saor Éire asserted that the money they 'expropriated' from banks was to be 'used to purchase arms and equipment for the forthcoming struggle in Ireland'.[106] In April 1970, 43-year-old Garda Richard Fallon was shot dead by them during a robbery in Dublin. There was widespread shock. The *Irish Press* asserted that the killing 'was not, and cannot be defended as a political act in any sense ... It was simply a brutal murder.'[107] A married man with five children, Fallon's funeral saw a huge turnout. His son, Richard, then 11, later recalled

> all along the route all you could see was a sea of uniforms. Old people were kneeling saying the rosary by the side of the road. It was still that kind of Dublin then, it was a very post Civil War scene ... everyone assumes that my father was given a state funeral. He wasn't: it just looked like one because so many Gardai turned out in force.[108]

Later that year, a Saor Éire member, Liam Walsh, died in an explosion near Dublin's McKee Barracks. Gardai suspected Walsh was planting a bomb, but his comrades claimed that he was dismantling a Loyalist device. Walsh's funeral saw a paramilitary display with shots fired at the GPO.[109]

1971

By 1971, the larger republican organizations were escalating their activities. In August, the Provisional IRA killed a British soldier, Private Ian Armstrong, during a gunbattle inside the Republic, close to the Louth/Armagh border. The shooting led to a diplomatic incident as the British claimed Gardai had not intervened.[110] Attacks from the southern side of the border became commonplace during the winter, *Hibernia* magazine estimating that there had been over 200 such incidents by early 1972.[111] On 19 November, Bríd Carr, a waitress from Lifford, was hit and fatally wounded when the Provisional IRA fired on troops near Strabane.[112] A few days later, Private Robert Benner, a locally born British soldier, was abducted and killed by the Official IRA outside Dundalk.[113] In early December 1971, an ex-British Army officer, C.R.P. Walker, died after a raid on his home near Navan, Co. Meath. Sixty-year-old Walker suffocated after being tied up while his house was ransacked for arms.[114]

1972

In February 1972, the Official IRA carried out two more killings in the 26 Counties. They shot David Seaman, an ex-British soldier accused of being a spy, and Thomas McCann, a 19-year-old British soldier, abducted while home on leave in Dublin.[115] In June, Garda Inspector Samuel Donegan was fatally wounded by a booby-trap bomb near the Cavan/Fermanagh border. An Irish

Army officer was seriously injured in the same blast.[116] The bomb was believed to have been planted by the Provisional IRA and aimed at British forces.

There were also several arson and bomb attacks attributed to republicans during late 1972. In October, bombs were found outside a Garda station in Buncrana and the courthouse in Letterkenny, Co. Donegal.[117] In November, a bomb destroyed the newly built home of a Garda sergeant in Monaghan.[118] Gardai suspected republicans of carrying out the Irish Film Centre blast the same month. Earlier that day there had been a shootout at the Mater Hospital as the IRA had tried to rescue their leader, Seán Mac Stíofáin. Gardai believed the bomb attack was carried out by IRA members acting on their own initiative, though in public memory it is associated with the loyalist bombs of a week later.[119]

The National Coalition
From 1973, the Republic had a new Fine Gael/Labour government which rapidly developed a hardline reputation. By then the Provisional IRA was increasingly carrying out aggressive activity, including robberies, south of the border.[120] By the mid 1970s, one of the key roles of the Provisional organization in the south was providing these funds.[121] Despite their ceasefire, the Official IRA remained active and Saor Éire and unaffiliated republicans also carried out actions. In July 1973, a bomb was found at a British Legion war memorial in Tullamore close to where Minister for Justice Patrick Cooney was due to speak later that day.[122] During August, a British officer was shot at while visiting relatives in Co. Meath.[123] In September, two Royal Ulster Constabulary (RUC) Reservists were wounded in a gun attack outside Westport, Co. Mayo. They had been part of a group of anglers visiting from Fermanagh.[124] In late October, John Doherty, a 31-year-old RUC detective from Lifford, Co. Donegal, was shot dead when home visiting his family.[125]

Ivan Johnston, an ex-RUC detective working as a lorry driver, was abducted in Monaghan during December, shot and his body dumped on the northern side of the border.[126] In January 1974, Cormac McCabe, a part-time UDR officer, was kidnapped from a hotel in Monaghan. His body was found a few days later, again just over the border.[127] On the morning of 30 January, a series of bus and lorry hijackings brought chaos to Dublin. Armed men took over vehicles and used them to block roads, while hoax devices were placed at bridges and intersections. The Provisional IRA claimed the actions were in order to draw attention to a campaign by their prisoners in Britain, notably the Price sisters, for political status. However, the hoaxes were blamed for an accident in which 3-year-old Brian Boylan and his infant sister Elaine were killed.[128]

The British Legion premises in Cork city were fire bombed during April.[129] During the spring there were a series of letter bombs at Dublin banks and finance houses and a primitive fire bomb at the Department of Justice.[130] In

March, Fine Gael Senator Billy Fox was shot dead.[131] The Provisional IRA were responsible, though they denied involvement.[132] During April, Gardai were held up and stripped of their uniforms in separate incidents in Cavan and Leitrim, while a soldier's family were 'terrorized' by an armed gang who stole uniforms from his Leitrim home in the same month.[133] In May, a container packed with explosives was found outside the Garda station in Swanlinbar.[134] During June, a Donegal-born British soldier, Eugene Patton, was kidnapped while visiting his parents in St. Johnston, but escaped unharmed after a day in captivity.[135] In July 1974, a pub owned by relatives of Patrick Cooney was bombed in Swanlinbar.[136]

Kidnap

In January 1974, Provisional IRA members including Rose Dugdale and Eddie Gallagher hijacked a helicopter in Donegal and used it to bomb Strabane RUC barracks from the air.[137] The same group then successfully stole the Beit collection of rare artwork, worth £8 million in May 1974. The paintings were to be exchanged in return for the freedom of IRA prisoners in Britain, but they were soon recovered.[138] After the death of Michael Gaughan on hunger-strike in England during June, Lord and Lady Donoughmore were kidnapped from their home in Tipperary to put pressure on the British to release other prisoners. The Donoughmores were released after five days.[139] The Gallagher group became estranged from the Provisionals and were forced into more dramatic efforts to raise the case of their jailed comrades. A former British Colonial Chief Justice, Sir Paget-Bourke, was briefly abducted from his home in Donnybrook in April 1975.[140] Three Limerick hotels had to be evacuated during May after bombs were found in them. The bombs were planted in support of Rose Dugdale who was on hunger-strike in Limerick prison.[141]

In early October 1975, Dutch industrialist Tiede Herrema of the Ferenka factory in Limerick was kidnapped. His captors issued a statement demanding the release of three IRA prisoners, though the Provisionals disassociated themselves from the action. After a massive security operation, the group was traced to a house in Monasterevin, Co. Kildare. A two-week siege followed, in which a Garda was shot and injured. Eventually Herrema was released unharmed and his captors arrested.[142] The kidnapping led to extensive Gardai and Army sweeps, roadblocks and searches, contributing to the sense of crisis. There had been another fatality after an attempted escape from Portlaoise in March 1975, during which an IRA prisoner, Tom Smith, was shot dead by troops.[143] In the same month a bomb exploded at a Co. Louth pub owned by Paddy Donegan, the Minister for Defence.[144] In February 1976, another bomb exploded late at night in Swanlinbar, where Gardai believed the IRA were retaliating for recent arrests.[145] These incidents occurred in the context of an increasingly bitter struggle between republicans and the authorities.[146]

State of emergency

During 1976, a showdown seemed imminent. A series of bomb attacks in Dublin targeting British-owned stores occurred in the aftermath of the death of hunger-striker Frank Stagg in Britain during February 1976.[147] In May, the IRA shot and wounded Ian Taylor, his wife and another woman in a bar in Cavan town. Taylor was a clerk in the supply section of Scotland Yard and was in Ireland for the wedding of his wife's sister. While making his escape, the gunman also fired at a Garda.[148]

In June, the Provisionals warned that they would consider any judge, civil servant or Garda operating the new Criminal Law (Jurisdiction) Act to be legitimate targets.[149] Gardai believed they prevented a bomb attack on the Governor of Portlaoise prison.[150] Letter bombs were sent to a judge and a court official. In July 1976, two bombs exploded in Green Street courthouse in Dublin, allowing four Provisional IRA men to escape.[151] A week later, the newly-appointed British Ambassador Christopher Ewart-Biggs and civil servant Judith Cooke were killed in a landmine explosion in Sandyford, Co. Dublin.[152] The most senior official at the Northern Ireland Office, Brian Cubbon, was seriously hurt in the blast. The IRA (who did not admit the killing until late September) alleged that Biggs was coordinating British intelligence in southern Ireland.[153]

In response, the government introduced a state of emergency. There was another wave of fire bombings targeting cinemas and pubs in Dublin city centre, for which an IRA member was jailed.[154] In October 1976, Gardai in Portlaoise received a phone call informing them about suspicious activity. When they investigated, a booby-trap bomb exploded, killing 24-year-old Garda Michael Clerkin and seriously injuring other officers.[155] Though the Provisionals denied involvement (claiming British dirty tricks) the bomb had been planted by them.[156] In 1977, there was another hunger-strike in Portlaoise, but the election of a Fianna Fáil government seemed to defuse the escalating conflict.

The more mundane aspects of the armed struggle continued, however. In March 1977, 55-year-old UDR soldier John Reid was shot dead by the IRA while on his farm, which straddled the border near Glaslough, Co. Monaghan.[157] In August 1978, British Army Lieutenant Gary Cass was shot and wounded when leaving the church during his wedding to a local woman in Trim, Co. Meath.[158] In October 1978, 55-year-old Letitia McGrory from Lucan, travelling to Belfast on a 'shoppers special' excursion, was killed by a bomb on the Enterprise train. The IRA claimed responsibility for the attack.[159]

Raids and robberies

Armed robberies remained commonplace, despite increased security. Between 1974 and 1976 there were 81 armed bank raids and 56 post office robberies.[160] In 1974, the Provisional IRA robbed Tralee's General Post Office, netting £74,000, and the Chase Manhattan bank in Shannon, taking £159,000.[161]

Between July and December 1976 there were 41 major robberies in the state, with over £200,000 stolen.[162] The number of armed robberies rose again in 1977 to 236, fell slightly to 217 in 1978 and rose again to 228 in 1979. Not all armed robberies were carried out by republicans. In 1977, two men were jailed in Dublin for a string of raids in which £27,000 was taken. The men had actually fled Belfast after being accused by the IRA of criminal activities.[163]

In other cases, such as the October 1978 robbery of a Donegal post office in which £225,000 was netted, it is unlikely that anyone but a paramilitary group could have managed the raid. Seven heavily armed men took over the local Garda station, smashed communications equipment and stole files before making off with the loot.[164] By 1978, some police and legal sources in Dublin would assert that while the major raids were carried out by republicans, perhaps just '30 per cent of robberies are political'. But as one lawyer explained, 'the majority of the non-political robbers here ... have been introduced to armed robberies by the example of the Northern para-militaries'.[165]

The INLA

The mid 1970s saw the emergence of the Irish National Liberation Army (INLA) after a split with the Officials. The INLA was associated with the Irish Republican Socialist Party (IRSP). From an early stage, supporters were being jailed for involvement in robberies.[166] In March 1976, four IRSP members were charged with the theft of £200,000 from a mail train in County Kildare. Despite evidence of Garda brutality in forcing their confessions, the men were convicted and sentenced to lengthy prison terms.[167] Unusually, in 1980 the Provisional IRA claimed that they, and not the INLA, had carried out that train robbery.[168] But one of the biggest robberies of the decade *was* carried out by the INLA, when a Brinks Mat security van was held up in Co. Limerick and £460,000 taken.[169] (The IRA publicly expressed regret that they had not carried out that operation.)[170]

'It is inevitable that life would be lost.'

The widespread use of arms during robberies had predictable results.[171] In August 1973, the Provisional IRA took £15,000 in a wages raid in Dublin. During the robbery, 54-year-old British Leyland employee James Farrell was shot dead and a colleague critically wounded.[172] In August 1974, Jerome O'Connor, a 52-year-old wages-clerk, was shot and killed during a robbery by dissident OIRA members in Galway.[173] In September 1975, £7,000 was taken in a bank robbery in Dublin. Off-duty Garda Michael Reynolds gave chase and was killed in a scuffle with the raiders.[174] Noel and Marie Murray, the married couple charged with Reynold's murder, were anarchists and ex-members of the Official IRA. Initially sentenced to death, after a retrial this was commuted to life imprisonment.[175] In December 1976, a detective was shot and critically wounded by IRA members during a robbery at Cornelscourt in Dublin.[176] In

November 1977, there was a 12-hour siege in Dublin during which a group of IRA men held several people hostage after a robbery.[177] In February 1978, Provisional IRA members fatally wounded a man during a robbery in Donegal. Fifty-one-year-old Bernard Browne was shot in the chest as he grappled with the raiders.[178] A female clerk was wounded and shots exchanged with detectives during a robbery by the Official IRA near Cork in September that year.[179] In August 1979, Eamon Ryan was shot dead by the Provisional IRA in Tramore, Co. Waterford. Thirty-two-year-old Ryan was with his young son when he entered a bank that was being held up.[180] The *Irish Press* noted after Ryan's death how, with 'three or four bank raids a week, with women and children held hostage … It is inevitable that life would be lost.'[181]

'Tear out their sentimental imperialist heart'

In August 1979, the IRA claimed its highest-profile victim in the Republic. Lord Louis Mountbatten, cousin of Queen Elizabeth, senior Royal Navy officer and the last Viceroy of India, died in an explosion on board a boat off Mullaghmore, Co. Sligo. Also killed were 14-year-old Nicholas Knatchbull (Mountbatten's grandson) and 15-year-old Paul Maxwell, while 82-year-old Lady Patricia Brabourne was fatally wounded. Nicholas Knatchbull's father, mother and twin brother Timothy were badly injured but survived.[182] Timothy Knatchbull recalled how 'the gelignite under the deck must have been between us … we rose in the air (and) went in different directions. I remember a sensation, as if I had been hit with a club, and a tearing sound.'[183] Seventy-nine-year-old Mountbatten had holidayed at Classiebawn Castle, near Mullaghmore, for years and was well known in the area. The IRA were unapologetic about his 'execution', warning the British public that they would 'tear out their sentimental imperialist heart'.[184]

On the same day, the IRA killed 18 British soldiers at Warrenpoint, Co. Down. During the attack, British troops opened fire across Carlingford Lough, shooting dead Londoner Michael Hudson, a holidaymaker who was watching the events.[185] These killings garnered worldwide headlines, but few outside Ireland paid much attention to other fatalities later that year. In October, INLA member Anthony McClelland died in Monaghan hospital after a chase by Gardai ended in a fatal car crash.[186] The IRA shot dead RUC Reservist Stanley Hazelton as he shopped in Glaslough, Co. Monaghan in December 1979.[187]

Republican fatalities

Throughout the 1970s, republicans from the south died north of the border, while a number of northern republicans also suffered violent deaths in the Republic. In April 1971, a Provisional IRA member from Belfast, Tony Henderson, died after being shot in a training accident in Co. Laois.[188] In December that year, a senior member of the Provisional IRA, Jack McCabe, was killed while mixing explosives in his garage in Howth.[189] Two northern republicans, Patrick Casey and Eamon Gamble, badly injured in an explosion in Armagh, died in hospitals in the Republic during March 1972.[190] Cork IRA members, Anthony Ahern and Dermot Crowley, died in separate explosions in the North during the summer of 1973. Ahern was just 17 years old, Crowley 18. Both men were from Mayfield and had attended the North Monastery school.[191] Several thousand attended their funerals in Cork.[192] In August 1973, Seamus Harvey and Gerard McGlynn, from Tyrone, were killed in an explosion just inside Donegal.[193] In January 1975, Kevin Coen, an IRA volunteer from Riverstown in Co. Sligo, was shot dead by British troops near the Fermanagh border. Twenty-eight-year-old Coen, a lorry helper, had joined the IRA shortly after 1969. Sligo County Council observed a minute's silence in his memory.[194] In March 1975, IRA prisoner Tom Smith was shot dead during an attempted escape at Portlaoise. Smith was from Dublin's Harold's Cross and was 27 years of age.[195] Twenty-year-old Sean Campbell, a tiler from Faughart in Louth, was killed in a premature explosion in Armagh in December 1975.[196] Patrick Cannon and Peter McElcar were killed moving a bomb in Tyrone in July 1976. McElcar was 24 and from Ballybofey, Co. Donegal, while 20-year-old Cannon was from Edenmore on Dublin's northside and had been an active trade unionist.[197]

Southern-born republicans also died in British prisons. Michael Gaughan, originally from Ballina, Co. Mayo died after a 64-day hunger-strike in Parkhurst prison in June 1974.[198] Frank Stagg, also from Mayo, died after 62 days on hunger-strike in February 1976.[199] In October 1976, Meath native Noel Jenkinson, who was serving a 30-year sentence for the Aldershot bombing, died of a heart attack in Leicester prison.[200]

Civilians and British forces

There were also several civilians and members of the British forces, originally from the south, who were killed in Northern Ireland. In February 1971, RUC Detective Cecil Patterson, a native of Cavan, was shot dead in Belfast.[201] Another detective, Wicklow-born Dermot Hurley was killed by the IRA in Belfast during November of that year. Fifty-year-old Hurley, a Catholic, had joined the RUC in 1953.[202] In July 1972, British soldier Martin Rooney, a 22-year-old native of Carrick-on-Shannon in Leitrim, was shot by a sniper in Belfast.[203] In the same month Frank McKeown, originally from Monaghan but living in Belfast for 20 years, was shot dead by the British army. In August, 21-year-old hotel worker Philip Fay from Cavan was murdered by loyalists in the same city.[204] During October, Donegal-born RUC Constable Gordon Harron died after a confrontation with loyalists in Belfast.[205] During May 1973, Michael Leonard, a civilian from Donegal, was shot by police after a car chase near the Fermanagh border.[206] In August that year another Donegal native, 16-year-old Henry Cunningham, was killed in a UVF ambush near Belfast.[207] During June 1976, the IRA kidnapped RUC officer William Turbitt after an ambush in south Armagh. Turbitt, a native of Co. Monaghan, was later shot dead.[208] Another RUC officer, Samuel Davison, originally from Donegal, was killed in an IRA attack in Tyrone in June 1977.[209] Loyalists also killed two southerners north of the border during that year. John Lowther, originally from Mayo (though living in England), was murdered in Belfast by the UDA. Larry Potter from Clones was killed by a UVF bomb while working at a meat factory in Co. Antrim.[210]

Feuds and informers

The Official–Provisional split quickly led to bloodshed in the North. While there were shooting incidents in Dundalk during late 1970 and occasional physical clashes between the groups, deadly conflict was avoided in the south.[211] This was not the case in other disputes. In October 1971, Peter Graham of Saor Éire was murdered in Dublin. His death sent an 'unprecedented wave of shock' through Dublin's far-left, especially as it became known that he was killed by fellow members of the group.[212] In December 1973, a man was shot and wounded in Dublin's Abbey Street during another Saor Éire connected dispute.[213]

After the formation of the Irish Republican Socialist Party (IRSP) and its armed wing in December 1974, a violent feud with the Official IRA ensued. After two deaths in Belfast, this spread south in March 1975 when Seán Garland, a leading Official IRA member, was shot and critically wounded near his home in Dublin.[214] In May, the Officials tried to shoot the IRSP leader Seamus Costello after a meeting in Waterford.[215] In June, Larry White, a Saor Éire member, was shot dead by the Officials in Cork city. White's killing was the first political murder in Cork in decades and attracted huge public attention.[216] Though a truce was eventually agreed between the Officials and their rivals, in October 1977 Costello was shot and killed by an Official IRA gunman while sitting in his car in Dublin's North Strand.[217] As the Officials did not claim his murder (in fact, their political wing condemned it), speculation about the culprits persisted for several years.[218]

Republicans also targeted those they accused of betraying them. In October 1975, an Official IRA member killed Billy Wright at his barbershop in Dublin. Wright was alleged to have provided information to Gardai about an armed robbery.[219] In September 1977, John Lawlor was shot dead by the Provisional IRA in Dublin. Lawlor ran a haulage business and had moved arms on the IRA's behalf. He was accused by them of having 'gratuitously given important information to the authorities'.[220] In January 1979, Englishman Arthur Lockett died on the Dublin Mountains after being abducted and beaten by members of the INLA. They suspected him of being a spy.[221] In February 1979, Patrick Sills, a 27-year-old IRA member from Donegal, died after being beaten and shot by his own organization.[222] In October 1979, Christy Shannon from Ballymun was shot dead in a car near Croke Park in Dublin. Though there was no claim of responsibility, it was suggested that he had been targeted by republican paramilitaries.[223] (Republicans were also responsible for killing at least 12 people north of the border during the 1970s and secretly disposing of their bodies in the Republic, the so-called 'Disappeared'.)[224]

'Pointless and counter-productive'

The impact of deaths caused by republicans depended on the nature of the victim, the location and the circumstances of their death. In general, IRA military activity was viewed, even by sympathizers, as something that should be confined to the Six Counties. After Provisional IRA hoax bombings in Dublin during early 1974, the *Irish Press* warned that such actions were 'pointless and counter-productive'. If they meant 'a spread of any proportion of Northern violence to the South then not alone will those who perpetuate such happenings suffer, so too will the Price Sisters campaign, and the whole position of the Northern minority'.[225]

'Symbols of the State'

The killing of Gardai was treated as an attack on society itself. This was in part because it had been so unusual. As a Garda noted after the killing of Richard Fallon in 1970,

> it stunned the place for days. Like I mean, never in our lifetime, the previous shooting of a guard had been in 1942 or something. And it cast a pile of gloom over the whole force for weeks if not months you know because it hadn't happened for so long.[226]

The funerals of the Gardai who died between 1970 and 1979 were all huge public events. Samuel Donegan's saw a 'complete closedown' of business in Cavan, with blinds in houses drawn as his cortege progressed through the town.[227] Nevertheless, Donegan's family felt that his death was 'forgotten' quicker than those of Garda Fallon or Michael Reynolds who were gunned down tackling robbers.[228] The booby-trap killing of Michael Clerkin was regarded as particularly outrageous. When his cortege returned to Monaghan, local people 'shut their shops and lowered their flags for one of the most remarkable funerals the country has seen'.[229] *The Kerryman* described Clerkin as 'the symbol of the State to which the overwhelming majority of the Irish people owe their allegiance. The people who killed Garda Clerkin despise that vast majority which owes an allegiance to that State.'[230]

'Cowardly and heartless'

But many killings, especially those which occurred amid the maelstrom of the 1971–72 period, passed with relatively little comment. While both the Gardai and the Republican movement keep alive the memory of their members killed south of the border during the 1970s, commemoration of civilians is left to their loved ones. The deaths of members of British security forces in border areas were usually less remarked upon than attacks on British soldiers further south.

People also viewed these attacks differently according to when they occurred. During 1972, it looked as if the conflict was heading inexorably towards some final settlement. Violence, while perhaps not desirable, might ultimately result in a united Ireland. In contrast, by the late 1970s many killings seemed pointless. As the *Irish Press* asked after the shooting of Gary Cass in 1978, 'do the IRA seriously think that gunning down a young man on his wedding day is likely to force the British Government to change its policy?'[231] But while the death of Letitia McGrory later that year was described as a 'monstrous deed', it received tiny coverage compared to those of Christopher Ewart-Biggs or Lord Mountbatten.[232] Mountbatten's killing was universally condemned as a 'cowardly and heartless' murder of an elderly man and innocent children.[233]

However, loyalists made the deadliest intervention into southern life during the 1970s, killing nearly 50 people and injuring hundreds. Nobody was ever convicted of the major attacks. Neither were loyalists ever regarded as an existential threat to the state in the way that republicans were. In early 1974, a report into state security was compiled for Justice Thomas Finlay after consultation between government departments, Gardai and the Army. Finlay reported that the 'agreed view submitted to me (was) that the greatest long-term danger to the security of the institutions of the State comes from the activities of the Official IRA and of political groups or associations connected with it'. The Provisionals, in contrast, were thought to be focused on the North, though their 'apparent policy of avoiding militant action within the State could be changed' by factors such as the 'introduction of internment, or the institution of direct co-operation between the Gardai and the British Army'.[234] Loyalists, despite a number of deadly attacks by that stage, were seen as a relatively minor threat.

By the mid 1970s, the Provisionals had superseded the Official IRA as the main focus for the state, and rhetoric directed at them was far harsher than that aimed at those who bombed Dublin and Monaghan. During 1977, the Coalition Government would claim that those involved in the Portlaoise hunger-strike had organized 'a campaign in which almost 2,000 Irish people have been killed and nearly 10,000 injured'.[235] The assertion that republicans were responsible for *every* death and injury in Northern Ireland was a significant indicator of official attitudes.

Republicans themselves denied they were threatening the southern state, even as they robbed banks or carried out killings. In particularly embarrassing or unpopular cases, republicans denied involvement or claimed British agents were responsible. As one IRA activist recalled, 'we lied whenever we thought we could get away with it'.[236] Killings connected to the Troubles generated interest either through their awfulness or sometimes their usefulness in scoring political points. Reactions to them were varied. For many they simply illustrated how 'the North' was making all of Ireland a more dangerous place. Though the numbers of Gardai and civilians who died in bank raids were relatively low, they were a shock to a society with a largely unarmed police force, which regarded itself as being at peace. To those not involved in politics, the shootings and bombings often seemed bewildering and contributed to a pervasive feeling that the violence was 'all going to start down here'.[237]

Notes

1 *New Statesman*, 8 Dec. 1972.
2 *Irish Press*, 9 Aug. 1979.
3 *Irish Times*, 3 Nov. 1969.
4 Ibid., 25 Dec. 1969.
5 Houses of the Oireachtas, *Interim Report on the Report of the Independent Commission of Inquiry into the Dublin Bombings of 1972 and 1973* (Dublin, 2004) pp. 127–129.
6 *Irish Press*, 29 Dec. 1969.
7 Ibid., 5 March 1971.
8 *Northern Standard*, 3 March 1972.
9 *Irish Times*, 21 March 1972.
10 Ibid., 26 May 1972.
11 *Anglo-Celt*, 20 Oct. 1972.
12 *Irish Times*, 6 Nov. 1972.
13 Ibid., 30 Oct. 1972.
14 Ibid., 7 Nov. 1972.
15 Houses of the Oireachtas, *Interim Report, 1972 and 1973*, pp. 23–24.
16 *Irish Times*, 2 Dec. 1972.
17 Ibid., 4 Dec. 1972 and *New Statesman*, 8 Dec. 1972.
18 Houses of the Oireachtas, *Interim Report, 1972 and 1973*, p. 116.
19 *Irish Times*, 29 Dec. 1972.
20 Houses of the Oireachtas, *Interim Report, 1972 and 1973*, pp. 105–114.
21 Ibid., pp. 70–75.
22 Ibid., pp. 137–138.
23 *Leitrim Observer*, 30 June 1973.
24 Houses of the Oireachtas, *Interim Report, 1972 and 1973*, p. 123. *Irish Times*, 25 Oct. 1973.
25 *Irish Times*, 21 Nov. 1973.
26 *Anglo Celt*, 16 Nov. 1973.
27 18 Dec. 1973.
28 *Irish Times*, 22 Dec. 1973.
29 *Cork Examiner*, 23 Jan. 1974.
30 Houses of the Oireachtas, *Interim Report of the Independent Commission of Inquiry into the Bombing of Kay's Tavern, Dundalk* (Dublin, 2006) p. 165.
31 *Irish Times*, 13 June 1974.
32 Ibid., 15 April 1974.
33 'Brown' in Gillfillan, *Trinity Tales*, p. x.
34 Houses of the Oireachtas, *Interim Report on the Report of the Independent Commission of Inquiry into the Dublin and Monaaghan Bombings* (Dublin, 2003) pp. 1–6.
35 E. Conlon. (Ed.) *Later On: The Monaghan Bombing Memorial Anthology* (Dingle, 2004).

36 *Irish Independent*, 18 May 1974.
37 *Irish Times*, 20 and 28 May 1974.
38 *Irish Press*, 21 May 1974.
39 *Northern Standard*, 28 June 1974.
40 *Irish Times*, 27 July 1974.
41 *Guardian*, 3 Sept. 1974.
42 *Irish Times*, 9 Dec. 1974.
43 Houses of the Oireachtas, *Kay's Tavern*, pp. 170–171.
44 *Irish Times*, 10 March 1975.
45 *Irish Press*, 23 June 1975.
46 Ibid., 1 Aug. 1975.
47 Houses of the Oireachtas, *Kay's Tavern*, pp. 138–140.
48 Ibid., pp. 13–16.
49 *Irish Times*, 14 Feb. 1976.
50 Houses of the Oireachtas, *Kay's Tavern*, p. 145–147.
51 *Irish Press*, 20 Aug. 1976.
52 *Irish Times*, 5 July 1976.
53 *Donegal News*, 11 Sept. 1976.
54 *Irish Press*, 12 April 1977.
55 F. Callanan (Ed.) *The Literary and Historical Society 1955–2005* (Dublin, 2005) p. 211.
56 *Irish Press*, 16 May 1975.
57 É. Walshe, *Cissie's Abattoir* (Cork, 2009) p. 98.
58 *Irish Times*, 20 May 1974.
59 Ibid., 30 Dec. 1972 and 5 Jan. 1973.
60 Houses of the Oireachtas, *Kay's Tavern*, p. 16.
61 Ibid.
62 *Irish Times*, 20 Oct. 1972.
63 Ibid., 4 Dec. 1975.
64 *Sunday Independent*, 4 July 1976.
65 A. Cadwallader, *Lethal Allies: British Collusion in Ireland* (Cork, 2013) p. 222.
66 *Irish Press*, 21 July 1975 and 12 May 1976. *Magill*, April 1999.
67 *Sunday Times*, 12 Aug. 1973.
68 *Irish Press*, 1 Aug. 1975.
69 *Guardian*, 4 Dec. 1972.
70 *Irish Times*, 22 May 1974.
71 Ibid., 6 Dec. 1975.
72 Coogan, *The Irish*, p. 225.
73 *Hibernia*, 24 May 1974.
74 *Guardian*, 20 May 1974.
75 A. Galsworthy report to Cabinet Ministerial Committee on Northern Ireland, 21 May 1974, FCO 87/530 NAUK.
76 M. Hayes to K. Bloomfield, 25 June 1974, FCO 87/311 NAUK. However, Hayes admitted to having few contacts with Fianna Fáil supporters. I am grateful to Alan Power for providing me with this reference.
77 *Irish Times*, 15 May 1975.
78 *An Phoblacht*, 31 May 1974.
79 *Donegal News*, 9 Aug. 1975.
80 *Limerick Leader*, 15 Aug. 1975.
81 S. Travers and N. Fetherstone, *The Miami Showband Massacre: The Search for Truth* (Edinburgh, 2017) p. 58.
82 *Sunday World*, 3 Aug. 1975.

83 *Irish Times*, 1 Aug. 1975.
84 Hanley and Millar, *Revolution*, pp. 238–240, 260.
85 Ibid., pp. 243–244.
86 *Irish Times*, 23 April 1971 and 6 July 1971.
87 *An Phoblacht*, Jan. 1972.
88 *Irish Times*, 30 June 1970 and 6 July 1970.
89 Ibid., 7 Dec. 1970.
90 Ibid., 26 July 1971.
91 Ibid., 12 July 1971.
92 *Irish Press*, 17 Nov. 1972.
93 K. McCarthy, *Republican Cobh and the East Cork Volunteers* (Cobh, 2008) pp. 324–325. *Irish Press*, 11 Nov. 1971 and 15 Aug. 1972.
94 *Connacht Tribune*, 7 and 14 Jan. 1972.
95 *Drogheda Independent*, 28 Jan. 1972.
96 G. Ó Faoleán, 'Ireland's Ho Chi Minh trail? The Republic of Ireland's role in the Provisional IRA's bombing campaign, 1970–1976', *Small Wars and Insurgencies* 25:5–6 (2014) pp. 976–991.
97 Ibid.
98 *Irish Times*, 2 Feb. 1974.
99 K. McCarthy, *Republican Cobh*, pp. 331–334.
100 Hanley and Millar, *Revolution*, p. 63.
101 Ibid., p. 118.
102 *Irish Times*, 27 Oct. 1973.
103 Ibid., 1 Oct. 1971.
104 Ibid., 31 Aug. 1971.
105 *Fortnight*, Nov. 1971.
106 *Irish Times*, 2 Jan. 1970.
107 *Irish Press*, 4 April 1970.
108 L. Walsh, *The Final Beat: Gardaí who died in the Line of Duty* (Dublin, 2001) p. 8.
109 *Irish Times*, 20 Oct. 1970.
110 Ibid., 1 Sept. 1971.
111 *Hibernia*, 7 Jan. 1972.
112 Houses of Oireachtas, *Interim Report, 1972 and 1973*, pp. 101–104.
113 *Irish Times*, 9 Dec. 1971.
114 Ibid., 6 Dec. 1971.
115 Hanley and Millar, *Revolution*, pp. 175.
116 *Anglo-Celt*, 16 June 1972.
117 *Irish Times*, 28 Oct. 1972.
118 Ibid., 25 Nov. 1972.
119 Houses of the Oireachtas, *Interim Report, 1972 and 1973*, pp. 23–33. There are suspicions of links with associates of the Littlejohn brothers.
120 It would seem that the Provisionals did not embark on armed robberies in the Republic until 1973. See McGuill, 'Violence', p. 84.
121 J.J. Barrett, *Martin Ferris: Man of Kerry* (Dingle, 2005) p. 45.
122 *Irish Times*, 9 July 1973.
123 *Irish Independent*, 24 Aug. 1973.
124 *Irish Times*, 3 Sept. 1973.
125 Ibid., 30 Oct. 1973.
126 Ibid., 18 Dec. 1973.
127 Ibid., 26 Jan. 1974.
128 *Irish Press*, 31 Jan. 1974. *Sunday World*, 3 Feb. 1974.
129 *Irish Times*, 3 Sept. 1974.

130 Ibid., 19 Feb. 1974 and 7 March 1974.
131 *Irish Press*, 13 March 1974.
132 *An Phoblacht*, 22 March 1974.
133 *Irish Independent*, 30 April 1974.
134 *Anglo-Celt*, 10 May 1974.
135 *Irish Times*, 26 June 1974.
136 *Anglo-Celt*, 12 July 1974.
137 *Irish Times*, 26 Nov. 1974.
138 Ibid., 25 June 1974.
139 *Irish Press*, 7 and 10 June 1974.
140 *Irish Times*, 17 May 1975.
141 Ibid., 7 May 1975.
142 Ibid., 22 and 25 October 1975. P. Howard, *Hostage: Notorious Irish Kidnappings* (Dublin, 2004) pp. 120–184.
143 National Commemoration Committee, *Tírghrá* (Dublin, 2002) p. 165.
144 *Irish Times*, 27 March 1975.
145 Houses of the Oireachtas, *Kay's Tavern*, pp. 168–169.
146 'Miscellaneous incidents July–December 1976', in 2008/79/3109 NAI.
147 R. O'Donnell, *Special Category: The IRA in English Prisons, 1968–78* (Dublin, 2012) p. 365.
148 *Anglo-Celt*, 28 May 1976.
149 *Irish Times*, 1 June 1976.
150 'Miscellaneous incidents July–December 1976' in 2008/79/3109 NAI.
151 *Irish Times*, 15 July 1976.
152 Ibid., 22 and 24 July 1976.
153 Ibid., 20 Sept. 1976.
154 Ibid., 31 Aug. 1976.
155 *Irish Press*, 18 Oct. 1976.
156 *An Phoblacht*, 19 October 1976. L. Walsh, *Final Beat*, p. 69.
157 *Irish Press*, 10 March 1977.
158 Ibid., 28 Aug. 1978.
159 *Republican News*, 21 Oct. 1978.
160 'Level of violence in 26 Counties resulting in declaration of state of emergency', D/T. 2006/133/581, NAI.
161 Barrett, *Martin Ferris*, pp. 52–57.
162 Military Intelligence report, 15 Feb. 1977, D/J 2008/79/3109 NAI.
163 *Irish Times*, 29 Nov. 1977.
164 Ibid., 4 Oct. 1978.
165 *Magill*, July 1978.
166 *Irish Times*, 3 March 1975, 9 April 1975.
167 Irish Republican Socialist Party, *Framed Through The Special Criminal Court, The 'Great Train Robbery' Trial* (Dublin, 1979).
168 D. Dunne and G. Kerrigan, *Round Up the Usual Suspects* (Dublin, 1984) pp. 261–265.
169 J. Holland and H. McDonald, *INLA: Deadly Divisions* (Dublin, 1994) pp. 128–129.
170 *Magill*, Aug. 1978.
171 *Irish Independent*, 19 Oct. 1974.
172 *Irish Times*, 4 Aug. 1973.
173 *Connacht Tribune*, 16 Aug. 1974.
174 *Irish Press*, 12 Sept. 1975. L. Walsh, *Final Beat*, pp. 39–59.
175 *Irish Times*, 10 June 1976.
176 Ibid., 18 Dec. 1976.

177 Ibid., 28 Nov. 1977.
178 *Donegal News*, 4 Feb. 1978.
179 *Irish Press*, 6 Sept. 1978.
180 *Munster Express*, 10 Aug. 1979.
181 *Irish Press*, 9 Aug. 1979.
182 Ibid., 28 Aug. 1979.
183 T. Knatchbull, *From A Clear Blue Sky: Surviving the Mountbatten Bomb* (London, 2010) p. 70.
184 *An Phoblacht/Republican News*, 1 Sept. 1979.
185 *Irish Press*, 29 Aug. 1979.
186 Ibid., 19 Oct. 1979.
187 *Irish Times*, 24 Dec. 1979.
188 Ibid., 6 April 1971.
189 National Commemoration Committee, *Tírghrá*, p. 30.
190 *Irish Press*, 9 March 1972.
191 National Commemoration Committee, *Tírghrá*, pp. 108 and 113.
192 *Irish Times*, 15 May and 29 June 1973.
193 *Donegal News,* 18 Aug. 1973.
194 *Irish Times*, 4 Feb. 1975.
195 *Irish Press*, 18 March 1975.
196 National Commemoration Committee, *Tírghrá*, p. 177.
197 Ibid., pp. 198–199. *An Phoblacht*, 13 July 1977.
198 National Commemoration Committee, *Tírghrá*, p142. *Irish Press*, 13 February 1976.
199 Ibid., p. 186.
200 *Irish Press*, 12 Oct. 1976.
201 *Anglo-Celt*, 5 March 1971.
202 *Irish Times*, 12 Nov. 1971.
203 *Leitrim Observer*, 22 July 1972.
204 *Anglo-Celt*, 21 July and 25 Aug. 1972.
205 P. Mulroe, *Bombs, Bullets and the Border: Policing Ireland's Frontier, Irish Security Policy, 1969–1978* (Dublin, 2017) p. 98.
206 J. McVeigh, *Taking a Stand: Memoir of an Irish Priest* (Dublin, 2008) pp. 120–121.
207 *Irish Press*, 11 Aug. 1973.
208 *Northern Standard*, 23 June 1976.
209 *Irish Press*, 3 June 1977.
210 Ibid., 26 Jan. and 29 March 1977.
211 *Hibernia*, 20 Nov. 1970.
212 *This Week*, 12 Nov. 1971.
213 *Irish Times*, 3 Dec. 1973.
214 Ibid., 3 March 1975.
215 *Irish Press*, 8 May 1975.
216 Hanley and Millar, *Revolution*, pp. 299–300.
217 *Irish Times*, 6 Oct. 1977.
218 Hanley and Millar, *Revolution*, pp. 347 and 402.
219 Ibid., p. 309.
220 *Irish Times*, 12 Sept. 1977.
221 Ibid., 16 June 1979.
222 *Donegal News*, 27 Feb. 1979.
223 *Irish Times*, 20 Oct. 1979. McGuill, 'Violence', p. 106.
224 Ibid., 10 Aug. 2005 and 2 Aug. 2010.
225 *Irish Press*, 31 Jan. 1974.
226 V. Conway, *Policing*, p. 113

227 *Irish Times*, 12 June 1972.
228 L. Walsh, *Final Beat*, p. 23.
229 *Irish Press*, 20 Oct. 1976.
230 *The Kerryman*, 22 Oct. 1976.
231 *Irish Press*, 28 Aug. 1978.
232 Ibid., 13 Oct. 1978.
233 Ibid., 28 Aug. 1979. *Magill*, Sept. 1979.
234 Joint Committee on Justice, Equality, Defence and Womens Rights, *Report of Independent Commission of Inquiry into the Dublin and Monaghan Bombings* (Dublin, 2003) pp. 34–35.
235 L. Cosgrave to Ambassador, Holy See, 6 May 1977 in G. FitzGerald Papers, UCDA P215/403.
236 K. Conway, *Southside*, p. 93.
237 *New Statesman*, 8 Dec. 1972.

4

Offences against the state, 1970–72

The southern state's tried and tested response to subversion had always been emergency law. Internment, military courts and restrictions on the press had all been implemented during the Civil War, the Emergency and the IRA's 1956–62 campaign.[1] But the situation after 1969 was unfamiliar. The emotional upsurge that accompanied the outbreak of conflict in the North made security measures against republicans problematic. During 1969 and again in 1972, plans to introduce repressive laws were stymied by public solidarity with nationalists. But there was also a contradiction in southern nationalism that was to prove crucial. As British diplomats noted in late 1972

> 'Nationalist struggles' in the North, whether about civil rights or reunification, deeply affect emotions in the South. To many action against 'Irish patriots' is unacceptable: action against those threatening the institutions of the Republic is a different matter.[2]

While in popular memory repression is associated with the 1973–77 coalition, and censorship almost entirely with Conor Cruise O'Brien, when Fianna Fáil left power in 1973 they had acquired a much harder-line reputation on law and order than their rivals. Jack Lynch's administration had introduced the Forcible Entry Bill, the Prisons Bill, the Special Criminal Court and the Offences Against the State Amendment Bill. They had also tightened control of radio and television and sacked the RTE Authority for objecting to government broadcasting policy.[3]

'Immature minds'

The government had been on the verge of introducing special legislation against the IRA *before* the North exploded. In early August 1969, Jack Lynch met

RTE's Director-General and Deputy Head of News, along with the 'editors of Dublin and Cork newspapers' to express his concern at increased IRA activity. The Taoiseach suggested that the organization's campaign 'against foreigners might be broadened to include nationals who were considered to have too much land or wealth and that this economic campaign was a prelude to a military campaign'. He asked the media men to refrain from publicizing IRA statements or using language which he claimed romanticized them in 'immature minds'. Lynch also asked that the term 'illegal organization' be used instead of 'IRA'. He signalled that the government was intent on introducing new measures to deal with that organization's activities soon.[4] However, by September, events across the border had transformed the political mood and made this impossible.[5] Instead, republicans took advantage of the emotional period after August to intensify their training and arms procurement.

1970: 'The politics of underkill'?

During 1970, several cases of northern men captured with arms came before the courts. In Donegal during January seven Derry men pleaded guilty to unlawful possession of arms. They were given probation after the Donegal State Solicitor recommended 'Let them go in peace and leave their firearms behind them'.[6] Defendants in these cases tended to emphasize that weapons were not 'to be used against forces in the 26 Counties but for the protection of people in the 6 Counties' and were usually released on probation or with a small fine.[7] The policy was characterized by *This Week* magazine as the 'politics of underkill'.[8]

During 1970, an Irish civil servant explained to a British counterpart how there was a 'depth of public sympathy among Irish people of all kinds for men sentenced for political offences – irrespective of the logic or even of the merits'.[9] By the end of the year the mood had shifted somewhat. Frustration with republicans was accelerated by the killing of Garda Fallon in April. After the shooting, one detective stated that

> the honeymoon is now over. One of our men has been killed, a father of five, who never did harm to anybody. We've always been painted as the villains, the ones who were brutal. You go up and ask Dick Fallon's widow today who are the brutal ones.[10]

However, despite a large Gardai presence, no action was taken to prevent shots being fired at the GPO during the funeral of Saor Éire's Liam Walsh in October.[11] There was a sense though, by the year's end, that the government was getting tougher. During November, 15 Official IRA members were arrested at a training camp in Louth and a Dublin IRA member was

sentenced to seven years in jail for armed robbery.[12] Nevertheless, there was
shock when on 4 December Lynch announced that internment was to be
introduced.[13]

'A step on the road to dictatorship'

The government claimed this was in response to information that Saor Éire
were about to assassinate or kidnap politicians and civil servants.[14] Ministers
were adamant that the threat from a 'secret armed conspiracy' was credible. It
was suggested that Saor Éire was targeting either the Minister for Justice
Desmond O'Malley, Peter Berry of the Department of Justice or Chief Superintendent John Fleming of the Special Branch. Reports that the Curragh camp
was to be reopened and that lists of potential internees had been drawn up
were soon in circulation. A series of Garda raids on republican activists during
December was seen as a dry-run for internment.[15] The announcement provoked
initial shock, followed by outrage. Most commentators felt that the threat,
even if credible, hardly justified such a measure, the *Irish Times* warning that
'internment camps mean a step on the road to dictatorship'.[16] The *Irish Press*,
on the other hand, while expressing 'surprise and puzzlement', nevertheless
considered that 'in a country in which there is a tradition of not recognising
the courts, intimidating jurors and, above all, not giving evidence against
political defendants ... some such recourse as detention camps is inevitable if
distasteful'.[17] Republicans, the left, the labour movement and civil liberties
groups were united in opposition. Northern activists, from Paddy Devlin of
the SDLP to Michael Farrell of People's Democracy, noted that internment
in the south would only embolden the Unionist government in its use of
repression north of the border.[18] (Indeed, Reverend Martin Smyth of the
Orange Order applauded Lynch's proposal.) Eamonn McCann and Bernadette
Devlin, along with Official Sinn Féin's Máirín de Burca, Labour's John Horgan
and solicitor Con Lehane of Citizens For Civil Liberty, were among those
who addressed a rally of 1,000 people at the Dáil. Walkouts and 'teach-ins'
took place in several universities, and leading trade unionists forcibly expressed
their opposition.[19] Four Labour TDs were suspended from Leinster House for
criticizing the government's refusal to allow debate on the issue. Limerick TD
Stevie Coughlan warned that 'the Taoiseach knows where this is going to
end, in hunger strikes and civil war. Be it on the Taoiseach's head.'[20] Noel
Browne called for industrial action in protest, while Conor Cruise O'Brien
was physically accosted by Fianna Fáil TDs when he denounced the measure.[21]
Most of those who opposed the government suggested that its claims about
armed threats were fantasy. Provocatively, however, Saor Éire asserted that
they might indeed just do what the government alleged they were planning
to do.[22]

'If your people are responsible for internment down here you're all dead'

Tánaiste Erskine Childers dismissed the 'the wails of protest from a limited number of people' to the proposed measure.[23] But less than a fortnight later the issue had disappeared from the political agenda.[24] Desmond O'Malley later claimed that Gardai had information that Saor Éire were planning a major operation. But the authorities were also aware that neither of the two IRA organizations wanted a clampdown in the Republic. By signalling that they were about to introduce internment, the government hoped that the IRA(s) would head off such a threat by neutralizing Saor Éire themselves. So, O'Malley argued, the government would 'threaten to do it (introduce internment) and convey to a much more sizeable subversive organisation the fact that we were considering that and let them exert pressure to see that this matter didn't happen. It wouldn't have suited the more sizeable organisation. And that's the way it worked, and it did work.'[25] Provisional IRA Chief of Staff Seán Mac Stíofáin later claimed that he had 'sent two people to the two people in Saor Éire. I said "look if your people are responsible for internment down here you're all dead".' [26] The whole issue was forgotten remarkably quickly, though when internment was introduced north of the border during August 1971, Unionists were quick to point out that Lynch had threatened to introduce it less than a year before.

'A blind eye'?

The escalation of violence during 1971 brought another upsurge in solidarity with northern nationalists. There was a widespread perception that this was felt by members of the security forces as well as the general public. In December 1971, it was claimed that 'there is already considerable sympathy for the Northern activities of the IRA amongst individual members of the Gardai up to Superintendent level and there have been cases where some Gardai have turned a blind eye to IRA activities'.[27] After internment was introduced, there were rumours that Gardai in Dublin met privately to discuss whether they would be forced to cooperate with the British and guard their Embassy. One was quoted as claiming that 'we will not stand idly by while Irishmen are being shot by British forces'.[28] There were a small number of cases of soldiers or reservists stealing arms or ammunition for use by republicans. [29] FCA Captain Joe Keohane, a Kerry All-Ireland medal winner, was court-martialled for stealing ammunition and fined £25. Keohane later joined the Aontacht Éireann party.[30] There were also men from nationalist areas of the North serving in the Irish Army and a few became involved in republican organizations. (One, John Starrs from Derry, was killed in May 1972.)[31] A report in late 1971 claimed that 'one of the Army's fears was that some groups of FCA men might decide to have a go on their own at British patrols. Along the border, some of these men made it clear last weekend that if there was any more cheek from the British Army or the Ulster Defence Regiments, they would let fly, and take the consequences.'[32] The mood became even more intense after Bloody Sunday. One IRA activist claimed that

> the southern police and army ignored us; some of them openly encouraged us. 'I hope you have one set up for those bastards'. That remark came from a patrol car of Irish police who met us at the border shortly after Bloody Sunday. There was an understanding between us and the southern Irish security forces. They wouldn't bother us and we didn't bother them.[33]

The British, frustrated by what seemed the unwillingness of the Irish Government to clamp down, reflected that

> rural areas of the Republic resent authority and Gardai are not accepted by the locals; the Gardai and the IRA traditionally seek to avoid one another. This system works unless the IRA engage in activities which the State cannot condone; then either the State allows law and order to break down, or it acts. The Irish Government fear at present that they may be forced to confront the IRA when they believe the IRA to command considerable public sympathy ... the Civil War is within living memory and the dangers of a renewed 'Republican/Free Stater' split are very real, and are so regarded by the Irish themselves.[34]

Those brought before the courts on arms charges still often received light sentences. A 70-year-old Kerryman caught in possession of a submachine gun got a £4 fine.[35] While some alleged fear of the IRA was a factor, Sinn Féin's Ruairí Ó Brádaigh claimed to have 'seen jurors shaking hands with men they had just tried after a recent court case in Dundalk ... it is because we have got juries like these that the accusations of intimidation are farcical'.[36] There appeared to be considerable opposition to special legislation, 15 Motions at the 1971 Fianna Fáil Ard Fheis demanding repeal of the existing Offences Against the State Act.[37] 'Wigmore' in the *Sunday Independent* warned that

> It's no secret that Britain is applying heavy pressure on the Government to get tougher with the IRA but we should not do so at the expense of the impartiality and fairness of our legal institutions. Once law becomes the servant of the State, it loses the respect of the general public. This has already happened in the North. Nobody wants it to happen here.[38]

The *Longford Leader* argued that 'the facts about the carnage (and) especially the nightly encroachments of British troops into Catholic (only) areas do not suggest that the IRA, who unfortunately appear to be their only reliable defence, should be attacked from this side of the Border. Illegal or not.'[39]

'Soft peddling'?

It was not only the British who were frustrated. Liam Cosgrave complained in October 1971 that 'we in the Republic have now come perilously close to political anarchy ... the illegal armies have become so active; their drilling and other activities so notorious up and down the country, that the one lawful army of the state appears to be upstaged by them'.[40] A Dublin businessman complained to the Taoiseach that

> your Government's position on the I.R.A. and subversive forces is ambiguous to say the least ... believe me, Taoiseach, when I say I am no way unsympathetic to the terrible plight of our Northern people but unless the Government of the Republic does its duty and Rule of Law is carried out, then credibility of any kind is hard to maintain.

The writer claimed that a recent case involving Official IRA leader Cathal Goulding was evidence of this 'apparent soft peddling'. Two 'international bankers' he had spoken to 'were appalled that no firmer action had been taken against Mr. Goulding'.[41] However, there had been legislative action by the government, with the Forcible Entry Bill becoming law in September 1971. This was particularly aimed at housing protesters and others who favoured direct action.[42] In a number of cases, Gardai were accused of carrying out only limited investigations for fear of upsetting local republicans. In Lifford, Bríd Carr's family later complained that Gardai made little effort to question locals after the gun attack in which she died, despite many people witnessing the IRA unit responsible.[43] After the shooting of Private Robert Benner near Dundalk, *Hibernia* magazine alleged that the Dublin government 'fearing that they might find out in an investigation that Benner was in fact taken hostage in the South, just did not want to know'.[44]

However, a series of provocations, including the armed holding up of FCA members in Co. Louth and stealing of rifles and machine guns from them, led to calls for action.[45] By January 1972, news reports suggested that the government was taking an 'extremely grave view' of cross-border incidents and interference with juries, and was considering setting up military courts.[46] But while Bloody Sunday forced postponement of these measures, the destruction of the British Embassy concentrated minds. The Minister for Defence Jerry Cronin was convinced that 'those who were capable of burning down an embassy were quite capable of burning down Dáil Éireann'.[47] Desmond O'Malley noted how 'known criminals' had taken advantage of the disorder but claimed not to be 'worried about them' in contrast to the subversives who had 'taken advantage of genuine sorrow of the ordinary people to pursue their own objectives'.[48] In the aftermath of the burning, a Dublin woman told Fine Gael's Garrett FitzGerald that she was ashamed of 'the way last night Irish people attacked our own police force. Gallant men who were there only doing their duty and with very little reward. These men arrest political extremists with sometimes a grave risk to themselves then see these men released with little or no sentences.'[49]

Encouraging 'subversive elements'?

The government's private frustration with the state broadcaster was already evident. After October 1968, the republican *United Irishman* had noted how 'the television set can be abused, but its potential for teaching lessons more vividly than countless books or exhortations was clearly shown by the events of Derry'.[50] At the time, about 70% of southern Irish households had televisions.[51] The importance of TV was also recognized by the influential civil servant T.K. Whitaker when he complained in August 1969 that RTE had given the republican movement 'quite disproportionate publicity' during the crisis, suggesting that an outsider might have thought they were the main opposition.[52] In late 1969, the Minister for Justice complained again about the appearance of IRA leaders on RTE.[53] Since 1960, the government had possessed power under Section 31 of the Broadcasting Act which enabled it to prohibit RTE from broadcasting material considered subversive. Sinn Féin had not been allowed party political broadcasts during the 1961 election, for instance.[54] However, between 1970 and 1971, representatives of both Official and Provisional IRAs were interviewed on radio and televison. In July 1970, the government complained that republicans and left-wingers were being given undue prominence in news and current affairs programmes.[55] The '7 Days' programme featured former IRA prisoner and Sinn Féin MP Tom Mitchell in a discussion on the northern elections, for example.[56] The Minister for Post and Telegraphs, Gerry Collins, believed that the 'left wing and even some pretty extreme elements of it' had influence at the station.[57]

In December 1970, Official Sinn Féin's Tomas Mac Giolla walked out of the studio in protest at the exclusion of the Provisional leader Ruairí Ó Bradáigh from a discussion about internment on the 'Féach' programme. The programme's producer, Eoghan Harris (a supporter of the Officials), then publicly took issue with RTE management's decision to ban Ó Bradáigh.[58] In June 1971, Gerry Collins refused to take part in the radio programme 'This Week' because it featured representatives of the Provisional IRA. Fianna Fáil TD's complained afterwards that the Provos had been given a free platform 'to advocate violence'. Some opposition TDs disagreed, claiming that IRA spokesmen's lack of concern about civilian casualties and what seemed to be their 'approval for the polices of the Rev. Ian Paisley' would be counterproductive with southern listeners.[59] But Jack Lynch claimed that it was not in the public interest that a station funded by the taxpayer promote illegal organizations. In reply, Labour's Conor Cruise O'Brien stated that 'to have them argue and have them answered was the best way of dealing with them (the IRA) and not by silencing them on air as the Government had tried to do'.[60]

But Collins informed RTE that the show had been 'contrary to the national interest' and warned that 'subversive elements should not be given RTE facilities as a platform for their publicity'. On 28 September 1971, RTE's '7 Days' carried interviews with Seán Mac Stíofáin and Cathal Goulding. Collins then issued a written directive under Section 31 ordering the station to 'refrain from broadcasting any matter that could be calculated to promote the aims and activities of any organisation which engages in, promotes, encourages or advocates the attainment of any particular objective by violent means'. Eoghan Harris, who was also a leading activist in the Workers Union of Ireland (WUI), predicted 'strong and persistent resistance to this directive. There are many of us who feel that it would be better to transmit no programmes than to transmit programmes that were censored.'[61] The RTE Authority argued that it would be 'failing in its statutory duty were it to ignore the existence of significant elements in the community; legal or illegal'.[62] Despite the station's formal opposition to censorship, there was a wariness about being perceived as being sympathetic to republicans. Broadcaster Donnacha Ó Dúlaing, who helped organize a 'Santa Claus train' to Belfast and a programme featuring internee's families during December 1971, found management suspicious of his efforts.[63]

'Section 31, what Section 31?'

The exact legal status of interviews with republican activists on RTE was still unclear in early 1972. Both Fianna Fáil and Fine Gael TDs regularly claimed that the station was too sympathetic to the IRA. During June 1972, the Dáil heard complaints that RTE 'glorified men of violence' and Gerry Collins informed the House that he was conveying these views to the station's Authority. Eoghan Harris and his allies were increasingly prominent in disputes at the station.[64] Harris appeared on the 'Late Late Show' denouncing both EEC membership and 'the ruling class of six of our counties, who used a local and especially vicious form of social control called religious bigotry'.[65] In the *Irish Times* John Healy criticized the tone of RTE's Kevin Myer's reporting in the aftermath of the Official IRA's killing of a local soldier in Derry. Myers had claimed that despite clerical condemnation, the IRA in the city was not isolated. Healy commented that 'Myers' own value-free position is well understood'. He also claimed that Ruairí Ó Brádaigh had 'had a rather good spell of it on the State broadcasting service', leading Healy to wonder 'Section 31, What Section 31?'[66] Fianna Fáil TDs complained that after the Mountjoy riot RTE referred to prisoners as 'Republicans' giving them 'an aura and status to which they were not entitled'.[67] Collins told the Dáil that 'an undue amount of time has been given to these people (who) represent nobody but themselves, to express their viewpoints and philosophies which are clearly unacceptable to the vast majority of Irish people'.[68] In its defence, RTE claimed that between October 1971 and June 1972 Sinn Féin had only been interviewed four times in the '7 Days' programme, three times in the Irish language 'Féach', and seven times in news bulletins.[69] Indeed, some TDs such as Labour's Seán Treacy complained that RTE should not discriminate against republicans when it continued to give coverage to 'bloodthirsty maniacs Bill Craig and his colleagues'.[70] Nevertheless, relations between Fianna Fáil and RTE continued to deteriorate.[71]

'Deal effectively with these illegal organizations'

In late February 1972, just a few weeks after Bloody Sunday and shortly after the Aldershot bombing, the Fianna Fáil Ard Fheis had heard an appeal from the Minister for Justice. O'Malley argued that

> illegal organisations had done more to hinder the reunification of the country over the past few years than any other single factor. The stupid policies of the British Government and of the Unionist Government could not go on forever. Their day is very nearly at an end now, but unfortunately they can justify themselves in their own eyes – and justify the sort of measures they have taken to one another – by the activities of the IRA.

O'Malley asserted that the end of partition was 'now within our grasp but (the) one group of organisations that can thwart us in achieving the objective are, the illegal, subversive organisations ... This we cannot allow ... We have existed as a party for 46 years to achieve this objective. We almost have it. Let us achieve it in the lifetime of our great founder.' A motion from the Brothers Pearse cumann calling on the government to take steps to control and suppress illegal organizations was passed.[72] There was little indication at the Ard Fheis of the sympathy that republicans presumed existed for them from the rank and file of the governing party.

'The ultra-liberals'

In May 1972, the government made the first move, re-introducing the non-jury Special Criminal Court. Section 30 of the Offences Against the State Act also allowed Gardai to arrest and detain for 24 hours those suspected of being involved in subversion. The matter of jury tampering was brought to a head after Cathal Goulding was acquitted of incitement after a belligerent speech at the funeral of Official IRA member Martin O'Leary in Cork. Goulding had warned of 'the bomb and the bullet' being deployed by the Officials.[73] The case was adjourned several times as the Official IRA made a concerted effort to intimidate the jury. An RTÉ tape recording of the speech was found to be blank and ten jurors failed to show up for Goulding's trial.[74] The government's position was also boosted by the wrecking of Mountjoy jail in a riot by IRA prisoners on 18 May.[75] An Act authorizing the Minister for Justice to put selected persons convicted or awaiting trial into custody under the Minister of Defence was rushed into law. This meant prisoners could be transfered to military prison in the Curragh. The setting up of the new courts would normally have been extremely controversal. But May was an exceptionally bloody month in the North, with car bombings claiming widespread civilian casualities. A grassroots peace movement emerged in Derry after the Official IRA killed an off-duty soldier home on leave, and there were signs that pressure was growing on republicans to end their activities. The legislation was supported by Fine Gael and by most of Labour's TDs. The fear that the violence was spreading south weakened opposition. The *Irish Press* felt that both 'unusual court decisions' and the 'recent atrocities in the North' had forced the government to 'put security of the State above the niceties of legal principle'. The paper asserted that

> the Government has a clear duty to remain in absolute control of the situation (and) must be seen to exercise its full constitutional authority no matter what huffings and puffings may emanate from the ultra-liberals ... those who do not themselves observe the Queensbury Rules can hardly expect the same in return.[76]

There was strong support for the measures within Fianna Fáil and only a handful of TDs voted against them, Michael O'Leary arguing that those opposed were betraying the peace women of Derry.[77] For a period in the summer of 1972, it seemed as if a cessation might be in prospect. The Official IRA declared a ceasefire and the Provisionals followed suit and took part in talks with the British Government. But these talks broke down and in July the Provos went back to war in what proved to be the bloodiest month yet. Refugees fled south and street conflict escalated. In government circles there were worries that 'as Northern militants find less opportunity for demonstrating in the North, they are turning their attention to the Republic'.[78] There were also increasing indications that public opinion was becoming 'revolted by the activities of subversives within the Republic'.[79] On 6 October, Gardai raided and closed offices used by Provisional Sinn Féin in Dublin.[80] By then, the government felt confident to move against the IRA, but also provoked the most intense opposition to any security measure of the 1970s.

'Continuous crisis'

In November, three issues combined to provoke two weeks of 'continuous crisis'.[81] The government wanted to introduce an amendment to the Offences Against the State Act which would 'shift the burden of proof onto the defendant' and meant that a suspect could 'be convicted by a judge on the say-so of a senior police officer'.[82] There was broad opposition to the proposal, which ranged from trade unionists to academics. Dozens of Trinity College staff publicly denounced the measure.[83] The *Longford Leader* felt the proposal made it appear as if Irish government policy was 'being decided by the British authorities'.[84] The *Kilkenny People* was dubious about the need for new laws, claiming that 'it has yet to be shown that the IRA is in any way a major threat to civil order in the Republic'. While agreeing that 'something must be done to stop armed bank raids' the paper contended that 'otherwise the forces of law and order ... have shown themselves to be completely in control of the situation'.[85] Labour were determined to oppose the bill, as were Fine Gael. Although Liam Cosgrave broke ranks and announced that he would vote for the measure in the interests of national security, it looked as if the government would be defeated and a general election triggered.

'Bring RTE to heel'

But tension between the government and RTE produced another crisis. In the early hours of 19 November, Seán Mac Stíofáin was arrested leaving the home of RTE reporter Kevin O'Kelly. The following day O'Kelly repeated statments from his interview with Mac Stíofáin (though RTE did not broadcast the IRA leader's voice). The government informed the station that it had contravened Section 31 and demanded that the RTE Authority meet and explain their position. When, on 24 November, the Authority asserted that their staff had not broken the law, the government promptly dismissed them. By then, Kevin O'Kelly had been arrested and charged with contempt for refusing to hand over a tape of his interview to Gardai, and Mac Stíofáin, who was sentenced to six months in jail, had begun a hunger and thirst strike. The British believed that the tension between the government and RTE had become 'personal' and the Mac Stíofáin interview was an excuse to 'bring RTE to heel'. Having dismissed the Authority, Lynch replaced them 'with a collection of retired civil servants, party hacks and Corkmen'.[86] Gerry Collins explained that as '600 people had met violent deaths recently', RTE, which had given illegal organizations disproportionate coverage, could not be allowed become a 'recruiting platform to increase the death total'.[87] The sacking of the Authority shocked many and there was much anger at the jailing of O'Kelly. But some RTE staff, such as Liam Ó Murchú a senior editor at 'Féach', supported Lynch, privately informing him that 'most ordinary people understand the difficulties you are going through and they also understand, in my opinion, that there are no ways of dealing with them other than the measures you have taken'.[88]

Within hours of O'Kelly being jailed, RTE staff had walked out, halting broadcasts for three days. Reporter Kevin Myers resigned from the station in protest saying that he 'could not be associated with a news service which had been deprived of the freedom fundamental to the journalistic profession'.[89] Print journalists struck for 24 hours in support of O'Kelly, halting the production of evening and daily papers in Dublin and Cork.[90] The one-day stoppage was accompanied by growing street protest. Students in Cork and Maynooth boycotted lectures, condemning Section 31 for denying 'the people of Ireland their basic right to have all the facts that are vital to the welfare of the nation made known'.[91] A large group of staff at UCD publicly 'deplored' both O'Kelly's jailing and the proposed amendment to the OASA.[92]

'An activist clique'

In contrast, the *Irish Press* asserted that 'the question by whom and how RTE is to be controlled' was valid and that the government had a 'right and duty' to sack the Authority if necessary, though it was 'debatable' that they needed to do it on this occasion.[93] Industrial action in support of O'Kelly was described as 'unwise', leaving 'the country without Irish newspapers, dependent only on a British press'.[94] In Leinster House, Fianna Fáil's George Colley dismissed 'all the claptrap about freedom of the press' and said he 'felt sorry for many of the sensible journalists who had been maneuvered skillfully in the past few days by an activist clique who did not give a damn about free speech'. Colley alleged that an IRA leader in Meath had 'walked into the home of one of their fellow-journalists and kicked him around in the presence of his wife and children, because he disapproved of something that man had written, and ended up by threatening to shoot him'. He questioned why the unions were not protesting about this. Colley defended not only the sacking of the Authority but also the OASA, saying that 'I want to make it clear here that whatever Fine Gael will do, we in Fianna Fáil will not fail the Irish people … the issue facing this House is whether this State is to be governed by the Houses of the Oireachtas and elected Government or whether illegal groups are to hold sway'.[95]

'I will be dead in six days'

Dublin was increasingly on edge. When sentenced, Mac Stíofáin had shouted 'I will be dead in six days. Live with that', while a youth roared 'British traitor' at the judge. Removed to the Mater Hospital for treatment, the IRA leader was visited by archbishops Charles McQuaid and Dermot Ryan and by Labour TD David Thornley.[96] There were strikes and walkouts in support of Mac Stíofáin (and against the Offences Against the State Act) in Dublin, Cork, Limerick, Tralee, Navan and Monaghan. Dozens of union branches, GAA clubs and local councils called for his release.[97] Republican leaders called for protests to 'bring down the government' while Saor Éire threatened retaliation if the IRA leader died. The mood of the rallies was 'emotional', though 'almost innocent of political content'. At one a Catholic priest 'broke down and wept talking of Mac Stoifain' comparing him to Terence MacSwiney and Thomas

Ashe.[98] On Sunday 25 November, 10,000 rallied at the GPO and Ó Brádaigh said he wanted to see 'the workers of Ireland downing tools' the next day. While Dáithí Ó Conaill claimed that 'we want no confrontation with the forces of this state. Our fight is with the politicians', Adrian Corrigan appealed to the crowd to 'get Jack the Rat out of his office'. Seven thousand people then marched to the Mater Hospital, which was surrounded by several hundred Gardai, backed up by an army unit.[99] Shots had been fired inside the hospital earlier and several people injured during a failed IRA escape attempt. Later that night, a bomb injured over 40 people at the Irish Film Centre. After the failed rescue, Mac Stíofáin was moved to the Curragh military prison. On 28 November, he announced that though he was remaining on his fast, he was ending the thirst-strike so as to prevent further violence in the south. But protests, merging with those against the Offences Against the State Act, continued. A couple of days later, 4,000 joined an evening march to Leinster House where 1,000 Gardai, backed up by troops, were deployed. Ó Brádaigh claimed that republicans 'are not at the top of the hill yet, but we are climbing', but stressed that their fight was not with the 'Garda Siochana, the Free State Army or with the courts. It is with the politicians.'[100]

'If the IRA want to fight it out, then so be it'

When Mac Stíofáin ended his thirst-strike, British sources sensed that the movement was losing momentum and the government gaining in confidence.[101] Even though they expected to lose the vote on the Offences Against the State Act, Fianna Fáil deputies were confident of winning a general election fought on the issue of law and order, one asserting that 'if the IRA want to fight it out, then so be it'.[102] Reflecting the views of Fianna Fáil's base, the *Irish Press* opined that

> we are living in bad times. The violence that has been spawned obscenely in the North has spread down into the heart of Ireland ... if the IRA chooses to mount an assault now on Southern personnel or institutions, then there is no length to which public opinion here will not go in supporting measures to suppress the organisation ... the South is not the North ... we have a Government elected by the people, and the will of the people must prevail.

Despite what the paper described as the 'furore over the Bill from the usual so-called liberal forces', it was clear that the authority of the state needed to be upheld.[103] On Friday 1 December, a 'general election atmosphere' gripped Leinster House, Fianna Fáil believing that the 'opposition had been wrong-footed on (the) issue of law and order'.[104] Labour's Noel Browne predicted 'a very dirty general election. The horror, wounds, agony, suffering and deaths of fellow Irishmen and women in the North had become a good issue for the

Fianna Fáil Government.'[105] Nevertheless, most Fine Gael TDs remained set to vote against the Offences Against the State Act, along with Labour. Urging rejection of the bill, the ITGWU warned that 'Irish trade unionists are anxious that their country should not be lined up with South Africa, Rhodesia and the Portuguese territories at the top of the repressive legislation league'.[106] The ATGWU described the bill as 'a threat to all trade unions, tenant's associations and minority political groupings' and called for a general strike in protest. Bus workers' leader Tom Darby warned that 'any Government capable of enacting such panic legislation would have no hesitation in introducing measures to shackle workers in times of industrial unrest'.[107] One thousand five hundred students from Dublin universities, addressed by USI leader Pat Rabbitte, rallied against the bill outside Leinster House.[108]

'Soft-headed liberals'

The debate, covered live by RTE TV's '7 Days', was rancorous. Jack Lynch claimed that by opposing the bill the Labour Party 'had identified themselves with the Provisional IRA'. Breaking ranks with his own party, Liam Cosgrave complained of subversives 'whingeing about civil liberties when brought before the courts' and alleged that only 'Communist fellow travellers and soft-headed liberals' opposed stricter security. Minister for Social Welfare Joe Brennan stated that 'the only people who wanted to see this legislation defeated were the people (who) slung bottles at the police, and used tactics copied from other countries where mob-rule had to be stamped out by strong measures'.[109] In contrast, David Thornley described the bill as 'a piece of disgraceful, fascist, totalitarian legislation which, if introduced by the Greek colonels, would be opposed by every delegate we sent to the Council of Europe'. Seán Treacy claimed the bill was a 'despicable sellout of our national interests' and described Fianna Fáil as the 'Unionist party of Southern Ireland'. Neil Blaney told a tense Dáil that 'I and a lot of others, helped to bring … into existence what is now condemned as the terrorists and gunmen of the Provisional IRA'.[110]

'Like a Kilburn pub on a Friday night'

At 8pm, deputies heard the sound of an explosion followed by another a quarter of an hour later. Soon, news of deaths and injuries reached the chamber. When Fine Gael's T.F. O'Higgins was speaking, he was asked by Fianna Fáil's Noel Davern as to whether he supported 'the two bombings in this city?' O'Higgins replied by telling Davern not to be a 'bloody ass' while his colleague Gerry L'Estrange interjected that he 'would not be surprised if some of you (Fianna Fáil) set them off'. But an hour later, Paddy Cooney announced that Fine Gael would not oppose the second reading of the bill, because an election 'might have the effect of plunging the country into the turmoil of a political crisis when, above all, in view of recent events, stability is required'.[111] Most Fine Gael TDs then abstained and the bill was passed by 70 votes to 23.[112] Afterwards, the atmosphere in the Dáil Bar as Fianna Fáil celebrated victory was described by journalist Mary Holland as being 'like a Kilburn pub on a Friday night'. Despite the deaths and injuries just across the river, TDs sang rebel songs and shouted 'Up the Republic!'[113] The ITGWU asserted that the new laws had been 'born in the tragedy of death, injury and destruction and the double talk of confused politicians who have put party before country and made nonsense of our democratic institutions'.[114] Labour Senator Mary Robinson was among those who spoke at a Citizens for Civil Liberties meeting which condemned the 'cynical and shameless exploitation' of the bomb attacks to force through the new laws.[115]

'But they're even more against us'

The government had emerged victorious from a series of crises. The scale of industrial action and local protests during the hunger-strike had been the most extensive since Bloody Sunday.[116] But though Mac Stíofáin ultimately spent 57 days on his fast, protests in his support dwindled after early December. O'Kelly was released, but Section 31 had been enforced and the Offences Against the State Act had been passed. During the protests, Mary Holland recounted how journalists who had been marching to Leinster House changed route when they spotted a similar demonstration for Mac Stíofáin arriving. A republican leader explained to her that 'there's a lot of people in this country who are against oppressive legislation but they're even more against us'.[117] Many of the organizations who opposed the Act stressed that they were in no way sympathetic to the IRA. [118] A Geography lecturer at Maynooth, who forwarded a motion from his students denouncing the Offences Against the State Act and the jailing of O'Kelly, pointed out that 'personally, I have little objection to the conviction and imprisonment of Mr. Mac Stíofáin; but the other developments referred to above are a different matter altogether'.[119] Similarly, Con Houlihan in the *Kerryman* explained that he opposed

> the amending Bill as does the opposition in the Dail, and I should like to think, the mass of the Irish people. No one wants their opposition to the Bill to be interpreted as support for illegal organisations – they are not the same thing at all and it is dishonest on the part of anyone, whether it be Mr. Jack Lynch or Mr. Daithi O Conaill to suggest as such.[120]

For many, Mac Stíofáin was an unsympathetic character ('Stephenson ... an Englishman living 145 miles away in the South', as the Derry peace women put it).[121] David Thornley's suggestion that he had visited the IRA leader for humanitarian reasons had been mocked by Fianna Fáil TD Joe Dowling, who asked him 'what about all the other people who are seriously ill in hospital?'[122] Indeed, Mac Stíofáin's image never recovered from his taking fluids, the British Ambassador gleefully noting that he had become an 'object of ridicule to many who previously held him in some respect'.[123] Journalist Henry Kelly noted the irony of the IRA leader ending his strike because he did not want bloodshed in the 26 Counties, and asked whether this proved that the Provisionals were in fact 'the real partitionists'.[124] Despite the extent of the protests, there were in fact several different movements, mutually antagonistic and unlikely to cooperate.

'Cancer of evil and violent men'

The government was aware that there was broad opposition to their policies, including from some of their own supporters, one Fianna Fáil member writing to Lynch that 'I never thought I would see the day that a Fianna Fail government would arrest and imprison an Irishman for trying to free his country'.[125] But they also knew that there was a constituency that backed the measures. A Killybegs fisherman informed Lynch that 'I wish to give you my support in your action to bring in tougher laws against Terrorists, and I am sure the vast majority of honest working people echo this'.[126] Another supporter of the government, a Galway Christian Brother, suggested that in contrast to those who 'make noise on the streets' the 'ordinary people do not say much but they have their own thoughts ... a time would inevitably come when democracy would have to be put to the test'.[127] A Tipperary farmer assured Lynch that 'the silent majority are with you ... I would like you to know that the ordinary farmers and workers down the country are with you all the way.'[128] Another man stressed that 'you can be assured that whatever measures you take as Head of Government to eradicate the cancer of evil and violent men from our society will recieve the fullest support from my immediate family (which in the Cork area as you know is quite large) and also my circle of friends'.[129] Lord Wicklow, who for 20 years had been vice-president of the Irish Civil Liberties Association, wrote to Lynch to make clear 'how completely I am behind you in the courageous stand you are taking. I was very glad that the bill was passed with such a large majority.'[130] The 5,000-strong National Organisation of Ex-Servicemen stated that it fully supported the 'lawfully-elected Government of the Republic of Ireland in its efforts to bring peace and unity to the country' and offered the assistance of its members in an emergency.[131]

By the time the government did go to the country, the issue was superceded by economic concerns. Of those polled in February 1973, only 3% thought security was the most important matter for the government, while just 12% regarded what was happening in the North as paramount.[132] Despite this, Fianna Fáil's George Colley warned that 'security against subversion was one of the most vital issues in the election' and that paramilitaries might make 'merry hell' under a Fine Gael government.[133] One of his party's TV broadcasts featured

footage of the bombs in Dublin and suggested that more could occur if Fine
Gael came to power. John Healy had claimed that with Mac Stíofáin 'a forgotten
man in the Curragh, law and order, as an issue, was dead'.[134] However, in
border areas, evidence suggests that Fianna Fáil may have benefitted from their
hardline stance on security.[135]

'On par with the Reichstag fire'

There was little doubt that 'the passage of the (Offences Against the State Act)
was assured by the two bomb blasts in Dublin'.[136] Republicans soon alleged
that British agents were involved as the 'only beneficiaries (were) those who
advocate more repression'.[137] These allegations were given wider credibility by
a series of inter-connected events. In October 1972, £67,000 was stolen from
the Allied Irish Bank in Dublin's Grafton Street.[138] The raiders were led by
two English criminals, the brothers Keith and Kenneth Littlejohn, who were
arrested in London a week later. The Littlejohns had associated with Official
IRA members from Newry, but later admitted they had been working for
British intelligence in order to discredit republicans. They claimed to have
petrol bombed Garda stations in Louth and carried out other actions to provoke
a clampdown on the IRA.[139] The British Ministry of Defence later admitted
contact with the Littlejohns but denied approving any illegal activities in
Ireland.[140] The brothers were extradited to Dublin after an assurance they
would not be prosecuted for political offences, and in August 1973 were jailed.
Both men then escaped from Mountjoy prison in May 1974. They were later
recaptured and were finally released in 1981. The saga increased suspicion of
British intelligence involvement in the republic. There was other evidence
involving 'spies in Ireland'.[141]

On 18 December 1972, Gardai arrested an Englishman named John Wyman
at a Dublin hotel. The following day they apprehended a Garda detective
named Patrick Crinnion at the same hotel, in the process of attempting to
contact Wyman. When Crinnion tried to flee, confidential files were found
in his car. Wyman admitted to being a British intelligence agent and to be
cultivating Crinnion as an asset. Both men were tried under the Official Secrets
Act at the Special Criminal Court. The case was heard in camera and the men
were found guilty of relatively minor offences and jailed for three months.
After their release, both were flown to England.[142] The revelations that both
British agents and criminals were operating in Ireland prompted a widespread
view that the bombings and other incidents were their work and that events
in December 1972 were 'on par with Reichstag fire'.[143]

During August 1973, special reports in the *Evening Herald* and the *Observer*
detailed British involvement. In the *Observer* Kevin Myers claimed that military
intelligence agents were involved in the December bombings, while the *Evening
Herald* suggested an SAS link.[144] That month, Jack Lynch told a news programme

that he suspected British involvement, and a Coalition minister was quoted as saying 'you would have difficulty finding anybody in Dublin political circles who does not believe that those bombs were the work of British agents'.[145] Despite official denials, many agreed with the *Sunday World* when it asserted that 'no one doubts that the British bombed Dublin'.[146] Suspicions about dirty tricks would resurface again and again throughout the 1970s and lent credibility to republican allegations after every mysterious bombing or shooting.

The 1973 election saw the return of a new government, the 'National Coalition' of Fine Gael and Labour. In opposition, TDs from both parties had warned that Fianna Fáil's security legislation was dangerous, but they were soon embroiled themselves in a conflict with republicans that both sides would compare to the Civil War.

Notes

1 A legal analysis of these powers is contained in M. Robinson, *The Special Criminal Court* (Dublin, 1974).
2 J. Peck to A. Douglas-Home, 12 Dec. 1972, FCO87/11 NAUK.
3 *Magill*, Feb. 1978.
4 Notes on Programme Policy Meeting, 8 Aug. 1969, RTE Archives (courtesy of Rob Savage). Tim Pat Coogan refers to such a meeting in his memoirs, but crucially not to its context. M. O'Brien, *The Fourth Estate: Journalism in Twentieth Century Ireland* (Manchester, 2017) p. 139.
5 *Hibernia*, 29 Aug. 1969.
6 *Donegal News*, 10 Jan. 1970.
7 *Irish Times*, 17 Nov. 1970.
8 *This Week*, 17 Dec. 1970.
9 K. Rush, 6 May 1970, in P. Hillery Papers, P205/36 UCDA.
10 *Irish Times*, 4 April 1970.
11 *Irish Times*, 20 Oct. 1970.
12 *Irish News*, 11 Nov. 1970 and *Irish Times*, 8 Dec. 1972.
13 *Hibernia*, 20 Nov. 1970.
14 *Irish Independent*, 5 Dec. 1970.
15 *Irish News*, 15 Dec. 1970.
16 *Irish Times*, 5 Dec. 1970.
17 *Irish Press*, 5 Dec. 1970.
18 *Irish Times*, 10 Dec. 1970.
19 Ibid., 11 Dec. 1970.
20 Ibid., 10 Dec. 1970.
21 *Hibernia*, 18 Dec. 1970.
22 *Irish Times*, 5 and 7 Dec. 1970.
23 Ibid., 12 Dec. 1970.
24 *Hibernia*, 18 Dec. 1970.
25 *Magill*, Jan. 1986. Indeed, Lynch intimated this to the British Ambassador during 1971. J. Peck, 30 July 1971, Prem 15/478 NAUK.
26 McGuill, 'Violence', p. 128
27 *Sunday Independent*, 19 Dec. 1971.
28 *Cork Examiner*, 11 Aug. 1971.
29 *Connaught Tribune*, 7 Feb. 1972.

30 *The Kerryman*, 19 Feb. 1972. *Irish Times*, 10 March 1972.
31 National Commemoration Committee, *Tírghrá*, p. 56.
32 *Connacht Tribune*, 20 Aug. 1971.
33 T.A. McNulty, *Exiled: 40 Years an Exile* (Monaghan, 2013) p. 75. See also P.M. O'Sullivan, *Patriot Games: Resistance in Ireland* (Westchester, 1972) p. 229.
34 J. Peck, 21 Dec. 1971, in FCO 87/7 NAUK.
35 *Fortnight*, 12 Jan. 1972.
36 Ibid., 12 Nov. 1971.
37 *This Week*, 26 Feb. 1971.
38 *Sunday Independent*, 19 Dec. 1971.
39 *Longford Leader*, 3 Dec. 1971.
40 *Fortnight*, 12 Nov. 1971.
41 Name Abstracted to Taoiseach, 26 Aug. 1971, in D/T 2002/8/251 NAI.
42 Hanley and Millar, *Revolution*, p. 240.
43 *Irish Independent*, 24 Nov. 2012.
44 *Hibernia*, 17 Dec. 1971.
45 *Irish Times*, 21 Dec. 1971.
46 *Sunday Press*, 30 Jan. 1972.
47 J. O'Leary, *On the Doorsteps: Memoirs of a Long-serving TD* (Kerry, 2015) p. 153.
48 *Irish Times*, 5 Feb. 1972.
49 A. Howlett to G. FitzGerald, 3 Feb. 1972, in FitzGerald Papers, P215/4 UCDA.
50 *United Irishman*, Nov. 1968.
51 Ivory, 'RTE' p. 32.
52 T.K. Whitaker to Lynch (draft) 15 Aug. 1969, T.K. Whitaker papers, UCDA, P175 (1).
53 J. Horgan, *Broadcasting and Public Life: RTE News and Current Affairs, 1926–1997* (Dublin, 2004) p. 83.
54 R. Savage, *A Loss of Innocence: Television and Irish Society 1960–72* (Manchester, 2010) p. 381.
55 Horgan, *Broadcasting*, p. 88.
56 *United Irishman*, July 1970.
57 *Irish Press*, 3 March 1976.
58 Ibid., 8 Dec. 1970.
59 *Irish Times*, 21 June 1971.
60 Ibid., 3 May 1973.
61 *Irish Press*, 2 Oct. 1971.
62 *Irish Independent*, 2 Oct. 1971.
63 D. Ó Dúlaing, *Donncha's World: The Roads, the Stories and the Wireless* (Wexford, 2014) pp. 128–129.
64 *Irish Independent*, 11 March 1972.
65 N. Meehan, 'Eoghan Harris fed the hand that bit him', *Village*, Sept. 2009.
66 *Irish Times*, 27 May 1972.
67 Ibid., 14 Dec. 1972.
68 *Dáil Debates*, 8 June 1972.
69 Ivory, 'RTE', pp. 31–51.
70 *Fortnight*, 30 Nov. 1972.
71 F. Dunlop, *Yes Taoiseach: Irish Politics from Behind Closed Doors* (Dublin, 2004) pp. 4–8.
72 *Irish Times*, 21 Feb. 1972.
73 *Hibernia*, 16 July 1971.
74 *Irish News*, 14 March 1972.
75 *Irish Times*, 19 May 1972.

76 *Irish Press*, 27 May 1972.
77 *Irish Times*, 27 May 1972.
78 Ibid., 5 July 1972.
79 Ibid., 25 Sept. 1972.
80 Ibid., 23 Nov. 1972.
81 J. Peck to Sir Alec Douglas-Home, 12 December 1972, FCO 87/11 NAUK.
82 *New Statesman*, 1 Dec. 1972.
83 *Irish Press,* 1 Dec. 1972.
84 *Longford Leader*, 10 Nov. 1972.
85 *Kilkenny People*, 10 Nov. 1972.
86 J. Peck, 12 December 1972, FCO 87/11 NAUK.
87 *Irish Times*, 14 Dec. 1972.
88 *Sunday Tribune*, 12 Jan. 2003.
89 *Irish Times*, 8 Dec. 1972. *Irish Socialist*, Jan. 1973.
90 Ibid., 29 Nov. 1972.
91 Ibid., 28 Nov. 1972.
92 *Irish Press*, 29 Nov. 1972
93 M. O'Brien, *De Valera, Fianna Fáil and the Irish Press: The Truth in the News* (Dublin, 2001) p. 142.
94 *Irish Press*, 28 Nov. 1972.
95 Ibid., 1 Dec. 1972.
96 *Irish Times*, 27 Nov. 1972.
97 *Irish Press*, 27 Nov. 1972, *Irish Times*, 28 Nov. 1972. *Meath Chronicle*, 2 Dec. 1972.
98 *New Statesmen*, 1 Dec. 1972.
99 *Irish Times*, 27 Nov. 1972.
100 Ibid., 29 Nov. 1972.
101 J. Peck, 12 Dec. 1972, in FCO 87/11 NAUK.
102 *Irish Times*, 27 Nov. 1972.
103 *Irish Press*, 27 and 29 Nov. 1972.
104 Ibid., 1 December 1972.
105 *Irish Times*, 1 Dec. 1972.
106 *Liberty*, Dec. 1972.
107 *Irish Times*, 29 Nov. 1972.
108 Ibid., 2 Dec. 1972.
109 Ibid., 1 Dec. 1972.
110 *Irish Press*, 1 Dec. 1972.
111 *Irish Times*, 2 Dec. 1972.
112 The Labour party, two Fianna Fáil, two Fine Gael, one independent and one Aontacht Éireann TD voted against.
113 *New Statesman*, 8 Dec. 1972.
114 *Liberty*, Dec. 1972.
115 *Irish Press,* 2 Dec. 1972.
116 SWM *Bulletin*, No. 23, May 1975.
117 *New Statesman*, 1 Dec. 1972.
118 *Irish Times*, 29 Nov. 1972. *Liberty*, Dec. 1972.
119 F. Walsh to J. Lynch, 5 Dec. 1972, D/T 2003/16/591 NAI.
120 *The Kerryman*, 2 Dec. 1972.
121 *Irish Times*, 24 June 1972.
122 Ibid., 1 Dec. 1972.
123 J. Peck, 12 Dec. 1972, FCO 87/11 NAUK.
124 *Irish Times*, 2 Dec. 1972.
125 Louis J. O'Connor to J. Lynch, 28 Nov. 1972, in D/T 2003/16/590 NAI.

126 S. Tully to J. Lynch, 4 Dec. 1972, in D/T 2003/16/590 NAI.
127 Rev. Brother J.F. Dowling to J. Lynch, 29 Nov. 1972, in D/T 2003/16/590 NAI.
128 D. Hunt to J. Lynch, 28 Nov. 1972, in D/T 2003/16/590 NAI.
129 T. Horgan to J. Lynch, 4 Dec. 1972, in D/T 2003/16/591 NAI.
130 Lord Wicklow to J. Lynch, 11 Dec. 1972, in D/T 2003/16/591 NAI.
131 *Irish Times*, 4 Dec. 1972.
132 *Irish Independent*, 26 Feb. 1973.
133 *Irish Times*, 9 Feb. 1973.
134 Ibid., 1 March 1973.
135 Mulroe, *Bombs*, pp. 112–113.
136 *Liberty*, Dec. 1972.
137 *Irish Times*, 22 Jan. 1973.
138 Ibid., 13 and 21 Oct. 1972.
139 *Time Out*, 4 April 1974.
140 Houses of the Oireachtas, *Interim Report, 1972 and 1973*, pp. 12–13.
141 Clann na hÉireann, *Spies in Ireland* (London, 1974).
142 Houses of the Oireachtas, *Interim Report, 1972 and 1973*, pp. 14–15.
143 *Guardian*, 22 Dec. 1972.
144 *Irish Times*, 10 Jan. 1973. Cadwallader, *Lethal*, pp. 215 and 389.
145 *Sunday Times*, 12 Aug. 1973.
146 *Sunday World*, 19 Aug. 1973.

5

'Are we trying to create a new Chile here?'

In September 1976, the *Sunday World* reacted to new security legislation by asking 'are we trying to create a new Chile here?'[1] The government had just declared that 'arising out of the armed conflict now taking place in Northern Ireland, a National Emergency exists affecting the vital interests of the State'.[2] New laws allowing for seven-day detention on 'reasonable suspicion' and permitting the Army to make arrests in certain circumstances were introduced. Failure to provide information such as a name and address to the Gardai became an offence in itself. Encouraging people to join illegal organizations could carry a penalty of ten years in jail. Already that year a new Criminal Law Jurisdiction Act allowing for the trial of suspects in the Republic for offences committed in Northern Ireland had been introduced.[3] By that stage, newspaper editors had also been brought before the courts for publishing material thought to be subversive of the Gardai or Special Criminal Court.[4] But the government contended that the measures were justified as

> Notwithstanding the measures taken by the authorities to deal with them, terrorist activities have continued, and have increased in intensity and seriousness. Within recent months, a bomb was sent by post to the home of a Judge, bombs were exploded in a Courthouse in the centre of Dublin during the trial of a number of persons charged with terrorist-type offences, and the Ambassador to Ireland of the United Kingdom and a civil servant of the Government of the United Kingdom were assassinated by a bomb attack in the outskirts of Dublin.[5]

The previous three years had seen conflict intensify between republicans and the state. Both sides viewed the struggle through the lens of the Civil War. A young man charged with IRA activity told a court that 'it was a Fine Gael Free State Government which had murdered 77 Republicans and others in

1922–23. This was now 1973 and they will not murder any more. They are doing their utmost, but they won't beat us.'[6] From the other perspective, at the 1977 Fine Gael Ard Fheis Liam Cosgrave asserted that 'not for the first time has this party stood between the people of this country and anarchy'.[7]

'A point never before attained in peace-time'

The state's response included an increasing role for the army. When British Prime Minister Edward Heath visited Dublin in 1973, the city became a 'virtual armed fortress' ringed with soldiers at roadblocks backed up by armoured cars.[8] Prior to the Bodenstown commemoration in 1974, a 'huge force of Gardai in riot helmets stopped and searched cars. They were covered by soldiers in battledress, half-hidden in ditches and behind bushes. The soldiers were armed with automatic weapons, they wore helmets, flak jackets and carried gas masks.'[9]

In 1977, Liam Cosgrave boasted that

> we have built up the security forces to a point never before attained in peace-time … the Army now stands at 14,500 which is an increase of 4,000, or 40%, since early 1973. More important, perhaps, the Army has received modern equipment to enable it to carry out its peace-keeping duties in support of the Gardai with the highest efficiency.

The Taoiseach asserted that 'the purpose of these measures is to make it quite clear to that small and unrepresentative minority (who) use violence for political ends that they cannot win against this Government'.[10]

In February 1974, Garda strength stood at 7,853 officers, of which 1,028 were in border stations (13% of force). Of the 11,257 soldiers in the Army, 1,142 were in border posts (30% of available Army strength).[11] Between 1974 and 1975, 6,000 military parties were supplied for 13,000 joint Garda/Army checkpoints. There were 3,500 border patrols and 1,200 army escorts for explosives and blasting operations.[12] Increased funding made the Permanent Defence Forces (PDF) a far more 'modern (and) professional' force than they had been in 1969.[13] But the routine presence of troops led to several serious incidents. Twenty-year-old James Hughes was left paralysed after being shot four times in the back at a checkpoint near Slane during August 1973.[14] Enda Magee, a republican and ex-internee, was shot twice at a checkpoint near Bandrum in Monaghan in August 1974. There had been no Gardai present when Hughes was challenged by soldiers.[15] In March 1975, troops opened fire on IRA prisoners attempting to escape from Portlaoise, killing Dubliner Tom Smith and wounding six others.[16]

'Devoid of the thing called tradition'

The use of troops in internal security roles increased friction between them and republicans. One Cork army recruit recalled that during basic training some soldiers boasted about having fired on the IRA prisoners in Portlaoise.[17] Republicans for their part ridiculed the 'Free State' army as a 'mercenary' force, 'devoid of the thing called tradition' whose roots lay the crushing of the IRA during the Civil War.[18] Then, according to *An Phoblacht*, the Free State had recruited a 'vastly inflated army of youngsters from the garrison towns of the South. Their fathers had been reared for the British Army ... the "Civil War" was as a god-send to them.'[19] There were some clashes between off-duty soldiers and locals in border areas.[20] There were also occasional attacks on soldiers, such as on the home of an Army Sergeant in Leitrim during 1974 (though republicans usually denied responsibility for them).[21] But the Irish Army was largely recruited from among the urban working class and had also been affected by the upsurge in emotional nationalism between 1969 and 1972. In 1975, two soldiers were jailed for stealing explosives from a depot they were guarding. One claimed that their motivation was financial – to sell the material to a 'bit of an IRA man' – rather than political.[22] Nevertheless, the Army was aware of the potential for republicans exploiting dissatisfaction. There were press reports that Military Policemen disliked having to behave like 'screws' while in charge of IRA prisoners at the Curragh.[23] In 1977, some army officers made approaches to a government minister regarding the ill-treatment of prisoners at Portlaoise.[24] In 1976, Army Intelligence noted that there were

> approximately 30 discharges on security grounds in the PDF and somewhat more in the FCA ... Although recent changes in recruiting procedures have reduced the problem considerably those procedures are not foolproof and for obvious reasons have no effect on those who become disloyal in service nor those who enlisted prior to the change in procedures. It is apparent, therefore, that the problem of disloyalty continues even if it is in decline and will require persistent efforts and good intelligence in all units to eliminate it completely.

However, in general the army felt that 'a satisfactory state of loyalty and morale' existed which was 'reflected in the attitudes of soldiers to subversive organisations and their willingness to take on extra duties when called on'.[25]

'Thank God for the IRA'

For the Gardai, increased funding brought tangible benefits. As a columnist in *Garda Review* pointed out in 1974

> we can all remember the blue murder and screaming which resulted in the past from even very modest requests for increases in manpower and equipment. The undeniable fact is that whatever improvements in these areas have been secured in the past three years have been due largely to the political crisis. Five years ago most districts in the country still had no radio and extra manpower was just out of the question. Today five hundred new gardai can be delivered like so many hot dinners ... Maybe we should thank God for the IRA.[26]

However, these benefits came with increased dangers. The perception that they were aiding the British Government made some officers uncomfortable. As British diplomats noted 'many Gardai share the hope of a united Ireland and are therefore uneasy about our continuing presence in the North'.[27] Some in the force harboured sympathy for republicans. *An Phoblacht* claimed that after the Portlaoise breakout in 1974, Gardai in nearby Gorey turned a blind eye despite spotting some of the escapers.[28] In 1976, Sergeant Martin Hogan, a Guard with 21 years service, was disciplined after he attended the funeral of Frank Stagg. Hogan had also flown a black flag from his home during Michael Gaughan's hunger-strike.[29] In 1978, an ex-Garda, Brian Kirby, admitted selling confidential documents to the IRA over two years.[30] The intimate nature of rural Ireland also meant that occasionally Gardai and IRA activists could have been neighbours, school friends or teammates.[31]

'Thugs in uniform'

But sympathy was likely to be limited while Gardai were in the frontline of conflict with republicans. Officers suffered physical injuries, threats to their families and disruption to their lives while in and out of uniform.[32] By 1976, Military Intelligence believed that the IRA's prohibition on attacks on the southern state forces was no longer in force and that they were 'approaching a dangerous period where desperation may begin to take over'. That year, a young Garda was killed and several maimed by a booby-trap bomb and a detective shot and critically wounded during a robbery. On a number of occasions Gardai were held up, assaulted and had their uniforms stolen or their cars disabled.[33] As one put it 'the Provisional IRA was threatening to take over … there was a very thin blue line between anarchy and democracy … the politicians knew how close the whole thing was to falling in around their heads'.[34] But for republicans, the Garda were increasingly 'thugs in uniform intent on proving their ability to be just as brutal as their RUC counterparts in the Six Counties'.[35] In 1977, when hunger-strike protesters invaded the pitch at Croke Park, they faced not only uniformed Gardai but Dublin and Kerry footballers who were themselves members of the force. *An Phoblacht* claimed that youngsters were 'brutally assaulted' by the 'Garda-players'.[36] Republicans also alleged that one of the Dublin players had tried to entice a Sinn Féin member into a fight when questioning him while on Garda duty one night.[37]

While uniformed Gardai were in the frontline at demonstrations, it was the Special Branch who were dedicated to policing 'subversion'. An IRA activist described 'the Branch' as 'a tough bunch' who 'hated us with a vengeance'.[38] Detectives routinely pressurized young activists, visiting their families and issuing 'dire warnings about the consequences of involvement with the Movement. Parents are told that their sons and daughters are engaging in criminal activities.'[39] Detectives even became 'well informed' about the membership of small left-wing groups.[40] One activist recalled that

> people became more careful about what they said and did ... detectives began watching hoardings and abandoned shops and stopped, questioned and sometimes arrested people who attempted to post up political posters. Not even the smallest and most innocuous group of republicans, socialists or militant trade unionists could hold a meeting without a Special Branch presence.[41]

On occasion, *An Phoblacht* admitted that 'we are well aware that there are many good, honest men and women members of the Garda ... good and honest in so far as they try to administer the law justly and humanely'.[42] Indeed, some republicans cautioned that Gardai should be regarded 'as fellow Irishmen not yet converted to the Republican cause; secondly, as fellow Irishmen whom it would be very useful to convert to the Republican cause'. But the routine conflict contributed to a sometimes visceral hatred, as did republican allegations that the Gardai were allowing 'entire towns, cities and parts of cities to become jungles of crime and violence, while they patrol England's border in Ireland'.[43]

Civil liberties

Opposition to these government policies came from a number of sometimes mutually antagonistic sources. First there were republicans and their supporters. But the Provisionals rarely cooperated with other organizations. In 1974, there were complaints from the organizers of a march in support of IRA prisoners in Britain that not only had Sinn Féin boycotted the event, but republicans had 'harassed' those taking part.[44]

A partial exception was the Irish Civil Rights Association (ICRA) founded in December 1972.[45] Initially intended to be a broad civil liberties organization, it was sponsored by, among others, Thomas MacAnna of the Abbey Theatre, writer Edna O'Brien and the Aontacht Éireann TD Sean Sherwin. It rapidly faced allegations that it was a 'provo front' and, though it denied this, in practice it was an alliance between some politically active Provisionals, unaligned nationalists and far-leftists.[46] Despite claiming 1,000 activists in 1973, the group had only 82 members on paper a year later. [47] The Labour party had opposed the Offences Against the State Act in 1972, but by 1974 several of its leading figures were vigorous defenders of hardline security policies. Nevertheless, the party was divided, Labour conferences continuing to see motions from local branches denouncing the Offences Against the State Act and other legislation.[48] Evidence of these divisions came at the 1974 Labour conference. The West Dublin branch submitted a motion condemning internment in Northern Ireland as both a 'cause of violence' and a 'primary obstacle' to peace. But a counter-motion from Clontarf described the 'murderous' IRA campaign as the 'principal cause of the continuation of internment'.[49] Further to the left, the Communist Party had a certain influence in some trade unions, rivals recognizing it as in 'very restricted areas … the militant workers organisation'. [50] Warning in 1976 that the 'Government are in a headlong flight to a full police state', the party played an important role in developing a broad civil liberties campaign.[51]

Even smaller groups, such as the Movement for a Socialist Republic and the Socialist Workers Movement, also put a high priority on opposing state repression.[52] Though numerically tiny, they could have an influence beyond their ranks and were often to the fore in protests over issues like the death penalty. Indeed, there might not have been any such campaigns without them. After 1974, the IRSP, many of whose members were facing serious charges within a short period of the party's formation, were also prominent anti-repression activists. (The jailing of four IRSP members for a train robbery in 1976 would become one of the major cases concerning Garda brutality.)[53] In 1977, several left groups cooperated in the Trade Union Co-Ordinating Campaign Against Repression (TUCCAR) which gained affiliation from trades councils in Dublin, Navan, Waterford and Sligo. Some workers were still willing to take industrial action over these issues, though in smaller numbers than during the early 1970s. Such protests usually occurred where left activists had some influence, but militants benefitted from the unwillingness of many workers to cross picket lines which were still widely regarded as 'sacrosanct' whatever the issue.[54]

'A certain kind of Irish liberal'

While TUCCAR was highly critical of union leaderships for not taking 'concrete action' beyond resolutions, the major trade unions generally opposed government security policy.[55] Senator Michael Mullen of the ITGWU was expelled from the parliamentary Labour party for opposing the Criminal Law Bill in 1976. That year, Mullen, along with members of Official Sinn Féin and the Communist Party, helped form the Irish Council for Civil Liberties (ICCL). The ICCL was based at the ITGWU's Liberty Hall.[56] The bitter divide with the Provisionals meant the Officials were generally unwilling to campaign on any issue that concerned their former comrades. However, Official Sinn Féin opposed the ban on the 1976 Provisional Easter commemoration as an 'attack on the right of peaceful assembly (which) allied to the stringent censorship operated in RTÉ, helps glamourise rather than expose the perverted ideas of the Provisionals'.[57]

The ICCL was founded in June that year, its leading figures including Senator Mary Robinson (a Labour member) and anti-Apartheid leader Kadar Asmal, both lecturers at Trinity College. 'Non-party and non-denominational' and concerned with 'civil liberties within the State', the ICCL was not an activist organization and included vocal opponents of the IRA; Provisional supporters walked out of an early meeting.[58] Nevertheless, in the atmosphere

of 1976 it was seen by government supporters as giving comfort to those who
wished to destroy the state. Cruise O'Brien had earlier described the willingness
of Robinson to address an anti-internment rally as a 'confusing alliance between
militarist Republicans and a certain kind of Irish liberal'.[59] In contrast, Robinson
argued that 'it did not take much courage in the Ireland of September 1976
to denounce the IRA; it took courage to denounce the IRA or any other
organisation that used violence, including institutional violence'.[60]

'Hammer away on security issues'

Criticism of Coalition policy was increasingly heard in the *Irish Press*, whose
editor, Tim Pat Coogan, would become embroiled in a major row over censorship
with Cruise O'Brien.[61] The *Irish Times* was sceptical about the moves towards
ever more drastic security measures and broke major stories about Garda brutality
during 1977. *Hibernia* editor John Mulcahy was a sponsor of the ICCL, and
the magazine ran an anti-internment campaign during 1974. Perhaps the most
consistent critic of the government was the tabloid *Sunday World*, the best-selling
Sunday paper in the state. From an early stage it 'hammer(ed) away on security
issues when every other editor in town was dodging the flak and ducking for
cover'.[62]

'A riot of one degree or another'

Those campaigning against state abuses faced many obstacles. Some were
alienated by the violence that seemed to accompany demonstrations concerned
with the North. In 1973, ICRA lamented that one reason for its failure to
mobilize wider numbers was that 'peaceful marches organised in good faith ...
invariably ... ended up in a riot of one degree or another'.[63] After clashes
outside Portlaoise in 1973, Ruairí Ó Brádaigh blamed 'unruly elements and
hangers on' for the trouble.[64] ICRA discussed ending street actions entirely
unless they could 'ensure that they were well conducted'.[65] Republican protests
attracted young, often working-class, crowds who had little compunction about
clashing with Gardai. But republican leaders were aware that such violence
frightened off many others. Second, as Gene Kerrigan noted, to the general
public allegations about Garda brutality often 'seemed to come from individuals
who would themselves have little compunction about punching your ticket if
that was what they thought the occasion demanded'.[66] Campaigning in the
general election of 1977, Cosgrave complained that 'to listen to commentators
... you'd think the Portlaoise prisoners were a lot of baby-sitters ... They are
in for the most heinous crimes against the people of this country ... (not)
because they had no lights on their bikes.'[67]

Since most people were not political activists, they were unlikely to
encounter state repression in their day-to-day lives. Outside of some urban

areas, the Gardai were generally respected. Though the IRA claimed that it was not engaged in aggressive actions in the Republic, this claim became increasingly threadbare. When republicans described the government as 'Quislings', 'cowards' and 'traitors' it suggested that they might turn their attentions south.[68] Hence, several polls seemed to show approval for government security policy (which in any case always lagged behind economic issues as a concern). In September 1976, 38% thought the government was 'doing well' on law and order while 20% thought it 'doing badly'. By December that year, 49% thought it 'doing well' and only 16% 'doing badly' on the same issue. By April 1977, the number approving government security policy reached 47%, with just 23% feeling it was 'doing badly'.[69] British diplomats (who admittedly regarded Coalition policies in a very positive light), thought that the policy of being

> hard on terrorism but aloof from the British is a popular one. It is in tune with the average Irishman's growing weariness with the North, his fear that terrorism will become endemic in the South, his apprehension about the impact of violence on tourism and investment and his pathological dislike of feeling dominated by his British neighbour.[70]

Those who regarded paramilitary activity as far more serious than alleged state abuses would point to the level of popular mobilization against violence. In December 1974, over 20,000 marched in Dublin demanding peace in the North. Relatives of those killed by bombs in Dublin, Monaghan, Belfast and Birmingham took part. Several thousand took part in similar demonstrations across the state on the same day.[71] One commentator observed how in Dublin 'it was deeply moving' to see 'the young, middle-aged and old; people of different religious beliefs; people of varying political convictions; people of all social classes; people of conflicting ideological attitudes, city people and country people – all were united as they walked'.[72] But when Sinn Féin members tried to join the march, they were 'physically restrained' by Gardai.[73] In August 1976, around 50,000 joined a march in Dublin in support of the 'Peace People' in the North. Again, a diverse crowd ranging from 'Clontarf bus conductors' to Methodist clergymen took part. Once more, Gardai prevented members of the 'No Hanging Here' group joining the march. [74] While the motivation of those joining the peace protests varied, their numbers were far larger than those mobilized by republicans in the mid 1970s.

'An atmosphere of fear inside RTE'

In 1972, Official Sinn Féin complained about the 'silencing of RTE under the famous s.31 directive' which it claimed prevented 'all radically dissenting opinion from being voiced ... Republicans were banned ... while fascists like Craig and Imperialists like Heath can utter whatever blood-curdling threats they like against a mainly defenceless population in the North'.[75]

The Coalition years would see a significant expansion in the use of Section 31. During 1972, Fine Gael and Labour TDs, including leading figures such as Garrett FitzGerald, had defended RTE's independence.[76] Once in power their opinions changed quickly. By 1976, Cruise O'Brien, as Minister for Posts and Telegraphs, had extended Section 31 to include not only the IRA but also Provisional Sinn Féin. But pressure was being felt being prior to this.

In 1974, an RTE journalist asked whether O'Brien did 'not trust RTE journalists to do a proper job' or whether he accepted the 'lie propagated by some influential columnists that most of them are Provo fellow-travellers?'[77] Shortly after taking office, O'Brien had approached the RTE Director General Tom Hardiman complaining about the presence of Eoghan Harris and other Official republicans at the station.[78] Some noted that the sacking of the Authority by Fianna Fáil had already created 'an atmosphere of fear inside RTE'.[79] In early 1973, staff were being urged to use 'extreme caution and consultation through a hierarchy' when researching anything to do with 'subversive' or 'dubious' groups related to Northern Ireland.[80] Later that year, Lochlin MacGlynn in the *Kerryman* noted how the BBC's coverage of the Mountjoy helicopter escape had provided more historical context than RTE's 'ultra-objective' report which 'might have been the story of three Swallows taking off for Spain from a tree in O'Connell Street'.[81]

'Scarcely a tittle of support'

There were a variety of political viewpoints represented at the station, some of them very hostile to the IRA. In 1973, reporter Arthur Noonan refused to cover the Sinn Féin Ard Fheis as he believed the party was a front for an 'undemocratic' organization.[82] RTE's chief political correspondent Joe Fahy claimed that 'the men of violence' had been depicted on the station 'as if they were the elected leaders of the Irish people'. He believed that the government had been forced to take action to prevent the use of broadcast media in 'favour of illegal groups'. He also suggested that the National Union of Journalists (NUJ) knew that any attempted strike against Section 31 was 'doomed to failure'.[83] As Fahy illustrated, there were RTE employees who agreed with government policy. But there were also republicans and left-wingers working at the station, some of them recent arrivals from political activity in nearby UCD. [84]

There was some initial resistance to censorship. Tom McGurk was due to interview Claire Price, whose sisters were then on hunger-strike, on RTE radio in early 1974. Ten minutes prior to the broadcast, RTE management decided that the interview might contravene Section 31. In response, McGurk walked out of the studio. The Dublin branch of the NUJ asserted that

> this Union has already warned of the threat to balanced journalism inherent in
> the application of Section 31 … today's incident was an inevitable example of the

kind of ethical dilemma which RTE's application of the instruction was bound to create for our members in their day-to-day working. The union is particularly concerned if today's decision means that the interpretation of the Ministerial instruction is being widened to include material which could possibly breach it.[85]

P.K. Downey, the *Irish Times* radio critic, applauded McGurk but noted that there was 'scarcely a tittle of support from the Liberal Belt'. While in 1972 there had been protests about censorship, the 'champions of free speech have been mostly mute for the best part of a year. The rebels of RTE shut up like clams. Nobody bitched anymore about the lack of balance in new coverage: suppression became acceptable under Doctor's orders.'[86]

'7 Days'

In November 1974, there was another public confrontation over the issue. After his removal from 'Feach', Eoghan Harris secured a post at the current affairs programme '7 Days'. In October 1974, the show broadcast a special on internment, featuring interviews with ex-internees and their families, interspersed with footage of British troops attacking protesters. Cruise O'Brien asserted that Section 31 had been breached and verbally attacked Desmond Fisher, the head of RTE current affairs at the Labour party conference (though O'Brien at this point had not seen the actual programme).[87] O'Brien also alleged that the IRA were in 'spiritual occupation' of RTE.[88] Harris was accused of 'publicising (the) IRA' and suspended, along with other members of the '7 Days' production team.[89] Members of their union, the WUI, took unofficial action and refused to work on the programme.[90] There was a strong reaction from the union's leader Denis Larkin and threats of an official strike. However, unlike during 1972, the RTE Authority did not defend their staff, and after an internal inquiry Harris and his colleague Gerry Murray were transferred from current affairs.[91]

'Government control of RTE'

There were consistent complaints about censorship. When O'Brien addressed the ITGWU conference in 1973, he heard strong criticism of Section 31.[92] The following year there was particular unease that during the Ulster Workers Council strike people associated with Loyalist paramilitaries had been interviewed by RTE. Fr. Denis Faul claimed that 'people in the South seemed to care little about the plight of the minority (and) that was due to Government control of RTE'. Meanwhile, Faul asserted, loyalists were allowed 'pour out their hate for Catholics' on the station.[93] At that year's ICTU conference, a delegate from the Irish National Teachers Organisation claimed that

in the 26 Counties there is a peculiar situation directed by somebody who has come to the Congress … whereby certain political forces in this country… are denied the right of television and media on the grounds (that) to give them that right would be to encourage subversion (but) that same media provide facilities for Northern politicians to appear and say it is understandable and excusable that people should be murdered.[94]

In July 1974, Provisional Sinn Féin councillors had picketed RTE in protest at their exclusion from local election coverage.[95] In 1976, the ITGWU's *Liberty* reflected that if, like O'Brien the 'chief censor', 'you believe that you are right and your interpretation of our history and the reason for the present violence is the only correct one' then you endorsed a censorship which ultimately 'bodes ill for our democracy'. [96]

'Boastful emotive slogans'

But critics also noted that a large section of the TV viewing public were able to see interviews with republicans on British channels. When Thames Television screened a special programme on the 60th anniversary of the Rising 'Men of Easter', it featured not only Cruise O'Brien and 1916 veteran Seán MacEntee (his father-in-law), but also Seán Mac Stíofán and Dáithí Ó Conaill. Ken Gray in the *Irish Times* thought it remarkable that O'Brien could reconcile 'the hamstringing of his own television service through the operation of Section 31' with his own participation '(in) a British current affairs programme which featured, as well as Ó Conaill, Sean Mac Stiofan, and which was readily available to more than half the viewers in Republic through U.T.V and Harlech'. For Gray and some other opponents of censorship, the problem was that the views of republican leaders went unchallenged. He claimed that Ó Conaill had 'talked largely in cliches and boastful emotive slogans' and that 'one inescapable conclusion was that Section 31 ... may be one of the best things he has going for him'.[97]

Others pointed out the incongruity of banning people from the airwaves when if 'Irish people want the full version of the news they can tune into any BBC radio station, whilst a great number can tune in to a choice of Harlech, BBC or UTV news reports where the Provisional viewpoint is reported'.[98] In 1977, Section 31 was extended to include bans on interviews with the Provisional IRA and Sinn Féin and the Official IRA, Cumann na mBan, Na Fianna Éireann, Saor Éire, the UVF, Ulster Freedom Fighters and the Red Hand Commandos.[99] However, even without a formal ban, discussion of prison protests and other issues were also avoided by RTE staff who feared breaking the law.[100] By 1977, many agreed with playwright Neil Jordan that

> R.T.E. has been more completely muzzled than ever before, under a man, while he might be a lousy playwright, seemed once to be a logical thinker and an excellent historian. Is it not amazing to have to turn to I.T.V.'s 'News at Ten' to find out what's happening in Ireland or to have a series of revelations about police brutality relegated to 'It says in the papers.'[101]

However, despite the change of government that year, Section 31 was not rescinded. Instead, in 1978 the UDA were added to the list of proscribed organizations.[102] By then Mary Holland considered that in RTE 'self-censorship had been raised to the level of an art. Caution lay like a thick cloud over everything.'[103] Indeed, some of the previous oppositionists in RTE, particularly Eoghan Harris and his allies, were actually becoming supporters of censorship themselves.[104]

'A new generation believe in the same thing'

The treatment of republican prisoners generated much conflict. There were three major hunger-strikes in 1973, 1975 and 1977. Prisoners became seriously ill before these disputes were resolved. Female republicans in Limerick prison also undertook fasts and other protests.[105] There were recurring allegations of ill-treatment and brutality and several major escapes. In November 1973, the IRA hijacked a helicopter and flew it into the exercise yard of Mountjoy before taking off with three prisoners.[106] IRA prisoners were then moved to the high-security prison in Portlaoise. In August 1974, 19 IRA men escaped from there, with explosives used to blast prison gates open.[107] In March 1975, there was another escape attempt which was foiled but led to the death of a prisoner.[108] In July 1976, two bombs were exploded inside Green Street courthouse in Dublin, allowing four IRA men to escape.[109]

The prison issue led to intense street campaigning. There were also mobilizations around the conditions of Irish prisoners in Britain, such as the Price sisters, Michael Gaughan and Frank Stagg. These issues were so emotive that they could even affect supporters of the government. In 1973, one man wrote to Cosgrave reminding him that political status was what 'your noble father fought for. Oh it is so sad to see young lads today on hunger strike in the prisons of our own state, because they, a new generation believe in the same thing.'[110]

'A spirit of youthful idealism'

In August 1973, Irish troops fired rubber bullets for the first time during demonstrations outside the Curragh. Two army huts were burnt and a flare fired at an Air Corps helicopter during rioting by about 1,000 marchers.[111] During September, 100 Dublin bus workers, angered at allegations of British complicity in the bombs that had killed three of their colleagues, protested at the visit of Ted Heath.[112] There was trouble after several demonstrations outside Mountjoy during a three-week hunger-strike in October. After its resolution, *An Phoblacht* suggested the mobilizations 'could have been a real beginning, in a big way, of street politics in the 26 Counties'.[113] In November, a small People's Democracy march ended in scuffles near the Curragh. Forty protesters were met by 'troops in full riot gear, including fibreglass helmets and perspex riot shields'.[114] In December, serious trouble erupted at another protest outside Portlaoise. A squad car was burnt out and Gardai accused of batoning people indiscriminately. The fighting had been so confused that several Sinn Féin speakers were struck by stones as they appealed for calm.[115] During early 1974, there were several demonstrations in support of the Price sisters and their comrades, including an ICRA march of 400 to the British Ambassador's residence.[116] One thousand people took part in a rally at the Mansion House against force-feeding.[117] Dozens of local councils, trade union branches and GAA clubs passed motions supporting the repatriation of the Prices, while the *Sunday World* added its voice to the campaign.[118] Most stressed that this support did not imply sympathy for the armed struggle. One Dublin man was 'certainly opposed to the present violent activities of the I.R.A.' and agreed that 'their campaign of violence must be brought to an end'. But he felt that 'if any of these young people die, it will surely create a very bitter situation'. He contended that the prisoners 'were probably activated by a spirit of youthful idealism (however misguided)'.[119]

'Stamping, booing (and) shouting'

In June 1974, there was a huge turnout for the return of the remains of Michael Gaughan (though there had been little campaigning during his hunger-strike).[120] Three thousand people followed Gaughan's coffin through Dublin city centre, accompanied by a uniformed colour party, while thousands lined the streets. On the way from Dublin to Mayo, crowds awaited in towns and villages. In Ballina many shops were shut and, despite large numbers of troops and Gardai being present, it appeared the republican movement controlled the proceedings.[121]

Broad opposition to internment north of the border was evident with over 1,000 attending a rally sponsored by *Hibernia* at Dublin's Mansion House. The magazine's campaign had won widespread trade union and political support, including from Labour and Fianna Fáil TDs. Among the speakers were Mary Robinson, Fr. Denis Faul, trade unionist Noel Harris and actress Siobhan McKenna.[122] But the rally exposed the divide between republicans and other campaigners. When Faul criticized the IRA in passing, the rest of his speech was drowned out by 'stamping, booing (and) shouting' from elements in the hall.[123]

A few weeks later, there was another rally at the Mansion House to condemn the jailing of *An Phoblacht* editor Eamonn Mac Thomáis for possession of IRA statements. Speakers included veteran republican Peadar O'Donnell, editor of the *Roscommon Champion* John Costello, NUJ chairman Niall Connolly and writer Ulick O'Connor.[124] Commenting on the awarding of the Nobel Prize to former IRA leader Seán MacBride, the *Sunday World* asserted that it was 'most ironic that in a week a great honour is bestowed on such an outstanding Irishman, the editor of a paper he once was chief of himself is arrested and jailed'.[125] Mary Robinson also criticized what she called the 'Alice-in-Wonderland' nature of the charge, given that IRA statements were widely sent to media outlets and Mac Thomáis himself had only recently been released from prison.[126]

'Worse than any other ... prison'

The successful breakout from Portlaoise in August had led to further trouble at the prison. In December, troops and Gardai stormed part of the jail where prisoners were holding hostages, firing rubber bullets and using fire hoses to subdue them.[127] In the aftermath, one inmate recalled how the 'Garda riot squad, military and some screws vented their anger on the prisoners', beating them and destroying their clothes, shoes, letters and radios.[128] Gardai were placed on permanent duty inside the prison. While the prisoners' complaints were dismissed as propaganda, a Garda later admitted that 'things went on we'll say in searches ... that shouldn't have gone on ... it was fairly grotesque at times, no point saying otherwise ... there were episodes that were fairly severe, that shouldn't have happened'.[129]

With tension still high over conditions, in January seven men began a fast 'to the death'.[130] As the weeks went on more prisoners joined the strike. Siobhan McKenna, Denis Faul and Michael Mullen were among those calling for an inquiry, Mullen pointing out that there were 19 ITGWU members in the prison.[131] The *Sunday World* claimed that the inmates in Portlaoise were treated 'worse than (in) any other regular prison ... in the EEC'.[132] The paper's political correspondent suggested that 'anyone who cries a tear about what went on in Russian jails or in jails in Spain or Greece but who takes no interest in what is being done in his or her name to Irish prisoners now is a fraud and a hypocrite'.[133] During the hunger-strike, 5,000 marched in Portlaoise.[134] In Dublin, workers struck at the Setanta building site and the Williams and Woods factory.[135] There were fears that one of the prisoners, Pat Ward, who had taken part in two previous fasts, was seriously ill. One Dublin man wrote to convey his 'distress that a native govt should let a Donegal man, ie a 26 counties man, die as a result of a hunger strike. I am well aware of the difficulties and it is not as a member of the Provisional IRA nor as a protest that I wish to express my concern.'[136] The strike lasted for 44 days and only ended after Ward was admitted to hospital in a critical condition.[137]

'The lowest depths of brazen indecency'

For much of 1975, the IRA was on ceasefire north of the border. But there was no let up in clashes in the south. In March, there was another attempted escape from Portlaoise, during which Tom Smith was shot dead. In the aftermath, prisoners were rounded up and there were 'strip searches and a bit of a hiding for everyone'.[138] The government was determined that there be no show of strength for Smith's funeral. In Dublin, 1,000 Gardai blocked all streets leading into the city centre and the cortege was surrounded.[139] At Glasnevin cemetery there was a 'short but sharp series of incidents' where detectives and uniformed Gardai batoned mourners. *Irish Press* and *Sunday World* staff were among those struck and both papers gave extensive coverage to the incidents.[140] Republican Sean Keenan contrasted the behaviour of the Gardai with that of the British who, he claimed, 'have always respected the dead and refrained from interfering with funerals'.[141] The government's position was summed up by minister Richie Ryan who asserted that

> the lowest depths of brazen indecency were reached last week when the dead body of the misfortunate victim of the criminal attack on Portlaoise prison was hawked through the country draped in the Tricolour. That young man was in jail because after a fair trial he was convicted of murder. He is now in God's merciful hands, as is the innocent Dublin wages clerk who was killed by him in a wages snatch at the instigation of the evil men who accompanied his remains to the grave.[142]

'Assisting maiming, death and destruction.'

The sense of crisis did not abate during the winter. In September, Garda Michael Reynolds was shot dead. Noel and Marie Murray were sentenced to death for his murder. The killing of an unarmed Garda was a highly emotive issue and campaigning for a reprieve was unpopular. Allegations of ill-treatment and questions about political speeches prejudicing the case were dismissed by many. As the *Irish Times* argued, 'the country at present is plagued by thieves and murderers who rip their way into banks and post offices. Such persons are enemies of society. Garda Reynolds was a public servant and chose to stand against these obvious enemies.'[143]

Initially only a handful of left-wing activists were involved in the Murray Defence Campaign. They feared that if the executions took place the 'stage would be set for the suppression of the whole anti-imperialist movement'.[144] At the 1976 ITGWU conference, Michael Mullen called for commutation of the sentences as 'capital punishment had been abolished in most countries which shared values with us and should be abolished here'.[145] Campaigners always faced accusations that they were 'assisting maiming, death and destruction'. Kadar Asmal responded that this was 'a dangerous argument that has been used in the past to justify the curtailment of civil liberties'.[146] *Liberty* complained that it was 'a sad day if any criticism of the "security" or law and order approach of our Government for party political purposes is dismissed as Provo propaganda'.[147]

'Section 30 him'

During 1974, Mary Robinson had complained that 'it is a somewhat daunting experience to have made a most serious allegation of abuse of our court system, to offer evidence in support of this allegation, and to be greeted by complete silence at official level'.[148] Despite official silence, claims that the Offences Against the State Act and the special courts were being abused were being widely aired by the mid 1970s.[149] The *Sunday World* was reporting beatings in Garda stations from 1973 onwards.[150] The powers given to Gardai under Section 30 of the Act allowed them huge leeway;

> Section 30 became a verb, as in 'Section 30 him', or more likely, 'any more lip out of you, sonny, and I'll Section 30 you'. Special Branch detectives went about their business of sitting outside meetings, photographing demonstrations, 'visiting' people at home for a 'little chat', stopping people in the street and following them. People who had never seen a gun, let alone fired one, were being questioned about their politics and their friends, their work and their relations. The gardai had no right to answers to such questions, but failure to adopt a compliant attitude could get you pulled in for a few hours under Section 30.[151]

Between 1972 and 1980, there were 8,105 arrests under Section 30 of the Offences Against the State Act; 1,545 people were charged.[152] The atmosphere was such that even small left-wing groups advised their members that they should 'stop talking too loud in pubs', treat all 'phones with caution' and guard internal documents carefully.[153] Emergency legislation was even used to arrest activists protesting about censorship of feminist literature.[154]

The 'Heavy Gang'

Conor Cruise O'Brien later recalled that a detective told him how they had convinced a suspect to give crucial information in the Herrema case; 'they beat the shit out of him'.[155] Allegations about such tactics were first aired in the republican and left press, then taken up by *Hibernia* and the *Sunday World* and finally by the *Irish Times*. Many of the revelations centred around claims that a 'Heavy Gang' of detectives, based at the Garda Technical Bureau, were deployed in cases involving subversion. This group routinely used violence to extract information. People claimed to have been 'punched, kicked and pulled by the hair' deprived of sleep and told that 'we'll break you mentally and physically on the seventh hour of the seventh day – that's when they all break'. Christy Lynch, convicted and later acquitted of a murder with no political connotations, remembered that detectives questioning him claimed to be 'the special boys. We're experienced at getting confessions … (we) know a murderer just by looking at him.'[156]

In May 1976, the *Sunday Independent* interviewed a Garda detective who argued that 'there is nothing sinister in what we do. We deal with tough criminals ... we know they are guilty ... there is no use treating them with kid gloves. They just laugh at you.' However, he asserted that 'we are not torturers ... if you read what some of these fellows have said themselves you will see they were not tortured. They were treated in the only way they understand. How would they treat their prisoners, I wonder?'[157]

Generally, allegations that a 'heavy gang' was operating were viewed as malicious propaganda. As the *Leitrim Observer* saw it, Gardai had been 'shot, maimed and bombed' but not all those who attacked them had been armed; 'some have used the modern revolutionary weapon of propaganda'.[158] The fear of being associated with terrorism meant that there were difficulties getting doctors and lawyers to intervene in 'subversive' cases.[159]

'The Gardai are doing a good job'

In 1977, Paddy Cooney told the Dáil that of 58 allegations of Garda brutality, 22 had been sent to to the DPP, just eight had resulted in court cases and there had been no prosecutions.[160] Many saw ill-treatment, if indeed it occurred, as understandable. As *Garda Review* explained during 1977, it would be 'close to a miracle ... in the face of guns and bullets, in the face of loss of life, serious injury, assassinations, pistol whippings and beatings ... the hardship and misery which they see inflicted by criminals ... if the odd Guard did not over-react'.[161] The official view tended to be that emergency powers were not 'real fears for people unless they are on the side of the enemies of the state'.[162] Where Gardai clashed with demonstrators, many agreed that 'had they not come under direct attack, there would have been no baton charges and no injuries'.[163]

British diplomats noted that the allegations were a problem for the Coalition but that, in general, 'the Irish media pay more attention to allegations of brutality by our Security Forces, especially by the RUC'.[164] A priest who raised the issue to his parishioners in Monaghan was amazed at the hostile response. 'I could say what I liked about the north and about the RUC, but I soon discovered that criticism of the gardai was not tolerated in this close-knit community in the twenty-six counties.' [165] At a Kerry GAA meeting, one delegate responded to a motion about Garda brutality by stating that 'the Gardai are doing a good job ... we must realise that there must be law and order down here. I do not agree that there is ill-treatment in our jails and I congratulate the Gardai and prison officers who have to do their duty.'[166] The GAA was one body where both republicans and Gardai were represented in large numbers, along with supporters of the main parties. At a Tipperary GAA Convention in 1976, calls for support for hunger-striker Frank Stagg were rejected as being 'propaganda ... in a partisan manner'. A motion 'condemning all kinds of violence in this country' was passed instead.[167]

'Too soft'

A further complication was that there was intense fear of rising crime, particularly in Dublin. A *Sunday World* poll found that while 54% of readers
believed that suspects were being ill-treated in custody, most (59%) also
thought that Gardai were 'too soft' when dealing with criminals; 90% agreed
with more severe sentences for law-breakers.[168] The position taken by Fianna
Fáil reflected this, condemning emergency laws as unnecessary but demanding
greater Gardai attention on non-political crime.[169] Jack Lynch asserted that
'old people, indeed even young able-bodied people' were 'afraid to walk the
streets at night' and were no longer 'secure from attack and robbery in their
own homes'. Government obsession with security legislation was therefore a
diversion from protecting the general public.[170] Similarly, Fianna Fáil were
careful not to criticize the Gardai for whom that party had 'the highest
regard'.[171]

Emergency powers

The death of Frank Stagg in February 1976 led to a 'ghoulish cat and mouse
game' between the state and republicans.[172] There had been comparatively little
protest during Stagg's 62-day fast, though 350 workers at the ESB station in
Tarbert, Co. Kerry had struck, arguing that his death would 'only lead to an
intensification of bitterness and an escalation of violence in Northern Ireland.
This, as working people, we would deplore.'[173] But after Stagg's death just
250 rallied in Dublin.[174] At Monaghan Town Council, a Sinn Féin representative
walked out after he was unable to gain a seconder for a motion of sympathy
with Stagg.[175] Stung by the Gaughan funeral, the government determined that
there would be no repeat, claiming that they would not allow a 'propaganda
jaunt' in Dublin.[176] Taking advantage of a split in the Stagg family, his body
was flown to Shannon and with tight security buried under concrete in his
family plot in Ballina. The following day, 5,000 republicans rallied in the town,
despite the presence of 1,000 Gardai and troops. Soldiers fired rubber bullets
during clashes in the cemetery.[177]

  While the local *Western People* strongly supported the government's action,
others were conflicted. The *Longford Leader* bemoaned how 'in trying to show
the British how willing they are to smash the IRA' the Coalition had 'trod
on the inherited philosophy of the Irish – that is that the treatment of the
dead is sacred'. This would, the paper concluded, only play into the Provisional's
hands.[178] Some months later, republicans removed Stagg's body and placed it
in the republican plot. The *Leitrim Observer* applauded this action, arguing that
this was 'fitting justice, in proper and fitting compliance with (the) last wishes
of the dead hunger-strike patriot'.[179]

'We salute the "1916 Men of Violence"'[180]

In April, the government also prohibited the Provisional's 60th anniversary Easter commemoration. There were warnings that those attending could face arrest and that public servants taking part could lose their jobs. But in a major show of defiance, thousands turned out for the commemoration at Dublin's GPO. Despite large numbers of soldiers and Gardai in riot gear being present, and the tense atmosphere, there were only minor scuffles.[181] Estimates of numbers varied widely according to their source (*An Phoblacht* claimed 20,000, the *Irish Independent* 10,000, the *Irish Press* 5,000).[182]

The ability of republicans to hold the event illustrated that they had a substantial nationwide organization and also that there was a widespread desire to identify with the Rising.[183] The relatives of several 1916 participants were present on the platform, along with Labour's David Thornley who defied his party to attend (but was nevertheless booed by many of the crowd).[184] Rather sourly the *Irish Press* contended that the government's ban had given 'a potentially nondescript occasion, which few people would have known or heard about … a hundred times the publicity it would otherwise have got'.[185]

'No prospect of a fair trial'

In 1976, the government introduced a new Criminal Law (Jurisdiction) Bill allowing trial in the Republic for offences committed in Northern Ireland. Matt Merrigan of the ATGWU argued that there was 'no prospect of a fair trial' for suspects in the North and that the government was responding to the 'crack of the whip in London' by introducing the law.[186] The IRA's response was to threaten to kill those involved in administering it. An armed breakout from the Special Criminal Court and the assassination of the British Ambassador followed that summer. By September, the Coalition were responding with the Emergency Powers Act. There was opposition from the ICCL, from the ITGWU and the left, but significantly Fianna Fáil were also critical of the measure. Dick Walsh of the *Irish Times* wrote that 'it is ironical that … the ogres of 1972, are cast in the role of defenders of liberty and moderation while the Labour Party which, in 1972, clung to its libertarianism even after the bombs, should now proclaim the necessity for intensifying repression'.[187] Workers at the Asahi site in Mayo struck against the bill and there were protest stoppages in Navan, Sligo and Clarecastle.[188] Writers Liam O'Flaherty, Brian Friel, Ulick O'Connor, Seamus Deane and Jim Sheridan were among those signing a letter of protest arguing that the laws were 'quite inconsistent with the freedoms which were fought for by those who established this State'.[189] In the *Sunday World* the laws were described as 'a charter for torturers' that would 'help kill civil rights here'.[190] Columnist Liam MacGabhann argued that journalists 'should not be used as touts for any organisation including the police'.[191] Opposition was assisted by reports of an interview with the *Washington Post* by Cruise O'Brien, where he seemed to suggest that newspapers would be prosecuted for publishing material, including letters, deemed subversive.[192] Nevertheless, campaigners against the legislation recognized that people's 'revulsion' at some of the Provo's activities made them wary of identifying with them.[193] Expecting a clampdown, *An Phoblacht* published a cut-out guide outlining how to respond legally to the powers.[194] Such a clampdown looked even more likely after the murder of Garda Michael Clerkin in Portlaoise during October. The *Irish Press* warned that 'the large body of opinion in this country that felt misgivings about this declaration will today be saying grimly: "Bad as the law is, the situation obviously merits something like it."'[195] A constitutional crisis followed as President Cearbhall Ó Dálaigh, who had referred the bill to the Supreme Court before signing it, was publicly insulted by Paddy Donegan. Ó Dálaigh resigned shortly afterwards and the 'outrageous affront' to him contributed to a sense that members of the government were out of control.[196]

'Enough Is More Than Enough'

As 1977 began, the slogan 'Brits out – Peace in' appeared on walls across the state as Sinn Féin launched a major propaganda campaign.[197] Another hunger-strike also took place at Portlaoise. Complaints had mounted about the treatment of prisoners there, ranging from 'visitors having to wait outside the gate for long periods after the scheduled opening time, to crude probings of the back passage by jeering warders'.[198] Commentators noted the irony of the fact that the government was still pursuing a case against the British Government at the European Court of Human Rights over internment while allegations mounted about Portlaoise. The *Sunday World* noted that 'it looks as if some Gardai earning Irish money and acting for and on behalf of the Irish government are doing precisely the same things to Irish prisoners that English torturers were found guilty of'.[199] On 20 March, that paper ran a front page and centre spread entitled 'Enough Is More Than Enough' and outlined a regime at Portlaoise of random strip searches, beatings, harassment and solitary confinement.[200] By then, ten IRA prisoners were on strike, demanding an inquiry into these conditions.

The issue once again sharply divided opinion. Leitrim Fianna Fàil council-lor Joe Dolan asserted that 'the majority of the prison service were doing a good job but ... there were also people in the service who could only be described as sadists ... people ... who think they can put down the Republican movement single-handed'.[201] The government believed that the IRA were in a weak position and that the strike was a 'last ditch effort behind a flagging cause'.[202] At a local level, Fine Gael representatives were warned not to endorse calls for inquiries, which the government claimed were attempts 'to gain support for groups trying to subvert the lawfully established institutions of the State'.[203]

'Our bastards'

As protests gathered momentum, pleas for compromise were directed to politicians. One Dublin man wrote to Cosgrave claiming that 'the only people who will rejoice in the death of Irish hunger-strikers will be the Brits and their Orange supporters'. The prisoners he accepted, 'may be bastards, Taoiseach, but they are, after all, our bastards'.[204] A Killarney man stressed that he did 'not support these mens organisation ... I detest the killing of people for political motives (but) I don't think you are going to beat the Provos by sheer oppression. What will beat them is their own violent actions.' He feared that the government's policies were 'renewing sympathy for them' and asked that they 'remember 1916 ... internment and Bloody Sunday'.[205] Derry bishop Edward Daly complained to Cooney that though the authorities in Northern Ireland were 'dealing with similar people (they) *appear* to deal with them in a more humane manner'.[206] Daly was one of several clerics who approached the government on the issue, one priest from Dundalk writing 'on behalf of scores of friends both lay and clerical' to ask for concessions that would 'save lives and possibly spare the country serious trouble'.[207] The Bishop of Killaloe, having met relatives of the prisoners, suggested that allowing them unhindered visits 'would tend to moderate rather than encourage the convictions of the hunger strikers'.[208]

As tension mounted, the numbers at protests grew. One thousand people marched to Portlaoise in early April, where clashes erupted that left 'scores of Republicans (and) Gardai ... bleeding and unconscious'.[209] Two weeks later, 2,500 joined a Dublin march organized by ICRA, led by foot-stamping youths in military formation. The following day, there were chaotic scenes when young protesters invaded the pitch at the Dublin–Kerry League final at Croke Park.[210] Shop stewards at Asahi, workers at Tara mines, Ardnacrusha power station and a number of trades councils and ITGWU branches expressed support.[211] There was also a stoppage at the Fiat factory in Dublin.[212] TDs Neil Blaney, David Thornley and Noel Browne joined calls for an inquiry. In Tralee, this demand was supported by Labour TD Dan Spring and Fine Gael Senator Blenner Hasset.[213] Many local councils accepted that grounds existed for an inquiry into prison conditions, though usually with the same caveat as Wexford Corporation that they did not 'condone acts of violence'.[214] The strike ended after 47 days, with several prisoners very ill, after intervention by Michael Mullen and the Auxiliary Bishop of Dublin James Kavanagh.[215] Though some believed that the government had faced down the strike without concessions, republicans claimed that it had 'succeeded in stirring the conscience of some of the most influential organisations and individuals in the country'.[216]

'Let That Be A Lesson'

In the run up to the June 1977 general election, polls found that only 2.3% thought the North was the most important issue, and just 2.5% security, though taken with unemployment and other matters, 20% considered them a factor in their voting.[217] Though initially favourites to win, the Coalition were trounced, Fianna Fáil coming to power in a landslide victory.

It is unclear how much of this was due to the government's record on repression.[218] But the *Sunday World* was in no doubt it was a key factor, its front page declaring 'Let That Be A Lesson'. The paper asserted that while it had taken Fianna Fáil 12 years in power to become arrogant, it only took the Coalition 12 months. It 'shed no tears' for Paddy Cooney who had been completely 'out of touch' with the 'humanity of the electorate' nor Cruise O'Brien 'whose attitude to the media has been little short of menacing'.[219] *Liberty* regarded the government's 'arrogance' and 'refusal to listen to critical but deeply concerned people on such matters as civil liberties' as key factors in their defeat; 'instead of dialogue we were read lectures, instead of a more open society, we were given a strengthened directive under Section 31 (and) threats against newspapers'.[220] *Magill* magazine claimed that an internal Fine Gael review found that the issue was 'a significant factor in the defeat. People, including even some Fine Gael candidates themselves, were dismayed by the "inhuman" face of security policy as represented by Liam Cosgrave and more particularly by Paddy Cooney.'[221] Others were unimpressed by the delight the Coalition had seemed to take in its policies. Cosgrave's intemperate speech to the Fine Gael Ard Fheis, where he denounced media critics as 'blow-ins', was seen by *Hot Press* magazine as evidence that 'given another five-year "mandate" the present bosses will prove themselves capable of the ultimate despicable militarist authoritarian repressive maneuvers'.[222]

'A successful ploy'

Many people expected changes in security policy under Fianna Fáil. Republicans suspected that the new government might make a difference, noting that 'Fianna Fáil always locked them up, admittedly, but (they) did not beat them up'.[223] There were 'some improvements' in conditions in Portlaoise, for instance.[224] There were also markedly fewer reports of ill-treatment in Garda custody and a less abrasive tone from government ministers.[225] However, the British were relieved to report during 1978 that 'so far' Fianna Fáil 'have followed their predecessors's hard line, modifiying it only slightly and in non-essential areas. In general, their aim has been to cultivate a less repressive image (but) without any loss of vigilance. This was a successful political ploy which earned the Government good marks in their early days.'[226]

Though it might not have seemed apparent to either side in the midst of the conflict, they were not re-fighting the Civil War. Large parts of the state's population were observers, rather than participants in this battle. Both sides also exercised restraint or were constrained by a variety of factors from engaging in greater violence (however horrific some of the events seemed at the time). Nevertheless, the northern crisis allowed the Irish state to implement draconian security measures, which ultimately became permanent legal fixtures.

Notes

1 *Sunday World*, 5 Sept. 1976.
2 Report, 1 Sept. 1976, in Office of the President, 2006/149/211 NAI.
3 *Irish Independent*, 4 March 1976.
4 V. Conway, *Policing*, pp. 100–102.
5 Sec. Dept of Taoiseach, 13 Sept. 1976, in 2006/133/580 NAI.
6 *Irish Times*, 8 Nov. 1973.
7 Ibid., 11 June 1977.
8 *Hibernia*, 16 Nov. 1973.
9 *Irish Times*, 17 June 1974.
10 Ibid., 10 June 1977.
11 Houses of the Oireachtas, *Interim Report on the Dublin and Monaghan Bombings*, p. 38.
12 Aspects of Security Situation, 31 Aug. 1975, in FitzGerald Papers, P215/164 UCDA.
13 *Magill*, May 1979.
14 *Irish Times*, 6 Aug. 1973 and *Hibernia*, 30 Aug. 1974.
15 Ibid., 22 Aug. 1974.
16 See Chapter 3.
17 K. McCarthy, *Republican Cobh*, p. 355.
18 *An Phoblacht*, 5 July 1974.
19 Ibid., 23 July 1976.
20 *Sunday World*, 5 Aug. 1973.
21 *Anglo-Celt*, 10 May 1974.
22 *Irish Times*, 3 Jan. 1975.
23 *Sunday World*, 2 June 1974.
24 E. Wynne to O.J. Flanagan, 18 April 1977, in D/T 2007/116/794 NAI.
25 Intelligence Assessment – Spring Period 1977, 15 Feb. 1977, 2008/79/3109 NAI.
26 *Garda Review*, Feb. 1974. I am grateful to John Johnston Kehoe for this reference.
27 Mulroe, 'The Gardai, Violence and the Border', p. 291.
28 *An Phoblacht*, 30 Aug. 1974.
29 *Sunday Independent*, 28 March 1976.
30 *Irish Times*, 11 Jan. 1978.
31 Barrett, *Ferris*, pp. 55–56.
32 See testimonies from Gardai, Jim Gallagher, Tim Kelly, B.J. Kealy and Maurice Walsh, INCORE, www.green-and-blue.org.
33 Mulroe, *Bombs,* p. 261.
34 V. Conway, *Policing*, p. 145.
35 *Irish Times*, 17 Oct. 1972. See also McNulty, *Exiled*, p. 169.
36 *An Phoblacht*, 19 April 1977.

37 Ibid., 7 Sept. 1977.
38 K. Conway, *Southside*, p. 184.
39 *An Phoblacht*, 15 March 1977. R.W. White, *Out of the Ashes: An Oral History of the Provisional Republican Movement* (Dublin, 2017) p. 144.
40 SWM *Bulletin*, No. 16, May 1974.
41 Dunne and Kerrigan, *Suspects,* p. 92.
42 *An Phoblacht*, 24. Aug. 1973.
43 Ibid., 5 March 1976.
44 M. Moynihan to R. Ó Bradáigh, 8 May 1974, in O'Mahony Papers, Ms. 44,279/1 NLI.
45 ICRA press release, 16 Dec. 1972, in O'Mahony Papers, ibid.
46 *Irish Times*, 6 Jan. 1973.
47 ICRA Paid membership list, Jan. 1974, in O'Mahony Papers, Ms. 44,279/1 NLI.
48 Labour Party conference agenda 1973, in John De Courcy Ireland Papers, P29/A/21 UCDA.
49 Labour Party Conference report 1974, in John De Courcy Ireland Papers, P29/A/26 UCDA.
50 SWM *Bulletin*, No. 4, 1972.
51 *Irish Socialist*, May and Aug. 1976.
52 Ibid., No. 7, April 1973 and (N/D) 1974. The SWM had only 45 members in 1973, but it sold around 3,000 copies of its monthly paper, *The Worker*, many to active trade unionists.
53 Irish Republican Socialist Party, *Framed Through The Special Criminal Court, The 'Great Train Robbery' Trial* (Dublin, 1979).
54 C. McCarthy, *The Decade of Upheaval*, p. 17.
55 TUCCAR *Newsletter* (N/D) 1977.
56 *Irish Times*, 16 March 1976. Hanley and Millar, *Revolution*, p. 326.
57 *Nuachtsheirbhis Sinn Féin*, 22 April 1976.
58 *An Phoblacht*, 23 July 1976.
59 *Irish Times*, 28 Oct. 1974.
60 Ibid., 6 Sept. 1976.
61 M. O'Brien, *De Valera, Fianna Fáil and the Irish Press,* pp. 149–150.
62 *Magill*, Nov. 1978.
63 *Irish Times*, 30 July 1973.
64 Ibid., 3 Dec. 1973.
65 Eibhlín na Cruadhlaoidh, 21 Aug. 1973, in O'Mahony Papers, Ms. 44,279/1 NLI.
66 *Magill*, 1 Feb. 1984.
67 *Irish Times*, 14 June 1977.
68 *An Phoblacht*, 15 June 1973.
69 R. Sinnott, 'The Electorate' in H. Penniman (Ed.) *Ireland at the Polls,* p. 56.
70 W.R. Haydon to A. Crosland MP, 1 Jan. 1977, Republic of Ireland: Annual Review for 1976, FCO87/603 NA.
71 *Irish Independent*, 23 Dec. 1974
72 Ibid., 25 Dec. 1974.
73 Ibid., 23 Dec. 1974.
74 *Irish Times*, 30 Aug. 1976.
75 Official Sinn Féin, 'Fight Repression 1972'.
76 *Irish Times*, 24 Nov. 1972.
77 *Hibernia*, 26 April 1974.
78 *Irish Times*, 10 March 1979. Niall Meehan, 'Eoghan Harris fed the hand that bit him', *Village*, Sept. 2009.

79 Quoted in 'Conor Cruise O'Brien and the Media', *Belfast Bulletin* No. 9 (1981) pp. 2–8.
80 *Irish Times*, 22 Feb. 1973.
81 *The Kerryman*, 16 Nov. 1973.
82 *Sunday World*, 21 Oct. 1973.
83 Horgan, *Broadcasting*, pp. 122–123.
84 B. Purcell, *Inside RTE: A Memoir* (Dublin, 2014) p. 37 and 114.
85 *Irish Times*, 10 Jan. 1974.
86 Ibid., 21 Jan. 1974.
87 *Irish Times*, 24 Oct. 1974. Desmond Fisher, 'Getting Tough with RTÉ' in M.P. Corcoran and M. O'Brien (Eds) *Political Censorship and the Democratic State: The Irish Broadcasting Ban* (Dublin, 2005).
88 Meehan, 'Eoghan Harris'.
89 *Irish Independent*, 5 Nov. 1974.
90 *Irish Times*, 13 Nov. 1974.
91 *Hibernia,* 8 Nov. 1974.
92 *Liberty*, July 1973.
93 *Irish Times*, 17 Oct. 1974.
94 *ICTU Annual Report* (Dublin, 1974) p. 509.
95 *An Phoblacht*, 12 July 1974.
96 *Liberty*, Dec. 1976
97 *Irish Times*, 3 May 1976.
98 *Leitrim Observer*, 30 Oct. 1976.
99 RTE, *Handbook 1977 and Annual Report 1976* (Dublin, 1977) pp. 21–22.
100 M. O'Brien, 'Disavowing Democracy: The Silencing Process in the South' in Corcoran and O'Brien (Eds) *Political Censorship*, pp. 48–58.
101 *Hot Press*, 9 June 1977.
102 RTE, *Handbook 1979 and Annual Report, 1978* (Dublin, 1979) p. 29.
103 *Irish Times*, 1 April 1978.
104 Hanley and Millar, *Revolution*, pp. 429–430.
105 *An Phoblacht*, 5 May 1975.
106 *Irish Press*, 1 Nov. 1973.
107 *Irish Times*, 19 August 1974.
108 Ibid., 18 March 1975.
109 Ibid., 15 July 1976.
110 A. O'Halloran to L. Cosgrave, 2 Oct. 1973, in D/T 2004/21/105 NAI.
111 *Irish Times*, 13 Aug. 1973.
112 *An Phoblacht*, 28 Sept. 1973.
113 Ibid., 12 Oct. 1973.
114 *Irish Times*, 5 Nov. 1973.
115 Ibid., 3 Dec. 1973.
116 *An Phoblacht*, 18 Jan. 1974.
117 Ibid., 26 April 1974.
118 See examples in G. FitzGerald Papers, P215/705 UCDA. *Sunday World*, 13 Jan. 1974.
119 Noel Davies to G. FitzGerald, 18 Jan. 1974, in G. Fitzgerald Papers, UCDA P215/705.
120 *Hibernia*, 21 June 1974.
121 *Irish Times*, 10 June 1974.
122 *Hibernia*, 11 Oct. and 25 Oct. 1974.
123 *Irish Times*, 28 Oct. 1974.
124 *Irish Press*, 26 Nov. 1974.

125 *Sunday World*, 13 Oct. 1974.
126 *An Phoblacht*, 18 Oct. 1974.
127 *Irish Times*, 30 Dec. 1974.
128 M. Ferris, *Prison Struggle: Portlaoise Gaol 1917–1985* (Dublin, 1994) p. 32.
129 V. Conway, *Policing*, p. 122.
130 *An Phoblacht*, 17 Jan. 1975.
131 Ibid., 24 Jan. 1975.
132 *Sunday World*, 26 Jan. 1975.
133 Ibid.
134 *An Phoblacht*, 14 Feb. 1975.
135 Ibid., 21 Feb. 1975.
136 J. Gibbons, 15 Feb. 1975, in D/T 2006/149/8 NAI.
137 *Irish Press*, 17 Feb. 1975.
138 *An Phoblacht/Republican News*, 15 Nov. 2007.
139 *Irish Times*, 22 March 1975.
140 Ibid., 24 and 26 March 1975. *Sunday World*, 23 March 1975.
141 *An Phoblacht*, 28 March 1975.
142 *Irish Times*, 25 March 1975.
143 Ibid., 12 Sept. 1975.
144 *Socialist Republic*, 1976.
145 Ibid., 12 June 1976.
146 *Irish Times*, 29 Jan. 1976.
147 *Liberty*, Sept. 1976.
148 *Hibernia*, 6 Dec. 1974.
149 Report, 18 Aug. 1975, in FitzGerald Papers, P215/160 UCDA. See also examples
    in Irish Council for Civil Liberties (ICCL), *The Emergency Powers Act 1976 – a
    Critique* (Dublin, 1977).
150 *Sunday World*, 8 July 1973.
151 Dunne and Kerrigan, *Suspects*, p. 99.
152 *Magill*, July 1987.
153 SWM *Bulletin*, Vo. 2, No. 2, April 1976.
154 See, 'Case Study: The Marie McMahon Case' in Connolly and O'Toole, *Documenting*,
    pp. 39–44.
155 C.C. O'Brien, *Memoir: My Life and Themes* (Dublin, 1998) p. 355.
156 *Magill*, 1 Feb. 1984.
157 *Sunday Independent*, 2 May 1976.
158 *Leitrim Observer*, 5 March 1977.
159 *Irish Times*, 14 Feb. 1977.
160 Ibid., 18 Feb. 1977.
161 V. Conway, *Policing*, p. 143.
162 ICCL, *Critique*, p. 9.
163 *The Echo and South Leinster Advertiser*, 8 April 1977.
164 Republic of Ireland: Annual Review for 1977, 7 Jan. 1977, FCO 87/603 NAUK.
165 McVeigh, *Taking a Stand*, pp. 143–144.
166 *An Phoblacht*, 15 April 1977. However, the Kerry GAA did bring a motion on
    Portlaoise to Congress in 1977. *Irish Times*, 5 April 1977.
167 *Irish Times*, 26 Jan. 1976.
168 *Sunday World*, 27 Feb. 1977.
169 *Irish Press*, 28 April 1976.
170 C. Meehan, *A Just Society for Ireland 1964–1987* (Basingstoke, 2013) p. 135.
171 *Dáil Debates*, 10 Sept. 1976, Vol. 292, No. 7.

172 *Sunday World*, 22 Feb. 1976.
173 *An Phoblacht*, 6 Feb. 1976
174 *Irish Times*, 14 Feb. 1976
175 Ibid., 24 Feb. 1976.
176 Ibid., 20 Feb. 1976.
177 *Irish Times*, 23 Feb. 1976.
178 *Longford Leader*, 27 Feb. 1976.
179 *Leitrim Observer*, 12 Nov. 1976.
180 Sinn Féin poster, Easter 1976.
181 *Irish Independent*, 26 April 1976.
182 *An Phoblacht, Irish Press*, 26 April 1976.
183 Ibid., 30 April 1976.
184 *Irish Times*, 28 April 1976.
185 *Irish Press*, 26 April 1976.
186 *Irish Times*, 29 Jan. 1976.
187 Ibid., 29 Oct. and 31 Aug. 1976.
188 *An Phoblacht*, 20 Sept. 1076. *The Worker*, 18 Oct. 1976.
189 *Irish Independent*, 15 Sept. 1976.
190 *Sunday World*, 5 Sept. 1976.
191 Ibid., 12 Sept. 1976.
192 *Irish Press*, 7 Sept. 1976.
193 *The Worker*, April 1976. *Irish Socialist*, May 1976.
194 *An Phoblacht*, 26 Oct. 1976
195 *Irish Press*, 18 Oct. 1976.
196 *The Kerryman*, 22 Oct. 1976.
197 *An Phoblacht*, 18 Jan. 1977.
198 J.H. Stagg, ICRA, 28 Jan. 1977, Ms. 44,279/1 NLI.
199 *Sunday World*, 6 March 1977.
200 Ibid., 20 March 1977.
201 *An Phoblacht*, 1 March 1977.
202 *Sunday Independent*, 17 April 1977.
203 Senator J.W. Sanfey to all Fine Gael representatives, 6 April 1977, in D/T 2007/116/794 NAI.
204 J. Clancy to L. Cosgrave, 18 April 1977, in D/T 2007/116/794 NAI.
205 J. O'Donoghue to L. Cosgrave, 19 April 1977, in D/T 2007/116/794 NAI.
206 E. Daly to P. Cooney, 28 Dec. 1976, in D/T 2007/116/794 NAI.
207 Rev. Padraig MacAodhagain to L. Cosgrave, 14 April 1977, in D/T 2007/116/794 NAI.
208 Bishop M. Harty to L. Cosgrave, 15 April 1977, in D/T 2007/116/794 NAI.
209 *Irish Independent*, 4 April 1977.
210 *Irish Times*, 16 and 18 April 1977.
211 *An Phoblacht*, 20 April 1977.
212 *Irish Times*, 22 April 1977.
213 *An Phoblacht*, 20 April 1977.
214 *The Echo and South Leinster Advertiser*, 8 April 1977.
215 Ibid., 23 April 1977.
216 *An Phoblacht*, 20 April 1977. Ferris, *Portlaoise*, p. 71.
217 *Irish Times*, 31 May 1977.
218 Lee, *Ireland*, p. 484
219 *Sunday World*, 19 June 1977.
220 *Liberty*, Aug. 1977.

221 *Magill*, May 1978.
222 *Hot Press*, 9 June 1977.
223 *An Phoblacht*, 31 Aug. 1977.
224 Ferris, *Portlaoise*, p. 73.
225 *Magill*, Feb. 1978.
226 Republic of Ireland: Annual Review for 1978, 12 Jan. 1979 CJ 4/2577 NAUK.

6

Refugees and runners

During 1976, when researching her book *A Place Apart*, the writer Dervla Murphy reported hearing

> anti-Northern sentiments with increasing vehemence and frequency. Some such outbursts may be excused on grounds of frustration and despair but most, I fear, are symptoms of a spreading infection ... a new form of intolerance ... between Southern and Northern Catholics.[1]

A few years later, Vincent Browne also asserted that 'the divide between the Catholic community in Northern Ireland and the rest of the population ... is deeper than ever'. Indeed, he felt that the northern minority 'must now bear whatever further tribulations arise ... as an isolated case, ignored and reviled by the rest of Ireland'.[2]

'They wrecked every place they went'

But such hostility was not new. As early as 1972, Mayo TD Joe Leneghan had claimed that 'the northern people were the authors of their own destruction and when thousands of them were given sanctuary down here, they wrecked every place they went'.[3] Indeed, Mícheál MacGréil's study of popular attitudes in Dublin (conducted between 1972–73) found that 55.2% of respondents agreed that 'Northerners on all sides tend to be extreme and unreasonable'; 59% also believed that 'Catholics in Northern Ireland have more in common with Northern Protestants than they have with Catholics in the Republic'.[4] From an early stage, Liam de Paor noted a widespread perception that 'they were all bigots in the North (and) we are better off without them'.[5] Many northern nationalists also saw the Republic as at best indiffferent and perhaps even hostile. Dónall Mac Amhlaigh reported in 1972 how 'northern Catholics who have been to the Free State as they call it, are particuarly bitter' feeling that 'they don't give two hoots about us down there'.[6] In 1979, a Belfast schoolteacher expressed the widespread perception that the 'South doesn't give a damn about us. It never did.'[7]

'This State doesn't need northerners'

Northern activists soon recognized this as well. Writing from Long Kesh in 1973, Provisional Seamus Loughran complained that 'apathy would appear to be the watchword of the southern Irish, if their reactions of this past few years is anything to go by'.[8] But for a period in the early 1970s, northern leaders had been household names. Nationalists such as the veteran Eddie McAteer, Ivan Cooper, Austin Currie and John Hume, labourites Gerry Fitt and Paddy Devlin, republicans Joe Cahill and Maire Drumm and radicals Eamonn McCann and Bernadette Devlin featured on TV and radio and were invited to speak across the state. But, in 1973, the *Irish Times* editor Douglas Gageby wondered if 'public opinion … may be reverting to its pre-1969 attitude. Prominent Northern politicians have noted a certain coolness to them down south, even from the man or woman in the street.'[9] This coolness was apparent earlier when those politicians commented on affairs in the Republic. Responding to statements by Paddy Kennedy MP during the Arms crisis, the *Irish Press* contended that 'this State doesn't need northerners either coming or being brought to take sides in its internal affairs … any efforts made to discredit Mr. Lynch and the Government now at this crisis are blows struck in the cause of anarchy'.[10] When Kennedy predicted growing support for a united Ireland in late 1971, the response of the *Sunday Independent*'s Wigmore was to assert that

> a very substantial number of people in the Republic are bloody well sickened by killings in the North and are no longer very much interested whether the blame can be put on the British Army, the Provos or the Officials. Hostility against them is fairly evenly divided … The North today is a gross obscenity. And to hell with the Faulkners, Maudlings and Paddy Kennedys who keep it that way![11]

'Dog in the manger'

There had long been a southern perception that northern nationalists could be abrasive or aggressive. This co-existed with sympathy for their plight and a tendency to see these attitudes as the result of Unionist misrule. Thus, Kerry GAA officials could describe how during a dispute with their Down counterparts the Ulster men's 'dog in the manger' attitude showed that not all intolerance in the North came from Unionists. Kerry Chairman Dr. Jim Brosnan explained that 'the men of the six counties were brought up in a different atmosphere and, possibly, were more bitter because of the historical background'.[12] There was also a belief that those in the North enjoyed far greater social security than southerners, one Dubliner claiming that 'it isn't just the Protestants who don't want a united Ireland, there's plenty of Catholics too. People living in a Welfare State know what sides their bread's buttered on.'[13]

'Separated brethren'

But the years between 1969 and 1972 saw unprecedented solidarity with nationalists, when thousands of people tried to help their 'separated brethren' in practical ways. [14] After August 1969, a series of organizations had come together to aid those affected by the violence. A National Relief Fund Coordinating Committee was established, under the Chairmanship of Fine Gael's Declan Costello. It included Catholic, Protestant and Jewish clergy, employers and trade unionists.[15] A leading figure was Dublin businessman Dermot Ryan, who had visited Belfast and seen 'the extent to which the Catholic popula-tion … are obliged to fight to defend their houses and lives'. He personally donated £1,000 for relief.[16] Republicans, meanwhile, formed the National Solidarity Committee, which included left-wingers, cultural activists and trade unionists.[17]

The ITGWU's Michael Mullen was a member of both committees. He visited union members in Belfast, Derry and Newry and all 140 ITGWU branches were instructed to offer accommodation to refugees if necessary.[18] His union donated £5,000 for use by members in the North and its southern activists collected over £6,500 for relief.[19] The Workers Union of Ireland also donated £500. Dublin Trades Council collected £1,500, while Cork dockers worked one hour overtime to raise £400 for a fund established by the city's Lord Mayor.[20]

'Give until it hurts'

Thousands of people offered to open up their homes to their 'stricken brethren'.[21] Branches of the GAA, the Irish Countrywomen's Association, the National Farmers Association and a myriad of local clubs began to collect money, clothes and food. [22] Drogheda Trades Council organized factory collections for the Red Cross. In Louth, the singer Tommy Makem housed a woman and her five children. Cabarets and concerts were organized with Ronnie Drew, Luke Kelly and others performing at Dublin's Gresham Hotel.[23] A cross-party meeting in Wexford, attended by trade unionists, GAA members, Old IRA veterans and the Chamber of Commerce collected £736.[24] One thousand pounds was raised at churchgate collections in Limerick and the city's Archconfraternity established a relief fund.[25]

The *Limerick Leader* reminded its readers that 'not so long ago the starving people of far-flung Biafra cried out for aid. Limerick answered the call. Let us now answer the call from our compatriots north of the Border. Let every organisation, every business man, every man, woman and child give – and give until it hurts.'[26] There were donations from young people, groups of workers and residents committees, with £2,000 later sent to Belfast.[27] Fifty-two boys from Ardoyne stayed for some weeks at the city's Redemptorist Retreat House. They were taken to the Limerick Horse Show and had dinner with Lord Mayor Stevie Coughlan, followed by a sing-song, where they 'showed that they had a great repertoire of rebel songs'.[28] Similar scenes were replicated across the state.[29] There were numerous donations by individuals. The Anglican Dean of Killaloe, Rev. Edwin Owen, offered £25 in 'heartfelt sympathy for Roman Catholic brethren in their terrible hour of suffering' while racehorse trainer P.J. Prendergast donated a prize bull worth £100 to aid the refugees.[30]

'Army billets'

The most obvious sign of the crisis was the refugees themselves. They were accommodated in military camps with the aid of the Red Cross. During August, the Irish Army looked after 720 people, the majority at Gormanstown Camp in Co. Meath. Smaller numbers went to Donegal's Finner Camp or to Kildare.[31] The majority were women and children. They included Anita Currie, wife of Tyrone MP Austin Currie, and their baby daughter, and Jacqueline Gogarty, whose husband, Frank, was a leading civil rights activist and their three children.[32] Though the vast majority was Catholic, a handful of Protestants also crossed the border.[33] In Gormanstown, facilities were basic, one woman remembering that

> our living quarters were the army billets. To me they were huts bordering on the likeness of a garden shed … No kitchen, no bathroom, the toilets were public toilets as were the shower facilities on the campsite. There was a cast iron burner in the centre of the hut to provide warmth … we spent our time gathering the turf from a turf stack to keep the burner alight day and night as the hut always felt cold.[34]

However, there was widespread praise for the soldiers and their efforts.[35] The nearby Butlin's Holiday Camp offered free admission to the refugees and the Army transported children there daily. By the end of August, 300 people remained at Gormanstown.[36] One hundred people were still there when a new influx arrived in July 1970.

'The Northerns cried with relief and joy'

Not all those who crossed the border were looked after by the army. Some refugees slept in parish halls in Donegal, while 100 people stayed at the republican movement's Northern Relief Centre in Dublin's Parnell Square. A number of people from Belfast were accommodated in Mullingar, due to a personal contact between a local woman with a friend in Andersonstown.[37] After a phone call in early August, a committee was established, but due to the escalation of violence far larger numbers than expected arrived. People travelled by train to Dundalk and were then ferried by car to Mullingar. On arriving 'the Northerns cried with joy and relief to find such a welcome awaiting them. Before long, they had been taken into Mullingar hearts and homes.' Numbering almost 200, they were housed in St. Loman's Hospital and St. Finian's Diocesan College.[38] One of the Belfast women gave birth to a child while there.[39] Some were taken on a tour of Dublin by the Red Cross, given gifts of toys and footwear and allowed to visit Dublin Zoo after closing hours.[40]

Contact was maintained and £1,300 was collected after the refugees returned to Belfast. During 1970, a delegation from Mullingar visited Andersonstown and donated £481 to the local St. Theresa's Relief Centre. There were public meetings in the Lake County Hotel, where Paddy Devlin, Austin Currie and Máire Drumm spoke. The committee also sponsored a 'Childrens' Holiday Scheme' and over 100 youngsters were brought to Westmeath. After Bloody Sunday, they collected £209.98.[41] This was only one of many similar bodies which maintained personal connections with those in the North.

'Give a kid a break'[42]

The northern child on a holiday from the 'Troubles' became a feature of southern life in the early 1970s. The fictional Riordans of RTE's popular drama series were among those who brought children south for Christmas.[43] In early 1972, 500 Belfast youngsters visited Dublin as guests of the Rotary Club and Lady Wicklow. CIE provided transport, there was lunch in the RDS and the pantomime 'Robin Hood' at the Gaiety, Maureen Potter and cast performing for free.[44] Similar trips were organized by the 'Children Together' group established to 'give holidays to children from the troubled part of this island'. This organization was sponsored by Catholic and Protestant clergy, trade unionists (among them the eponymous Mickey Mullen), Lady Wicklow (Eleanor Butler), businessman Victor Bewley and academic Augustine Martin.[45]

Republicans organized similar ventures. Sixty children whose fathers were interned were given accommodation in Wicklow by Official Sinn Féin in early 1972.[46] By September that year there were an estimated 1,200 northern children on holidays in the Republic. Those involved in accomodating them included political activists and religious and community groups.[47] The Cork-based Assocation for Human Rights in the North organized holidays for around 300 people from Belfast during 1972.[48] There were also breaks for the elderly, 20 pensioners from Derry being given a weekend in Limerick at the invitation of its Mayor during June 1972.[49]

'They can't offer comfort'[50]

By mid 1970, it was apparent that the refugee crisis was not over. The authorities were taken by surprise by the numbers who fled south in July that year. The Army was forced to open new camps in Coolmoney, Co. Wicklow and Kilworth, Co. Cork. Soon, 1,558 people were being cared for. The numbers proved difficult to deal with and conditions basic; 'twenty to a hut and no privacy except in the showers and toilets'.[51] Though the Army ran the camps, responsibility for refugee needs was assumed by the Red Cross. They supplied pocket money at the rate of 10/- (later increased to £1) weekly to each adult and 2/6d a week a child. They also supplied clothing and footwear, toiletries, washing powders, baby bottles and baby foods. Red Cross workers provided first aid, cared for the sick and elderly, washed and dressed children, organized school buses, brought patients to hospital and met hospital bills. A full-time trained social worker was also provided for a time. The cost of all transport for refugees, including the free travel vouchers for their return to their homes, was met by the Red Cross.[52] In February 1972, the organization outlined its spending since the crisis began: £102,735 had been provided to relief organizations, £14,657 spent on clothing and footwear, £11,702 on transport, medical expenses totaled £3,440 and £5,677 had been provided to refugees as pocket money. The total came to £138,211.[53]

Internment

After August 1970, most refugees returned to the North. But a year later the introduction of internment saw a much larger deluge. Officially 5,409 people arrived, forcing the Army to seek aid from other state and religious bodies. By 12 August 1971, cars and vans were crossing the border 'many ... carrying crude Red Cross signs or flags'. As well as Gormanstown, Finner, Kilworth, Coolmoney and Kildare, camps at Kilkenny, Mullingar, Waterford and Tralee had to be opened. A further 250 people arrived in Dublin on a special CIE train and were placed overnight in the Old Coombe Hospital. [54] Another 600 refugees stayed at the Garda training college at Templemore. Gormanstown operated as a transit camp for those moving elsewhere and its resources were soon overstretched. Army medical staff struggled to cope with a number of injured persons and Red Cross personnel and local volunteers were reportedly not getting more than one hour sleep. There were numerous complaints about conditions in the camps, RTE and BBC reports describing the accomodation as 'primitive'. The Central Citizens Defence Committee in Belfast expressed disappointment, claiming that some refugees were 'preferring to brave the bullets' rather than stay in such conditions.[55] At least 1,000 people were supposed to have left Gormanstown with the intention of travelling home.[56] Labour TD Stevie Coughlan claimed that the refugees were 'just thrown together in these primitive camps ... its little wonder that many are annoyed and angry at the Government'.[57]

The Department of Defence was forced to ask for help from local authorities and religious bodies. Archbishop McQuaid of Dublin announced provision for refugees in 38 convents and other church properties across the state from Leitrim to Waterford.[58] By 14 August, around 6,000 people were being housed in camps, schools, convents and hospitals. Special leave with pay was granted for civil servants who were members of Civil Defence, Red Cross, St. John's Ambulance brigade and Order of Malta to help with the crisis.[59]

'Citizens of the future 32 county republic'

There was a huge popular response. In Dublin, the Phibsboro and District Residents Asssocation offered accomodation. Its chairman Michael Keating stated that 'this is just a Christian gesture ... We feel that they should be able to stay here if they wished, in the surroundings of a private home, which might be more congenial and comfortable – Army camps are Army camps, and are not designed to be like home.'[60] The GAA and the Irish Country-women's Association called on their members to help. Trade union and Labour party branches held collections and relief committees were established, or reestablished, across the 26 Counties.[61] In Sligo, 100 refugees from Derry were housed in the Ursaline College. TV sets were donated by local shops. There was a 'fantastic response' by businesses to an appeal for children's clothing and footwear. The refugees were given access to the swimming pool at Summerhill College.[62]

PJ Carrolls Ltd donated 10,000 cigarettes for refugees in Meath. People with cars were urged to 'take the refugees out to sporting and other functions; entertainers to come to the centres and perform for them; and volunteers to give at least four hours service in any area'. Clothing, games, toys, books and comics were donated to the Catholic Young Women's Society (CYWS) Hall, Navan in response to appeals in the parish bulletin, which asserted 'don't refer to them as refugees, they are citizens of the future 32 county republic'.[63] In Lanesboro, Co. Longford Bord na Mona workers collected £138.55 for the Red Cross fund, workers at Tuam Co-operative Mart Ltd donated £200, while in Bailieborough £400 was collected door to door. [64]

'Did these people think they were going to Butlins?'

There had been much criticism of the camps, but a group of Belfast women refuted the complaints asserting that 'it is very ungrateful of some people to make so little of the hard work the soldiers are doing for us ... did these people think they were going to Butlins?'[65] At Gormanstown, another woman reflected that 'last week back in the Ardoyne we got no sleep at all, we got a cup of tea now and again if we were lucky … so we can hardly complain here'. The press reported that eight army cooks had been working to serve 4,000 people:

> work began at 6.30 a.m., it ended far into the small hours; and always there were the extra loose ends to be looked after, not just the food and bedding, but the split families looking for lost children in other camps, for news of home, for prams, for Paddi-pads, for tranquillizers, for Entero-Vioform …[66]

But reports also noted the politics of many of the refugees. Children on a trip to Dublin sang 'No surrender is the warcry of the Belfast brigade'.[67] They played war games and identified with the IRA, as did some of their parents. The *Irish Times* described how

> the first sign from the leading coach was a waved fist and a cry to the soldiers lounging around. 'Why can't yiz get on up there and give some help? Go on with ye and join our men above.' … the door opened and poured onto the gravel drive a trio of women, almost speechless in their anxiety to talk themselves out of tension, quite frightening in their explosion of hate and fear. It burst out of the coach, flooding in strong, high-pitched Belfast accents …[68]

Others noted 'among some of the small children (the) stone-throwing habit which, no doubt, was acquired by imitating their elders during the riots'.[69] Large numbers returned home by September, though several hundred people remained in the camps for the winter. Local groups continued to provide them with support. The Blarney Development Association organized for 62 children from Kilworth camp to be 'feted' and 'treated to supper' at a local hotel. The Lord Mayor of Cork Tim O'Sullivan addressed the children and assured them that 'the day is fast approaching when this land of ours will be ruled by both Protestants and Catholics and not by the military junta of aggression and discrimination that has forced you to leave the shelter of your homes and the environment of your childhood'.[70]

'Deprived … of … breadwinners'

Support for those interned after August was also apparent. In December 1971, a group of academics, writers and clerics formed the Association of Committees for Aiding Internee's Dependents. Among the sponsors were historians Sister Benvenuta (Margaret McCurtain) and Liam de Paor, journalists John Horgan, John Mulcahy and Prionsias MacAonghusa, his wife activist Catherine McGuinness, Fr. Austin Flannery and the Reverend Terence McCaughey. Their aim was to help alleviate the distress of those families who had been 'deprived … of their breadwinners'. The committee sponsored individual families at £20 a month. They asked that committees be formed from 'a street, a firm, a factory, a family, a village, an office …'. By March 1972, 400 such committees existed across the 26 Counties.[71] An indication of the breadth of sympathy was the fact that a Fine Gael supporter in Dublin's Blackrock 'collected and passed on some £750 from some thirty or forty neighbours here to help the families of half-dozen internees'.[72] Dublin Trades Council collected £9,000 for its internees fund.[73] In Kilkenny, several workplaces, including Smithwicks and Castlecomer Mills, sponsored internees' families.[74]

Fundraising

In August 1971, the GAA established their own 'non-political (and) non-sectarian' fund.[75] At a game between Offaly and Antrim in Tullamore, £1,808 was collected; £4,555 was raised by raffles at Croke Park and fundraising by Dublin's Scoil Chaitríona and Colaiste Mhuire.[76] On Sunday 2 January 1972, the Cork GAA collected £8,600 at church gates,[77] while £1,500 was collected in a similar fashion in Wexford.[78] Eight thousand pounds was raised in Dublin during January. Altogether, £60,000 had been collected by February 1972.[79]

Several funds were also established for the victims of Bloody Sunday. The ITGWU collected £15,163 from its members.[80] Thousands of workers donated wages from the Day of Mourning. The miners at Arigna in Co. Leitrim gave £736.95 and their management matched the amount, raising £1,500.[81] Sixty pounds was donated by the staff, including nuns, at St. Louis Secondary School in Monaghan. Waterford United star Alfie Hale personally collected £500 for the fund. [82] Various efforts continued throughout 1972. One thousand pounds was raised at a Dubliners concert in New Ross. Management and workers at the local Albatros plant presented two cheques, the hotel staff worked for free and bar takings were also donated at an event where Ivan Cooper MP was the main speaker. The Clonmel Golf Club raised £250 during February.[83] Another £2,500 was collected at church gate collections in the Ardagh and Clonmacnoise Diocese.[84]

July 1972

However, July 1972 saw both the biggest crisis and the most equivocal response. After the breakdown of the IRA's ceasefire, violence escalated, and thousands again fled south. By then the Irish Army were no longer directly involved in accommodating refugees. Now, local authorities and regional health boards were given the prime responsibility for dealing with the 10,000 people who arrived. The *Irish Press* reported how at Dublin's Connolly Station there were 'blue uniformed Civil Defence workers; the mobile canteen on the roadway … Dutch and American television crews; the press photographers – and an air of slightly suppressed tension'. Civil Defence was providing 'gallons of tea (and) mountains of sandwiches which disappeared into hungry, thirsty mouths in 20 minutes'.[85] CIE reported that, despite their experience of dealing with refugees since 1969, this was 'the first time that the bubble burst'.[86]

By mid July, there were 4,000 refugees in Dublin in 35 centres including the RDS, Cabra's Dominican Convent, Clonliffe College, the Oblate Fathers in Belcamp and St. Brendan's and St. Ita's hospitals.[87] Five hundred children already staying in private homes in Dublin as part of the Belfast Children's Holiday Project remained, as it was too dangerous for them to return home. Two thousand five hundred people were housed in Counties Cork, Kerry and Waterford and 1,800 in Cork city itself.[88] Others were placed in Donegal, Sligo, Roscommon, Leitrim and Co. Limerick. [89]

'As tough as they come'

As in 1971, there was a sympathetic public response. The Catholic Youth Council provided 300 volunteers to help refugees in Dublin.[90] There was a 'tremendous response' to an appeal from the Women's Emergency Volunteer Services for clothes for women and children.[91] In Castleblayney, workers at a local quarry paid for northern children's transport costs so they could go on excursions. The local cinema gave free passes for the children each night. [92] In New Ross, Co. Wexford, 49 people, mostly children, were accomodated at St. Mary's School by the Mercy Nuns. The local public were

> magnificent ... numerous people called to bring them on a day's outing, and they had all been taken out for the day by 2.30pm on Monday. We hope to get most of them boarded out. We hope also that people will continue to take them on day's outings. Instead of bringing them all to one seaside resort it was decided to bring them to different areas to get them away from the ghetto way of life in which they have been reared and brought up.[93]

But even among the sympathetic there was a perception that experience was hardening northerners; 'the Catholics of Belfast are a determined people' began a report about Mrs. Gibson from Ardoyne, who was 'friendly, outgoing, but clearly as tough as they come ... Now even she has had enough.' Housed in a school in Dublin's Drumcondra, her 2-year-old son Peter was 'enjoying a freedom he has never experienced before' but asking 'where are the soldiers?' Mrs. Gibson and her friends 'clustered around the television set, watching the news bulletins, they scanned newspapers for names of dead and injured ... they sat around surmising, reassuring each other or just thinking'.[94]

No need to leave Belfast?

However, as refugees arrived at Dublin's Connolly Station that July, one man 'disgust on every line of his face' claimed that 'some of them have only come down here for a free holiday. They've no need to leave Belfast, not one of them.'[95] That accusation was increasingly common. The *Evening Herald* reported how one Belfast woman said her husband was about to pay for a holiday 'but when people came around rapping on the door asking if we would like to go to the South we came'.[96] By 1972, a system was in place whereby

> people arriving at Royal Victoria (St) Railway Station in Belfast, and declaring themselves to be refugees, are issued with free rail travel vouchers to Dublin by the Railway authorities, the cost being recouped later from the Irish Red Cross Society.

The official view was that 'all and sundry can take advantage of this and many who have no good reason to leave their homes inevitably do'. Privately, civil servants considered that in 1972 'the exodus appeared to have been organised by different people from the various Catholic areas of Belfast'. There were reports from across the state that the refugees understood that their 'holiday' was being paid for by money collected for them.[97]

'We don't take cheek from anyone.'

The idea that the refugees expected a 'holiday' was partly stimulated by widespread reports of discontent among them. Thirty-two youngsters from the Falls Road returned to Dublin's Busarus and spent the night there rather than stay in a former sanatorium in Newcastle, Co. Wicklow.[98] Civil Defence responded that there would 'complete chaos' if refugees were allowed choose their accomodation and told the children it was 'back to Wicklow or back to Belfast'. One Belfast woman complained that 'we were refugees coming here, now we are gypsies'. However, she praised the efforts of CIE staff at Busarus, asserting that 'they were more than good to us'. A compromise was eventually reached that saw the group sent to Limerick.[99]

At the Royal Dublin Society, 30 women and children from Ballymurphy held a sit-down protest after they were told they were to be split up and sent to separate locations. The women sang 'Take It Down From The Mast' and 'We Shall Overcome' and there were 'dark murmurings about hijacking a bus (and) going to O'Connell Street to stage a protest'. One woman explained that 'it's the children mostly. They all know each other and want to play together.' Another suggested that 'it was just this one high-up person came and told us if we didn't go on the bus, we could go whereever the hell we liked. And we don't take cheek from anyone.' The group were given accomodation with the Jesuits at Rathfarnham Castle.[100]

'Atrocious, dirty and mean'

Another group of 46 refugees from Belfast reportedly returned home complaining that the living conditions in a former sanatorium outside Portlaoise were 'atrocious, dirty and mean'. The women claimed that 'we had one toilet between us, the sinks were filthy, and the food was tasteless. We took our children into Portlaoise everyday to eat in the cafes there.' A spokesman dismissed the claims as 'ridiculous' saying that there were ten toilets and ample supplies. George Crean of the National Refugee Control claimed that 'the refugees organised this episode to get themselves a fortnight in Dublin'. One aid worker explained that

> we are treating the Belfast people as refugees in a war-time situation. Given that definition, we provide them with emergency accomodation, and do the best we can to see that they have a nice time as well. Unfortunately, from the Belfast end, our offer is seen as an invitation for a holiday away from the troubles, and they come down expecting just that. Sometimes, it must be admitted, conditions are not exactly like Butlins.[101]

In other areas, Civil Defence maintained that they were expected to baby-sit while mothers went to local pubs and that refugees wanted to be ferried around in ambulances.[102]

'People cannot have long faces all the time'

The arrival of northerners increasingly placed burdens on local resources. In Donegal, 'evacuees are coming to Buncrana in hundreds, sampling the goodness of local people, but also imposing strains on a domestic communal life that is not geared for this sort of change …'.[103] Young northerners were often perceived as cheeky. There was a 'mini-riot' in Kilworth camp when children were denied sweets.[104] Their street-wise demeanour could raise smiles as when 'an eight year old refused to throw away a cigarette so the Sister told him "go down there and report to the Reverend Mother". Five minutes later the same nun caught the same boy returning, smoking the cigarette. "I thought I told you to see the Reverend Mother" she said. "I did" said the youngster, "She lit it."'[105] Tony Meade in *The Kerryman* cautioned that

> it is easy to say that many of the refugee families are on holiday, particuarly if their accents are different, perhaps loud, and if they tend to do the things which most of us do anyway but which we feel the refugee should not do. People cannot have long faces all the time, they cannot be conscious of their miserable lot all the time.[106]

But notherners also felt the resentment, noting that 'on O'Connell Street' people looked 'at you … as if you had horns'.[107]

'Demanding and ungrateful'

July 1972 marked a sea change in how refugees were seen at an official level. A report regarding future policy argued that

> the refugees that came down from the North in appreciable numbers in 1969, 1970, and again in 1971 … did so largely through fear of their personal safety.

Most of them them came on the spur of the moment and in great haste, bringing with them only what they wore.

In contrast, it claimed in 1972 that many had 'made preparations in advance for a holiday in the South' and 'most of them had suitcases' while some children brought 'swimming gear, tennis racquets (and) fishing rods'. The report asserted that

> refugees are not always just frightened people who are thankful for the assistance being given them. Some of them can be very demanding and ungrateful, even obstreprous and fractious – as well as, particularly in the case of teenage boys, destructive.

Civil servants believed that those 'who came South in 1972 were not driven from their homes and were largely holiday makers', but felt that it was neccesary that 'all be accepted without question and treated to the best of our ability as groups of Irish people in need of help at a very difficult time'. However, the report suggested that as the 'mainly "holiday" motivation of the 1972 influx' was, 'widely known and commented on throughout the country' there were now 'indications from some of the religious communities of an intention not to become involved in future'. [108]

'Misfits no matter where they were'

The report also claimed that some of those who arrived would be 'misfits no matter where they were'. These were people who,

> through ineffectuality of one sort or another (mental subnormality, marital break-downs etc.), find it difficult to cope with the stresses and strains of life and are reluctant to leave any place where there is free food and accommodation. There are still these kind of people (men, women and children) being taken care of by the Army at Kilworth Military Camp and more (men, women and children) being looked after by Dublin Corporation. [109]

An RTE report made similar claims about Gormanstown, stating that

> refugees were taken into the camp without question. Some of them undoubtedly came mostly for the 'free holiday.' But they were of course the first to go home. Among those who remain are some who are hiding from other things as well as petrol bombs. Gormanstown can also provide a refuge from marital problems or even just a comfortable retreat for the mildly neurotic or over nervous. It can be difficult to make such people face up to a world, which has made them suffer. It can be easier to forget in a warm hut with meals included, a laundry service round the corner, clothes and £1 pocket money …[110]

'Go back to Strabane'

By 1972, northerners were increasingly associated with disorder, especially after a number of serious confrontations in border towns. There was a riot in Lifford, which was blamed on protesters from Strabane.[111] In Lifford Hospital, doctors remarked to one of those injured that he should 'go back to Strabane and get … fixed up over there'.[112] In Buncrana, during October, the town's Garda station was attacked as 'hundreds of Northern Ireland people rioted'.[113] Ballybofey saw clashes between Gardai and revellers after a dance in December. Four hundred people surrounded the Garda Barracks and all its windows were smashed. Reports suggested that 'an element of the mob were from Northern Ireland' and that 'at least a dozen locals assisted the Gardai in dispersing the crowd'.[114] Some months later, youths 'from across the border in Clady' attacked a Garda squad car near Cloughfin.[115] Similiar incidents occurred in later years.[116]

In June 1973, there were serious clashes between inner-city Dublin youth and republicans returning north from the Bodenstown commemoration. After scuffles broke out in O'Connell Street, the trouble escalated into 'a three-way struggle between Northerners, Gardai and Dublin skinheads'.[117] Shop and bus windows were smashed, a car with northern registration was hijacked at knifepoint and Gardai reinforcements in riot gear had to be deployed.[118] There were accusations from *An Phoblacht* that the Gardai 'stood idly by' while the republicans were attacked and blamed 'Northern bastards' for the trouble.[119] A week later, northern members of Official Sinn Féin were attacked by youths in Drogheda on the way back from their Bodenstown event.[120] A year later, there were nine arrests as northern members of the Officials clashed with youths in Dublin's Gardiner Street.[121]

'Northern youths' were again blamed for a riot at the Butlin's holiday camp at Mosney in July 1973.[122] Later that month, Butlin's cancelled a booking for 200 Belfast children because of 'trouble caused by groups from the North in the past'.[123] A sense that northerners were predisposed to conflict was evident in the comments of one Galway Garda: 'Salthill would be … very well attended by people from Northern Ireland and invariably there would be trouble … it did seem to follow that when we got a large contingency of people from Northern Ireland, that you had troubles on the streets at night … that was a fact of life'.[124] What type of northerner made a difference, however. During 1976, a young Garda in Buncrana explained that

> You can talk to a Derryman. If you can get a word in edgeways, that is. Keep talking and he'll go away. You might have sore ears listening to him, but you won't have a riot squad out on the street fighting with him. Now, a Belfast man …[125]

Indeed, a young woman from that city felt that her accent alone could 'put people's backs up' and recounted how, in Donegal, she and her friends were told 'You can't do what you want down here. You're not in the back streets of Belfast now.'[126]

'Some kind of invasion force'

Crowd trouble emerged as a problem at GAA games during the 1970s. One of the first incidents involved Derry fans at a match against Kerry in April 1973. Missiles were thrown at Gardai and the referee and officials attacked. In the *Irish Times*, Paddy Downey suggested that

> in an effort to understand the behaviour of a section of the Derry following, but not to condone it … perhaps this thought is worth consideration: a people who have been so long striving for justice in other spheres may have been too quick to imagine that injustice was again their lot … in a place where they expected the very opposite, even in such a transient and relatively unimportant event as a game of football.[127]

In 1977, there was 'considerable anxiety' about trouble at the All-Ireland final between Dublin and Armagh, in part because Armagh supporters came from 'an area where respect for the security forces had been eroded' and might be 'sympathizers of the IRA'.[128] The *Irish Times* cautioned that 'some people have talked, foolishly, of the Armagh supporters … as though they were some kind of invasion force. That is nonsense: they have as much right in Croke park, and in the streets and pubs of the capital, as anyone else.'[129] Despite heavy security, the game passed off peacefully. However, in 1978 there were clashes between Dublin and Down fans. The GAA's Seán Ó Sochain explained that while such incidents were rare 'unfortunately, they have always been associated with occasions when teams from the North of Ireland have played here. I suppose it is reasonable to presume that because of the troubles in the North, actions of this type have come to the fore.'[130]

'Runners'

The year 1972 was the last time northern refugees were a public phenomenon, though there were still 16 people being housed in Kilworth camp as late as 1974.[131] But many continued to leave the North and settle in the Republic.[132] In 1971, there were 26,183 people born in the Six Counties residing in the south; by 1981 this had risen to 40,557. The number was highest in Leinster, particularly Dublin, Meath and Louth, and in the three Ulster counties.[133] Though there were considerable numbers of northerners in Dublin, they were relatively diverse and did not form a distinctive community in the city. Many of them avoided contact with each other, and while 'there was an attitude that everyone from the North was a Republican' that was often far from the case. (Some indeed had left the North to escape the IRA.)[134]

But specific local authority housing estates in or around Dundalk and Cavan and Monaghan towns became associated with people of 'northern' origin, sometimes being labelled 'Little Belfasts'.[135] Among those living there were republicans escaping arrest or people fleeing sectarian threats. These 'runners in' tended to choose areas popular with people from their locality. Many Belfast people settled in Dundalk, while nearby Omeath was a popular holiday destination. Republicans from south Armagh gravitated there too. Derry and Fermanagh activists tended to go to Donegal and those from north Armagh and east Tyrone to Monaghan.[136]

'El Paso – the bad man's town on the Border'[137]

The Muirhevnamor housing estate in Dundalk was an area of substantial settlement and the town itself became strongly associated with the Troubles. RTE reports and a BBC documentary during 1972 solidified Dundalk's reputation as 'El Paso', much to the chagrin of many locals.[138] There was some resentment of republicans residing in the area, with 'fellows being in local pubs on the run since 1969'. The IRA leaderships in Dublin received a litany of complaints about the behaviour of some of their members in the town.[139] During 1972, local judges commented on the number of cases involving northern youths before the courts.[140] After the riot of September 1972, a priest in the town asserted that republicans

> are fooling themselves if they think goodwill is unqualified or that having welcomed many hundreds of refugees from Northern terror, the people of Dundalk will allow their town to be turned by young thugs into a town of terror. Let the message be loud and clear – no one but Republicans will suffer if this ever happens again.[141]

The *Dundalk Democrat* blamed ' "runners" from outside areas, who have duped a number of susceptible teenagers (into) committing acts more likely associated with the less civilised tribes of Africa, and (who) then disappear into the night when confronted with a few determined men'.[142] Those who moved to the town noticed that sentiment. One woman remembered 'never feeling you belong ... local people resented people from the North being housed'.[143] One man recalled that 'people from the North were not immediately welcomed ... (they) tended to socialise together around a number of bars/pubs frequented by northerners ... I would hear through my work this part of the town being referred to as Provo Land.' One republican accepted that 'there were tensions, particularly in the early years ... wild stories were spread ... but likewise I have seen Northerners not afraid to misuse this fear and act in a bullying fashion'.[144]

There was also settlement elsewhere. One woman who arrived as a 10 year old in Gormanstown camp and whose family moved to Drogheda felt the full 'impact of being a refugee ... when I went to school ... it was the first time I was called a refugee and from then on I was constantly referred to as such ... to this day I am still jokingly referred to as a "runner in".'[145] As far south as Shannon, Co. Clare, the Cronan estate was sometimes called 'little Belfast', One woman moved there from Belfast as a child;

> there was a lot of work to be got in this new town and lots of houses to rent. It was like moving to a foreign country. TV didn't start until about 4pm and ended at 11pm with the National Anthem ... My Mum was beside herself with us – we wouldn't drink the milk as it was different. We wouldn't eat a lot of the food as it was different.[146]

'A very argumentative race'

A perception that Northerners were gripped by fanaticism was commonplace. Councillor J.J. Quigley told Carrickmacross urban Council in 1972 that 'the people of the South ... could not know or understand the feelings of the Catholics or Protestants in the North, and the politicians in the South should keep out if it. No one could understand the bigotry which was in the North.' Though Quigley was 'from the North himself', even he 'could not understand it'.[147] In the aftermath of the 1974 bombings, a Dublin man wrote to the Taoiseach to demand that people from the North be forced to carry an identity card. He argued that

> it is apparent to most people here that the people from the six counties are a very argumentative race and very difficult to please unlike people from the West of Ireland or other parts of the country ... If you had a referendum in the Republic in the morning to see if we wanted (them) as part of our country it would be a hundred to one against.[148]

These views seemed to be mirrored at the official level. The British Ambassador claimed that Minister for Foreign Affairs Patrick Hillery told him in 1972 that

> while the Irish were very emotional, the people in the South, on the whole and with exceptions, were not given to violence and murder. It was the men from the North who were cruel and violent and it was noteworthy that many of the recent bank raids and other crimes of violence in the South have been committed by northerners.[149]

Kerry Fianna Fáil TD John O'Leary recalled that 'it was well known in the corridors of power that senior Gardai and army people believed that a lot of the protests in Dublin were being fuelled by IRA members and supporters coming down from the North'.[150] Desmond O'Malley publicly complained that the task of the government was 'not made easier by the influx of dozens of gunmen from the North, whose "patriotism" expresses itself in armed robberies' as well as those who wanted to 'instigate civil strife and revolution down here as well as in the North.'[151]

'Doomsday'?

During 1975, the Coalition Government became very worried at the prospect of a British withdrawal and a subsequent 'Doomsday' scenario.[152] One of their concerns was of a major refugee influx. A report by a senior Garda argued that while

> refugees in the normal way are usually law abiding citizens fleeing from advancing enemy forces (and) are usually happy to be provided with shelter and food supplies on friendly soil until they return home (a) good percentage of those we would be likely to receive from Northern Ireland would not fall into this category.

He asserted that 'it is an accepted fact that the Queen's Writ does not run in many areas of Northern Ireland' and some teenagers had grown up knowing only 'violence, indiscipline and destruction'. Indeed, among those who had come south previously were people who were 'demanding, indisciplined and destructive'.

Problems of anti-social behaviour would accompany any large influx, but more problematically 'many of these people will be bitter towards the Northern Ireland Establishment, Gt. Britain and possibly the Republic, depending on the stand taken by the latter in their defence'. The Garda suggested that the refugees would be unlikely to appreciate the problems of the Republic, would be sympathetic to radical alternatives and 'a serious threat to the security and stability of the host country itself could be posed'. Comparing the situation to that of the Palestinians in Lebanon, the officer suggested that 'small numbers from Belfast or Derry could create much greater problems than larger numbers from rural areas'. He warned that 'Dundalk, Monaghan, Buncrana, etc. could well become shades of the Bogside, Ballymurphy or the Falls if there was no refugee dispersal policy'.[153]

'Will not stand idly by'

In contrast, during 1974, the IRA leader Dáithí Ó Conaill had claimed that in the event of civil war 'the people of the South will create an army that will not permit the slaughter of Catholics and that 'Irish people right across the line will not stand idly by irrespective of what the politicians would say'.[154] This view was echoed by Gery Lawless in the *Sunday World* who argued that 'any Dublin Government (that) did not go to the aid of the Nationalist areas of the North … would be overthrown'.[155] Left-wing activists were less sure, one group concluding that even in a civil war situation the 'Southern population would hardly stir'.[156] Indeed, Conor Cruise O'Brien had explicitly ruled out any intervention, claiming that the Army was not capable of mounting it and that the arrival of huge numbers of refugees, including some who were 'tough, violent and virtually ungovernable', could spell disaster for the south.[157]

But in the same period, senior military officers were tasked with considering options in the case of British withdrawal. It was their view

> that public opinion in the Republic will demand the intervention by the Defence Forces if the minority population comes under Loyalist attack. Failure to respond would have the most serious effects on the status and morale of the Defence Forces. It is also our belief that the government must have the option of military intervention and that the military capability to do so must be seen to exist.[158]

A further report also suggested that 'it is extremely doubtful that a decision NOT to provide military protection to the limit of our potential capabilities would be accepted by the Irish people ... It may be that we are to a great extent prisoners of our past – but that does not alter the reality of the situation'.[159] The report's conclusions were rejected, but nevertheless signalled that a section of the armed forces believed that popular sympathy for nationalists remained a factor in southern politics.

Attitudes to northern nationalists were diverse and complex. A basic sympathy informed most public responses during the early stages of the conflict. While refugees were seen primarily as victims they seem to have been welcomed. However, when they complained or appeared ungrateful attitudes could change very quickly. Anything other than gratitude and passivity was evidence of deviancy. The official view that many of those who arrived in July 1972 were holiday makers is remarkable given the situation in Belfast (where the majority were from). July 1972 was the worst month of the worst year of the Troubles and saw almost 100 people killed. Lenadoon, where at least 500 of the refugees came from, was the site of a breakdown of the IRA ceasefire. In Ballymurphy, from which hundreds fled, several people, including children, were killed by the British army. Sectarian assassinations escalated and that month also saw the carnage of Bloody Friday. The tone of the official reports does not convey this sense of terror. Nor is hard to discern an element of class judgement on the people seeking help (80% of whom were children) and their behaviour. By and large, those who came in 1972 were from urban working-class backgrounds, while the officialdom they dealt with usually was not. Added to a growing distancing from the North itself, this suggests that the reception for future waves of refugees might have been less than welcoming.

Notes

1 D. Murphy, *A Place Apart* (London, 1978) p. 12.
2 *Magill*, Dec. 1980.
3 *Irish Times*, 14 July 1972.

4 M. Mac Gréil, *Prejudice and Tolerance in Ireland: Based on a Survey of Intergroup Attitudes of Dublin Adults and Other Sources* (Dublin, 1977) pp. 377–380.
5 *New Statesman*, 11 Feb. 1972.
6 *Irish Times*, 23 Nov. 1972.
7 Ibid., 24 Oct. 1979.
8 *Sunday World*, 23 Sept. 1973.
9 *Irish Times*, 13 Feb. 1973.
10 *Irish Press*, 9 May 1970.
11 *Sunday Independent*, 19 Dec. 1971.
12 *Irish Independent*, 27 Jan. 1969. I am very grateful to Dónal McAnallen for this reference.
13 *Fortnight*, 8 June 1972.
14 *Nusight*, March 1969.
15 *Irish Press*, 21 Aug. 1969.
16 *Irish Times*, 18 Aug. 1969.
17 *United Irishman*, Sept. 1969.
18 *Liberty*, Aug. and Sept. 1969.
19 Ibid., Dec. 1969 and Jan. 1970.
20 *Irish Times*, 18 Aug. 1969. Cody *et al.*, *Parliament*, p. 226.
21 *Drogheda Independent*, 22 Aug. 1969.
22 *Irish Times*, 18 Aug. 1969.
23 Ibid., 18 and 25 Aug. 1969.
24 *Wexford People*, 30 Aug. 1969.
25 *Limerick Leader*, 30 Aug and 1 Sept. 1969.
26 Ibid., 18 Aug. 1969.
27 Ibid., 29 Nov. 1969.
28 *Limerick Leader*, 25 Aug. 1969.
29 *Irish Press*, 23 Aug. 1969.
30 *Irish Times*, 23 and 29 Aug. 1969.
31 Ibid., 21 Aug. 1969.
32 Ibid., 25 Aug. 1969.
33 O. Long, 'The Land that Made Us Refugees: North-South Population Movements at the Onset of the Political Troubles' (MA, UCC 2008) pp. 26–27.
34 Drogheda Community Forum, *Dispelling the Myths: Research on Displacement from Northern Ireland to Drogheda at the Onset of the Troubles* (Drogheda, 2004) p. 12.
35 Long, 'Land', p. 14.
36 *Irish Times*, 29 Aug. 1969.
37 *Westmeath Examiner*, 20 Sept. 1969.
38 *Irish Times*, 20 Aug. 1969.
39 *Westmeath Examiner*, 30 Aug. 1969.
40 Ibid., 6 Sept. 1969.
41 Ibid., 18 March 1972.
42 Children Together leaflet, D/T 2004/21/494 NAI.
43 H. Sheehan, *Irish Television Drama: A Society and its Stories* (Dublin, 1987). p. 182.
44 *Sunday Press*, 23 Jan. 1972.
45 'Children Together' leaflet in D/T 2004/21/494 NAI.
46 *Wicklow People*, 21 Jan. 1972.
47 *An Phoblacht*, 1 Oct. 1972 and 1 March 1974.
48 *Irish Times*, 12 July 1972.
49 Ibid., 27 June 1972.
50 Long, 'Land', p. 16.
51 Ibid.

52 Memorandum for the Government Catering for Northern Refugees, 1 Feb. 1973, D/T 2004/21/494 NAI.
53 *Western People*, 5 Feb. 1972.
54 *Irish Times*, 12 Aug. 1971.
55 *Irish Independent*, 17 Aug. 1971.
56 O. Long, 'Land', p. 22.
57 *Irish Times*, 14 Aug. 1971.
58 Ibid., 13 Aug. 1971.
59 O. Long, 'Land', p. 24.
60 *Irish Times*, 13 Aug. 1971.
61 Ibid., 14 Aug. 1971.
62 *Sligo Champion*, 20 Aug. 1971.
63 *Meath Chronicle*, 21 Aug. 1971
64 *Longford Leader*, 10 Sept. 1971. *Anglo Celt*, 24 Sept. 1971. *Irish Independent*, 11 Sept. 1971.
65 *Irish Times*, 14 Aug. 1971.
66 Ibid., 19 Aug. 1971.
67 Ibid.
68 Ibid., 11 Aug. 1971.
69 *Munster Express*, 27 Aug. 1971.
70 *The Kerryman*, 22 Jan. 1972.
71 Association of Committees for Aiding Internees' Dependents, Sighle Humphries Papers, UCDA, P106/1585 (1–2).
72 L. Barry to G. FitzGerald, 11 Oct. 1972, G. FitzGerald Papers, UCDA P215/4.
73 Cody *et al.*, *Parliament*, p. 229.
74 *Kilkenny People*, 11 Feb. 1972.
75 *Irish Press*, 3 Oct. 1973.
76 *Sunday Press*, 6 Feb. 1972.
77 *Irish Press*, 3 Jan. 1972.
78 *New Ross Standard*, 14 Jan. 1972.
79 *Irish Press*, 7 Feb. 1972.
80 *Liberty*, Aug. 1972.
81 *Leitrim Observer*, 26 Feb. 1972.
82 *Kilkenny People*, 25 Feb. 1972
83 *Nationalist* (Clonmel) 26 Feb. 1972.
84 *Leitrim Observer*, 4 March 1972.
85 *Irish Press*, 17 July 1972.
86 *Evening Herald,* 4 Aug. 1972.
87 *Irish Times*, 13 July 1972.
88 Ibid., 17 July 1972.
89 Ibid., 15 July 1972.
90 Ibid., 19 July 1972.
91 *Irish Press*, 21 July 1972.
92 *Irish Times*, 18 July 1972.
93 *Munster Express*, 28 July 1972.
94 *Sunday Independent*, 23 July 1972.
95 *Irish Press*, 17 July 1972. The report claimed that the man was a Sinn Féin supporter.
96 *Evening Herald*, 4 Aug. 1972.
97 Memorandum, 1 Feb. 1973 D/T 2004/21/494 NAI.
98 *Irish Times*, 5 Aug. 1972.
99 *Evening Herald*, 4 Aug. 1972.
100 *Irish Times*, 13 July 1972.

101 Ibid., 28 July 1972.
102 'We Couldn't Understand the Peace', RTE Radio Documentary on One, 2016.
103 *Irish Times*, 7 Aug. 1972.
104 Long, 'Land', p. 48 and 69. RTE, 'We Couldn't Understand the Peace'.
105 *This Week*, 17 Aug. 1972.
106 *The Kerryman*, 15 July 1972.
107 *This Week*, 17 Aug. 1972.
108 Memorandum, 1 Feb. 1973 D/T 2004/21/494 NAI.
109 Ibid.
110 Drogheda, *Dispelling the Myths*, p. 17.
111 *Donegal Democrat*, 10 Nov. 1972.
112 Jim Gallagher transcript, INCORE, www.green-and-blue.org.
113 *Irish Times*, 16 Oct. 1972.
114 *Derry Journal*, 19 Dec. 1972 and *Donegal News*, 31 March 1973.
115 *Donegal News*, 7 July 1973.
116 *Irish Press*, 17 Oct. 1975.
117 *Irish Independent*, 11 June 1973.
118 *Irish Times*, 11 June 1973.
119 *An Phoblacht*, 22 June 1973.
120 *Irish Independent*, 18 June 1973.
121 *Irish Press*, 24 June 1974.
122 *Irish Independent*, 10 July 1973.
123 *Irish Press*, 30 July 1973.
124 Joe Lynch transcript, INCORE, www.green-and-blue.org.
125 *Irish Press*, 15 Nov. 1976.
126 *Irish Times*, 2 April 1974.
127 Ibid., 10 April 1973.
128 Ibid., 6 Dec. 1977.
129 Ibid., 20 Sept. 1977.
130 *Irish Press*, 22 Aug. 1978.
131 *Hibernia*, 7 June 1974.
132 Ralaheen Ltd Dublin, *All Over the Place: People Displaced to and from the Southern Border Counties as a Result of the Conflict 1969–1994* (Dublin/Monaghan, 2005) p. 57.
133 Long, 'Land', pp. 51–52.
134 Ralaheen, *All Over*, p. 76.
135 Ibid., p. 33.
136 Ibid., p. 64.
137 *Hibernia*, 17 Dec. 1971.
138 *Irish Times*, 23 Sept. 1972.
139 Ibid., 4 Oct. 1972.
140 *Hibernia*, 22 Sept. 1972.
141 *Dundalk Democrat*, 23 Sept. 1972.
142 Ibid., 23 Sept. 1972.
143 Ralaheen, *All Over*, p. 69.
144 Ibid., p. 73.
145 Drogheda, *Dispelling the Myths*, p. 12.
146 Christina Bennett, *Clare People*, 12 Aug. 2016.
147 *Northern Standard*, 4 Feb. 1972.
148 J. Malone to L. Cosgrave, 18 May 1974, in D/T 2005/7/660 NAI.
149 J. Peck to W.K.K. White, 2 March 1972, in FCO 87/11.
150 J. O'Leary, *Doorsteps*, p. 153.

151 *Irish Times*, 1 Aug. 1972. Of 524 convicted by the Special Criminal Court between 1972–74, 59% were from Northern Ireland. D/T 2005/151/718 NAI.

152 G. FitzGerald, 'The 1974–5 threat of British withdrawal from Northern Ireland', *Irish Studies in International Affairs* 17 (2006) pp. 141–150.

153 Chief Superintendent to Sec. Dept of Justice, 1 Aug. 1975, in D/Justice 2005/155/6 NAI.

154 Transcript of interview with Ó Conaill on LWT TV, D/T, 17 Nov. 1974, 2005/7/663 NAI.

155 *Sunday World*, 2 Feb. 1975.

156 People's Democracy leadership document, N/D (1976?), Sean O'Mahony papers, MS. 44,241 NLI.

157 *Irish Independent*, 26 Sept. 1974.

158 Assessment of Possibilities of Military Intervention in Northern Ireland in Support of Besieged Groups, 14 June 1974, D/T 2005/7/484 NAI.

159 Annex G, Military Study – Northern Ireland, February 1975, 2008/79/3109 NAI.

7

'The other minority'[1]

On the 2 February 1972 (the National Day of Mourning), people in Newbridge, Co. Kildare awoke to find the town's Anglican church, St. Patrick's, and shops belonging to local Protestants had been daubed with sectarian slogans.[2] It was one of a number of such incidents, illustrating how war in the North was reviving dormant questions about southern Protestant loyalties. Most, however, denied that sectarianism played any part in southern life. Shortly after Bloody Sunday, Jack Lynch assured a correspondent that there had been 'no ... threats to the Protestant minority in the Republic. Neither is there any discrimination against them so they are in a very much more fortunate position than the Catholic minority in the North.'[3] Indeed, during May 1972, over 100 prominent southern Protestants published an open letter to Ulster Unionists in which they stressed they had 'every opportunity (to) play a full part in the affairs of the community'. They also asserted that in the Republic, 'Protestants hold positions of importance and trust at least in proportion to their fraction of the population'.[4]

'A very Protestant looking man'

In 1971, Protestants of all denominations made up less than 5% of the Republic's population. Their social position was perceived as relatively privileged:

> as a working citizen, the Protestant in the Republic certainly has little to complain of. Among the poor, he is unlikely to be poorer for being Protestant. Among the wealthy, he is likely to be wealthier for it. And outside the small-farm areas, his status is likely to be comfortably middle-class.[5]

Nevertheless, stereotypes abounded in a society in which religion had until comparatively recently been a marker of status. When people spoke about a 'very Protestant-looking man', they mean a distinct type: 'fair-haired, neat, usually with an upper-class English accent – and prosperous.'[6] For some there was still a 'Protestant air of relaxed superiority', Protestants 'had money and an edge' or were 'English who ride horses and hunt foxes'.[7] As late as 1966, Trinity College could be described as the 'last bastion of the English establishment and Protestant Ascendancy' in Ireland.[8]

Though southern Protestants were represented in all the mainstream political parties, many still associated them with the British connection. Indeed, some Protestants did identify with it, particularly service in its military. As emotions rose after 1969, there was still 'a view that you couldn't be a true Irishman if you were a Protestant'.[9] Such feelings were sharper along the border. The Ulster counties had much more substantial Protestant populations than elsewhere, including larger numbers of Presbyterians and other denominations.[10] The Orange Order was still a factor in community life in a way that it had long ceased to be in the rest of the 26 Counties.[11] In Monaghan, a Protestant Association contested council elections and the 'Protestant vote' was judged to be an important factor there and in Cavan and Donegal. (In 1970 two of three Monaghan TDs were Protestant.)[12]

'A vote for Fox is a vote for Paisley'

Though the North was not a major issue in the June 1969 general election, the growing tensions there were used for electoral advantage along the border. Billy Fox, a young Monaghan Fine Gael councillor and secretary of the local National Farmers Association, faced graffiti and a whispering campaign alleging that a 'vote for Fox was a vote for Paisley'. Posters asserted that a 'Vacancy exists in B Specials. Must be anti-Catholic. Contact Billy Fox or Paisley.'[13] In Donegal, where Bertie Boggs stood for Fine Gael, roads were painted with slogans proclaiming 'Vote Boggs No. 1: No Pope Here'. Rumours circulated that Boggs, a butcher from Malin town, was a B-Special and had been part of the mob who attacked civil rights marchers at Burntollet.[14] Both candidates blamed elements within Fianna Fáil for the allegations.

In both men's constituencies there was a belief that the existence of a 'large minority group of planter stock' meant that 'if they choose … to cast their votes for one particular candidate or party this means that the party in question has a great advantage when it comes to the matter of who will get the second seat'.[15]

In 1969, this rivalry was intensified by the fact that Fianna Fáil's only successful Dáil candidate in Monaghan was Erskine Childers (a member of the Church of Ireland). The belief in the potency of the 'Protestant vote' was such that Peter Berry of the Department of Justice later contended that the government threatened to introduce internment in December 1970 because they wanted to win Protestant votes in the Donegal–Leitrim by-election.[16] (In fact, the by-election took place on 2 December and the government did not announce their internment plan until two days after that.)[17]

'Fears of reprisals'

The wave of emotional solidarity with nationalists after August 1969 saw some incidents where anger was directed at Protestants. In Arklow, the small Presbyterian Church was fire bombed.[18] Guests fled a Christian evangelical holiday home at Greystones after it was visited by masked men and received bomb threats.[19] In Enniscorthy, Co. Wexford a petrol bomb was thrown at a Protestant-owned shop. Gardai were then stationed outside other businesses in the town in response to 'fears of reprisals against Protestants in the Enniscorthy area for happenings in Northern Ireland'.[20] In Sligo, local demonstrations of solidarity were 'charged with (a) tenseness and blood-belling (sic) atmosphere ... and fed on rumours, current in the town ... that some people living in the locality were members of the B-Special Force and supporters of the Orange Order'.[21] In Newbliss, Co. Monaghan a petrol bomb was thrown at the home of Derek Scott, who had been accused of being a B-Special.[22] There was also an arson attack at the home of Ivan Knox in Ballybofey, Co. Donegal. He was one of several Donegal Protestants who received letters from a group calling itself the United Catholic Front alleging that they were Specials. (Knox, a Presbyterian, offered £500 to St. Vincent de Paul if anyone could prove he was a B-Special.)[23] A caravan was burnt out at Milford, and Protestant holiday makers from across the border received threats.[24]

'Disgraceful incidents'

Condemning the intimidation, Ruairí Ó Brádaigh asserted that 'hundreds' of such letters had been sent to Donegal Protestants and that they 'were sent out on such a scale that one couldn't help being driven to the conclusion that there was some form of organisation behind it. That was clear especially when these letters were often addressed to people by their colloquial and nick names.'[25] Sinn Féin in Monaghan condemned the 'throwing of a petrol bomb at Newbliss, damage to a shop in Castleblayney, an attempt to burn a hall in north Monaghan, verbal intimidation of a family in Monaghan town and disgraceful incidents in Kingscourt, Co. Cavan'.[26] In Donegal, the party denounced as 'Catholic Paisleys and Craigs' those who threatened Protestants.[27]

But accusations that locals were B-Specials continued to be aired. In Monaghan, on 19 August, Austin Currie MP condemned attacks on Protestants but asserted 'I don't like "B" men, whether they are from the north or south, but please do not interfere with them. If you have "B" men crossing over the Border, just give us their names and let us deal with them when they come into Northern Ireland.'[28] Strabane republican Ivan Barr told a rally in Lifford that they were 'aware that men were coming across border, donning uniforms in Strabane and taking out rifles' but 'if they are attacked or interfered with on this side of the border it will bring retaliations in Strabane. Leave them alone for now.'[29] In contrast, the *Northern Standard* advised those engaged in this 'foolishly vicious "B" Special witch-hunt' that 'many quite innocent people have been falsely labelled with membership ... and thus wrongfully exposed to the distrust and odium of their neighbours'. The paper conceded that there possibly were a 'small number' of men living close to the border who were Specials (but the) number was 'altogether insignificant'.[30]

But most of the protests across the south had no sectarian dimension and Protestants often associated themselves with them. The statement by the Dean of Cork, the Very Reverend F.K. Johnston, that 'today one is ashamed to be a Protestant', and repudiating the 'so-called Protestant spirit that deliberately sets out to suppress ... that allows and encourages ghettoes (and) victimisation of men and women because of their religious and political convictions' was fairly typical. Johnston asserted that 'we have known no such ghettoes in the South. Fifty years of Unionist and Protestant Government in Northern Ireland has produced the present holocaust.'[31]

Rossknowlagh

Tensions arose again in Donegal during the summer of 1970. The eastern part of the county had a strong Orange tradition. An ITGWU official recalled that during the 1960s mill workers in the region were '50/50 Protestant and Roman Catholic' and many union members were also 'members of the Orange Order ... all of East Donegal had this kind of religious divide, which always had to be taken into consideration when organising'.[32] In July 1970, Fianna Fáil Senator Bernard McGlinchey predicted trouble if the Orange parade at Rossknowlagh was allowed go ahead. He claimed that during August 1969 Donegal Orangemen had crossed the border 'to help B Specials in their foul work' and had 'marched through three towns in Donegal while the city of Colmcille was ablaze'. He also alleged that there was local involvement in the UVF bombing of an RTE mast at Raphoe earlier in the year.[33]

There was a hostile reaction to McGlinchey's assertions. The Donegal Ancient Order of Hibernians supported the Orange Order's right to march, as did both Official and Provisional Sinn Féin. Republicans blamed 'Blaneyite' elements for introducing tension into what Ó Brádaigh described as 'a completely harmless affair'.[34] However, the parade *was* cancelled and did not take place again until 1978. In the midst of the controversy there was an attempt to burn the Orange Hall in Lifford (which would be targeted again on a number of occasions over the next few years).[35] Such incidents in the 26 Counties were eagerly seized on by Unionists across the border. During July 1970, speakers at the Fermanagh Orange parades claimed that lodges in Cavan had been warned that if they took part, Kilmore Cathedral would be burned in retaliation. Gardai were unable to find any evidence of these threats, though the Very Rev. R.C.H. Turkington, Dean Of Kilmore, confirmed that he had been told that it would be better if the Kilmore band did not travel across the border. There were in fact six southern lodges at the main parade in Fermanagh, two from Cavan and four from Monaghan.[36]

'The least said about it the better'

As conflict began to escalate in the North, there were more incidents in Donegal. In January 1971, the home of a Church of Ireland Rector, Rev. Canon McDonald, at Tamney was damaged by an explosion. When this was condemned locally as a sectarian attack, Councillor Harry Blaney responded that 'some of the people concerned didn't know what they were talking about … he felt it was not on a sectarian basis and many others of both denominations felt the same. There were good relations between the two communities and the least said about it the better.' However, in July windows were broken in Stranorlar's Presbyterian Church, during September Carrigan's Memorial Orange Hall was burnt down and in December the St. Johnston Orange Hall was damaged in an arson attack.[37]

'These people were in our midst'

There were also continuing allegations that border Protestants were involved with loyalist paramilitaries. In September 1971, an independent member of Monaghan County Council, James Deery, claimed that there had been a major arms find on the Farnham Estate in Cavan and that local business people were involved with the UVF. He warned that 'these people were in our midst, training in our midst and it is up to us to defend ourselves'. After the allegations were repeated in the *Sunday Independent*, the Minister for Justice was forced to issue a statement that they were 'wholly false and without foundation of any kind whatsoever'.[38] At Avra that month a Sinn Féin anti-internment rally heard calls to ignore the 'rumours of UVF training and arms finds in the county which, the speakers said, were calculated to drive the communities apart'. [39]

However, it is clear there were starkly different views as to the responsibility for the escalating violence. At Monaghan Urban District Council in August 1971, motions condemning internment, welcoming Irish army support for refugees and expressing sympathy with victims of violence were passed almost unanimously. But Victor Heasty of the Protestant Association disassociated himself from all of them bar the resolution of sympathy.[40] This reflected the position of the main Protestant churches who, controversially (and with some reservations), had supported the introduction of internment.[41] This in turn led some southern Protestants to criticize the leadership of their churches.[42] Protests in August 1971 saw some anti-Protestant feeling. At an anti-internment meeting in Sligo, socialist Declan Bree condemned the 'drunken bigot' who had broken windows in a Protestant-owned shop in the town.[43]

'Unease and insecurity'

During 1971, there had been a growing number of attacks on British-owned property, symbols of the British connection and the homes of British citizens living in Ireland – some of whom were also Protestants. When the British Ambassador compiled his assessment of events in the Republic, he stated that his review

> would be incomplete without a mention of that loosely knit group known variously and at different times as the Ascendancy, the Anglo-Irish, or West Britons, including the old Southern Unionists and those of which ever extraction, many of whom served in Her Majesty's Forces, who have felt and experienced no difficulty in feeling or being both English and Irish. One has met a violent death, another has been badly beaten up. The British Legion offices in Dublin have been burnt, and the Cork office of the Department of Health and Social Security blown up. There are increasingly frequent stories of threats and minor harassment. The ex-service associations have cancelled most of their annual dinners and similar manifestations which could provoke violence against members' families. Measured against the space of a year and the length and breadth of the Republic, these incidents are few and scattered. Nevertheless there is a growing sense of unease and insecurity among them, due more to doubts about what will happen if the strength and influence of the IRA continue to grow than to anything that has happened so far.[44]

'Brutal attack'

The majority of southern Protestants would not have regarded themselves as 'West Britons' nor part of the 'Ascendancy'. However, incidents such as the daubing of slogans like 'Up the IRA' and 'Down with Orangemen' on Mount Falcon Castle in Ballina, the residence of Major Robert Aldridge, showed how lines could be blurred.[45] More seriously, a retired British officer, Lt. Col. Stuart-French, was badly beaten up during a raid on his home in Cobh. Shortly afterwards he and his wife left the country following threats of arson.[46] (The Provisional IRA condemned the 'brutal attack' on Stuart-French).[47] In early December, another ex-British Army officer, C.R.P. Walker, died after a raid on his home near Navan, Co. Meath.[48] Threats, including arson attacks, against British citizens continued over the next year.[49] These were not directed at Irish Protestants per se, and the 'Anglo-Irish' themselves were divided politically.

Lord Kilbracken of Leitrim, for example, a decorated veteran of the Second World War, described the British version of events after Bloody Sunday as lies, returned his war medals and renounced his British passport.[50]

Bloody Sunday

But it was in the context of the mobilizations after Bloody Sunday that the issue of threats to Protestants arose again. The day after, students from the High School in Rathgar were among those protesting outside the British Embassy where 'for a few hours, south Dublin Protestant schoolboys were shoulder to shoulder with Sinn Féin'.[51] The national Day of Mourning saw some sort of event in almost every town in the state, and there was widespread participation by Protestant clergy in the various services. At the rally in Waterford, on the platform with Catholic Bishop Michael Russell were Anglican Bishop John Ward Armstrong of Cashel, Emly, Waterford and Lismore, the Reverend Fergus Day-Dean of Waterford, Reverend Dudley Cooney of the Methodist church, Presbyterian Reverend S. Watt and Mr. Maurice Wigham of the Society of Friends.[52] There were special Church of Ireland services in Ennis and throughout the Diocese of Killaloe and Clonfert, in Longford town, Navan, Trim, Kells, Ballinasloe, Westport, Aughrim, Carlow, the Curragh, Cavan, Cootehill, Westport, Ballinrobe, Carrick on Shannon and Kilkenny.[53] Anglican clergy were present at many of the cross-party protest meetings. At a factory mass on the Shannon industrial estate, one of the lessons was read by a Church of Ireland minister.[54] There were also Methodist and Presbyterian services in several areas, including Longford, Carlow, Cootehill, Dunmanway and in Dublin. Tánaiste Erskine Childers attended a special service in St. Patrick's Cathedral, along with an estimated 2,000 others.

At many meetings, speakers from Protestant backgrounds identified themselves as such. Jack Boothman from the West Wicklow Board of the GAA mourned the '13 of our people murdered in a few bloody seconds' and asserted that though 'I belong to what some people call a religious minority ... I have never regarded it so'.[55] On Bray Trades Council, both the outgoing president Thomas Sutton of the ATGWU and his successor Desmond Hedley Wright were members of the Church of Ireland, Sutton stating that 'my fellow Protestants have nothing to fear in a united Ireland'.[56]

However, there were also sectarian incidents. In Co. Wexford, shots were fired in the vicinity of three Protestant homes, hitting one. Petrol bombs were thrown into the Congregational Church in St. Johnston, Co. Donegal.[57] In Monaghan, there was an attempt to burn the Jackson Memorial Hall in Carrickmacross. In Newbridge, the Anglican church and shops belonging to Protestants were daubed with sectarian slogans. The windows of the Methodist Church in Dublin's Blackrock were smashed.[58] A protest meeting in Navan heard that a Protestant farmer living near Mountnugent had been burnt out, and there were reports of damage to Protestant property in Co. Longford, Arklow and Sligo.[59]

In west Cork, there were widespread reports that Protestant families had been threatened, with Anglican clergymen confirming that such rumours were 'definitely circulating in their communities'. Some form of intimidation was reported from Kinsale, Bandon, Ballydehob, Schull, Skibbereen, Roscarberry, Ballinadee and Clonakilty.[60] However, apart from a few specific cases of telephoned threats, the bulk of these remained 'confused and unconfirmed'.[61] There was almost universal condemnation of the incidents. In Newbridge, local people painted over the sectarian slogans the morning they appeared.[62] In Wexford, it was stressed that 'relations are very good down here' and that the people attacked were 'held in high regard'.[63] In Cork, the threats were 'attributed either to hooligans, misguided patriots or jealous neighbours'. Fianna Fáil TD Flor Crowley described them as

> the work of a very sick element in our society who are using the tragic situation in the North as an outlet for their own malady ... the Protestant community ... have played a very important part in the development of our part of Ireland since the foundation of the State ... We are all Irishmen and Irishwomen.[64]

Activist priest Fr. Austin Flannery denounced the attacks at a Dublin solidarity rally on Sunday 6 February.[65] Both Official and Provisional republicans condemned the incidents and in some cases threatened retaliation.[66] In Clare, the Provisional IRA warned those behind threats to 'non-Catholics and non-nationals' that they would have to 'answer to this command'.[67] A hint of the atmosphere is evident from the social column of the *Leitrim Observer* where, reporting on a fundraising event in the aftermath of Bloody Sunday, the writer gave a 'BOO: To the Master of Ceremonies at the Northern Aid Concert for his tasteless jibes at the Protestant community. We are above that, I hope.'[68]

'A Quisling approach'

There were exceptions. The heated rhetoric about Ulster Unionists, aired at numerous meetings, and the use of terms such as 'planter' might have appeared to be directed at all Protestants. The most blatant example of this was an editorial in west Cork's *Southern Star*, which began by criticizing Unionists and suggested that if they were 'not prepared to live in an Ireland governed by Irishmen, let (them) get out'. It then suggested that 'unless the Irish minority, can pledge full and undivided allegiance to an Irish state, the outlook for them is blue'. In this, the *Star* argued, 'the Southern Protestant bears a heavy responsibility' because, though Protestants in the Republic knew accusations of discrimination against them were false, they 'nonetheless persevere(d) with a Quisling approach to nationhood'. While 'one or two Church of Ireland clergymen very occasionally have made declarations of allegiance to the Irish State ... for the rest the approach is tongue-in-cheek'.[69] Among those responding was local farmer J.W. Pollard, who had served in the Local Defence Forces during the Emergency and been prominent in community organizations. He claimed that 'the support given to national activities by the Protestant portion of the community is far greater than might be expected from 5 per cent of the population'.[70]

'Mafia like methods'

Closer to the border, such tensions were nearer the surface. On Clones council there were heated exchanges alleging intimidation during the post-Bloody Sunday protests, when the town had shut down for two days and been patrolled by vigilantes. Councillor Maureen Magee claimed that 'Mafia like methods were used' and people ordered not to go to work on Tuesday 1 February. The council heard that 'some Protestant citizens in the town were confined to their homes in fear for two days'. It was also alleged that at least one man was physically threatened.[71] On Monaghan Council there were complaints that Victor Heasty of the Protestant Association had not attended the special meeting after the Derry massacre. Councillor Francis McCarron hoped that Heasty's absence did not represent Protestant attitudes to what occurred in Derry. McCarron stressed that in contrast to Northern Ireland, the minority in Monaghan were 'treated very fairly' making up '33% of those on local bodies while only 15% of population'. However, Councillor Ronaghan claimed that he could 'well understand why Protestants did not participate in any great numbers' in the protests, because these had begun at the Catholic Cathedral. While stressing that he had no quarrel with Protestants, James Deery 'did object to the Monaghan group that went down last 12th July and painted their car. He had their names and they had better be careful.'[72] While many speakers noted the good relations that existed locally, they tended to assert that the onus was on Protestants to stress this to those across the border; 'If the Protestant people of Co. Monaghan came out and testified that they were getting more than fair treatment they would decrease the fears of the Protestant people of the North – the fears they have of coming into a united Ireland.'[73]

'Relations ... were particuarly good'

The *Church of Ireland Gazette* reflected that in the aftermath of Derry it could

> scarcely have been expected that the Protestant minority would entirely escape the attentions of those who equate 'Protestant' with 'British', 'Unionist' or even 'Orange'. Minor incidents have taken place here and there involving threatening letters or telephone calls, the daubing of church walls or business premises owned by Protestants. Some of the latter incidents have been chiefly notable for the speed with which the Roman Catholic community has acted to make good the damage.[74]

At a local level, there seemed little desire to complain. During May 1972, six Protestant boy scouts were beaten up in Dundalk after being confronted by a gang of youths who demanded to know their religion before attacking them. There was anger about the incident because the scouts had collected money for northern refugees, and it was condemned from the pulpit at all Catholic churches in Dundalk. However, when the Rector of St. Nicholas (Anglican) Parish Church was asked for his views, he replied that he had 'no comment … because inter-religious relations in Dundalk were particularly good'.[75]

'Catholics went berserk'

July 1972 saw the most serious incident of large-scale sectarian disorder in the 26 Counties since 1935. There were two nights of rioting in St. Johnston, Co. Donegal with over 70 people injured, widespread damage to Protestant property and troops called in to back up Gardai. The trouble started when local Orangemen returned from their parade across the border at Garvagh and formed up to march to their hall. They were attacked by a large crowd who had gathered outside a pub. Stones and bottles were thrown and Orange banners broken and torn. Though calm was restored, trouble broke out again that night. The town's Masonic hall was burned down, an attempt was made to set fire to the Orange hall, a petrol bomb was thrown into the Presbyterian church hall, all the windows in the Congregational church were broken and a Protestant-owned store and its contents were gutted by fire. Several Protestant homes also had their windows broken, and in one case an attempt was made to break into a house. One of the Protestant homeowners fired a shotgun at men outside his house, wounding three. A squad car was overturned and set on fire and a fire engine hijacked.[76]

The *Irish Press* reported that one Protestant woman claimed that 'local Catholics went berserk' and smashed their way into her home after damaging her car. They had also attacked the home of a 77-year-old pensioner. But local Catholics stated 'the Orangemen started the trouble'. There were reports that several Protestant families had fled to relatives in Derry.[77]

'A great tradition in East Donegal'

In the aftermath of the violence, a local barrister explained that relationships between the communities had been good in a town where the religious makeup was 'roughly 50–50'. The *Derry Journal* condemned the violence and asserted that Orangemen had a 'perfect right to their parade' in 'their native village'.[78] The Donegal Provisional IRA stated that the rioting 'had nothing to do with them, and that in fact they deplored it'. Local republican Frank Morris described 'Orange marching (as) a great tradition in East Donegal'.[79] In the midst of the trouble, Senator Bernard McGlinchey had phoned the Department of Justice warning that 'Protestants in St. Johnston (are) terrified that they will be burned out tonight' and asking that 'there should be a show of strength by the security forces *early* today'. The Department noted that 'The Gardai are also being told locally that there are two sides to the question – but if they are ... (to) accept the Protestant complaints at the moment.'[80] Gardai were detailed with protecting Protestant property for a period afterwards.[81]

'Law-abiding citizens'

In early August, local Orange Order leader David Beattie wrote to the Taoiseach outlining the damage caused by the riot. Beattie stated that 'we are particularly concerned at the level of intimidation which has been directed against Protestants in the area for past 2/3 years and the fact that eleven families have felt compelled to leave their homes and seek refuge in Northern Ireland may well be the beginning of a general Protestant exodus'. He confirmed rumours that the Provisional IRA had approached him, disclaiming responsibility for the violence and offering protection to local Protestants. The UDA had also contacted him. Beattie claimed that 'we have politely refused both offers as we would prefer to rely, in the first instance, on the protection of elected Government forces'. He concluded by asserting that 'since the State was formed we have been among its most law-abiding citizens, taking our full part in the social and economic life of the community, and we are entitled to full protection from all forms of attack'.[82]

'Settle now or a bomb'

Sectarian factors were also at work in a long-running industrial dispute in Letterkenny. Joe Patterson claimed that his victualling business was boycotted because he was Protestant and rumours were spread that he discriminated against Catholics.[83] Two strikes involving the ITGWU took place, during which Patterson was called a 'Protestant bastard' and received death threats, including a note which stated '2 strikes in seven months under "you" Settle now or a bomb (regret no warning)'. However, Patterson gained little support from officialdom, the Minister for Labour, Michael O'Leary, writing to him that the Department was 'satisfied that the industrial action, both official and unofficial, to which your Company was subjected was not motivated by political or sectarian factors'.[84] Interestingly, Patterson claimed that both the local IRA, and the Derry Provisionals, offered him support and disavowed any involvement in the campaign against him.[85] Ultimately, however, he closed his business and emigrated with his family to Canada.

Loyalists

There was no repetition of the scale of the trouble in St. Johnston, though its ripple effect was felt for years afterward.[86] But tension in east Donegal also increased because of loyalist attacks during the winter of 1972. The Ulster Defence Association claimed responsibility for five bomb attacks in Donegal in that period, targeting several factories and a pub. A young couple were murdered by the UDA near Burnfoot late that year, and in early 1973 a UDA member from Derry died in a premature explosion in Cloughfin.[87] In February 1974, republican Jack Brogan was shot and critically injured in Ballybofey. Brogan had been acquitted a few weeks before of the murder of RUC detective John Doherty, who was shot dead visiting his family in Lifford in October 1973.[88] As late as March 1975, the UDA bombed fishing trawlers at Greencastle, Co. Donegal.[89]

Aside from the worries and fears such incidents produced, there were suspicions of Donegal involvement. When investigating a bomb blast at a Catholic school in St. Johnston in September 1970, Gardai searched a local foundry and the homes of its owner, his son and seven employees. They believed the device, similar to the one used on an RTE mast at Raphoe earlier that year, was made by an ex-British soldier with an address in Derry, but who spent most of his time locally.[90] Gardai also thought that some of the UDA's bombs in east Donegal in late 1972 were informed by local knowledge. They suspected an explosion at a fertilizer factory in Carrigans was in part related to the involvement of an employee in the rioting in St. Johnston in July.[91]

A measure of the complexity of religious influence on politics in the border region was the fact that the Donegal Progressive Party, which claimed to represent the bulk of that county's Protestant voters, called for support for Fianna Fáil in 1973.[92] In the same year, 16-year-old Inishowen native Henry Cunningham was murdered in a gun attack on the motorway outside Belfast while returning with family members from work in Antrim. Cunningham, a Presbyterian, was killed by the UVF, who did not claim the attack, and for years his family presumed the IRA was responsible as nobody told them otherwise.[93]

The murder of Billy Fox

Bombs and bomb scares, false alarms and rumours were part of border life in those years. There were several deadly attacks in Cavan and Monaghan. In November 1973, armed men shot and wounded Noel Thornberry at a house near Clones. Thornberry managed to escape, but the house where he had been staying was blown up.[94] Thornberry was a Lurgan republican and his comrades suspected that locals had provided information to his attackers. A few months later, Senator Billy Fox was murdered.[95] Fox was visiting the home of his fiancée, Marjorie Coulson, near Clones when he was shot. Up to 13 armed men had been ransacking the house and questioning the Coulsons (who were Protestant) about the whereabouts of arms and explosives. Fox arrived, was challenged by the IRA men, tried to escape and was shot. The Coulson's home and adjoining caravan were then burned down as the attackers made their escape.[96]

Fox's death produced outrage and confusion. The *Northern Standard* reported that 'the town of Clones is seething with rumours and counter-rumours as to the whys and wherefores of the awful tragedy'.[97] Initially it was unclear who had killed Fox. A statement from the Ulster Freedom Fighters claimed the murder, while Ruairí Ó Brádaigh blamed it on 'British or pro-British agents'.[98] *Hibernia* magazine stated that it was the 'opinion of local Gardaí ... that evidence suggested a raid by loyalists from across the border'.[99] But Fox had been killed by the Provisional IRA, and five of its members were jailed as a result of an episode 'that did the movement tremendous damage'.[100]

'B-Special Republican'

Shortly after the upheaval of August 1969, as a newly elected TD Fox had visited Derry and the Falls Road. On his return, he conveyed the Bogsiders' demands to Monaghan County Council.[101] As a result, he received hate mail from loyalists. However, in Leinster House he again faced allegations that he was a B-Special.[102] During 1970, Kevin Boland made the allegation during a Dáil debate.[103] Perhaps the reason Fox annoyed Fianna Fáil was because he consistently raised the issue of border incursions by British troops and alleged that the government was not doing anything about it. During one debate, he told ministers that 'we will see on which side you are, whether you support Irishmen or the British Army'. Fox was suspended from the House in December 1971, having produced a rubber bullet and a CS gas canister that had been fired into the Republic by British troops.[104] Eye-witness accounts of one border incident praised Fox for risking his personal safety to prevent a confrontation escalating.[105] However, during another debate on incursions by British troops, Fianna Fáil's Desmond O'Malley sarcastically welcomed what he called Fox's 'conversion'. In the row that followed, Brian Lenihan referred to Fox as a 'B-Special Republican'.[106] When Ian Paisley visited Monaghan to open a new Free Presbyterian church in early 1972, Fox condemned the move (ironically, Provisional Sinn Féin had asked Paisley to speak at an anti-EEC rally in the county).[107] During that year, Fox had argued that 'we must work towards the day when "Kevin Barry" and "The Sash" can be sung with equal safety ... in every pub in Ireland from one end to the other'.[108]

'Bogside Billy'

Being seen as a nationalist critic of the government affected Fox's standing among Monaghan Protestants. After 1969, he was nicknamed 'Bogside Billy', and several accounts suggest that his association with these issues cost him electoral support.[109] He lost his Dáil seat in 1973 by just over 200 votes.[110] Hence some of the confusion when he was killed.[111] In court, one of those accused of Fox's murder claimed that 'the whole thing began with the blowing up of McCooey's house in September 1973 and the shooting of Thornberry ... these explosions were carried out by the UVF with local help. The Gardai were well aware of this fact.'[112] The house where Thornberry was shot was about a mile from the Coulsons' home. It would seem that the IRA targeted the Coulsons because they received information claiming that loyalist weapons were stored by them.[113] In the opinion of a senior Garda, this was 'false information' motivated by 'pure spite'.[114] In the Thornberry raid, there had been a claim that loyalists had destroyed religious pictures. In the raid on the Coulsons, an IRA man had thrown their family bible into the fire.[115] Despite the widespread sorrow over Fox's death, whispering campaigns continued. Some claimed that on the night he was killed Fox himself was 'armed and fired the first shot', and that the May 1974 Monaghan bombing was a 'revenge massacre' for Fox's death.[116] In fact, that bomb exploded outside a Protestant-owned pub and one of the victims, 72-year-old George Williamson, was Presbyterian. However, local rumours about the events persist to this day.[117]

County of Intrigue

Many of these allegations were contained in Michael Cunningham's *Monaghan: County of Intrigue*, published in 1979. Cunningham contended that many Monaghan Protestants were members of the B-Specials and the Orange Order and that they occupied positions of influence and power far in excess of their ratio in the population. Ultimately, Protestants in Monaghan hankered 'back to the days of the Protestant Ascendancy' and had never accepted the independence of the 26 Counties. Among the book's assertions were that over 'the years since the Treaty, Dromard Bog in County Cavan was used by local Protestant members of the B-Specials or the UVF to do outdoor training ... During the 1960s B-Specials trained on Tuesday nights in Cavan's Kilmore Cathedral.' UVF weapons had indeed been found in Kilmore Cathedral, though that had been in 1925.[118] Since partition, a number of Protestants from border areas had also joined the northern security forces (several would be killed during the 1970s).[119] *An Phoblacht* considered *County of Intrigue* an 'interesting, if disjointed book' which 'drew heavily upon Catholic and conservative values' and was at times 'extremely eccentric if not ... fantasy'.[120] However, the book was significant as it contained many of the 'myths, rumours and hearsay' that often informed local attitudes with regard to sectarianism.[121] In some cases, this contributed to a situation where Protestants 'would not express a political opinion' for fear of drawing attention to themselves.[122]

'The Queen is part of the Protestant religion'

There were several anecdotal examples that testifed to residual Loyalism among some southern Protestants. One account noted how 'a Dublin minister spoke impatiently of reactionary Orange Lodge influence upon Presbyterian political attitudes in Monaghan, Cavan and Donegal'.[123] A young Protestant complained of older Monaghan co-religionists that 'a lot of them ... seem to think that the Queen is part of the Protestant religion'.[124] There are hints that, for some, Loyalism ran deeper than portraits of Queen Elizabeth. Assertions that loyalists had assistance from inside the Republic were not confined to the border. After both the May 1974 bombings and the Dublin Airport attack in November 1975, Gardai received information that there was a 'unit of Loyalist students at Trinity'. They concluded, however, that while 'it is true that quite a number of students at Trinity are from Northern Ireland ... from information available none of them are involved with Loyalist subversives'.[125]

However, these allegations persisted about the border regions. *Hibernia* magazine would claim that one of the loyalist bombs in Clones had been organized from within Monaghan, while loyalists maintained arms dumps in Redhills, Co. Cavan.[126] In May 1970, civil servant Kevin Rush reported information from a 'reliable source' that after the force's disbandment 'weapons held by B Specials were taken across the Border and hidden in the Republic by members of the B Specials who, themselves, reside in the Republic, or whose families reside in the Republic'.[127] Indeed, one study of the border asserts that 'quite a number of Protestants joined the B Specials during the 1956–62 campaign and would cycle over for duty on Saturdays'.[128] After a fatal car bomb attack in Castleblayney in March 1976, Gardai searched the homes of several local Protestants they suspected of being loyalist sympathizers. Two of these men had been observed by Gardai in the vicinity of pubs frequented by republicans in Ballybay and Castleblayney. They were believed to have been in contact with loyalists in Armagh. The men had stepped up activity in early 1976 following the Kingsmills massacre by the IRA, and Gardai suspected that a retaliatory attack was being planned.[129] Republicans in the county continued to assert that loyalists retained support around north Monaghan, 'where there would be those who'd be in the Orange Order and in the Black (Preceptory) as well'.[130]

'We are Irish and we don't want to be anything else'

By the 1970s, however, most southern Protestants seemed to be 'identifying more and more with the Irish state'. Those interviewed for a July 1972 BBC programme 'Protestant and Proud of It' stressed that 'we are Irish and we don't want to be anything else'. A Cork farmer explained that he favoured a united Ireland because 'an insignificant minority would then be a big minority' and that aspects of the Republic that he found uncomfortable 'would have to be tempered'. A young woman, also from Cork, explained that she saw herself as having far more in common with southern Catholics than northern Protestants.[131] Most southern Catholics would have agreed, 85% of those polled in Dublin during 1972 asserting that southern Protestants had more in common with them than their northern co-religionists.[132]

In May 1972, over 100 Protestants had signed an open letter stating that they wanted 'it to be known in Northern Ireland – for it does not seem to be' that southern Protestants faced no discrimination and played a full part in the affairs of the Republic. They stressed that in the Republic 'opinions and points of outlook are exchanged easily and without acrimony whilst the respect of one man for another is habitually related to the man rather than his religious views'. When it came to the laws governing contraception and other matters, the letter stated that 'various sensitive issues which find continuing publicity are for most men far short of crucial, are in practice far less than repressive, and are in prospect adjustable by stages'. Among the signatories were businessmen Sir Basil Goulding, Gordon Lambert, Peter Odlum, Victor Bewley and Rodney B. Dockrill, conservationist Desmond Guinness, sculptor Oisin Kelly, civil servant Thekla Beere, former Lord Mayor of Limerick Frances Condell, trade unionist William McMullen and historian Theo Moody.[133] The letter was the brainchild of Basil Goulding, who had written to Jack Lynch with a draft earlier that year.[134]

'We're all right Jack'?[135]

Responding to the letter, John Horgan wondered if it represented the views of most Protestants. He noted that the 'median income' of the signatories was 'not only significantly higher than the national average, but significantly higher than the Protestant average'. With 'some dismay' he saw the dismissal of the importance of issues such as contraception as an attempt by Protestants to 'opt out' of the struggle for liberalization in which many Catholics were increasingly prepared to disobey *their* church. Horgan reflected that in

> dealings with Southern Protestants I have often encountered a sort of 'don't rock the boat' attitude based on the belief that Protestants have done tolerably well out of things here and that criticism might be construed as disloyalty … I would have thought Protestantism was all about rocking boats.

He concluded that 'the way to appeal to Northern Protestants is not to appeal to the worst aspects of their character … but the best aspect of their character – an adventurous and unrepentent Protestantism … it is that, rather than meek acceptance, which would be their most valuable contribution to a United Ireland'.[136]

'Nobody has ever questioned my Irishness'

Dick Spicer, an Official Sinn Féin member from a Protestant background, suggested that while 'people like Sir. Basil Goulding (or) Desmond Guinness ... would suffer no discrimination under the 1937 Constitution ... the difficulties that face working-class Protestants can indeed be crucial'.[137] More generally, there was evidence of some discomfort with the 'tense, republican atmosphere of the South since the pogroms of 1969'. A young clergyman in Dublin, Paul Cardew, noted that 'old animosities are coming to the fore ... appearing on the odd wall have been such comforting slogans as "IRA will get Proddy Bastards".'[138] Protestants were aware of the fact that many still saw them as a 'remnant of the ascendancy' and that in many areas there was very little contact, beyond business, between the communities. Where there were social relations between Catholics and Protestants, it was often the case that 'religion and politics have been avoided as topics for discussion by tacit consent, so that neither element has developed any real understanding of the loyalties and aspirations of the other'.[139]

One clergyman suggested that many of his parishioners were 'hoping for a united Ireland because then they will be a third of the country and the Government down here would have to sit up and take notice'.[140] Others were keen to place distance between themselves and Ulster Unionists; 'we did not create this situation, while the Northerner has brought himself to this pass'.[141] However, when Cardew asserted that he felt that being a southern Protestant placed him in an 'odd position', fellow Anglican and republican activist, Stephen Hilliard, responded that he had 'never felt myself to be a second-class citizen. And nobody has ever questioned my Irishness: perhaps that is because I have never questioned it myself. I doubt if Mr. Cardew's hang-ups in this matter are shared by many 26 County Protestants.'[142]

'Puny Prods'?[143]

For a few campaigners, southern Protestants were not critical enough of the Republic. One left-wing group, campaigning for separation of church and state, claimed that while Ulster Presbyterians were 'famous for their independence of spirit. The Church of Ireland, at least in the South, is famous for its collection of antique silver.' They argued that because southern Protestants were

> made up *mainly* of middle-class, well-to-do types they had little stomach for fight and so they bowed and crawled. Now there is little left save a few tired old men and their antique silver. The Protestant community in the South is practically

dead, killed by Ne Temere and their own cowardice ... the movement for democracy which has got underway in Ireland in the last few years owes nothing to them.[144]

'Given up the ghost'?

From a different perspective, *An Phoblacht's* 'Jemmy Hope' also discussed 'the Decline of Irish Protestantism' during 1975. 'Hope' pointed out that historically it was 'wrong to suppose' that southern non-Catholics 'were all horse Protestants maintained here by grace of the British Government. Many of them were modest farmers and trades people. A few lived close to the poverty line, although it is traditional among Protestants that they rarely show this. Some lived below the poverty level.' Outlining the diversity of Protestant life across the 26 Counties prior to partition, from inner-city Dublin to the small farmers and shopkeepers of the countryside, the writer argued that then Protestants 'were accepted as part and parcel of the social fabric of the community, of the molecules that make a people'. But in the Ireland of 1975, 'they have quite literally almost disappeared'. Hope asked if 'we want to be a multi-denominational society' how 'can we, where Protestants form less than four per cent of it, and where the few remaining seem more concerned with living a social hari kari as unmarrieds, odd bods, or queers than in out proliferating the Papes around them? Southern Irish Protestants seem quite literally to have given up the ghost of the struggle.'[145] Even in the Ulster counties he suggested that

> Protestant populations ... have decimated themselves – by non-marriage, and by emigration into the Six and elsewhere – and are now pale shadows of the lusty communities of forty or fifty years ago ... true enough, Paisley has established a bridgehead in Monaghan, but one can afford to smile at it. It is an aberration and will die with him. There may still be an Orange demonstration in Ballybofey, and the 'contingents' may cross the border to take part in Twelfth marches in the North; we can smile at them too. They are harmless old men on the way out.[146]

For 'Hope', the republican movement's Éire Nua policy offered an opportunity for Protestants to once again become a social and political force in a new federal Ireland.

'Community relationships remained strong'

Some have argued the Northern Irish conflict fostered understanding between Protestants and Catholics in the Republic.[147] In 1976, historian John A. Murphy asserted that a 'changing sense of identity' among southern Protestants had been

> hastened by the catalyst of the Northern crisis. The longstanding identity of Protestant and Unionist interests led the Protestant to resent the Irish State in

which he unwillingly found himself in 1922: resentment has given place through slow acceptance to complete identification with the Irish polity. Today very few Southern Protestants think of themselves as British and they are as mystified by, and alienated from, the Northern Protestant as the Southern papist is.[148]

Others have argued that even in the border counties 'community relationships remained strong (and) sectarianism was never allowed to take root'.[149] Evidence suggests that the reality was far more complicated. In fact, the eruption of violence after 1969 saw the re-emergence of old suspicions and resentments which produced fear and occasionally violence. Though expression of such prejudices was widely condemned, they were reminders of an element in Irish nationalism that never accepted Protestants as truly 'Irish'. Similarly, there were also those Protestants in the Republic who had remained 'loyalist' long after independence and whose politics were also a factor in border areas.

Notes

1 *Church of Ireland Gazette*, 11 Feb. 1972.
2 *Nationalist and Leinster Times*, 4 Feb. 1972.
3 J. Lynch to J.R. Purvis, 11 Feb. 1972, in D/T 2003/16/189 NAI.
4 *Evening Herald*, 17 May 1972.
5 M. Viney, *The Five Per Cent: A Survey of Protestants in the Republic* (Dublin, 1965) p. 10.
6 T.P. Coogan, *Ireland Since the Rising* (London, 1966) p. 248.
7 A. Madden, *Fear and Loathing*, p. 30. K. Conway, *Southside*, p. 4. *Southern Star*, 11 Oct. 1975.
8 *Hibernia*, June 1966.
9 P. Bray, *Inside Man: Life as an Irish Prison Officer* (Dublin, 2008) p. 15.
10 W.E. Vaughan and A.J. Fitzpatrick, *Irish Historical Statistics: Population 1821–1971* (Dublin, 1978) p. 72.
11 D. Fitzpatrick, *Descendancy: Irish Protestant Histories since 1795* (Cambridge, 2014) pp. 55–58. In July 1969, 13 men had marched behind the banner of the Dublin/Wicklow lodge at the 12 July parade in Belfast. *Nusight*, Aug. 1969.
12 P.M. Sacks, *The Donegal Mafia: An Irish Political Machine* (Yale, 1976) p. 54. *Anglo-Celt*, 6 March and 18 Dec. 1970.
13 *Anglo-Celt*, 31 Oct. 1969.
14 *This Week*, 24 July 1970.
15 *Anglo-Celt*, 6 March 1970.
16 *Magill*, June 1980.
17 *Irish Times*, 2 Dec. 1970.
18 *Irish Press*, 21 Aug. 1969.
19 *Irish Times*, 8 Oct. 1969.
20 *Wexford People*, 23 Aug. 1969.
21 *Western People*, 23 Aug. 1969.
22 *Irish Times*, 20 Aug. 1969.
23 Ibid., 19 Aug. 1969.
24 *Donegal News*, 6 Sept. 1969.
25 *This Week*, 21 Aug. 1970.
26 *Northern Standard*, 12 Sept. 1969.

27 *Donegal News*, 6 Sept. 1969.
28 *Anglo-Celt*, 22 Aug. 1969.
29 *Donegal News*, 23 Aug. 1969.
30 *Northern Standard*, 29 Aug. 1969.
31 *Donegal News*, 23 Aug. 1969. *Limerick Leader,* 30 Aug. 1969.
32 'George Hunter' in D.R. O'Connor Lysaght, *100 Years of Liberty Hall* (Dublin, 2013) pp. 73–77.
33 *This Week*, 24 July 1970. *Donegal News*, 4 and 18 July 1970.
34 *This Week*, 21 Aug. 1970.
35 *Donegal News*, 4 July 1970.
36 *Anglo-Celt*, 17 July 1970.
37 *Donegal News*, 30 Jan. and 6 Nov. 1971. *Donegal Democrat*, 28 Jan. 1972.
38 *Anglo-Celt*, 17 Sept. 1971.
39 Ibid., 17 Sept. 1971.
40 Ibid., 13 Aug. 1971.
41 *Irish Times*, 14 Aug. 1971.
42 *Cork Examiner*, 18 Aug. 1971. *Irish Press*, 25 Aug. 1971.
43 *Sligo Champion*, 20 August 1971.
44 Republic of Ireland: Annual Review for 1971, 10 Jan. 1972, FCO 87/7, NAUK.
45 G. Madden, 'Political Change', p. 37.
46 *Irish Times*, 12 Feb. 1972.
47 *Southern Star*, 9 Oct. 1971. This was one of a number of raids on the homes of retired British officers in west Cork. K. McCarthy, *Republican Cobh*, pp. 331–334.
48 *Irish Times*, 6 Dec. 1971.
49 *The Kerryman*, 12 and 26 Feb. 1972. There were claims that over 30 British families left the state in the week after Bloody Sunday. *Sunday Independent*, 13 Feb. 1972.
50 *Irish Times*, 8 Feb. 1972. *Sunday Press*, 13 Feb. 1972.
51 *Irish Times*, 16 June 2010.
52 *Munster Express*, 4 Feb. 1972.
53 *Anglo-Celt, Drogheda Independent, Donegal Democrat, Kilkenny People, Nationalist and Leinster Times, New Ross Standard, Northern Standard, Longford Leader, Roscommon Herald, Sligo Champion, Westmeath-Offaly Independent, Wicklow People*, 4 Feb. 1972. *Dundalk Democrat, Drogheda Independent, Kerryman, Kerryman* (North Cork edition), *Leinster Leader, Leitrim Observer, Limerick Leader, Nenagh Guardian, Mayo News, Meath Chronicle, Tipperary Star*, 5 Feb. 1972.
54 *Clare Champion*, 12 Feb. 1972.
55 *Nationalist and Leinster Times*, 11 Feb. 1972.
56 *Wicklow People*, 25 Feb. 1972. Although the reaction of the strongly conservative Trinity historian R.B. McDowell was to write to the British Ambassador expressing condolence on the loss of the Embassy. R.B. McDowell, *McDowell on McDowell* (Dublin, 2008) p. 30.
57 *Derry Journal*, 4 Feb. 1972.
58 *Evening Press*, 4 Feb. 1972.
59 *Drogheda Independent*, 11 Feb. 1972.
60 *Irish Times*, 12 Feb. 1972.
61 Ibid.
62 *Nationalist and Leinster Times*, 4 Feb. 1972.
63 *New Ross Standard*, 18 Feb. 1972.
64 *Southern Star*, 26 Feb. 1972.
65 *Irish Independent*, 7 Feb. 1972.
66 *Sligo Champion*, 11 Feb. 1972. *Nationalist and Leinster Times*, 4 Feb. 1972.
67 *Clare Champion*, 26 Feb. 1972.

68 *Leitrim Observer*, 26 Feb. 1972.
69 *Southern Star*, 5 Feb. 1972.
70 Ibid., 12 Feb. 1972.
71 It was claimed that he had chosen to play a game of golf on the Day of Mourning. *Northern Standard*, 11 Feb. 1972.
72 Ibid. *Anglo-Celt*, 11 Feb. 1972.
73 *Northern Standard*, 18 Feb. 1972.
74 *Church of Ireland Gazette*, 11 Feb. 1972.
75 *Irish Times*, 30 May 1972.
76 Ibid., 27 Oct. 1972.
77 *Irish Press*, 14 and 15 July 1972.
78 *Derry Journal*, 14 July 1972.
79 *Irish Times*, 15 July 1972.
80 Unsigned note, 14 July 1972, in D/T 2003/16/76 NAI.
81 Jim Gallagher testimony, INCORE www.green-and-blue.org.
82 D.V. Beattie to J. Lynch, 1 Aug. 1972, in D/T 2003/16/76 NAI.
83 L. Adair and C. Murphy, *Untold Stories: Protestants in the Republic of Ireland 1922–2002* (Dublin, 2002) pp. 179–180.
84 Michael O'Leary, 28 May 1974, in D/T 2005/7/585 NAI.
85 R. Bury, *Buried Lives: The Protestants of Southern Ireland* (Dublin, 2017) pp. 157–159.
86 See Farset Community, *Separated by Partition: An Encounter between Protestants from East Donegal and East Belfast* (Belfast, 2000).
87 Houses of the Oireachtas, *Interim Report, 1972 and 1973,* pp. 137–138.
88 See Chapter 3.
89 *Irish Times*, 10 March 1975.
90 Houses of the Oireachtas, *Report 1972 and 1973,* pp. 127–128.
91 Ibid., p. 132.
92 Mulroe, *Bombs*, p. 173.
93 *Irish Times*, 14 May 2005.
94 *Anglo-Celt*, 16 Nov. 1973.
95 *Irish Times*, 13 March 1974.
96 Ibid., and 21 May 1974.
97 *Northern Standard*, 22 March 1974.
98 *Irish Times*, 13 March 1974.
99 *Hibernia*, 15 March 1974.
100 K. Conway, *Southside*, p. 161.
101 *Northern Standard*, 22 Aug. 1969.
102 *Anglo-Celt*, 31 Oct. 1969.
103 *Irish Press*, 23 and 24 March 1972.
104 *Irish Times*, 10 Dec. 1971.
105 *Irish Press*, 14 Dec. 1971.
106 *Dáil Debates,* 22 and 23 March 1972.
107 *Sunday Press*, 16 Jan. 1972.
108 Speech, 25 Jan. 1972, Richie Ryan Papers, P272/172 UCDA.
109 *Sunday World*, 24 June 1973.
110 *Irish Times*, 14 March 1974.
111 Tim Pat Coogan's book *The IRA* still carries the erroneous claim that it was the Official IRA who killed Fox. T.P. Coogan, *The IRA* (London, 1995) p. 357.
112 *Irish Times*, 8 June 1974.
113 Ibid., 21 May 1974.
114 J. Courtney, *It Was Murder!* (Dublin, 1996) p. 63.
115 *Magill*, 1 Oct. 1984.

116 M. Cunningham, *Monaghan: County of Intrigue* (Donegal, 1979) pp. 2 and 110.

117 One of these conspiracy theories was once presented to me in a Monaghan student's essay on the bombings.

118 *Anglo-Celt*, 21 Nov. 1925.

119 See Chapter 3 for details.

120 *An Phoblacht/Republican News*, 20 Oct. 1979.

121 Ralaheen, *All Over*, p. 80.

122 B. Harvey, A. Kelly, S. McGearty and S. Murray, *The Emerald Curtain: The Social Impact of the Irish Border* (Monaghan, 2005) p. 59.

123 Viney, *The Five Per Cent*, p. 21

124 J. White, *Minority Report: The Protestants in the Republic of Ireland* (Dublin, 1975) p. 23.

125 Houses of the Oireachtas, *Kay's Tavern*, p. 143.

126 *Hibernia*, 15 April 1977.

127 Report, 5 May 1970, in P. Hillery Papers, P205/36 UCDA.

128 Harvey *et al.*, *Emerald Curtain*, p. 60.

129 Houses of the Oireachtas, *Kay's Tavern*, pp. 152–154.

130 *Irish Times*, 6 Sept. 1980.

131 Ibid., 6 July 1972.

132 Mac Gréil, *Prejudice*, p. 377.

133 *Church of Ireland Gazette*, 2 June 1972.

134 B. Goulding to J. Lynch, 25 May 1972, in D/T 2003/16/76 NAI.

135 *Church of Ireland Gazette*, 2 June 1972.

136 Ibid.

137 *Irish Times*, 18 May 1972.

138 Ibid., 2 March 1972.

139 *Irish Press*, 12 Feb. 1972.

140 Ibid., 5 Feb. 1972.

141 *Church of Ireland Gazette*, 4 Feb. 1972.

142 *Irish Times*, 6 March 1972.

143 *Comment*, 25 May 1973.

144 Ibid.

145 *An Phoblacht*, 21 Nov. 1975.

146 Ibid., 28 Nov. 1975.

147 K. Bowen, *Protestants in a Catholic State: Ireland's Privileged Minority* (Dublin, 1983) p. 200.

148 Text of lecture by J.A. Murphy, April 1976, FitzGerald Papers, UCDA P215/481.

149 'Caoimhghín Ó Caoláin' in Adair and Murphy, *Untold*, p. 163.

8

'But then they started all this killing'

In February 1981, RTE screened the final episode of Robert Kee's *Ireland: A Television History*. It featured an interview with Dubliner Vinny Byrne, a veteran of Michael Collin's 'Squad'. In a previous episode, Byrne had described in detail how he had 'plugged' a British officer on Bloody Sunday in 1920. But now he asserted that the Provisionals had 'destroyed the name of the IRA' and that 'they should never have been allowed call themselves IRA men at all'.[1] Byrne's argument was a common one during the 1970s. School textbooks stressed that the modern IRA were 'not to be confused with the "Old IRA" … the men who fought for Irish freedom between 1916 and 1923'.[2]

Similiar points were made across the political spectrum, but most often by supporters of Fianna Fáil. Sean MacEntee, a 1916 veteran, claimed that his comrades

> did not plant bombs in public places, caring not whom these might kill or maim, whether men, women or children. Neither did they fan sectarian hatred, as neither did they turn their guns on each other in furtherance of personal or organisational rivalries. They were true soldiers and fought a clean fight.[3]

Ruairí Brugha, an ex-IRA internee himself, asked rhetorically whether 'James Connolly or Patrick Pearse would send teenagers into the market place carrying bombs set to detonate?'[4] In November 1972, Jack Lynch asserted that his party was the 'direct descendent of the Old IRA: the true IRA, which would have nothing to do those who now claim to be the IRA'.[5] His Minister for Finance George Colley denounced 'the various groups who call themselves the IRA' for 'desperately trying to fool the Irish people into believing that they are fighting the same fight and have the same moral authority as the real IRA'.

These groups, who exposed 'civilians to the risk of death and injury when they placed their bombs', were blemishing the reputation of 'the real IRA (who) were the army of the democratically elected parliament of the nation'.[6] Colley was echoing the official view that

> the members of the Government and Parliament (Dáil Éireann) in Ireland are the legitimate successors of what is now known as the Old I.R.A. – i.e. the men and women (who) fought and died to obtain freedom for Ireland over half a century ago. The members of the present-day I.R.A. do not command the support of the people of Ireland and have no authority to act in their name.[7]

The events of 1916–21 were not that far removed from many of those listening to these arguments. In 1974, there were over 30,000 veterans of the 'Tan War' still alive.[8] There were also a significant number of former members of the post-Civil War IRA in public life.[9] Their arguments were a potent factor in the battle for legitimacy over the war in the North.

'Half-wits and savage old hillbillies'

While denying republican claims to continuity with the past, critics also stressed that they lacked popular support. In 1978, Jack Lynch told British Prime Minister James Callaghan that 'there was no passive support for the IRA in the Republic'. Indeed, the organization 'had alienated themselves completely from the mainstream of public opinion. There was no suggestion whatsoever of support for the group among any worthwhile section of the population.'[10] In a 1978 IMS poll on southern attitudes to the North, 51% said that they 'have no time whatsoever for the Provisional IRA'. Only 2% admitted to approving of them.[11] During 1979, Fine Gael TD John Kelly claimed southern support for the IRA was restricted to 'a few thousand half-wits and savage old hillbillies'.[12]

Election results seemed to bear this out. In 1973, Official Sinn Féin (still linked in the public mind to a military campaign) won just 1.14% of the vote in that year's general election. Kevin Boland's Aontacht Éireann, which described the struggle in the North as akin to the War of Independence, took just 0.91%.[13] In local elections the following year Official and Provisional Sinn Féin received 3.11% of the vote between them.[14] In 1979, Provisional Sinn Féin gained 2.16% in the local contests; hardly enough to claim mass popular support.[15]

'Snaking regarders'

But republicans suggested that there was far more backing for the IRA than apparent from elections or opinion polls. As *An Phoblacht's* columnist 'Freeman' asserted in 1974, 'practical sympathy with militant Republicans is not reflected in support for Republican candidates. There is a great disproportion between the one and the other, to put it mildly.'[16] This was something that even the IRA's critics feared was true. A Northern Irish civil servant reflected after the 1974 elections that 'support for Sinn Fein and various parties of that nature was minimal. However, this does not tell us very much except the Irish people tend not to vote for militant Republican parties.'[17] Journalist John Healy declared that

> the Irish will give the IRA everything but the vote ... we'll give them safe houses, we'll put money in the collection boxes, we'll give them big funerals, we'll give them verbal support – but when they put their names on the ballot paper, the Irish draw the line there.

Instead, Healy claimed, all of the mainstream parties have 'a proportion of "snaking regarders"'. These included the 'Fianna Fáil kind ... the Fine Gael kind of United Irelanders and the Connolly Republicans of the Labour party'.[18] Indeed, if there was no support for the IRA then how could songs celebrating the escape of prisoners from Mountjoy and Portlaoise prisons top the Irish charts as they did in 1973 and 1974?[19] Republicans believed the success of Dermot Hegarty's '19 Men', a number one hit despite being banned from radio, was 'confirmation that the Portlaoise jail-break had stirred the nation'.[20]

'A mixture of all political persuasions'

Formal political allegiance and adherence to republican shibboleths was not necessarily a guide to how people felt about armed struggle. One IRA man recalled that 'the people of Monaghan who kept me in their houses in the early 70's were a mixture of all political persuasions ... they saw the Dublin government as the legitimate government of the Irish people and accepted them as such'.[21] Sligo Fianna Fáil councillor Tom Deignan (an 'old' IRA man) moved a motion of sympathy for the relatives of local IRA volunteer Kevin Coen, describing him as having been 'killed by British forces (and) not the first Irishman to be killed by them'. Republicans would have hoped that this reflected rank and file feeling in Fianna Fáil.[22] *An Phoblacht* also recognized that Donegal TD Neil Blaney's 'extremely large personal following and his demands on the British in relation to the National Question are so identical with that of the Republican Movement' that, often, at grass-roots (Blaney's) supporters were 'indistinguishable' from Sinn Féin's.[23] Indeed, in 1973 Blaney had claimed that 'you cannot fight an organised army by orthodox methods. The IRA's present action does not qualifiy for something I could condemn.'[24]

'The Irish people are sound at heart'

There were very fluid and often contradictory attitudes towards the IRA from across the spectrum. In 1980, a columnist in the *Meath Chronicle* could wonder 'Can the Provos drive the Brits out of the Six Counties? Deep down in his heart, the average Irishman hopes so, I am convinced. And what of his head? This one shakes a negative.'[25] The *Sunday World's* political correspondent would assert in 1974 that 'the IRA is a product of the Irish mind (and) while any part of Ireland is occupied by troops of another country there will be Fenians and "subversives" determined to drive out these troops'.[26] Padraig Mooney of Aontacht Éireann believed that 'the Irish people are sound at heart. They will eventually be roused to demand the nation's right to self-determination.'[27] Labour TD (and former IRA man) Stevie Coughlan could also assert that 'deep down … all Irishmen are republicans'.[28] In 1972, the British Ambassador felt that there was a

> latent virus of violent Republicanism in many people in the Republic, which can quickly spread to infect the country's whole personality. Moreover, although few are willing to give their active support to the IRA, many share its aims and resent or dislike too open interference with it.[29]

This in turn encouraged some IRA supporters to believe that 'scratch an Irishman and you have a Republican'.[30] They could argue that successful IRA operations would gain '70% acceptance' privately, 'despite the public outcry about it', and that if people 'thought you were winning the war … you would get a landslide'.[31] When asked to explain how they could claim popular support for their actions in 1976, IRA leaders responded that

> you must take into account the massive turn-outs at our rallies and demonstrations, such as that outside the GPO to commemorate 1916 … furthermore we have a solid bedrock of hard support which ensures our continued survival, and through our 'fringe' support may ebb and flow, the significant support remains firm – how else could we have survived these 7 years?[32]

'The objective remains unchanged'

Furthermore, republicans did not accept that they represented a break with the 'old' IRA. Ruairí Ó Brádaigh claimed that the 'only difference' between the current armed struggle and that of the 1920s was 'that it has gone on longer, has achieved more, and is nearer ultimate success than anything in the past'.[33] In 1974, *An Phoblacht* stated that

> in no essential way are the leaders of the Republican Movement today different from those of the Irish Republican Brotherhood, of the IRA, of the Irish Volunteers

and members of the Citizens Army in 1916 ... the objective remains unchanged. The strategy remains unchanged. Only the tactics are different – but not all that different – and, of course the weapons.[34]

When Fine Gael's Garret FitzGerald contrasted the tactics of Michael Collins and Cathal Brugha with those of the Provisionals during 1971, one critic responded by asking was it 'not the same Collins who had Mr. Alan Bell, the elderly civil servant killed in the gutter in Ballsbridge; and was it not Cathal Brugha who suggested that machine guns be smuggled into the British House of Commons to be turned on the front bench?'[35] As *An Phoblacht* explained

> war in Ireland for almost 300 years, except for very brief periods in 1798 and 1922, has been more or less as it is today ... ambushes, sorties, executions. And middle class reaction to that war again was more or less as it is to the liberation struggle today.[36]

Additionally, there were veterans of the 'old' IRA who did endorse the Provos. In 1972, Tom Malone ('Seán Forde' of the Limerick IRA during the 1919–21 period) refuted the suggestion 'that veterans of the war do not support the fight in the North against Britain'.[37] Easter Rising veteran Commandant W.J. Brennan-Whitmore argued during 1975 that he could not 'see any difference, moral or legal, between the fight now being waged by the present generation IRA, and that waged by the IRA of my generation'.[38] Some accepted this logic, a Killarney man telling Liam Cosgrave during 1973 'I can and do believe that if the men who fought in 1916 were in Belfast in July 1970 they would have taken up arms against what is basically an occupation force – the British Army'.[39]

'Opposition to IRA activities is not overwhelming'

All these factors meant that it was difficult to ascertain the reality of sympathy for the IRA's campaign. What was clear was that any suggestion that the Provos did enjoy popular backing produced vitriolic responses. In 1979, an ESRI survey concluded that 'opposition to IRA activities is not overwhelming and certainly does not match the strong opposition so often articulated by public figures'.[40] That survey found that 21% claimed to support the IRA, though, of this figure, only 8% were 'moderately to strongly supportive'. Support was stronger among men than women, among rural rather than urban dwellers, and higher in those over 40 years of age and of lower occupational status. However, it was also the case 'those who are more interested in politics and involved in political discussion (and) ... attentive to political communication tend to be more anti-partitionist, more supportive of IRA activities (and) more sympathetic to IRA motives'.[41]

A majority (61%) of those polled remained opposed to IRA activities and 63% actually favoured tougher measures against the organization. But though there was 'no evidence that an attitude of support ... leads to any concrete actions', the report concluded that 'the stark fact remains that 21% of the population emerge as being in some degree supportive in their attitude to IRA activities'.[42] The authors, Earl E. Davis and Richard Sinnott, soon discovered that reaction to their findings was characterized by a 'remarkable consensus' spanning politicians, journalists and academics. This reaction was also marked by 'extraordinary vehemence and intensity'.[43] The survey was roundly condemned for being 'highly irresponsible' and likely to benefit the IRA.[44] It was contrasted with the earlier IMS survey in which only 2% had endorsed the IRA. But as Davis and Sinnott pointed out, that poll had also shown that 32% of respondents admired 'the idealism of the Provisional IRA' but thought that 'their use of violence is totally wrong'.[45]

'Lynch Up The Poll'

Predictably, republicans were delighted; *An Phoblacht's* front page declaring 'IRA Okay! Lynch Up The Poll'.[46] A member of Sinn Féin in Dublin's Rathfarnham explained how

> every Friday evening ... our Cumann sell 96 copies of *An Phoblacht/Republican News* in nine pubs in the Rathfarnham/Ballyboden area ... dealing with approximately 490 members of the public ... these data reinforce the results of the survey, despite the fact that the majority of the pubs are frequented by people of the middle-income bracket ... it should also be pointed out that in buying a copy of our paper in a pub in front of friends and neighbours, one is publicly expressing support for the Republican Movement. How many others support us but are afraid to admit it publicly?[47]

Buying *An Phoblacht* in a pub or on a street corner was most people's point of contact with republicans. Indeed, during 1975, opponents of the IRA in Limerick called for a ban on the sale of republican newspapers in pubs.[48] *An Phoblacht* had been selling over 30,000 copies a week that year, the majority of them in the 26 Counties.[49] During 1976, sales declined to just over 20,000 weekly. By mid 1978, sales had fallen further to 15,000 copies a week in the south. Over 2,000 were sold in Dublin, 1,000 in Cavan and Donegal and nearly 2,000 in Kerry. Though there had been a steady decline in sales over several years, it was still an impressive circulation for a newspaper that unashamedly backed the IRA.[50]

There were, of course, a variety of reasons why people purchased republican literature. Sinn Féin supporters at a book stall in Galway's Eyre Square noted how 'the country people are mad for songs'.[51] Others pointed out that the survey was carried out prior to the visit of Pope John Paul II, who had made a strong appeal to the IRA to end their campaign, and also before the assassination of Lord Mountbatten that autumn.[52]

'You can't make an omelette without breaking eggs'

Attitudes were complex. In the same documentary in which Vinny Byrne denounced the IRA, his fellow-veteran Martin Walton found it hard to criticize those facing 'enormous ... odds' while fighting for an 'objective dear to my heart'. Another 'old-IRA' man Matt Flood disagreed strongly with 'this bombing business,' but did not object to meeting the enemy 'man to man'. Different incidents produced conflicting responses. There were some, such as the Cork farmer, who could rationalize of the violence that 'you can't make an omelette without breaking eggs. We wouldn't be free down here if your father or mine was all that squeamish.'[53]

In 1979, critics of the IRA would note that there were those who would support the organization 'if they didn't use violence, those who would support them if they ceased attacking civilian targets; others who would be behind them if they didn't oppose the Southern Government and so on and so on'.[54] The IRA's ultimate aim was generally seen as legitimate. Most also accepted that they had emerged as a response to oppression. So, the *Roscommon Herald* could describe the Portlaoise hunger-strikers in 1977 as belonging to a 'discredited organisation' that had committed 'dastardly crimes'. But it still believed recruitment to the IRA was 'due, as it has been always due, to the activities of the British army in the North'. Until that was recognized, violence would continue.[55] What is clear is that, for a period, sympathy for the IRA had not been confined to the margins.

'The long wait is over'

During August 1969, it seemed possible that a real challenge to partition was in the offing. In Ballinasloe, a retired Irish Army officer announced that 'the long wait is over' and asked 'all comrades who soldiered with me during the Emergency and all others who may be interested' to mobilize.[56] In some areas Fianna Fáil speakers shared platforms with representatives of the IRA for 'the first time since the civil war'.[57] While not all were as jubilant as Monaghan Councillor James Deery, who announced that 'War is coming! War there must be', the *Connacht Tribune* recognized that 'the people of the twenty-six Counties were conditioned to take the North by force during those ugly early nights of killing'.[58] These emotions were felt across party lines. One Fine Gael supporter in Roscommon 'responded immediately and passionately on the side of the nationalists ... if Lynch had sent in the army, I think my father felt, we could all, once again, be on the same side'.[59]

As confrontation escalated during 1971, the British Embassy reported a 'rapid increase throughout the Republic of popular support, particularly among the young, for both branches of the IRA'.[60] In August that year, the Irish military estimated that while there were about 1,900 'active Republicans' in the South, they had perhaps '20/40,000 active supporters'. [61] In December 1971, the Irish Embassy in London asked that the British should 'appreciate that ... public opinion in the South is increasingly behind the IRA'.[62] Support expressed itself in a variety of ways. One IRA man described how Monaghan was

> a good town for support and for socializing and for good craic ... When we weren't out in the country we would stay in the town, have a drink and chase women. We were young and very popular with the local girls. There was a certain quodo's (sic) to being an IRA man![63]

Labour TD Barry Desmond later asserted that he was treated as a 'political leper' when he asked the government to condemn IRA activity, and warned by 'Deputies ... from all political parties' that he would 'never be re-elected'.[64]

'The IRA ... have brought matters to a head'

There was increasingly a view that political violence was both necessary *and* effective. In the *Munster Express* Proinsias Mac Aonghusa argued that

> the initative has been taken by the Provos in Belfast ... No matter how bad behaviour may have been in the past, if the Belfast Provos put the British on the run, put the fear of God into every British agent in the North and break down Britain's will to remain in Ireland, all will have to be forgiven them. Terrorism is a terrible thing. It has been used to keep down the nationalists and republicans in the North for more than fifty years; that it should now be used to gain freedom is also terrible, but inevitable.[65]

One young Limerick man (who subsequently became a prison officer) recalled that 'even quite respectable people supported the armed struggle. I remember myself and my parents and neighbours taking part in a huge rally in Limerick protesting against internment ... we were livid against the Brits.'[66] Former Fine Gael TD Patrick Lindsay told a college audience that 'if it was neccesary for the unification of the country to have a civil war, I would have it straight away'.[67] A priest from Westport Co. Mayo told Garret FitzGerald that he was 'sick and tired' of the condemnation of 'illegal organisations' when 'any sane man admits that it is the IRA who have brought matters to a head'.[68] Trade Unionist Matt Merrigan felt that while some of the Provisional IRA's tactics were 'repugnant to the more civilised and humane people in all communities ... taken in conjunction with the Civil Rights Movement, the civil disobedience campaign and the courage and generosity of the young' they had forced the breakup of the Unionist state.[69]

On Leitrim Council, J.J. McCartin admitted that 'the bomb, bullet and destruction had received results which they (politicians) had failed to up to now'. McCartin lamented that 'Michael Collins said that the Treaty was a stepping stone to complete freedom, but it had not been used as a stepping stone'.[70] Responding to criticism of the IRA's tactics, Labour TD David Thornley asked

> Are they supposed, like Patrick Pearse, to don the full regalia of uniform and to hoist the tricolour in Donegall Square and allow themselves to be machine-gunned by 22,000 British soldiers? They have to resort to the tactics which are forced upon them.[71]

The *Irish Press* suggested that 'we have to face the fact that over the last 50 years a terrible violence has been done to the minority in the Six Counties and terrible means have now been found in a crude attempt to redress the balance'.[72] Moreover, the paper's editor Tim Pat Coogan felt that 'this coming year may see historic steps being taken to end the 700-year-old Irish question'. But this meant, Coogan stressed, that 'none of us do anything to provoke a breach of the peace south of the border... perhaps, for all we know, the last Christmas before which the Border, as we know it, disappears'.[73] When the *Irish Press* warned in June 1972 that 'whoever is responsible for the shootings across the border at Belcoo and Clady will not help the embattled Northern minority, but will only create a situation in which internment becomes necessary here', it was hard not to conclude that the paper regarded action in the North itself as legitimate.[74]

'Some good in the Provos'

The fear of trouble spreading south was significant. The existence of two rival IRAs also complicated matters. The tone of both national and local press coverage of the Officials, who were seen as focused on activity in the south, was more negative than that of the Provisionals.[75] Fine Gael TD Paddy Belton claimed that among Fianna Fáil supporters the view was that 'the Official IRA were no good but there was some good in the Provos'.[76] On the 'Late Late Show', popular cleric Fr. Michael Cleary suggested that 'the Provisionals are the genuine successors of the Sinn Féin movement we knew some years ago. I don't always agree with their tactics (but) I do respect them and admire their sense of nationalism. The other crowd – the Officials – are Communist-inspired and controlled.'[77]

There were limits to what was popularly acceptable. In March 1971, the Provisionals killed three off-duty soldiers in Belfast and five people in a bomb blast in Tyrone. They denied involvement in both incidents and many chose to believe them.[78] Vincent Browne, the *Irish Press*'s Belfast correspondent, recalled that 'I and others were coaxed into believing this had been done by Loyalists, to provoke hostilities between the Nationalist community and the British army (by) IRA leaders in Belfast at the time and I absolutely believed them when they assured me they had nothing to do with (it)'.[79] The denials reflected the fact that many people, including republicans, would have found such killings unacceptable at that stage.

Bloody Sunday

By 1972, this seemed to have changed. Bloody Sunday produced not just a wave of anger but also what appeared to be mass support for the IRA. In Dublin the following Monday,

> when the full story had been unfolded on radio and television and press, busy newspaper offices were handing out the number at which both wings of the IRA could be contacted, to scores of telephone callers who obviously decided the time for talking to the British was over. In O'Connell Street and Merrion Square, where throngs threatened the British Embassy hundreds of people offered the Sinn Féin and IRA organisations whatever help they could. It was an emotional scene as people queued to have their names taken, committing themselves to whatever task the militant republican organisations gave.[80]

At council meetings across the state local representatives described the IRA as 'true freedom fighters'; praised their 'pluck and courage'; and called on them to 'finish the job that was started in '16'.[81] Demands for military intervention and aid for the IRA came from across the political spectrum. Cork trade unionist Pat Magner asserted that it was not enough to send messages of sympathy and that the government should 'declare a state of emergency and organise and arm the state forces to support the people in the North'. The *Irish Press* claimed that 'while there is grief in Derry and throughout Ireland, it is now a lesser emotion to that of total rage and an unstoppable determination to be free at last – free at once from the sight and sound of British soldiery and free from the evil domination of a corrupt, illegitimate regime which puts licensed killers on the streets'.[82] When direct rule was introduced in March 1972, it seemed proof positive that violence brought results. Fine Gael's John Kelly complained of being 'politely asked … to "lay off" the IRA in case we might lose votes because of total opposition to them'.[83] A Cork supporter of Kelly's party wrote that 'at least the IRA has caused Stormont to be prorogued. This can only be a step forward & Michael Collins would have approved.'[84]

'Never more cut off'

Yet, within four months, *Hibernia* would assert that republicans were 'losing public support North and South of the border. Indeed their isolation was almost complete … the IRA had never been more cut off from public support.'[85] In a remarkably short period of time the government had moved to establish special courts, with limited political opposition, leading one sceptic to conclude that 'there is no electoral bag in Sinn Féin or the IRA'.[86] The Official IRA's bomb in Aldershot just a few weeks after Bloody Sunday had a profound effect. The killing of female cleaning staff was perceived as having robbed Ireland of a moral superiority over the British; the 'dead of Derry dishonoured'.[87] Liam MacGabhann (deputy editor of *An Phoblacht* during the 1930s) wrote that 'on the afternoon of February 22 1972 all sympathy held by the ordinary people of Ireland with the organisation calling itself the Official IRA died. It is buried with the corpses of the women of Aldershot.'[88] He also suggested 'many people would accept drastic measures against the IRA, at present'.[89] While Anne Harris in *Hibernia* described reaction to the bombing as the 'most nauseating show of hypocrisy from the Irish middle class to date', the popular outrage was real.[90]

While some people may have initially differentiated the rival IRAs, by the spring frustration with them was growing as the death toll mounted, particularly through car bombings. Irritation was expressed with those who offered verbal sympathy for republicans, Meath Labour TD James Tully wondering 'If one side or the other blew up a factory in Navan would the residents of the town regard them as heroes? It was extraordinary how militant some fellows, who lived miles away from the border, got after consuming a few pints.'[91] Others expressed frustration that the fall of Stormont had not resolved the situation, a Dublin man complaining that 'I was all for them getting their civil rights … but they're carrying it on too far. I mean, if you want a settlement you can't expect to get everything. They should be content with what they've got.'[92] Nevertheless, the British Embassy still believed that identification with the IRA's aims was 'widespread and can fluctuate violently according to emotion over events in the North'. While

> a majority of the population support the IRA's main aim … only a minority – say 10% – are prepared to countenance the use of violence. Perhaps 3% are willing to take part in IRA activities, and the number of those doing so is even smaller. Nevertheless, the IRA groups to some degree speak for the conscience of "loyal" Irishmen and sympathy for them, however irrational and inert, should not be underestimated.[93]

A survey on popular attitudes in Dublin, conducted during 1972, reflected this complexity, finding both acceptance of the use of force *and* hostility to the IRA: 35.3% believed that violence, 'while regrettable', had been necessary for the achievement of rights for nationalists. However, 28.9% of those polled were in favour of jailing members of the Provisional IRA, with 22% in favour of locking up the Officials.[94] But, as an editorial in the *Kilkenny People* explained, while most people could not 'possibly condone the killings and maiming of innocent women (and) children' there was 'a general realisation that if the

IRA were to cease to be an active force then many people living in the Nationalist ghettos ... would be entirely without defence'.[95]

'Senseless bombings'

By the summer of 1972, there were widespread calls for the Provisional IRA to declare a ceasefire, just as the Officials had done in May. The Leinster Branch Association of Irish Priests asserted that while they did 'not question the motivation which led the IRA to defend Catholic areas from attack three years ago (and) we recognise that real fear still exists in Catholic areas ... we ask what moral right have you to engage in acts of bombing and shooting now'.[96] The ITGWU's *Liberty* also urged that 'the minority which embarked on self-defence measures in 1970 when the British Army was being used as a tool of the Unionist Junta' recognize that the 'bombings, the shootings must now cease' before a civil war ensued.[97] The fact that the Provisional IRA did declare a ceasefire, which broke down and was followed by escalating violence, further disillusioned southerners.

July and August saw mass casualties caused by bombs in Belfast, Claudy and Newry. There was no precedent for these in modern Irish history. The *Kerryman*, which held the British responsible for the conflict and saw violence as an inevitable response, now asked whether the 'IRA could surely find some more effective way of engaging the British Army ... than over the dead and mangled bodies of bomb victims?'. The organization had 'isolated themselves' because of these 'senseless bombings' in which 'men, women and children were killed or maimed for life, wounded or driven hysterical with fear ... stripped down to simple terms we have Irishmen killing their fellow citizens'.[98] In 1973, at Bodenstown, Liam McMillen (the commander of the Official IRA in Belfast) contended that

> the horror and revulsion generated by the Provisional bombing campaign has irreparably destroyed that vast reservoir of support and good will which existed ... We now find that the people of the 26 Counties have washed their hands of what they term the "troubles in the North", fearful that the awful violence there will overspill and engulf them.[99]

While such criticism might be expected from the Provisional's rivals, McMillen's assessment reflected the experience of his own organization who had also lost potential support in the south because of their association with violence.[100]

'For love of their country'

Attitudes remained fluid. In early 1974, journalist Con Houlihan argued that only a 'moral defective' could mourn Bloody Sunday but 'be indifferent to the death of Cormac McCabe'.[101] McCabe was a UDR officer and a school headmaster, who had been having dinner with his wife and teenage daughter in a Monaghan hotel when he was abducted and shot.[102] But an indication of how complex responses could be came in a letter from Monaghan Fine Gael TD Brendan Toal to the government, shortly afterwards. Toal wrote on behalf of over 100 women from Carrickmacross, asking that the government intercede on behalf of the Price sisters and other republicans in jail in Britain. The women made clear that they 'in no way' condoned either the Prices' 'violent action or the bloody campaign of their organisation' and expressed 'abhorrence (and) utter condemnation of the wanton slaying of Cormac McCabe a fellow-Irishman'. Nevertheless, in view of what they called the Price sisters' 'age and steadfastness to the goal they have set out before them for love of their country we feel they should be granted political status'.[103] It was possible for many people to oppose the IRA's campaign yet still feel empathy for its prisoners, especially in British jails.

'I too would be in the IRA'

Sympathy came from a variety of sources and for various reasons. A 67-year-old 'life-long voter for Fine Gael' wrote to Liam Cosgrave during the 1973 hunger-strike to ask that the prisoners' demands be granted. The Cork woman declared that she

> always supported the Treaty, my father before me believed in it. I still support it of course and will to my last breath, but I never had a doubt about the Treaty until I realised the position it left the Catholic minority in. Let me tell you right now, Mr. Cosgrave, that if I was a young man, brought up in N(othern) I(reland) I too would be in the I.R.A.

She claimed that her daughter's marriage to a Catholic businessman from the North had opened her eyes to the reality of life for nationalists.[104]

A survey of attitudes among 1,300 young people, published in 1976, found that there was a 'strong minority favouring the use of force to end British rule in Northern Ireland'. This was located primarily among younger students and those 'representing the farm and manual labour socio-economic groups. The slim majority who oppose the use of force on this issue draw their strongest support from the older students and from the professional-management and non-manual labour categories.'[105] In the view of one teenager, the 'old' and 'new' IRA were 'more or less the same … they were fighting to free the country way back. They are doing the same thing now.'[106] Of respondents, 29.6% agreed the IRA were 'doing what is neccesary', while 5.9% thought them 'national heroes'. But the same survey found that 18% thought the IRA 'vicious gunmen and killers' while 33.8% believed the organization was 'harming Ireland'.[107]

'Cowards and traitors'

In explaining lack of popular support, republicans offered a number of explanations, usually emphasizing the impact of repression and the hostility of the media. Aside from Section 31 of the Broadcasting Act, other forms of censorship also existed. In 1973, Gardai seized 10,000 copies of the IRA's pamphlet *Freedom Struggle*, plus type and plates from a Drogheda printers.[108] Another response was to blame southerners themselves and appeal to a sense of guilt. In early 1971, when addressing what she considered a poorly attended meeting in Limerick, Máire Drumm wondered 'if the people of Munster want us to be part of a free Ireland at all'.[109] In 1973, Martin McGuinness demanded that southerners

> take some course of action to impress on your cowardly government that unless something is done by them to remove the British Army by force of arms, the people of the 26 (counties) shall be regarded as cowards and traitors with a few honourable exceptions.[110]

A republican pamphlet complained that 'the people of the Six Counties are justifiably angry and bitterly disappointed that their suffering (has) been viewed as less important than the price of Guinness in the rest of Ireland'.[111] In 1976, *An Phoblacht* asserted that 'we are in dung to our tonsils ... How else do you explain the public acceptance of the SAS fire bombs in Dublin (and) the utter lack of protest by any creditable personality among the establishment over the antics following the death of Frank Stagg?'[112] Perhaps it was because southerners did not have the stomach for the fight. As a right-wing republican asserted:

> the war in the North is the first taste of real war this country has seen since '98 ... The vast majority of the Irish people are a most inoffensive weak-kneed bunch who think that warfare should be left to the better class of nations like Britain, Germany, Russia, etc. Mind you, when asked to serve in the foreign killing fields, they can be willing enough if fed the right type of propaganda.[113]

When their lack of electoral support was raised, republicans sometimes responded that it was not neccesary. In 1976, IRA leaders claimed that 'a revolutionary movement does not depend on a popular mandate as a basis for action ... The men of 1916 and of 1920 had no mandate from the people.'[114] Admitting that popular support was lacking during 1977, *An Phoblacht* suggested that

> we do not need to be unduly upset by the alienation of so many people on the national question, remembering that most of them believe that the 26 Counties is free, and remembering, above all, the truth Fintan Lalor expounded ... 'It is never the mass of a people that forms its real and efficent might. It is the men by whom the mass is moved and managed. All the great acts of history have been done by a very few men.'[115]

Much of the thinking of the Provisionals in the mid 1970s was dominated by the belief that British withdrawal was imminent and that winning significant support in the south was likely to be easy once the 'foregone conclusion' of victory had been secured.[116]

'Nauseating hypocrisy'

In reality, this meant that republicans were often isolated. Activists opposing new security measures in 1976 noted that 'the big difficulty ... is the fear many people – including class-conscious trade unionists (have) of being identified with the Provos'.[117] Even after the carnage of the Dublin and Monaghan bombs, some had seen the IRA as the ultimate source of the problem. Mayo's *Western People* described how

> in the town of Ballina on Sunday last, with prayers for the dead and maimed ringing in their ears, people streamed out from church to find the IRA hate sheets being peddled outside the Cathedral gates with a brazen effrontery equalled only by the nauseating hypocrisy of IRA condemnation of the Friday bombings. Since it was IRA outrages in the North and in London which led to these retaliatory massacres in Dublin and Monaghan, this was almost too much for decent people to swallow.

Hibernia, a journal not unsympathetic to republicans, described IRA condemnation of the bombs as 'shameless'.[118] Critics countered by asking how the Special Branch were so familiar with the 'minute details of the private lives of Easter Lily sellers' but were strangely uninformed about 'British and Loyalist agents known to be working in the state'. *An Phoblacht* argued that the 'Dublin Government must bear full responsibility for the enormous and tragic loss of life in Dublin today' and that the massacres were perpetrated 'to deal a body blow to the ideal of a united Ireland, by striking deliberately at the ordinary man in the street'.[119] But the republican response to Dublin and Monaghan was strangely muted, in part because they had been praising the loyalist campaign against Sunningdale as 'brought about by a minimum of physical force and suffering, and, largely devoid of sectarian brutality' and even somewhat in the 'Wolfe Tone tradition'.[120]

'Reversed the tenets of James Connolly'

Later that year, the death of 21 people in the Birmingham bombs resulted in another wave of condemnation, which in the view of the British Ambassador 'did more than anything else to damage the Provisional movement in the Republic'.[121] The *Sunday World* claimed that 'the Provos have reversed the tenets of James Connolly: the people as distinct from the chemical elements called Ireland, mean nothing to them'. [122] The *Kerryman* asserted that it

> was Pearse who said 'Beware of the Risen People.' We repeat it with a different emphasis. The people have had enough. It is time that those who kill and murder in our name pay heed to us. Soon, when they turn to us, they will find stony faces and no pity.[123]

Legendary Cork IRA leader Tom Barry had spoken in support of the Provisionals after Bloody Sunday.[124] But now he stressed that he 'wouldn't have done the Birmingham job ... if it was going to set Ireland free and flowing with milk and honey'.[125]

The next few years brought atrocities with monotonous regularity. Some provoked outrage, though many were barely noticed. Republicans noted the lack of anger over ongoing loyalist killings, but public opinion in the south was always more focused on the IRA. After the assassination of their ambassador in 1976, the British noted how 'the killings had an impact of shock and shame in responsible and educated circles'. They were also informed that these 'sentiments were and are widespread in the population'.[126] Condemning the killing, the *Irish Press* had noted that 'one of the first principles of civility between States has been violated – namely that ambassadors and diplomatic staff and their families should always receive safe conduct no matter what the relationship between the countries'.[127]

Irish Military Intelligence noted how the killing of Ewart-Biggs and his secretary, the murder of Garda Clerkin and other incidents had 'eroded' republican support, though there was still evidence of a 'vague fear of the power of the IRA in many quarters'.[128] There was also a widespread perception that 'the Provisional IRA hope one day to be free to transfer their attentions to the Republic'.[129] Above all else, armed action against Gardai and the 'alarming increase in robberies' all contributed to the feeling 'that violence is spreading to the South'.[130] Confrontational rhetoric, such as that of Sinn Féin leader Aindrais Ó Ceallacháin when he warned the 'Quislings in the Free State, that once we get the Brits out, we can deal with them too', contributed to that sense of threat.[131] By 1977, the claim by *Republican News* that 'we are coming back with a vengeance to overthrow partition, to demolish the Free State and to establish our people's republic' clearly seemed to signal a threat to the south.[132]

The intimate nature of much of Irish society also played a role. Attacks on Gardai had a ripple effect in the communities they came from and served in. Pat Boran was a Portlaoise schoolboy when Detective Thomas Peters was maimed by the same bomb that killed Garda Clerkin. He recalled how the Garda's wife 'had been my teacher in primary school (his) daughter had been my classmate ... I thought about his daughter, hoping she would somehow know how horrified and hurt we all were for her'. IRA graffiti on walls of the school toilets 'ceased now to have any meaning'.[133] The *Irish Press* described Clerkin's 'cruel murder' as 'one of the most fiendish pieces of coldblooded plotting that we have seen'. It warned

> that the average person in the South has become so sickened by the horrors from Northern Ireland that, far from being inclined to work actively for unity, they will be much more likely to subscribe to having a great high wall built around the North.[134]

'No vestige of patriotism here'

In early 1976, several Catholics were murdered by the UVF in Armagh. The Provisional IRA responded by killing ten Protestants. Seán Mac Stíofáin hoped that 'the IRA was not involved' and asserted that 'all the evidence is that the ten men shot dead were nothing more than ordinary workmen'.[135] Tim Pat Coogan called the killings

> the worst single episode since the current spate of the Northern troubles began. Other atrocities claimed more lives, but they were through the blanket effect of explosions. These were a set of coldblooded, premeditated, individual murders. They were, moreover nakedly sectarian … There was no vestige of patriotism here. It was simply the taking of an eye for an eye on a barbaric scale.[136]

Shortly afterwards, while acknowledging the bravery of hunger-striker Frank Stagg, the *Longford Leader* commented that 'whatever hope the Provisional IRA ever had of gaining the support of the people died away once their local battalions in Ulster undertook murderous retaliation in the war admittedly kindled by the "Loyalist" groups'.[137] By 1977, Tom Barry would be reluctant to support the demands of the Portlaoise hunger-strikers because in his view 'the men who were carrying out the recent killings … could not be called IRA'. Barry told Sighle Humphries that 'since the hunger strike began he had been approached to use his influence in certain quarters but had refused and told whoever approached him that he should realise that his organisation was losing support from all quarters and they had only themselves to blame'.[138]

Republicans were also accused of betraying the legacy of their earlier volunteers. The *Leitrim Observer* suggested that 'nobody in their wildest dreams' could agree anymore that the IRA were 'fighting a war of Irish liberation'. The paper's editor asked that

> the Provos … should examine their current strategies and see if they have ever dishonoured the fight for Irish freedom by cowardice or inhumanity. They should examine their conscience (and) see have they maintained the standards set by their volunteers such as Eamonn Lafferty, who was gunned down in the heroic defence

of the Bogside immediately after internment in 1971 … I would say to the Provos that their actions of the past four years have left much to be desired.[139]

'The execution of a 79-year-old man?'

Though the level of violence both south and north of the border declined markedly between 1977–79, the war continued to dominate much of public life. The horror of the La Mon hotel bombing in 1978 (in which 12 died) came just as people were 'becoming accustomed to the idea that the age of gross atrocities was past'.[140] One Cavan man who had 'stood, marched and spoken out' in support of republicans was appalled by this 'mindless slaughter', asserting that 'if this was done for the Republican Movement then I cannot be part of it'.[141] But the conflict returned far more dramatically to the forefront of southern consciousness with the blowing up of Lord Mountbatten and his boating party in Sligo during August 1979. Now, even where some understanding of the IRA's position might have been expected, there was revulsion.

In *Magill*, Vincent Browne asserted that the 'killing of a 79-year-old man, who has had no personal involvement in the Northern Ireland issue, simply because of his family connections, is unjustifiable in any circumstances'. Browne also argued that there was 'no moral justification whatsoever' for targeting those on board Mountbatten's boat.[142] *Hibernia* accused the IRA of showing 'despicable contempt for the lives of children and others of no political consequence'.[143] In the *Irish Press*, Tim Pat Coogan noted how the IRA's 'cold, cynical statement' contained

> Not a word of sympathy for the victims, two of them mere children, not a hint of regret, not a scintilla of compassion. Murder, whatever the supposed cause, never can be justified. But the murder of Lord Mountbatten – and that, it needs to be emphasised, is what it was – was particularly cruel. A friend of this country … a friendly, genial man, popular with local people, blown to pieces while on one of his regular visits to this country … In their statement the Provisionals talk of his murder as 'an execution.' The execution of a 79-year-old man? Such hypocrisy will sicken and disgust all Irish people.[144]

Colin McCelland of the *Sunday World* remarked how there had not been 'any cheering (or) any dancing in the streets' after Mountbatten's death. He suggested that the killings 'hurt a lot of people in Dublin and it hurt them for a lot of different reasons'. In part this was because of the victim's age and relationship with Ireland, but also because it

> brought the war back to Dublin. It is true that many people Down Here were trying their best to forget what was happening Up North. And that they were happy enough to 'let them get on with it.' But Mountbatten's death brought the real or imagined fear of war back to the streets of this city … people are scared.[145]

The British Embassy reported that 'people from all walks of life continue to come to the Chancery to sign the Book of Condolence; there have been many telephone calls and letters expressing sorrow, shock and shame and paying tribute to the late Earl Mountbatten'.[146] Fr. Michael Cleary, who had professed to 'admire' the IRA eight years previously, now joined in the chorus of denunciation, admitting that while 'of course, there are some brave young people in the IRA ... their bravery is being misused and their deeds are becoming more cowardly and savage every day'. In Cleary's view, 'any intelligent leader of the IRA would have confined their activities after Bloody Sunday to defence of Catholic areas because world sympathy was then with them, but their subsequent sheer stupidity and brutality has turned the tide and Paisley (John) Taylor and Co. can sit back and laugh as the IRA do their work for them'.[147]

'Those bastards deserved it'

Republicans might have answered that they did not have the luxury of choosing their battleground. Nevertheless, Cleary's opinions were reflective of wider views. But popular attitudes remained contradictory. The hysterical reaction in Britain to Mountbatten's assassination led to a backlash. The *Sunday World* noted how the British media had 'succeeded in turning the groundswell of anti-IRA feeling Down Here that followed the Mountbatten killing into a tidal wave of resentment against England'.[148] *An Phoblacht* also noted how the inital 'potential for an anti-Republican drive ... has apparently abated considerably'.[149] And reactions to the death of Mountbatten and his companions were not the same as those to the killing of 18 British soldiers on the same day. One republican recalled how on that day he had 'bumped into an old school friend ... He condemned the Mountbatten murder out of hand. "Callous, pointless, utterly stupid", he called it. Without prompting he then said. "The paratroopers, that's different. Those bastards deserved it."'[150]

A further factor in the outrage was the fact that the killings happened just a month before the arrival in the Republic of Pope John II, a hugely symbolic event for Catholic Ireland. Many saw his appeal in Drogheda to the 'men of violence to return to ways of peace' as aimed directly at the IRA.[151] The IRA countered that 'force is the only means of removing the evil of the British presence in Ireland' and claimed that 'upon victory the Church would have no difficulty' in talking to the organization.[152] Danny Morrison noted that while the Pope had used terms such as 'men of violence' and 'terrorism' which had 'Pro-Brit and anti-Republican connotations', his references to the 'beleaguered Catholic community' had acknowledged their devotion.[153] For the IRA's critics, their rejection of the Pope's appeal reinforced the isolation of the organization from the majority whose 'desire for peace (was) so spontaneously expressed by the instant applause from the whole congregation at Drogheda, the vast majority of which was composed of people to whom the IRA looked to for moral support'.[154]

'Obsession with the North'

Despite the hostility directed at them, republicans still managed to maintain a political (as well as military) organization across the 26 Counties. In 1979, Sinn Féin held 26 seats on local bodies in small towns across 14 counties. The party polled 5,000 votes in Dublin but did not succeed in winning a seat in the city. (Though its former comrades, in what was now called Sinn Féin the Workers Party, did.)[155] Sinn Féin claimed that a vote for the party was 'a vote against British repression ... indeed against the whole British presence in the North'.[156]

While the party was overwhelmingly associated in the public mind with the IRA, at a local level it become active on a range of issues. As early as 1975 it recognized that 'people on the sideline, broadly sympathetic to Sinn Féin aims, have been critical of the party's "obsession" with "the North". Every active member at some time has brought this message to Kevin Street.'[157] Local campaigns on issues such as housing and unemployment were undertaken.[158] Both republicans and their opponents began to note a distinct class basis to their following. (Jack Lynch's comments about lack of republican support among 'worthwhile' sections of the community are suggestive in this regard.) By the mid 1970s many of those southerners jailed for IRA activity were from working-class Dublin.[159] In 1977, An Phoblacht contended that while 'there are good and courageous Irish people in the various classes in Ireland today ... our experience tells us that the most obvious support for the armed struggle and those elements which back it against imperialism comes largely from the most deprived and oppressed, whose instinct remains uncorrupted'.[160]

But the movement's support remained diverse. Galway businessman Frank Glynn had been a councillor for Sinn Féin since 1967. Glynn claimed to 'get on the finest with the Guards in Tuam ... if you have a clash its your own fault. You have a chip on your shoulder.' Indeed, another Galway Sinn Féin candidate, Pat Hynes from Loughrea, was a former Garda.[161] Local politics threw up personal friendships and alliances that defied easy categorization and contributed to councils in Galway, Leitrim and Longford passing republican-inspired resolutions.[162] In fact, the IRA could rely not only on backing from among the poor but also a more middle-class, professional network of supporters, including journalists, lawyers and stockbrokers.[163] Indeed, there was an active Sinn Féin cumann at University College Dublin, which claimed 45 members and to be selling 140 An Phoblachts weekly. Both Gerry Danaher, one-time editor of An Phoblacht, and Sinn Féin Ard Comhairle member Aindrias Ó Ceallacháin were leading lights in the college's Literary and Historical Society.[164]

By the end of the 1970s, the movement was moving steadily left, though not without some resistance – particularly in the Republic.[165] IRA leader Dáithí Ó Conaill would contend that 'people in urban areas see capitalism as the first issue ... people in country areas see the fight on the land issue and partition as more important' but he still believed that the armed struggle was the 'main factor which wins us votes in national terms'.[166] Yet this support was clearly limited. During 1980, left-wing republicans would suggest that 'the confusion of the Irish working class in the face of the war of national liberation today is as great as was the bewilderment of the citizens of Dublin following the Rising of 1916'. [167]

Clearly a substantial minority of people south of the border supported the IRA in some way. Some did so for traditional republican reasons, some out of sympathy for northern nationalists, others out of an instinct for rebellion. Though the republican movement had its own sub-culture of commemorations, fundraising functions and paper sales that made it a feature of life in many parts of the country, it was 'not large enough to have decisive political clout in parliament or in the community'.[168]

'But then they started all this killing.'

Between 1969 and 1972, a significant number of people were supportive of the IRA's campaign – especially as it seemed to be a response to Unionist and British oppression. After 1972, the IRA's bombing offensive proved far harder for people to endorse. Many, rightly or wrongly, compared the modern IRA unfavourably with the 'old' variety. Eighteen-year-old Limerick woman June Fitzgibbon agreed that the British were 'doing no good ... at all' in Ireland, but nevertheless believed that the IRA 'used to be a great organisation at one time ... But then they started all this killing.'[169] In part this confusion arose because people were tired after ten years of violence, which by the late 1970s seemed to be primarily the responsibility of the IRA. In 1979, for instance, republicans were responsible for 104 of the 125 conflict-related deaths.[170] In contrast, during the 1968–72 period, nationalists were seen as the *victims* of violence. Perhaps southerners were uncomfortable with an IRA which, in the words of one of its supporters, had decided 'never mind all that MacSwiney stuff ... this time we're going to make those other bastards suffer'.[171] Observing a sparsely attended republican meeting in a country town during 1979, the writer Anthony Cronin suggested 'the fact is that response to the Provisional's appeals on any issue whatsoever, H-Block included, is really dead in the South. Even if the old Civil Strife and massacre of Catholics situation were to come about at last, the South would not respond.'[172] Cronin was only partially correct. In a few years, the H-Block protests would become the biggest mobilizing force since 1972. But even then support for the IRA would never return to the level it had reached in the early years of the conflict.[173]

Notes

1 Episode 13, 'Prisoners of History', *Ireland a Television History*, RTE, 1981.
2 M. Tierney and M. MacCurtain, *The Birth of Modern Ireland* (Dublin, 1969) p. 188.
3 *Irish Times*, 25 Sept. 1971.
4 *Dáil Debates*, 26 June 1974, Vol. 273.
5 *Irish Times*, 29 Nov. 1972.
6 Ibid., 20 Jan. 1973.
7 H. O'Dowd to M.T. Conroy, 22 Feb. 1973, in D/T 2004/21/539 NAI.
8 According to the Minister of Defence, there were 6,000 holders of Military Service pensions and 29,000 people altogether holding medals or allowances related to the war. *Southern Star*, 21 Dec. 1974.
9 Ruairí Brugha in Fianna Fáil, Michael Mullen Roddy Connolly and Steven Coughlan in Labour among them.
10 Lynch to James Callaghan, 8 April 1978, in D/T 2008/148/709 NAI.
11 Irish Marketing Surveys, *Northern Ireland: A Survey of Prevailing Attitudes in the Republic of Ireland* (1978) Table 17A.
12 *Irish Times*, 31 Aug. 1979.
13 *Irish Times*, 20 Sept. 1971. M. Gallagher, *Irish Elections: Results and Analysis* (Oxford, 2009). Provisional Sinn Féin did not contest the 1973 general election.
14 Analysis of local Elections 1974, in FitzGerald Papers, P215/161 UCDA.
15 *Irish Times*, 17 Oct. 1979.
16 *An Phoblacht*, 5 July 1974.
17 M.N. Hayes, 25 June 1974, FCO 87/311 NAUK.
18 *Irish Times*, 20 Oct. 1979.
19 Gogan, *Pop*, pp. 169–170.
20 *An Phoblacht*, 27 Sept. 1974.
21 McNulty, *Exiled*, pp. 125–126.
22 *Irish Times*, 4 Feb. 1975.
23 *An Phoblacht/Republican News*, 1 Dec. 1979.
24 *Donegal News*, 10 March 1973.
25 *Meath Chronicle*, 18 Oct. 1980
26 *Sunday World*, 7 April 1974.
27 *Irish Press*, 23 Nov. 1973.
28 C. Maguire, 'Defenders of the State: The Irish Labour Party, coalitionism and revisionism, 1969–77', *Irish Studies Review* 23 (2015) pp. 1–20.
29 J. Peck, 27 June 1972, FCO 87/11 NAUK.
30 *An Phoblacht*, 28 Sept. 1976.
31 *Irish Times*, 21 Feb. 1980.
32 *Sunday Independent*, 19 Sept. 1976.
33 *An Phoblacht/Republican News*, 20 Jan. 1980.
34 *An Phoblacht*, 20 Dec. 1974.
35 *Irish Times*, 1 Nov. 1971.
36 *An Phoblacht*, 15 July 1978.
37 Ibid., 10 Dec. 1972.
38 Ibid., 31 Jan. 1975.
39 P. McKevitt to L. Cosgrave, 4 Oct. 1973, in D/T 2004/21/105 NAI.
40 E.E. Davis and R. Sinnott, *Attitudes in the Republic of Ireland Relevant to the Northern Ireland Problem*: Vol. 1. Dublin Economic and Social Research Institute Paper No. 97 (September, 1979) pp. 98–99.
41 Ibid., p. 116.

42 Ibid., p. 98.
43 E.E. Davis and R. Sinnott, 'The controversy concerning attitudes in the Republic to the Northern Ireland problem', *Studies* (Autumn/Winter, 1980) pp. 179–92. A counter report was undertaken and published a year later. See T.J. Baker, D. Hannan, D. Rottman and B. Walsh, 'Critique of ESRI paper No. 97' (June–Aug., 1980) (NAI, D/T 2010/53/877).
44 *Irish Times*, 17 Oct. 1979.
45 Irish Marketing Surveys, *A Survey of Prevailing Attitudes*.
46 *An Phoblacht/Republican News*, 20 Oct. 1979.
47 *Irish Times*, 22 Oct. 1979.
48 *An Phoblacht*, 12 Dec. 1975.
49 There was a separate paper, *Republican News*, distributed in the North.
50 Figures from reports in Sean O'Mahony Papers, Ms. 44,175/5 NLI. The issue of 31 May 1978 sold 18,161 copies.
51 *Magill*, Sept. 1978.
52 *The Kerryman*, 19 Oct. 1979.
53 Murphy, *A Place Apart*, p. 12.
54 *Limerick Socialist*, Nov. 1979.
55 *Roscommon Herald*, 22 April 1977.
56 *Irish Press*, 15 Aug. 1969
57 G. Madden, 'Political Change', p. 27.
58 *Connacht Tribune*, 5 Sept. 1969. *Northern Standard*, 22 Aug. 1969.
59 J. Waters, *Jiving at the Crossroads* (Belfast, 1991) pp. 73–74.
60 J. Peck, 'Republic of Ireland: Annual Review for 1971', 10 Jan. 1972, FCO 87/7 NAUK.
61 C/S T.L. Ó Cearbhail, 'Military considerations', 23 Aug. 1971, Hillery Papers, UCDA P205/37.
62 Telex to Sir S. Crawford, 17 Dec. 1971, Hillery Papers, UCDA P205/37.
63 McNulty, *Exiled*, p. 78.
64 *Dáil Debates*, Vo. 292, No. 7, 10 Sept. 1976.
65 *Munster Express*, 28 May 1971.
66 Bray, *Inside*, p. 15.
67 *Irish Press*, 18 April 1971.
68 Fr. P.F. Malone to G. FitzGerald, 9 Nov. 1971, in FitzGerald Papers, UCDA P215/4.
69 *Irish Times*, 9 Sept. 1971.
70 *Leitrim Observer*, 11 Sept. 1971.
71 *Dáil Debates*, Vol. 257, No. 11, 16 Dec. 1971.
72 *Irish Press*, 2 Oct. 1971.
73 Ibid., 23 Dec. 1971.
74 *Irish Press*, 30 June 1972.
75 Though sympathizers of the Officials worked at both the *Irish Times* and *Hibernia* magazine.
76 *Irish Times*, 2 Dec. 1972.
77 *Sunday Independent*, 12 Dec. 1971.
78 *An Phoblacht*, April 1971. *Hibernia*, 16 April 1971.
79 I. Kenny, *Talking to Ourselves: Conversations with Editors of the Irish News Media* (Dublin, 1994) p. 111.
80 *Connacht Tribune*, 4 Feb. 1972.
81 *Southern Star*, 5 Feb. 1972. *Leinster Express*, 11 Feb. 1972.
82 *Irish Press*, 31 Jan. 1972.
83 J. Kelly to R. Ryan, 10 Aug. 1972, in R. Ryan Papers, UCDA P272/172.

84 Mary Taaffe to G. FitzGerald, 27 May 1972, in FitzGerald Papers, UCDA P215/4.
85 *Hibernia*, 9 June 1972.
86 *Irish Times*, 27 May 1972.
87 *Irish Independent*, 23 Feb. 1972. *Clare Champion*, 26 Feb. 1972.
88 *This Week*, 2 March 1972.
89 *Longford Leader*, 25 Feb. 1972.
90 *Hibernia*, 3 March 1972. *Kilkenny People*, 25 Feb. 1972.
91 *Meath Chronicle*, 1 April 1972.
92 *Fortnight*, 8 June 1972.
93 'State of Security –The Irish Republic', 19 May 1972, CAB 134/3574, NAUK.
94 Mac Gréil, *Prejudice*, p. 415.
95 *Kilkenny People*, 10 Nov. 1972.
96 *Irish Times*, 15 June 1972.
97 *Liberty*, June 1972.
98 *The Kerryman*, 29 July 1972.
99 *Irish Independent*, 18 June 1973.
100 Hanley and Millar, *Revolution*, p. 262.
101 *The Kerryman*, 8 Feb. 1974.
102 *Irish Press*, 21 Jan. 1974.
103 B. Toal to G. FitzGerald, 28 Jan. 1974, in FitzGerald Papers, UCDA, P215/705.
104 Ann O'Halloran to L. Cosgrave, 2 Oct. 1973, in D/T 2005/21/105 NAI.
105 John Raven, C.T. Whelan, Paul A. Pfretzschner and Donald M. Borock, *Political Culture in Ireland: The Views of Two Generations* (Dublin, 1976) p. 131.
106 Ibid., p. 129.
107 Ibid., pp. 127, 187.
108 *Irish Independent*, 16 July 1973.
109 *An Phoblacht*, March 1971.
110 Ibid., 15 June 1973.
111 S. Ó Riain, *Provos: Patriots or Terrorists?* (Dublin, 1974) p. 19.
112 *An Phoblacht*, 16 April 1976.
113 *The Kerryman*, 15 Feb. 1974.
114 *Sunday Independent*, 19 Sept. 1976.
115 *An Phoblacht*, 25 Jan. 1977.
116 Ibid., 1 March 1974. *Sunday Independent*, 1 June 1975.
117 *The Worker*, April 1976.
118 *Western People*, 25 May 1974. *Hibernia*, 24 May 1974.
119 *An Phoblacht*, 24 May 1974.
120 Ibid., 7 and 14 June 1974.
121 Republic of Ireland Annual Review, 18 Feb. 1975, FCO 87/416, NAUK.
122 *Sunday World*, 24 Nov. 1974.
123 *The Kerryman*, Nov. 1974.
124 Ibid. (North Cork edition) 5 Feb. 1972.
125 *Sunday Independent,* 7 March 1976.
126 W.R. Haydon to Anthony Crosland, 1 Jan. 1977, in FCO87/603 NAUK.
127 *Irish Press*, 22 July 1976.
128 Intelligence Assessment – Spring Period 1977, 15 Feb. 1977, 2008/79/3109 NAI.
129 Murphy, *A Place Apart*, p. 12.
130 Republic of Ireland: Annual Review for 1977, 8 Feb. 1978, FCO87/603 NAUK.
131 *Irish Times*, 9 Aug. 1976.
132 Ibid., 20 June 1977.
133 Boran, *Invisible Prison*, p. 200.
134 *Irish Press*, 18 Oct. 1976.

135 *Sunday World*, 25 Jan. 1976.
136 *Irish Press*, 6 Jan. 1976.
137 *Longford Leader*, 27 Feb. 1976.
138 Undated note of telephone conversation with Barry (1977) (UCDA, Sighle Humphreys
   Papers, P106/1566 (6)).
139 *Leitrim Observer*, 9 April 1977.
140 *The Kerryman*, 24 Feb. 1978.
141 *Anglo-Celt*, 24 Feb. 1978.
142 *Magill*, Sept. 1979.
143 *Hibernia*, 30 Aug. 1979.
144 *Irish Press*, 28 Aug. 1979.
145 *Sunday World*, 2 Sept. 1979.
146 Embassy to FCO, 29 Aug. 1979, PREM 19/13f143 NAUK.
147 *Sunday Independent*, 2 Sept. 1979.
148 *Sunday World*, 9 Sept. 1979.
149 *An Phoblacht/Republican News*, 15 Sept. 1979.
150 *Fortnight*, Oct. 2002.
151 *Irish Times*, 1 Oct. 1979.
152 Ibid., 3 Oct. 1979.
153 *An Phoblacht/Republican News*, 6 Oct. 1979.
154 *Anglo-Celt*, 5 Oct. 1979.
155 Ibid., 16 June 1979.
156 Ibid., 2 June 1979.
157 *An Phoblacht*, 24 March 1975.
158 Ibid., 26 Sept. 1975 and 11 Jan. 1978.
159 Ibid., 5 Oct. 1977.
160 Ibid.
161 *An Phoblacht/Republican News*, 2 June 1979.
162 *Irish Times*, 21 Feb. 1980.
163 K. Conway, *Southside*, p. 174.
164 Callanan, *The Literary and Historical Society*, pp. 189 and 211.
165 See *An Phoblacht* throughout 1977.
166 *Irish Times*, 20 Feb. 1980.
167 *The Starry Plough*, April 1980.
168 T. McKearney, *The Provisional IRA: From Insurrection to Parliament* (London, 2011)
   p. 147.
169 *Irish Times*, 18 Feb. 1980.
170 Of the other fatalities, loyalists were responsible for 18 and the British army for
   two. David McKittrick, Seamus Kelter, Brian Feeney and Chris Thornton, *Lost
   Lives: The Stories of the Men, Women and Children Who Died as a Result of the
   Northern Ireland Troubles* (Edinburgh, 1999) pp. 773–774.
171 Quoted by James Downey, *Irish Times*, 2 Aug. 1980.
172 *Magill*, May 1979.
173 F. Stuart Ross., *Smashing H-Block* (Liverpool, 2011).

9

'They want to tell lies about our history'[1]

A few days after Bloody Sunday, a left-wing group distributed leaflets to students at University College Dublin. In contrast to most commentary that week, their message asserted that it was the 'consistant refusal of the nationalist leadership (to) recognise the national rights of the Protestants to a distinct political life (that) has led in turn to the repression of the Catholic minority in Northern Ireland'.[2] The leafleters were members of the British & Irish Communist Organisation (B & ICO) a small, Marxist sect who would intervene noisily in debates about the North throughout the 1970s.[3]

They were not the only Irish left-wingers sceptical about nationalism. Labour TD Dr. Noel Browne, an iconic figure since his days in the first inter-party government, also dismissed the idea that Irish unity could be progressive. In 1971, Browne argued that 'a rigidly conservative Catholic dominated theocratic state' was not capable of satisfying the needs of Northerners; 'the Irish worker, whatever his politics or religion to our shame is better off under the Unionists in Stormont'.[4] Despite their claims to socialism, Browne saw the Official IRA, as much as their Provisional rivals, as 'bourgeois'.[5] By 1978, he would compare the IRA to the Mafia and argue that their version of republicanism was 'the most powerful single impediment' to the creation of a socialist Ireland.[6]

'Forgotten the terror'

Browne had little in common with the Catholic Church. But from an early stage some senior clergymen also expressed worries about republicanism. The Bishop of Ardagh and Clonmacnoise, Cahal Daly, asserted during 1972 that he was 'personally convinced' that the historic fight for 'national freedom was just and necessary (and) the heroism both of soldiers and civilians in that struggle wrote a glorious chapter in our history'. But in romanticizing the independence struggle, he suggested, 'we have forgotten the terror and the terrible cost' of that period.[7] Daly warned that contemporary violence would carry a similar cost for both republicans and the nation itself.

These views were all different expressions of the foment caused by the reality of the northern war. There were echoes of them at trade union meetings, in GAA clubs, in sermons at Sunday Mass and in pub arguments. The crisis provoked the most widespread questioning of how southerners viewed their history and the most ferocious reaction to these questions since independence.

'Revisionism' became the catch-all phrase to describe this trend. The term was particularly applied by republicans to those who they accused of seeking to 'disparage the separatist tradition, to pooh pooh it, and to pretend that there is no reasonable or rational foundation for seeking total separation'.[8] By the mid 1970s, the *Sunday World*'s 'Senator' summed up the widespread perception that many in government 'would rather honour John Redmond than Patrick Pearse'. He suggested that the idea that 'those who protested in arms against the British throughout the years were at best fools, at worst criminals, is to be encouraged in schools and on platforms'.[9] *An Phoblacht's* Dara McDara explained that

> the Liberal crowd that is in the saddle in Dublin has decided that our history needs rewriting, that the 'old myths', as they call them, need to be thrown out … the new 'historians' are serious; they are being taken seriously by the civil servants, especially since two of these architects of the new myths are ministers in the Dublin assembly; the new text books are being prepared; and it is clear there will be no difficulty in finding publishers – those awaiting Irish language textbooks can wait a little longer.[10]

'The glorification of force'

But those who advocated reinterpreting Irish history were convinced that its popular version had contributed to violence. The coroner at the Mountbatten inquest, Dr. Desmond Moran, argued that

> it is important to stress again the great responsibility that parents and teachers of any nation have in the way they interpret history and pass it on to the youth of the country. I believe that if history could be taught in such a fashion that it would help to create harmony among people rather than division and hatred it would serve this and other nations better.[11]

After the murder of Billy Fox, Cavan's *Anglo-Celt* reflected how 'the glorification of force and violence (and) unfortunately, their historic success, has created not only amongst the killers but amongst those who support them (a) fearful arrogance'.[12] The carnage of 1972 prompted the popular magazine *Ireland's*

Own to reflect that 'it has been a year in which the art of warfare – so often glorified in our literature – reached a new level of immorality and barbarism'. This was forcing people to accept that 'attitudes that may have been relevant a century ago, or even half a century ago … cannot be relevant now'.[13]

That there was a direct link between popular culture and northern violence became an article of faith. During 1975, a Cork man claimed that as a result of the lionization of

> the patriot gunman, the guerilla ambushes, the rebel risings, the heroes who died for Ireland … children were, of course, impressed and uplifted with patriotic fervour, and if they had ended their schooling at national level they might have joined the IRA … Do you remember the enormous upsurge of support for 'Our Own' in the North at the beginning of the 'Troubles' … It was fed and fostered by the propaganda and from Press, politicians and RTE – yes, and the Church, too. It has taken us 4 years to see that nationalist fervour for what it was – too late to save all those who have died, or been maimed, on both sides.[14]

Journalist John Healy contended that young people could not be blamed for supporting the IRA as they 'were products of an educational culture and a society which glorified violence and the gun and the men who wielded the gun'.[15] Broadcaster Olivia O'Leary later recalled coming 'home from primary school with stories of the famine, the suppression of the Irish language and religion … primed with poisonous warnings about pagan England, and slogans like "burn everything British but her coal"'.[16] Attempting to establish how history teaching actually 'influences the development of views of history is a complex and highly problematic matter'.[17] Nevertheless, the belief that it was teaching in Irish schools that helped produce 'the young bomber' was widely asserted.[18]

'Lamentable ignorance'

As early as November 1969, memoranda for discussion on northern policy had noted that 'in the schools emphasis should be given to the positive aspects rather than the aspects which tend to be divisive … care should be taken to avoid appearing to condone the activities of illegal organisations such as the I.R.A'.[19] Among the academic profession, 'revisionism' was already a factor long before 1969. Historian G. Hayes-McCoy and *Hibernia* magazine had already criticized what they considered to be nationalist bias in textbooks during the early 1960s.[20] As the ashes of Bombay Street were smouldering, Trinity Professor Louis Cullen was questioning whether the image of Gaelic society presented in Daniel Corkery's influential *The Hidden Ireland* was reality or myth.[21] In March 1972, M.F. Collins of the History Teachers Association of Ireland observed that those claiming Irish schools were producing republicans betrayed a 'lamentable ignorance' of teaching for the past thirty years, research, writing and teaching of Irish history has endeavoured to achieve a level of objectivity which is internationally recognised … as a result, one is less likely to get distorted history in the average classroom than in Dail debates.[22]

Nevertheless, it was views like those of a *Kerryman* editorial in early 1972 that 'revisionists' sought to challenge:

Irish history for hundreds of years tells of the struggle against British Crown forces and the Ascendency that held the Irish people in serfdom. Geography tells us that this small island of ours is one and that its only border is the sea. In backing their artificial statelet in the Six Counties with their army the British are defending the last remnants of ascendency and vested interests …[23]

'The most effective propaganda organ'

But these new interpretations were never unquestioned. In 1978, Conor Cruise O'Brien would complain that 'two of the three Dublin morning papers, one Sunday newspaper, and the solitary Dublin "intellectual" periodical regularly published material tending to legitimize the existence and objective of the Provisionals'.[24] O'Brien was suggesting that the *Irish Times* and the *Irish Press*, the *Sunday World* and *Hibernia* all 'legitimized' the IRA. The B & ICO would also claim that 'next to the *Sunday World*, the most effective propaganda organ for the Provos in the Republic has always been Fianna Fáil's *Irish Press*. *An Phoblacht* would come a very poor third (if that).'[25] The reality was of course more complex.

The *Irish Times* was notable for its extensive coverage of the North, which included giving space to radical and republican voices.[26] During 1972, its detailed reports from Derry by Nell McCafferty included sympathetic interviews with the Provisional's local commander, Martin McGuinness.[27] It also published regular 'letters from Long Kesh' by Official IRA internee Des O'Hagan.[28] A number of its writers had Official republican sympathies, while the editorial tone leaned towards the SDLP. The *Irish Press* was a popular nationalist paper, stridently anti-partitionist but wary of disruptive action in the Republic. During 1972, journalist Liam McGabhann claimed that the paper emoted on the Provisionals while simultaneously 'never daring to criticise' Fianna Fáil.[29] After 1973, the *Press* became a vocal critic of Coalition security policy and 'the fact that the paper had defended censorship under a Fianna Fáil administration' was largely forgotten.[30] The *Sunday World* carried extensive northern coverage and 'more original news-material every week than either of its two rivals'. The paper's first political correspondent was Proinsias Mac Aonghusa: 'the Senator… from the corridors of power'.[31] Mac Aonghusa had been active in the Labour party but was sympathetic to republicans. The paper also employed John Keane from Newry, a supporter of the Officials, the Derry socialist Eamonn McCann and Gery Lawless, a former IRA activist and left-winger. Liam MacGabhann, the paper's news editor, had been active in republican politics during the 1930s.

Both *Hibernia* magazine and, after 1977, *Magill* devoted extensive coverage to the northern issue. Cruise O'Brien had criticized *Hibernia* for being too close to the Official IRA in the early 1970s, but within a few years the Officials would regard the magazine as sympathetic to the Provos and the IRSP.[32] *Magill* featured interviews with the Provisional IRA leadership and articles on prison conditions, state repression and censorship.

While the *Irish Independent* was the traditional voice of Fine Gael support, in the mid 1970s the *Sunday Independent*, edited by Michael Hand, carried more critical northern coverage, including interviews with IRA leaders.[33] It was possible for articles denouncing the visit of Queen Elizabeth to Northern Ireland and describing the UDR as 'atrocious sectarian murderers' to appear in the paper.[34] The politics of the national (and local) press were fluid. In 1976, a reader could congratulate the *Sunday Independent* for their 'courage' in publishing extracts from Michael Farrell's *Northern Ireland: The Orange State*, stating that 'in these days of so-called historical revisionism it is refreshing to hear again how exactly the Unionist junta was set up in Northern Ireland'.[35] In *Magill*, journalists such as Kevin Myers would write empathetic accounts of life in Belfast's Short Strand and the growing H-Block crisis. Myers reminded readers in 1977 that the IRA 'were not the cause of this war but the consequence'. He also suggested that anyone who did not believe that the RUC were using brutality to obtain confessions was 'either a fool or illiterate'.[36] During 1977, *An Phoblacht* noted that the 'republicanism' of *Irish Times* editor Douglas Gageby, though not of the same variety as theirs, nevertheless worried the Dublin establishment.[37] The local papers, read by thousands in the 1970s, featured a spectrum of opinions, from support for republicans to complete condemnation. Indeed, the letters pages of any newspaper would illustrate the diversity of ideas about the North (which is perhaps why Cruise O'Brien flirted with the idea of censoring them).

'An appalling stream of factual errors'

The issue also filled the bookshelves. As the IRA was reenergized by the crisis (while splitting into rival organizations), perceptions of it were being shaped. There were some who saw a positive role for republicans in the 1970s. The journalist and historian Dermot Keogh argued that 'men who have dedicated their lives to securing political objectives, who have faced death, endured imprisonment and hunger strikes cannot ... be dismissed as "young toughs"'. Indeed, Keogh argued, the refusal of 'many capable IRA idealists' to enter the Dáil has 'unfortunately given too much scope instead to opportunists and self-seekers'.[38] Fortuitously, two books on the subject were published during 1970. Tim Pat Coogan's *The IRA* was serialized in the *Sunday Independent*, and both it and J. Bowyer Bell's *Secret Army* were widely reviewed as readers sought an introduction to what was suddenly a very topical subject. Both Official and Provisional reviewers were effusive about Bell's 'scholarly and beautifully-written ... sympathetic and understanding' book, while Coogan was damned for an 'appalling stream of factual errors and inaccuracies, misprints and mis-spellings'.[39] Both books sold well and were soon joined by the first modern republican memoirs and collections of interviews; Maria Maguire's *To Take Arms* and Rosita Sweetman's *On Our Knees: Ireland 1972*. Maguire had been a Provisional activist while Sweetman was sympathetic to the Officials. Bernadette Devlin's *The Price of My Soul*, originally published in 1969, was serialized in *Woman's Way* during 1972.[40] Conor Cruise O'Brien's *States of Ireland* was also published that year, introducing many of the themes that would dominate his critique of Irish nationalism. The book was described as 'pro-Unionist and pro-Imperialist' in *Hibernia*.[41] In contrast, Garrett FitzGerald's *Towards a New Ireland* offered a moderate nationalist analysis of the likelihood of Irish unity.

Former IRA leader Seán Mac Stíofáin *Memoirs of a Revolutionary* would be published in 1975, following Eamonn MacCann's *War and an Irish Town*. Extracts from McCann's book were published in the *Irish Times*, but the Eason's chain refused to stock it.[42] In 1976, the *Sunday Independent* serialized Michael Farrell's *Northern Ireland: The Orange State* over three issues. The paper claimed that Farrell, who it noted believed that 'the anti-imperialist struggle in Northern Ireland is both justifiable and necessary' had 'had a profound influence, ideologically, on many of the younger elements in the Provisionals in Belfast'.[43] Two critical reviews of Farrell's book by the SDLP's John Hume and Unionist MP John Taylor followed.[44] One of 1977's best-sellers was *Ireland: A Terrible Beauty* by Leon and Jill Uris. The book was well received by republicans, *An Phoblacht* gushing that 'Uris is not sympathetic; he is over sympathetic. Like Jews in many lands he has a kinmanship with oppression.'[45] From a very different perspective, Ruth Dudley Edward's biography of Padraig Pearse, *The Triumph of Failure*, provoked widespread discussion in the same year.[46] In late 1977, Kevin Boland's account of the Arms Trial and the 'betrayal' of republicanism by Fianna Fáil – *Up Dev!* – also sold well.[47] Travel writer Dervla Murphy's *A Place Apart* attempted to interpret the North for southerners during 1978, its title and overall tone summing up what was becoming a widespread view among commentators.

'Cosgrave knows his Brit'

The northern crisis provoked very public upheavals in Fianna Fáil and the Labour party. It has been suggested that as Fine Gael had 'no republican wing' it escaped such trauma.[48] However, many of Fine Gael's supporters responded as emotionally as other parts of Irish society after 1969. That year, Liam Cosgrave attributed the crisis to 'the British designed and enacted partition of

Ireland' which could be only 'remedied by granting to Ireland the unity to which her people are intended'.[49] When Fine Gael policy was criticized by the *Irish Times*, Cosgrave noted the 'alien background' of that paper, recalled its support for the suppression of the 1916 Rising and responded that he was 'not particularly disposed to be receptive to advice from that quarter'.[50] After Bloody Sunday, Cosgrave hoped that the tragedy would 'jerk the British Government into immediate action to find a political solution that will get the British Army out of this country forever'.[51] A 1975 profile of Cosgrave described him as 'very much at odds with the old Parliamentary Party tradition within Fine Gael, especially on the national question (he) is instinctively an old style nationalist ... jokes about British interference in Irish politics such as that made at the recent Ard Fheis, come easily to him'.[52] As conflict mounted with the Coalition during 1974, an *An Phoblacht* writer speculated that 'perhaps ... FitzGerald exemplifies the Fine Gael party as presently constituted to a much more accurate degree than does Cosgrave, its leader. One senses that Cosgrave knows his Brit.'[53]

'Reunite this country'

The most public evidence of this trend within Fine Gael came at their 1971 Ard Fheis. A Meath delegate urged the party to do 'everything possible to reunite this country within this generation'. Condemning Fianna Fáil for their inaction, he stated that 'Mr. Lynch had said he would not stand idly by, but he allowed half of Derry to be burned ... Mr. Lynch should have sent troops across the Border and created an international situation which would have the effect of enabling us to negotiate with Britain on partition.' A South Kerry delegate reiterated that getting 'the British out of the North was a problem for the whole nation ... It was up to Fine Gael to get the army out of the Six Counties and to settle the whole problem.' Ballsbridge delegate Garret Cooney moved a motion that the Ard Fheis call on the party to 'emphasise in its public statements ... their support and sympathy for the beleaguered minority particularly in Belfast and Derry'. Cooney complained that 'the impression had been given that Fine Gael was a pro-British party, it seemed to have been forgotten that the party had been founded from one wing of the Sinn Féin movement'. Another delegate, Donal Lowry of Dundrum, asked that Fine Gael 'should extend its activities to the Six Counties and set up branches there'.[54] The shift in emphasis towards conciliation of Unionists during 1972 annoyed some supporters, one telling Cosgrave that he was

> really amazed to think that the Party of William T. Cosgrave, Michael Collins, Arthur Griffith, Kevin O'Higgins, Dick Mulcahy, Sean McEoin and others, could for one moment, adopt a policy whereby we, in effect, said that the reunification of Ireland could be postponed indefinitely or didn't matter.[55]

'Doing John Bull's dirty work'

These views could co-exist with a fierce loyalty to the southern state and a determination not to allow republicans to 'subvert' it. By 1973, the majority of Fine Gael would back Cosgrave's hard line, in public at least. However, when reacting to criticism, some party members fell back on nationalism. After complaints about Garda brutality were publicized by the *Irish Times* in 1977, Fintan Coogan TD complained that the paper was 'doing John Bull's dirty work'.[56] Some Fine Gael supporters asserted that the allegations were designed to distract attention from the Irish Government's case against Britain at the European Court of Human Rights. Kerry TD Gerard Lynch claimed that complaints against the Gardai were given 'prominence in a section of the press that has been traditionally hostile to Irish institutions and who never cease to attack the moral and political standards by which Irish people live …'. It was not a coincidence the British media then publicized these cases to divert attention from the fact that their nation was 'on trial before the world for activities that more properly belong to Cromwellian days or the era of the pitch cap for the mere Irish …'.[57] Cosgrave put it more succinctly at the 1977 Ard Fheis when he claimed that some of the government's critics 'who comment so freely and write so freely – some of them aren't even Irish … some of these are blow-ins. Now as far as we're concerned they can blow out or blow up.'[58] By 1977, there were signs among Fine Gael members of 'resentment' at the idea of not stressing their 'United Ireland' policy and 'adverse reaction to a statement on Northern policy by Conor Cruise O'Brien which appeared to commit the Government as a whole to an anti-unity line'.[59]

Thornley's republicanism

O'Brien, of course, was a member of the Labour party, whose ranks contained a wide variety of views about the North. As Tadhg O'Sullivan explained to a meeting in Kerry in early 1972, the

> rank and file of the Labour Party rejected the two-nation concept of Ireland and any other concept other than that of the founder of the party, James Connolly. He fought and died for the establishment of an independent socialist republic for all Ireland. That and none other must be their aim too. It could not be repeated too often.[60]

As mainstream a Labour figure as Justin Keating could argue that 'the whole of Ireland is still a colony of Britain, while at the same time the Irish ruling class is involved with British imperialism … we have never enjoyed real independence, North or South'.[61] However, though few Labour TDs shared the same intellectual commitment to undermining nationalism as Cruise O'Brien, in government after 1973 they generally rallied to defence of the state.[62]

The most prominent parliamentary figure to disagree was David Thornley. A former academic and RTE presenter, Thornley earned the wrath of his party for opposing security legislation. He claimed that though he rejected

> the methods of the IRA I recognise that they stand for a view of Irish history which is indigenous to the country. I'm sick of the revisionist rewriting of history which tries to black out certain historical facts, for instance anyone who thinks that the 1918 election gave a mandate to Michael Collins for Bloody Sunday doesn't know history … Violence may be wrong today, but none can deny that it happened yesterday and is burned in the folk-memory.[63]

Fianna Fáil's George Colley had complained that some 'would-be historians avail themselves of every opportunity to try to discredit the achievements and traditions of the old IRA' by equating them with the 'militant groups operating today'.[64] In contrast, Thornley argued that those like Cruise O'Brien were being consistent in their opposition to republicanism. It was commentators who claimed the Provisional IRA represented something fundamentally different from the 'old' IRA who were the hypocrites. Thornley claimed that the 1918 election had not given the IRA any mandate for its campaign as the 'election was not fought on the issue of violence'. If young people joining the IRA had been misled, then it was mainstream society that had misled them, whether that was through 'stories they have read in the *Sunday Press*' or by 'the history books from which children were taught until recently'.[65]

When critics raised the issue of civilian casualties, Thornley responded that 'a fair few bystanders bit the dust between 1919 and 1923'. In 1971, he asserted that he saw 'no essential difference between the Official IRA as I understand it, in the use of guns to defend beleaguered nationalist ghettoes … and the role of the IRA men who were sent North with the collusion of Michael Collins and Liam Lynch for the same purpose in 1922. My father-in-law was one of those; I am not ashamed of him.'[66]

Thornley and O'Brien both accepted that Irish nationalist 'mythology' helped produce the IRA. But they drew very different conclusions about what that meant. Thornley's early death in 1978 was mourned by one left-wing activist for being 'as great a loss as (IRSP leader) Seamus Costello's murder. In the previous decade Seamus had changed little; David had moved from non-commitment to revolutionary politics.'[67] However, in the following decade, the Labour party would move even further away from any identification with republicanism.[68]

'The gentle jouster from Castleisland'[69]

Debates about Irish history were not confined to academia. Some of the most damning criticism of republican ideas was published by the *Kerryman* newspaper in the weekly columns of schoolteacher Con Houlihan. Much of Houlihan's critique was based on seeing Irish history through the prism of class. In early 1972, he reminded readers that under British rule not only were the Irish peasantry 'rack-rented so that the social life of Mayfair and Baden-Baden could continue unabated', but 'for bad measure were preyed upon by the gombeen class, good Catholics to a man and woman … more than one family of proud Irish merchants laid the foundations of its fortunes in the black market that flourished during the famine years'.[70]

For Houlihan, much of the rhetoric that had accompanied the outbreak of the northern crisis was hypocritical. He claimed that though Catholics were the 'victims of vicious discrimination', in general they possessed 'better houses than the working class here and have far better facilities in medicine, education, and social security'. The War of Independence had not changed social conditions, and 'in 1921 … when the small farmers in the west of Ireland took over and divided some of the big estates they were driven out at gunpoint by the IRA'. Successive governments though 'all dominated by the freedom fighters of the Five Glorious Years have had one philosophy in common – that property is sacred, no matter how it is acquired'.[71]

Skewering the pretensions of the green wing of Fianna Fáil, he recalled how Kevin Boland was

> a member of a government that introduced internment at a time when there was infinitely less pretext for it than there was last August. It is generally agreed that Proportional Representation would greatly advance the cause of democracy in the North: this was the system Mr. Boland worked so hard to abolish south of the border.[72]

Immediately after Bloody Sunday, Houlihan warned that rather than uniting Ireland the armed struggle was driving its people further apart. Houlihan asserted that

> if we want to end partition we must first build a decent society where wealth and power will be fairly shared, where people need not fear that they will be neglected in sickness or old age, where our young will be educated to lead full lives and not thrown into the world at fourteen to provide a pool of cheap labour for foreign capitalists and local gombeen men (and) above all, we must exorcise the poisonous bigotry that sees only the Catholic as the 'true' Irishman.[73]

'Courage and generosity are not enough'

Houlihan initially presented republican activists as sincere if misguided. He claimed to have a good many friends in all three branches of the physical 'force movement', but worried that 'most of them suffer from the same form of myopia – an inability to realise the real living people are infinitely more important than hazy conceptions. Most of them talk of an Ireland that never was and dream of an Ireland that will never be.' While he accepted that 'Ruairi O Bradaigh and his fellows never intended their movement to be sectarian', Houlihan concluded that 'it is and is seen to be such'.[74] By 1974, he lamented that

> the Provisionals may be tragically mistaken (but) they contain a backbone of people who are utterly sincere. These same people would share the proverbial last crust with you. But courage and generosity are not enough ... whatever grudging respect one has for them is now wearing very thin.[75]

Houlihan became increasingly embittered. After one IRA killing, he asked whether those who felt 'sympathy with the (Price) sisters because they could see their parents only infrequently' ever thought about 'the girl who will never see her father again. Or have the families of U.D.R. men any feelings?'[76] His columns provoked much resentment, one correspondent suggesting that

> the snakes are hissing once again as they did in 1916 and 1922–3, and have continued ever since, but this time Con we will draw their fangs. Every generation has seen anti-Irishmen willing to grasp the slimy hand of John Bull, so get back in your hole and drop dead. I refuse to buy *The Kerryman* from now onwards.[77]

The paper's management received reliable information that the IRA intended to take action against them. However, the editor, supported by the NUJ, continued to publish Houlihan's articles despite the threats.[78]

'Abstractions are all very well'

Even after the Dublin/Monaghan bombings, Houlihan blamed republicans, asserting that

> the architects of Belfast's Bloody Friday belong to the same moral order as those who committed last week's blasphemy in Monaghan and Dublin ... yet those of us who protest at dealings in such degenerate coin are labelled traitors ... those who believe in blood sacrifice, those who believe that people must be killed before progress can be made might have revised their ideas if they had been in the midst of Friday's carnage. Abstractions are all very well; the obscene reality is different.[79]

Houlihan drew praise from some readers, like one emigrant who had lived for 30 years in Britain and who recalled that his 'only education was national school, having enforced Irish at all times. Hatred of the British ... received priority and was often taught for a whole morning – and ironically, Catholicism was instilled with fanatic enthusiasm the same day.'[80] The logic of Houlihan's anger led him to support the Coalition Government's emergency powers in 1976. By then, he had concluded that the IRA was made up of 'politically ignorant youths and mentally-ill people and plain gangsters' and led by 'sinister and power-hungry men who have little chance of advancing by the ordinary democratic means'. Because the IRA leadership was 'utterly cynical and care nothing for other people's suffering' there was no alternative but new laws. While Houlihan noted that 'sentimental liberals' protested about civil liberties, the fact was 'ordinary courts are powerless against terrorists'. Anyway, he asserted, the 'innocent have nothing to fear from the Special Courts'.[81]

'Our man in the *Times*'[82]

A similar critique to Houlihan's, though without its social radicalism, was carried regularly by the *Western People*. John Healy was the author of the 1968 book *The Death of an Irish Town* about the decline of Charlestown, Co. Mayo. In the early 1970s, he was 'Backbencher' in the *Irish Times*, and was regarded as the voice of a rural Ireland suspicious of the metropole, a representative of the 'snipegrass country'.[83] He had supported both Fianna Fáil and Fine Gael on occasion, and ultimately became a prominent defender of Charles Haughey. He was also a bitter opponent of the IRA.

In early 1972, he noted that he had 'been getting under people's skin here because of what I had to say about the war in the North: because, mainly, I have refused to heroise the green lads who are doing their patriotic thing'.[84] He was one of those who blamed support for the IRA on the 'bad teaching and faulty and indeed perverted history to which most of us have been subjected at school ... we enobled violence and the sacrifices of the men who "died for Ireland"'.[85]

His commentary in the aftermath of the Dublin/Monaghan carnage was even more cutting than Houlihan's. Healy argued that 'death in Dublin isn't any worse or more brutal than the deaths of over 1,000 people in Belfast or the other Irish towns and villages in the North'. Why then, he asked, 'can (we) weep more and be shocked because it happens to "Irish" Irish people?'. Healy claimed that after the bombs some journalists 'who ran with the Provos for the last few years' went back 'shaken to media offices (to) pull out all the harrowing language and emotive stops as if they had no hand in the evening's grim work'. He contrasted the lack of reaction with other atrocities in the North, and asked was it because in Dublin and Monaghan 'the dead are "Irish" Irish?'. Healy then chillingly noted that there was 'a smug view that the Orange militants couldn't mount a Provo type campaign in the South ... we'd soon see how many indulgent supporters there'd be for the Provos if the sons and daughters of Mayo or Kerry or Sligo parents were at risk in Dublin city'.[86] Given that young men and women from outside Dublin had died in the bombs, Healy's prose seemed particularly vindictive. His accusations that some Dublin journalists had run 'with the Provos' was testament to the bitter divisions the conflict produced among the media.

In the aftermath of the bombings, *An Phoblacht*'s 'Freeman' examined 'Healy's savage doctrine' and remarked that the Mayo man had 'a lot to answer for'. Noting that Healy had consistently stressed that it 'doesn't matter a damn whether the bombers give a warning or don't give a warning ... all killing is the same', 'Freeman' suggested that Healy should reflect that 'some savages from Belfast took him at his word'.[87] But, like Houlihan, Healy, a former 'Mayo Man of the Year', was not the product of what 'Freeman' called 'Dubland'. Neither man was a typical 'RTE Trinity College–Irish Times Liberal'.[88] Admitting this, 'Freeman' speculated that Healy wrote what he did because 'he found that doing so is the way to success in contemporary Ireland, making him acceptable to important people'.[89] But Houlihan and Healy's writing also reflected the genuine divisions that the war produced in the views of people across the country.

'Made by the Mass'

As an all-Ireland institution and the faith of the vast majority in the Republic, the Catholic Church was a powerful force. The hierarchy opposed the IRA's campaign, with varying levels of intensity, from the beginning, arguing that it brought 'shame and disgrace' to the nationalist cause.[90] But there were a range of views among the clergy, including some supportive of republicans.[91]

A number of northern clerics, notably Fr. Denis Faul and Fr. Raymond Murray, gained prominence in the south during the 1970s for exposing abuses by the British army, links between loyalist paramilitaries and the state and prison conditions.[92] A few priests, such as Fr. Sean Cunningham of Tralee, openly endorsed the IRA. Cunningham argued that the 'Provisionals are made by the Mass, the Family Rosary and the lives and writings of the classical Republican authors such as Pearse, Plunkett and Connolly. Indeed the Mass alone is enough sometimes.'[93] Fr. Padraic Campbell took issue with clerical condemnation of the IRA in late 1971, arguing that 'conditions (were) so intolerable in Northern Ireland that people were entitled to use force to restore true justice'.[94] On the other hand, there were also those priests who from an early stage were taking the lead in condemning republicans. After the riot in Ballyshannon in late 1971, local priest Fr. Patrick Gallagher described the IRA as 'inhuman and un-Christian. Whether their leaders admit it or not their gospel has far too much hatred, bigotry, intimidation and violence ... too much of a spurious, narrow and fanatical nationalism.'[95]

Cahal Daly: Violence in Ireland

Intellectually, it was Bishop Cahal Daly who intervened most directly in debates concerning the national question. Daly argued that the Provisional IRA's campaign was morally unjustified, lacked the mandate given to the 'old' IRA and was intensifying inter-communal division. A collection of his sermons and speeches – Violence in Ireland and Christian Conscience – was published in 1973 (and dedicated to Fr. Hugh Mullan and Fr. Noel FitzPatrick, both of whom had been shot dead by British troops).[96]

Daly argued that in 1918 'revolutionary violence was endorsed and the subsequent struggle legitimated by the most democratic and conclusive election perhaps ever held in Ireland. The army that fought for freedom was the Army of the elected Parliament and Government of the Irish people.'[97] He complained that despite the iconic status of the 1916 Proclamation, 'most people do not seem to even know about the Democratic Programme of the First Dáil. If this were given equal honour in our classrooms it would help to restore a sense of balance and a sense that freedom is still something to be achieved.'[98] Daly recognized that the modern IRA was capable of 'courage, endurance and even nobility'. Criticized for this, he responded that there was a distinction between 'moral condemnation' and 'moralistic condemnation'.[99] He also admitted that 'like most nationally-minded Irish youth' he once shared the IRA's 'emotions … I still share many of the ideals of their tradition'.[100] However, by 1973, he felt that 'physical force' had been 'conspicuously disavowed by the Irish electorate'.[101]

Daly warned that the armed campaign was also damaging republicanism itself. Contrasting the hope of the 1916 leaders that their forces avoid unnecessary killing, he asked whether the 'present leaders of republican violence want to be the men who dishonour the Republic by condoning the inhumanity, brutality and intimidation being practiced in its name? Republicanism, once a proud and honoured name, is being dragged in the gutter, made a synonym of shame.'[102]

'The ideology is new'

A native of Co. Antrim, Daly remembered that in his youth 'there were still surviving traces of Presbyterian liberalism and radicalism'.[103] The IRA campaign made it impossible for this type of politics to survive in the Protestant community. For Daly, northern Protestants were a 'sturdy, manly, honest, industrious, shrewd, loyal and loveable people'.[104] Winning their consent was the only way to a united Ireland. Debating with Daithí Ó Conaill on the merits of armed struggle, Daly argued that the rise in sectarianism 'was a totally foreseeable and predictable consequence of the decision to launch and sustain a campaign of violence'.[105] He accepted that while it would be difficult to convince Unionists of the logic of a united country, 'they can be persuaded. The task will be demanding, slow, difficult. It would be to take a poor view of the Irish to think they are not capable of the task.'[106]

Daly appealed to southern nationalism's deeply felt affinity with the 'old' IRA, asserting that 'the term, 'Irish Republican Army', with the noble name and record which it earned 60 years ago, can still evoke powerful emotional responses. It cannot be too emphatically asserted that those who usurp the name now have no right or title, historical or moral, to use it.' Interestingly, Daly also claimed to see a difference between the IRA of the late 1970s and the founders of the Provisionals, claiming that

> only the name has remained unchanged. The leadership is new. The structures are new. The ideology is new. The ultimate aims are new. The mentality and the methods have a new and amoral ruthlessness. The new IRA is a radically new phenomenon – and it is a sinister one. It is now taking shape as a movement alien to Irish tradition and values. Some of the men who mobilised it in 1970 must now have difficulty in recognising it as the same movement. What they created has become a Frankenstein, out of their control, with which many of them must now be disillusioned, and many of them now may even be frightened.[107]

'Apologise for Irishness'

Writing in *An Phoblacht*, Des Fennell claimed that 'Daly has been an ally and much-quoted darling of the Dublin liberal secularist establishment. For them, too, the chief object of assault has been Irish Catholic nationalism ... since they rightly reckon that, once it is destroyed, the way is clear for them to rule the Irish colony as quislings of London.'[108] But while Daly welcomed the 'demythologising' of some historians, he was no liberal. In fact, he saw the IRA's campaign as creating conditions which would undermine Catholicism. In 1974, he argued that 'probably no greater factor of de-Christianisation is at present at work (than) the continuing violence'. He wondered if the IRA leadership realized that 'because of what is being done in the North, some people are being given the excuse to belittle Irish history, decry nationalism and patriotism (and) apologise for Irishness'. He asked if the IRA wanted to

> be the people who will be the occasion for some to turn to any form of a vulgar cosmo-provincialism or genteel West Britonism, on the pretext that they wish to espouse the direct cultural opposite of the republicanism whose ugly face they have seen in the North? Men of an older and nobler republican tradition should raise their voices to protest against what is being done today to besmirch its name.[109]

Indeed, some who rebelled against the dominance of the Catholic Church in Irish life also rejected any association with nationalism. Daly's arguments were significant because they came from within the Catholic nationalist tradition. Republicans could denounce him and other 'well-heeled Cardinals', but arguments from 'one of our most logical bishops' carried far more weight than those of anti-republican government ministers. [110]

'The people will not forget 1916'

In 1977, Daly took part in a debate on RTE television about Padraig Pearse, prompted by the publication of Dudley Edward's biography. The programme featured Edwards herself, Cruise O'Brien, David Thornley, Michael Farrell, Oliver Snoddy and Professor John A. Murphy. Murphy was one of the most prominent Irish historians of the 1970s and featured centrally (often on radio or television) in many of the debates concerning the relationship between Irish history and the northern conflict.[111] Reviewing the debate, *An Phoblacht* concluded that while O'Brien was a 'revisionist Unionist', Murphy represented revisionist nationalism.[112]

Murphy had spoken at protests in Cork after Bloody Sunday and been sympathetic to the Official republicans, giving evidence at Cathal Goulding's trial for incitement during 1972.[113] While Dudley Edwards considered that the IRA were the 'natural successors' of those who followed Pearse, Murphy disagreed.[114] He also stressed that he did 'not regard 1916 as a tragedy'. Nor did Murphy agree that commemorating the Rising contributed 'in any substantial way to the Northern troubles ... if 1916 was never commemorated in the South, it seems to me that the unfulfilled nationalist aspiration of the northern minority would still latch on to 1916'.

Murphy contended that if the use of force to attain independence was played down, 'you are prostituting history in the cause of another political ideology'.[115] He had warned the Coalition Government that they were wrong if they thought that 'soft-peddling' on commemorating the Easter Rising would appease Unionists. After all, Murphy considered, Orangeism was far more offensive to many people and there was no sign of Unionists downplaying that tradition. Instead, he warned that even 'if the present government wants to forget 1916 ... the people will not forget 1916'. For Murphy, it was far more dangerous that the government should 'leave the celebrations in effect to the para-militaries'.[116] In 1978, Murphy challenged Cruise O'Brien, arguing that his 'revisionism ... involved not a little distortion as well as compromise with intellectual honesty'. Condemning O'Brien for being 'abrasive and intolerant' and for seeing those who disagreed with him as 'conniving at subversion', Murphy concluded that O'Brien had arrived at a 'neo-Unionist position'. He claimed there was little difference in O'Brien's position and that of 'Tory spokesmen like Mr. Airey Neave and, indeed, from the fatuities of the "two nations" thesis, as enunciated by the British and Irish Communist Organization'. Noting how unpopular O'Brien had become with the public, Murphy speculated that this was linked to 'an instinctive popular feeling that he had begun to challenge the basis of Irish nationality itself'.[117]

Echoing Official republican rhetoric, Murphy believed that 'the men of 1916 were standing for an Irish Republic ... that was essentially secular and fraternal. On the other hand I see the Provisionals as the logical outcome of aggressive Catholic nationalism ... "armed Hibernians".[118] At the end of the decade, Murphy reflected that 'there was a moment there between 1969 to 1971 when it seemed Ireland as a whole was being involved in a new kind of ferment ... an excitement which brought liberation for many people', but this had passed as the conflict escalated.[119] To republican critics, Murphy was a revisionist, yet there were clearly important differences between his views and those of O'Brien.

'Bloody folly'

The historian Liam de Paor had chronicled events north of the border from 1968 onwards. Then he had praised People's Democracy radicals for having 'the acumen to regard the Unionist government in Stormont and the Fianna Fáil government in Dublin as common (and in spite of the rhetoric of Mr. Blaney and Mr. Boland) collusive enemies of those who wish to transform Irish society'.[120] By 1972, he noted how, despite widespread sympathy for nationalists, not only had 'the Republic ... its own troubles' but a

> very large section of the population was uneasy about the crisis in the North. The Irish Establishment, the business people, the professional classes, the large farmers, would give sympathy to a Nationalist agitation for a united Ireland – although even then they would mostly probably prefer the happy day to be deferred to a more convenient time – but they were not at all happy about the hints of social revolution in the North.[121]

By the mid 1970s, de Paor, though a critic of revisionism, would argue that it was 'the bloody folly of the Provisional IRA in their bombing campaign in the North' that had made it possible to 'mount a sustained attack on the principles of Irish republicanism under the guise of an attack on the use of violence'. But he continued to assert that the crisis 'however hard many in the South may wish, will not go away' and that its effect on Irish life had to be confronted.[122]

But in academia in general, and University College Dublin in particular, wishing the North would go away was becoming the orthodoxy. A significant number of graduates from UCD made careers in the media, particularly in RTE.[123] One student recalled that 'if there was a forbidden "f" word or a forbidden "c" word while we studied there, they were "Fenian" and "colonial"; all the Irish history we studied was parliamentary and constitutional'. The object was 'cleansing history, concentrating on those aspects of our past which would make us good, worthy citizens who would keep the Irish 26-county state safe from the IRA and IRA fellow travellers'.[124] But it was also a period of intense activism at the college, with all strands of republicanism and radicalism represented on campus; 'they were not quiet times'.[125] Speeches by government ministers were disrupted, and during one visit to the college by Liam Cosgrave, a special branch car was overturned.[126] On another occasion, 1,000 students heard Adrian Hardiman of the Student Representative Council and Professor Augustine Martin call for support for the Price sisters.[127]

'Swept under the carpet'

In 1976, historians, journalists and activists responded to the debate by organizing a conference at Liberty Hall on the relevance of 1916. Among the speakers were Padraig Ó Snodaigh, George Gilmore, Dick Walsh of the *Irish Times*, Captain James Kelly and Michael Farrell.[128] The symposium was chaired by *Hibernia* editor John Mulcahy and arose 'out of a mutual feeling that 1916 was being swept under the carpet … a lot of Irish history was being re-written and many of the fundamental assumptions of the raison d'etre for this State were being forgotten about or put aside for various dubious reasons'.[129]

A year later, the second annual 1916 seminar 'The State of the Nation's Culture' featured a smiliar mix of academics and activists, including Seamus Deane, Miriam Daly, Gearóid Ó Tuathaigh, Nollaig Ó Gadhra, Ann Speed, Nora Connolly O'Brien and playwrights Margaretta D'Arcy and John Arden.[130] But by the decade's end it was still not clear how exactly revisionism might be defined. *An Phoblacht* would contend that if Ernie O'Malley's books were 'required reading in schools and universities, instead of the Shoneen or revisionist (or simply non-existent) versions of modern Irish history, then the people of Ireland would be better prepared to achieve a true independence'.[131] But the same paper could heartily recommend David Fitzpatrick's iconoclastic *Politics and Irish Life* as a 'remarkable study … based on impressive contemporary sources with a clear relevance to the present times'.[132]

The 'British Imperial Collaborators Organisation'?[133]

In April 1972, a group of protesters occupied the Department of Foreign Affairs, demanding the Irish state 'recognise Northern Ireland'. They were members of the rather ungainly titled Workers Association for a Democratic Settlement of the National Conflict in Ireland. The group was largely made up of B & ICO members and their publicity material made it clear that they regarded that the 'ultimate responsibility' for the ongoing 'terrorist campaign' as lying with the 'Southern state' and its decades of 'one-nation propaganda'.[134] In contrast, B & ICO contended that the cause of the conflict was 'not Unionism, nor the Unionists'.[135] B & ICO member and Dublin housing activist Denis Dennehy explained that 'we recognise, as democrats, the separate national rights of the Northern Protestant nationality … More than that, we recognise the democratic validity of the present Northern Ireland State.'[136]

Such views were unusual on the left. For many socialists, even those who protested at the Vietnam War and 'turned up at anti-apartheid rallies ... no issue was ever as serious, as personal and as emotional as the "eight hundred years"'.[137] B & ICO, in contrast, regarded the nationalist version of Irish history as largely mythology. The group's roots were among working-class Irish emigrants in London, attracted to communist politics in the 1960s, who then divided along Maoist and Trotskyist lines. Initally, the group held a left-republican perspective, but this had changed by 1971, in part because their reading of Stalin's writings on the national question suggested that Ulster Protestants were a separate nationality. Furthermore, B & ICO contended that Unionism had created a progressive, industrial society, while Irish nationalism had established 'one of the most bizarre little states this side of Middle Earth'. [138]

The B & ICO regarded the Provisional IRA's armed struggle as aiming at 'the realisation of the century-old ambition of forcing the Ulster Protestants into a state run by gombeen men and priests'.[139] The armed campaign itself was the logical consequence of Irish nationalism:

> The Provos are in the true tradition of Catholic Nationalist Republicanism. The conflict of Catholic and Protestant has always been the true core of the 'republicanism' deriving from the Volunteers of 1913. Its basic passion was to bring the Protestants to heel. The war with Britain was never fought with half the ferocity of the Catholic–Protestant war in Belfast: either that today or that of the early twenties. In the Southern war with Britain there were restraints caused by human feeling. That kind of restraint was not operative in the war in Belfast fifty years ago, nor is it today.[140]

'Extradition Now'

Logically, then, the B & ICO supported the northern state's right to defend itself. They also demanded that the southern state take action against the IRA. In 1974, *Comment*, one of their several publications, called for 'Extradition Now', arguing that it was

> high time the Government began to extradite IRA terrorists to Northern Ireland. The Republic is a rest-home for tired murderers who need to put their feet up for a bit before they get back on the job .... by providing a safe hiding-place, we all contribute to the terror and destruction being carried on in the North.[141]

As the IRA's campaign was illegitimate, then the other evils that flowed from it were their responsibility. Hence, B & ICO argued that the way to stop the growth of anti-Irish feeling in Britain was to 'stop anti-British bombing'.[142] They regarded loyalist terrorism as an unfortunate but inevitable reaction to the IRA's campaign, the Protestants having 'endured five years of bombing, shooting and murder'.[143] B & ICO saw the Ulster Workers Council strike as a triumph of working-class power and a victory for democracy. They argued that this should have made it clear to even the 'most stupid Southerner' that the 'majority community in Northern Ireland must be granted the right to self-determination'.[144]

Though often vitriolic in their rhetoric, the group did have a mischievious sense of humour (as long as the joke was not on them). Pro-IRA leftists in the group Revolutionary Struggle were caricatured as student hippies; 'we really relate to the Catholics, and we really get turned off by the Protestants, and in the coming civil war, you can count on Trinity College'.[145] When, in 1977, the Mac Gréil survey found that 42.8% agreed with the contention that 'Northern Ireland and the Republic are two separate nations', B & ICO responded that

> 43% of the people of Dublin have arrived at the conclusion that Northern Ireland and the Republic are in fact quite separate nations. We in the B & ICO have for long been arguing precisely this. We never dreamed we were so successful nor did we imagine we had become so influential a force on the political thought of the people of Dublin. However, now we know.[146]

The group's publications justified Cromwell's crushing of 'Royalist counter revolution' in the Ireland of the 1640s, comparing it to the de-Nazification of Germany after 1945.[147] They were also adamant that 'there was nothing unique about Stalin except that on matters of importance he was always right'.[148] Even their critics conceded that B & ICO were a 'model of how a dedicated and disciplined group' could have a 'totally disproportionate influence'. But it was not surprising that the group aroused hostility. Critical articles alleged that they were aiding loyalist paramilitaries, and even implicated them in the Dublin/ Monaghan bombings.[149]

'The game is not worth the candle'

The group's high level of activity and multitude of publications brought them attention. In 1972, Garret FitzGerald wrote to a B & ICO member claiming to 'have been struck for some time past by the courageous and sane approach adopted by B & ICP (sic) in Northern Ireland – while not going along with it in other respects!'.[150] B & ICO also impressed activists inside the Official republicans, many of the key arguments of 1977's *The Irish Industrial Revolution* lifted directly from B & ICO's *The Economics of Partition*.[151] But they also had an impact on working-class politics in Limerick.

In 1972, Jim Kemmy and a number of others left the Labour party because of the reactionary policies of the local organization, dominated by Stevie Coughlan TD. Kemmy was strongly influenced by the B & ICO and, though he did not join, he incorporated many of their key ideas into his new Limerick

Socialist Organisation. Kemmy was elected to Limerick Corporation in 1974, for a working-class ward, having campaigned for, among other things, the deletion of Articles 2 & 3 of the constitution (which claimed jurisdiction over Northern Ireland) and the right of northern Protestants to opt out of a united Ireland.[152] In a city noted for its Catholic conservatism, his was a notable victory. The extent to which it could be related to Kemmy's views on the national question was debatable. Nevertheless, B & ICO felt able to claim that 'Limerick workers' had seen 'through nationalism'.[153] In the 1977 general election Kemmy, though unsuccessful, won 2,333 votes. In the same election Eamonn O'Brien, of the Socialist Party of Ireland, took 2,189 votes (6%) of the poll in Dublin North. The Socialist Party also supported the idea of a 'two-state' solution to the Northern crisis. In 1978, the B & ICO, the Socialist Party and Kemmy's group formed Socialists Against Nationalism.[154] In November 1979, Kemmy's *Limerick Socialist* gave its verdict on ten years of conflict:

> we believe that unity can only be achieved through bloodshed and violence, that it would bring no material benefit to the majority of the people in the South, that unification would be used as a distraction to impede progress and the concept is just another of these sentimental, empty, meaningless myths on which the citizens of this state have been nurtured. The game is not worth the candle.[155]

'A lot of violence coming'

Some accounts suggest the term 'revisionism' itself was introduced 'into Irish debate by Desmond Fennell'.[156] Fennell was a Catholic intellectual, living in the Connemara Gaeltacht when the northern crisis began. He rapidly gained prominence for encouraging discussion with loyalists about a federal solution to the Irish question. During the early 1970s, he worked with both the Provisionals and the SDLP and was associated with a variant of the 'two-nations' idea.[157] Fennell, however, rejected such a label, arguing instead that in Ireland there was 'one nation and part of another'.[158]

By the mid 1970s, he was aligned with Sinn Féin, a regular *An Phoblact* columnist and credited with influencing the Provisional's Éire Nua policy. Though some on the left branded him a 'fascist', Fennell and his ideas, which he himself described as 'revisionist', were part of a broader debate, as republicans struggled to understand why their early hopes of victory had receded.[159] In 1973, Fennell asserted while that in the 26 Counties there had been 'progress of sorts' until the 1940s, now the Dublin establishment had gone 'beyond the Redmondite position and reacted right back to the attitudes and aims of the Anglo-Irish Protestant Ascendancy'.[160] In early 1972, Fennell warned that there was 'a lot of violence coming'. But while he thought that this would 'be fanned by the war in the North', he also believed that it would 'lack anything like the rational purpose of "getting the British out." It will be more like the irrational, deliberately desecrating violence of the French revolution.' This impending violence was aided by an 'assault on the nation's system of values by what you might call "top people."' Fennell contended that in the first decades after independence, 'the Irish nation in the 26 counties built up a public value-system which was also accepted, in its essentials, by the nationalist people in the North'. The 'sacred-cows' of this value-system included

> the Easter Rising, the Friday fast and sexual purity ... the politician with a national record, the minister of religion, and loyalty to our people in the North ... High in honour stood the Irish language, the idea of rural life, the inviolability of marriage, the virgin (especially if consecrated to God) national ballads and the Angelus on the national radio, and Radio Eireann itself ... This was the public value system which was restraining the latent violence in our nation.[161]

Fennell suggested that 'the two pillars of this system of civil values were Irish Catholicism and Sinn Féin nationalism – that remarkable synthesis of all the elements in Irish nationalism which was achieved between 1916 and 1921'.[162] Now, Fennell saw the same forces that favoured liberalization as intent on undermining nationality. Despite his desire to include Ulster Protestants in a new Ireland, he rejected the idea that an Irish Republic would have to liberalize to accommodate them. Thus he welcomed Leinster House's rejection of a bill to legalize contraception in 1972, asserting that 'the liberal establishment and Dublin bourgeois interests may want such a law' but 'the vast majority of citizens don't'.[163]

'Seoinin or conformist'

Writing in *An Phoblacht*, Fennell proposed the republicans cease referencing Wolfe Tone as their ideological touchstone. He asserted that if Tone arrived in the Ireland of 1974

> nothing in it would worry him except that there was a majority of Papists in the Dublin Parliament. He expressly stated that care must be taken to prevent this. As a Jacobin, he would be delighted to note the fine job of centralising government in Dublin done over the past 150 years. And he would rejoice that nearly all the Gaelic-speaking peasants had been civilised and taught to speak English. He might regret that there weren't men of more mettle at the head of government but he would see that as something which the next election could set right. Clearly, it is absurd to say that Irish Republicanism today means 'what Wolfe Tone wanted.'

Fennell argued that republicans should recognize 'that, in the first 20 years of this century, Irish republicanism was reborn and "changed utterly"'.[164] Some activists were uncomfortable with this. Critics noted that he was not actually a member of the republican movement.[165] But his regular attacks on Cruise

O'Brien, Garret FitzGerald and the 'Dublin establishment' struck a chord, as did his critique of liberalism. Fennell asserted that 'it is a fair rule of thumb to say that "liberal" means seoinin or conformist ... a slave-soul' and the 'direct opposite of a nationalist'.[166]

While Fennell's use of terms such as 'our British fellow countrymen' and his willingness to discuss an independent Ulster illustrated a desire to accomodate loyalists, he displayed a hard, sectarian edge on occasion.[167] Following the Kingsmills massacre in early 1976, *An Phoblacht* carried a range of views on the spiralling series of killings. Fennell proposed that if loyalist attacks did not cease then republicans should warn of a 'massive Catholic' backlash 'backed up by the full force of the IRA-600lb car-bombs and all'.[168] Deasún Breathnach countered that such a policy could not be justified 'morally, politically, strategically or tactically'.[169] Fennell also provoked an angry response when he wrote that the working class in Ireland was 'a minority of the nation (and) not uniquely oppressed'. He argued that 'the people of Connacht ... suffer more oppression and have considerably less power. The same might be said of the people of the Gaeltacht, or the people of Cavan and Monaghan or the small cattle-farmers or the young married couples of the Dublin suburbs.' In contrast, he asserted, many workers were highly paid and some of them remained 'mentally more in England than in Ireland'.[170] Among those responding, 'working class republican' described Fennell's article as 'reminiscent of the worst of the British Tory gutter press'.[171] By the end of the 1970s, Fennell was no longer welcome at the newly leftist *An Phoblacht/Republican News*. However, what he called his 'revisionist crusade' had helped establish a nationalist critique of liberalism.[172]

The northern crisis shaped much of the debate in southern Ireland during the 1970s. It was far more than an academic discussion and driven as much by confusion as by a desire to refute old mythologies. People could agree with aspects of the revisionist argument but recoil from others, while many retained a basic republicanism but were disillusioned by the ongoing war. For some it was reaction to a particular atrocity that changed their viewpoint. In the aftermath of the Birmingham bombs, sculptor Desmond McNamara reflected that 'it looks as if Conor Cruise O'Brien is right. I always thought he exaggerated.'[173] In the 1979 edition of his study of the IRA, Bowyer Bell suggested that 'CS gas did more for the Provos than all the legends of heroes and the patriot graves'.[174] Similarly, far more views are likely to have been changed by events such as Birmingham than by revisionist histories.

Notes

1 *An Phoblacht*, 22 June 1973.
2 *Irish Times*, 9 Feb. 1972.
3 H. Patterson, 'Unionism, 1921–1972' in A. Jackson (Ed.) *The Oxford Handbook of Modern Irish History* (Oxford, 2014) p. 695.
4 *This Week*, 5 March 1971.

5 J. Horgan, *Noel Browne: Passionate Outsider* (Dublin, 2000) p. 244.
6 *Irish Times*, 16 May 1978. See also *Magill*, July 1978.
7 Ibid., 3 Jan. 1972.
8 *An Phoblacht*, 28 Sept. 1977.
9 *Sunday World*, 7 April 1974.
10 *An Phoblacht*, 22 June 1973.
11 *Irish Times*, 10 Jan. 1980.
12 *Anglo-Celt*, 15 March 1974.
13 *Ireland's Own*, 29 Dec. 1972.
14 *Sunday Independent*, 19 May 1975.
15 *Irish Times*, 8 Jan. 1972.
16 O. O'Leary, www.ewartbiggsprize.org.uk2013–2/olivia-olearys-speech [accessed 2 Jan. 2018].
17 J. O'Callaghan, *Teaching Irish Independence: History in Irish Schools, 1922–72* (Cambridge, 2009) p. 62.
18 *Irish Times*, 1 Dec. 1972.
19 Memoranda for the Information of the Government Policy in relation to Northern Ireland, 28 Nov. 1969, in Hillery Papers, P205/36 UCDA.
20 *Hibernia*, March–April 1962. I am grateful to Carole Holohan for this reference.
21 *Irish Times*, 29 Aug. 1969
22 Ibid., 4 March 1972.
23 *The Kerryman*, 1 Jan. 1972.
24 C.C. O'Brien, *Herod: Reflections on Political Violence* (London, 1978) p. 11.
25 *Comment*, 30 June 1978.
26 F. O'Connor, 'Gageby's Northern crusade' in A. Whitaker, A. (Ed.) *Bright, Brilliant Days, Douglas Gageby and the Irish Times* (Dublin, 2006) pp. 83–89.
27 *Irish Times*, 9 Feb. and 19 April 1972.
28 Ibid., 22 and 29 Jan. 1972.
29 *Longford Leader*, 11 Feb. 1972.
30 M. O'Brien, *Irish Press*, p. 153.
31 *Magill*, Nov. 1978.
32 Hanley and Millar, *Revolution*, pp. 205 and 307.
33 *Sunday Independent*, 20 Sept. 1976.
34 Ibid., 14 Aug. 1977.
35 Ibid., 9 May 1976.
36 *Magill*, Dec. 1977 and Jan. 1978.
37 *An Phoblacht*, 13 July 1977.
38 *Word*, March 1971.
39 *Republican News*, May 1971. See also *This Week*, 17 Dec. 1970 and *Hibernia*, 18 Dec. 1970.
40 *Woman's Way*, 18 Feb. 1972.
41 *Hibernia*, 20 Oct. 1972. By Official Sinn Féin's Tomas Mac Giolla.
42 *Irish Times*, 13 Feb. and 23 March 1974.
43 *Sunday Independent*, 25 April 1976.
44 Ibid., 30 May 1976.
45 *An Phoblacht*, 19 Oct. 1977.
46 *Irish Press*, 15 April 1977.
47 *An Phoblacht*, 1 Feb. 1978.
48 B. Harvey, *Cosgrave's Coalition* (London, 1980) p. 75.
49 *Irish Times*, 20 Aug. 1969.
50 Ibid., 23 Oct. 1969.
51 *Irish Times*, 31 Jan. 1972.

52 *Sunday Independent*, 1 June 1975.
53 *An Phoblacht*, 5 July 1974.
54 *Irish Times*, 15 May 1971.
55 T.F. Roe to L. Cosgrave, 6 Oct. 1972, in FitzGerald Papers P215/4 UCDA.
56 *Irish Times*, 18 Feb. 1977.
57 Ibid., 19 Feb. 1977.
58 Ibid., 11 June 1977.
59 *Magill*, May 1978.
60 *The Kerryman*, 12 Feb. 1972.
61 *Profile*, Dec. 1973.
62 Maguire, 'Defenders of the State', pp. 1–20 .
63 *Sunday Independent*, 29 May 1977.
64 *Irish Times*, 20 Jan. 1973.
65 *Dáil Debates*, 16 December 1971, No. 12, Vol. 257.
66 *Irish Press*, 11 Oct. 1971.
67 *Magill*, July 1978.
68 A measure of the divisions is illustrated by Barry Desmond's claim that 'Dr. John O'Connell, Justin Keating, David Thornley and Michael Mullen (in effect) supported the murderous IRA campaigns'. Review of J. McGinley (Ed.) *Frank Cluskey: the Conscience of Labour* (Dublin, 2015) in *Dublin Review of Books,* Feb. 2016.
69 *The Kerryman*, 21 July 1974.
70 Ibid., 15 Jan. 1972.
71 Ibid., 29 Jan. 1972
72 Ibid., 12 Feb. 1972.
73 Ibid., 5 Feb. 1972.
74 Ibid., 19 Feb. 1972.
75 Ibid., 26 April 1974.
76 *Irish Independent*, 8 Feb. 1974.
77 *The Kerryman*, May 1974.
78 *Irish Independent*, 8 Feb. 1974.
79 *The Kerryman*, 24 May 1974.
80 Ibid., 17 May 1974.
81 Ibid., 13 Aug. 1976.
82 *Irish Times*, 12 Jan. 1991. The phrase was John Water's.
83 Ibid.
84 *Western People*, 15 Jan. 1972.
85 Ibid., 4 March 1972.
86 Ibid., 25 May 1974.
87 *An Phoblacht*, 31 May 1974.
88 Ibid., 17 Oct. and 14 May 1976.
89 Ibid., 31 May 1974.
90 D. Ó Corráin, *Rendering to God and Caesar: The Irish Churches and the Two States in Ireland, 1949–73* (Manchester, 2008) pp. 161–162.
91 *Irish Times*, 29 Dec. 1971.
92 *Irish Press*, 8 Dec. 1975.
93 Ibid., 24 Oct. 1972.
94 *Irish Times*, 29 Dec. 1971.
95 *Irish Press*, 25 Dec. 1971.
96 Though their deaths were described somewhat ambiguously as from 'street violence.'
97 C. Daly, *Violence in Ireland and Christian Conscience* (Dublin, 1973) p. 41.
98 Ibid., pp. 149–151.
99 *Irish Times*, 28 Aug. 1976.

100 C. Daly, *Violence*, p. 53.
101 Ibid., p. 67.
102 *Irish Times*, 19 March 1974.
103 Ibid., 28 Aug. 1976.
104 C. Daly, *Violence*, p. 90.
105 *An Phoblacht*, 25 Jan. 1977.
106 C. Daly, *Violence*, p. 49.
107 *Irish Times*, 1 Jan. 1980.
108 *An Phoblacht*, 22 June 1973.
109 *Irish Times*, 19 March 1974.
110 *Sunday World*, 13 Jan. 1974. *The Kerryman*, 15 Feb. 1974.
111 *Irish Press*, 15 April 1977.
112 *An Phoblacht*, 26 April 1977.
113 *Irish Times*, 15 March 1972.
114 Ibid., 18 April 1977.
115 *Irish Press*, 19 April 1977.
116 Ibid., 31 March 1975.
117 J.A. Murphy, 'Further reflections on Irish Nationalism', *The Crane Bag* 2 No. 1/2 (1978) pp. 156–163.
118 *Irish Press*, 28 Dec. 1978.
119 R. Sweetman, *On Our Backs: Sexual Attitudes in a Changing Ireland* (London, 1979) pp. 231–239.
120 Liam de Paor, 'UCD and the Pattern of Revolt' in P. Pettit (Ed.) *The Gentle Revolution: Crisis in the Universities* (Dublin, 1969) pp. 60–66.
121 *New Statesman*, 11 Feb. 1972.
122 *Irish Times*, 21 Aug. 1973.
123 Purcell, *RTE*, p. 37.
124 Colm Tóibín, 'New ways of killing your father', *London Review of Books*, 18 Nov. 1993.
125 Ibid., p. 33.
126 *An Phoblacht*, 14 Feb. 1973 and 14 Feb. 1975.
127 Ibid., 1 Feb. 1974.
128 *Irish Independent*, 24 May 1976.
129 *Irish Times*, 31 May 1976.
130 *An Phoblacht*, 11 May 1977.
131 *An Phoblacht/Republican News*, 14 April 1979.
132 Ibid., 12 May 1979.
133 People's Democracy internal document, 1972. Sean O'Mahony Papers, Ms. 44,241/1 NLI.
134 *Irish Times*, 5 April 1972.
135 Ibid., 12 June 1971.
136 Ibid., 27 July 1972.
137 A. Madden, *Fear and Loathing*, pp. 17–18.
138 *Irish Press*, 3 Dec. 1973.
139 *Fortnight*, 8 March 1972.
140 *Workers' Weekly*, 18 May 1974.
141 *Comment*, 29 July 1974.
142 Ibid., 11 June 1976.
143 *Irish Times*, 29 June 1974.
144 WADSNCI leaflet, 1974, John De Courcy Ireland Papers, UCDA P29/A/27.
145 *Comment*, 11 June 1976.
146 *Irish Times*, 5 Oct. 1977.

147 British & Irish Communist Organisation, *The Rise of Papal Power in Ireland* (Belfast, 1979).

148 British & Irish Communist Organisation, *Stalin and the Irish Working Class* (Belfast, 1980).

149 *The Kerryman*, 21 July 1974. *Republican News*, 15 June 1974. *Irish Socialist*, Sept. 1974. Since the 1990s, the organization has performed a volte-face and are strongly nationalist. See 'From Peking to Aubane' www.Indymedia.ie/article/80451 [accessed 2 Jan. 2016].

150 G. FitzGerald to M. O'Riordan, 27 Sept. 1972, in FitzGerald Papers, UCDA P215/4.

151 D. Finn, 'Challengers to Provisional Republicanism: The Official Republican Movement, People's Democracy and the Irish Republican Socialist Party, 1968–1998' (PhD: UCC, 2013). pp. 185–188.

152 *Limerick Socialist*, May 1974.

153 *Comment*, 21 June 1974.

154 Ibid., 21 April 1978.

155 *Limerick Socialist*, Nov. 1979.

156 Conor McCarthy, *Modernisation: Crisis and Culture in Ireland 1969–1992* (Dublin, 2000) pp. 17–18.

157 *Irish Times*, 26 Aug. and 15 Sept. 1969.

158 D. Fennell, *Nice People and Rednecks: Ireland in the 1980s* (Dublin, 1986) p. 57.

159 *An Phoblacht*, 12 Oct. 1973.

160 Ibid., 21 Sept. 1973.

161 *Sunday Press*, 2 Jan. 1972.

162 Ibid., 9 Jan. 1972.

163 Ibid., 13 Feb. 1972.

164 *An Phoblacht*, 18 Jan. 1974.

165 Ibid., 17 Oct. 1975.

166 *An Phoblacht*, 7 Nov. 1975.

167 Ibid., 27 June 1975.

168 Ibid., 23 Jan. 1976.

169 Ibid., 30 Jan. 1976.

170 Ibid., 7 and 14 Mar. 1975.

171 Ibid., 14 Mar. 1975.

172 D. Fennell, *The Revision of Irish Nationalism* (Dublin, 1989) pp. 30–31.

173 Desmond McNamara to Seamus De Burca, 14 December 1974, in De Burca Papers, Ms. 39,142 NLI. I am grateful to Fearghal McGarry for sharing this reference.

174 J. Bowyer Bell, *The Secret Army: The IRA* (Dublin, 1979) p. 376.

10

'Practically a foreign country'?[1]

In 1966, Tim Pat Coogan suggested that 'the level of physical contact between North and South is low. The average Southerner does not go North either for holidays or day excursions.'[2] Two years later, a British writer contended that 'to the majority of people in the Irish Republic ... Ulster is practically a foreign country ... Most Southern Irishmen have never been "up there" and they seem to have little desire to go.' He quoted a Waterford businessman who told him that 'Northern Ireland just doesn't come into the sweep of my thinking ... I went up there once. It didn't seem very Irish.'[3] Liam de Paor claimed that until the outbreak of the Troubles, most people in the Republic 'knew little and thought less about Northern Ireland, a place which for many of them was far more remote than (London's) Paddington or Notting Hill'.[4]

'All kinds of magic'

Yet according to the first Gallup survey of Irish attitudes, published in 1968, 41% of southern respondents had visited Northern Ireland in the previous two years and one in five had been there more than once.[5] Indeed, many living in the border counties travelled back and forth daily. For others, such as one Dublin youngster, the North was 'the place where bus excursions used to go on shopping trips, and we, as a group of teenagers, found all kinds of magic ... from men-only magazines to fireworks, to the latest English fashions and people with funny accents'.[6] One northern nationalist discerned during the 1960s that 'a sizeable gap had developed between the northern six counties and the twenty-six counties' with many southerners believing that 'we were better off economically and that we had a better education system and of course better roads! Some of them seemed to think that they would have been better off under British rule.'[7] Even in the midst of the conflict, southern visitors could find the North 'very modern compared to the Republic ... like entering a mini Britain. You had all the high street shops ... there were great car accessory shops, cool clothes and instruments you simply could not get in the South at the same price.'[8]

Unity

In 1968, there was a strong emotional attachment to idea of united Ireland, with 67% believing that the border would eventually go and only 22% thinking that it would remain.[9] But by 1978, 52% of the respondents to an IMS poll had never been in Northern Ireland. Of those who had, 9% had visited in the previous year and 10% had been there in the previous five years; 28% had not been in the North for a decade or longer.[10] This was obviously linked to the ongoing violence, though along the border interaction had continued if not as normal, then certainly as routine. A majority of those questioned still desired a united Ireland, 57% believing that the partition would eventually end, while 27% thought the border would stay. Most people (65%) rejected the idea of getting rid of Articles 2 and 3 (the Republic's territorial claim).[11] The poll confirmed the results of a previous survey by *Magill* magazine which found 63% of respondents wanted a united Ireland, 64% were opposed to dropping Articles 2 and 3 and a sizeable 33% desired unity whatever the cost.[12] Despite almost ten years of violence, the ideal of a united Ireland remained strong.

'It might as well be Vietnam'

Yet throughout the 1970s there was a pervasive sense of a widening gap. In 1974, one writer was dismayed to find that 'in the pubs of Dublin and Limerick and Cork men spoke of the North in the same unknowing and uncaring way as they might be expected to speak of Saigon or the Golan Heights'.[13] The same year, Belfast school student Brigid Cowan complained that 'people down here ... don't give a damn about the North. As far as they are concerned it might as well be Vietnam. They just don't understand and they don't come up either.'[14] Dervla Murphy thought that 'south of the Dublin–Galway line there is little sense of personal involvement with Northern Ireland; it seems much further than Britain, where so many people have lived and worked, or even the USA'. However, 'beyond Athlone' she 'noticed the North beginning to impinge, if only through complaints about the tourist trade; most of the Northerners who used to holiday in the Midlands or the West do so no longer'.[15] In 1966, Coogan had noted how 'a casual ear cocked in a Dublin restaurant or a Southern holiday resort will ordinarily pick up a considerable volume of northern cadences'. But violence had also led to a decline in the number of northerners coming south.[16]

The impact on counties such as Monaghan was considerable. Before the Troubles, 'people travelled across the border a lot and people took holidays on either side of the border. After 1969, all that stopped. There was a sense of decline ... young people left and the county became more elderly.' Towns such as Clones suffered particularly badly.[17] Even places far from the border felt the conflict's impact. Portlaoise in the midlands became defined as the town 'where the prison is', the scene of 'another story of prisoner transfers, mass protests or, now and again, attempted or even successful escapes'.[18] Residents became used to the considerable military presence and for some of the young this brought excitment: 'it was like a game ... the marching and shouting and roaring, boys up on the roof taking tiles off and smashing the windows'.[19] One of the most obvious signs of how the war had impacted on southern life was soldiers outside banks and army landrovers escorting security vans. In 1979, Anthony Cronin watched troops standing 'uneasily with their weapons at the ready' outside a bank in Roscrea, and pondered how 'more precautions (and) more armed men were needed to convey money from place to place in Ireland than ever were necessary to ferry gold dust from camp to railroad in the American West'.[20]

'Baffling complexity'

During early 1975, the British Ambassador reported a decline in sympathy for republicanism in southern Ireland. He described it as 'a commentary on the baffling complexity of the Anglo-Irish relationship' that the single event which contributed most to this was the Birmingham bombings. He concluded that because the bombs happened

> on the evening of the day when public opinion in Dublin had shown much warmth to Earl Mountbatten of Burma, the Prime Minister and the leader of the Opposition for their attendance at President Childer's funeral (it) produced a tremendous impact of shock on opinion in the Republic, no doubt because it was feared that the large Irish Community in Britain would suffer a backlash.[21]

He also suggested that Birmingham seemed to have had a bigger impact than the bombs in Dublin and Monaghan. From the South, the conflict was not only viewed in terms of how it might 'spill over' the border but on how it affected Irish people in Britain. Shortly after Birmingham, an emigrant in London complained in the *Irish Press* that 'the IRA has made the lot of the Irish in England an unhappy one; they're embarrassed and repelled by the savagery, and disturbed by the understandable hostility of English people'.[22] In the midst of the agitation for the Price sisters' repatriation in 1974, a Tralee woman, Pauline Carmody, wrote that she was 'Irish, 24 years old, and love my country as much as anyone. I ... am nursing in one of the London hospitals, where some of the injured were taken after the London bomb blast in which the Price sisters were involved.' She asked whether the campaigners had seen 'the horrible injuries that some of these innocent people received (the) limbs and eyes that some of these people lost'? How, she asked 'would they react, if one day, while doing their shopping ... their wives were blinded and scarred by a bomb. Would they then talk about the human dignity of the bombers?'[23]

Some years later, another Tralee man on a visit to see a friend who played for Middlesbrough Football Club recounted how 'everything was going wonderfully well for us until the Monday of the Lord Mountbatten bombing. I could hardly speak ten words that day. You would be ashamed to open your mouth.'[24] Civil servants reported that among the Irish in Britain, reaction to the same incident ranged from keeping their heads 'very much down' to the feeling that they had been 'let down' by people at home.[25] IRA activities in Britain produced a range of emotions in the Republic ranging from fear to shame. To the dismay of northern nationalists, they often seemed to provoke more outrage than what was happening in the North itself.

'England is always seen as our enemy'

In 1971, there were 709,235 Irish-born people in Britain.[26] Many thousands of southerners had relatives or friends in England's cities, while fewer had contacts north of the border. Emigrants could potentially be victims of IRA bombs (among those injured in Birmingham were people with surnames like Farrell, O'Brien, O'Connor, O'Connell, Twomey and O'Gorman) and of either police harassment or anti-Irish abuse in their wake.[27] In December 1974, the Donegal-born parents of the brothers Desmond and Eugene O'Reilly, killed in Birmingham, led a peace march in Dublin.[28] Many Irish people had also lived in Britain and maintained contact with the country. After the IRA attempted to kill a Scotland Yard employee in Cavan during 1976, the Bishop of Kilmore's statement condemning the shooting was read at all masses in the district. Bishop McKiernan described how there were many

> families in Cavan whose sons and daughters went to Britain in search of a livelihood and married English spouses. Up to now a feature of every Christmas and summer in the town was their visits home. It was not only in the immediate families that the English in-laws were made welcome. Neighbours always joined in making them feel at home. There was no discrimination on grounds of their religion, their politics or their means of livelihood. They were married to our own and that was enough to entitle them to our friendship. Now the gunman has come to Cavan town, how can we explain to our relatives, that there is a minority in our midst whose idea of patriotism, of love of homeland, is so monstrously perverse, that it leads them to shoot down a young mother in the very street in which she was born and reared and loved?[29]

At the funeral of hunger-striker Michael Gaughan, the officiating priest caused uproar when he stated that while 'England is always seen as our enemy … one might think how good a country it has been to us in the past, giving us work, opportunities and money'.[30] Objecting to a call for a boycott of British visitors to Kerry, another emigrant asserted that 'my husband is a builder's labourer. What chance would my children have if we lived in Tralee? They would be lucky if they were road sweepers.' She hoped that the boycotters 'will not burn our British money or car when we visit the town next August'.[31] As a Tipperary man explained during 1971, 'socially London is nearer than Dublin to the plain people of Wexford, Kilkenny, Clonmel, Limerick and Tralee'. Irish people there were 'breadwinners of parents and relatives at home' where many depended on 'emigrants remittances and pensions'.[32] Claiming that independent Ireland had failed its own people, Noel Browne noted how since 1921 'one million Irish Republicans were hunted by hunger from the Republic to be fed, clothed, and cared for by the British'.[33]

'All West Britons'?

Cultural links with Britain had become even stronger during the 1960s through fashion, music and sport. One future IRA man recalled how in Dublin he 'knew no one who didn't cheer when England won the World Cup in 1966; no one for whom London or Liverpool wasn't a spiritual capital'.[34] By the early 1970s, thousands were travelling across the Irish Sea to support English football teams.[35] In May 1970, the England World Cup's squad song, 'Back Home', reached No. 2 in the Irish charts. Even Chelsea FC's League Cup song 'Blue Is The Colour' made the Irish Top Ten in 1972.[36] Since the 1950s, sales of English newspapers had been growing along with interest in British radio and, where available, television. By the early 1970s, British Sunday papers *The People* and the *News of the World* were selling almost 250,000 copies in Ireland. By the mid decade, the *Daily Mirror* sold over 50,000 a day.[37] Children in the Republic were avid consumers of British war comics such as *Warlord* and *Victor*.[38] Sociologist Mícheál Mac Gréil suggested that the large number of Dubliners who saw Northerners as 'extreme and unreasonable' was not unrelated to the popularity of British mass media in the city.[39]

In 1971, 63% of those with television sets received RTE only.[40] But in the north and east people could access British channels, and by 1972 RTE was losing large numbers of viewers to the British stations.[41] In 1970, cable television arrived in Dublin, but was not accessible across much of the country. The demand for cable to facilitate receiving British channels was widespread and even became an election issue in Cork during 1973.[42] Given the popularity of British sport, television and music, it might appear that if 'culture is to be defined by the daily lives of ordinary people, then we were all West Britons of one sort or another'.[43]

'Our culture is dying'

Gene Kerrigan suggested Dublin teenagers in the 1960s identified with British culture not because 'we were Anglophiles' but because 'we just preferred the bright to the grey, the exciting to the dull' and England 'outshone our grey surroundings'.[44] But there also remained some feeling of cultural inferiority; as Ed O'Riordan recalled, 'British pop-stars were regarded as more glamorous, exciting and interesting. An Irish band getting a number one hit in the Irish charts was not really as good as number twenty in the British charts. An English accent was always more authoritative than an Irish one.'[45]

Some elements of British culture remained controversial. In November 1973, RTE provided live coverage of the wedding of Princess Anne and Mark Philips.[46] But over 2,000 householders in south Dublin were unable to watch the event because their coaxial cable had been deliberately sawn through and a note objecting to the coverage left beside it. Clearly some agreed that it was only 'sycophantic, slavish and servile sheep' who would contemplate watching 'the wedding of the representatives of our conquerors'.[47] That some British children's comics glorified war and promoted the British military was also a source of worry.[48] Calling for a boycott of RTE in 1978, one republican complained that 'Gaelic football ... is by far the most popular sport in Ireland. Nevertheless, RTE is at constant pains to suggest that rugby and association football (soccer) are almost as popular.'[49] During 1975, an angry GAA supporter complained that on RTE 'we saw Manchester United play West Ham ... our culture is dying and the shame of it is that we, the Irish, are killing it'.[50] Sports writer Tom O'Dea responded to the emergence of crowd trouble at Croke Park by arguing that

> football violence has drifted across the Irish Sea to the multi-channel area, borne on the airways from Britain. Soon, it will drift further inland, like poison gas, and spread to the rest of the country, because on October 4, RTE will begin its rebroadcasting of 'Match of the Day'.[51]

Such issues would have troubled some anyway during the 1970s, but they were sharpened by the fact that a war was raging north of the border.

'Be a bit more Republican'

It was possible to watch British TV, follow English soccer and still resent everything that England 'represented in our own history'.[52] Footballer Eamon Dunphy might remember how in his youth

> we read English newspapers, followed English soccer, spoke the English language and listened to the BBC. Soon those who could afford it would be watching English television ... the idea that you could prove you were a patriot by hating England was frankly ridiculous in the Ireland I grew up in.[53]

But after Bloody Sunday, while playing for Millwall, Dunphy donned a black armband in memory of the Derry dead. During 1974 (while at Charlton Athletic), he spoke at a rally in London in support of the Price sisters.[54] Indeed, many of those joining the IRA 'were the type of ordinary young men you would find in any British or Irish city. They listened to the same music, wore similar fashionable clothes and often followed the same English soccer clubs.'[55] The 1970s saw the emergence of the Dublin Gaelic football team as a popular phenomenon. Much of their fans' iconography was drawn from the terraces of English soccer, down to the singing of 'You'll Never Walk Alone' on Hill 16. This drew suspicion from within the GAA. However, League of Ireland footballer Fran Gavin suggested that it was also a way for some Dubliners to express republican sentiments:

> it was the height of the Troubles … it was a very tense time in Ireland, so people felt that this was their game and they felt a loyalty to it. Dublin never did (before) because it was a Culchies' game and soccer was always Dublin … but now we had a very strong Dublin GAA team and the soccer fans had a reason to follow the Gaelic team and to be a bit more Republican.

While the team's success was the reason for their popularity, 'we also had this little Republican thing going in the background and those soccer fans who didn't like GAA' had 'an excuse to say … it is not really GAA, it is the Dubs'.[56]

'A pretty decent people'

By 1971, the relationship between Ireland and Britain was no longer a question of history. In the words of the Barleycorn song, 'Cromwell's men' *were* here again. Images of British soldiers shooting Irish people in their own country were flashed across TV screens. In early 1972, Dublin cinemas were forced to censor the Movietone news segments that were played before the main feature. A spokesman for the Capitol cinema explained that recently one had shown

> the Lord Mayor of Belfast making a speech in which he referred to the IRA as 'murdering gunmen.' We deleted it for fear of reprisals. In the present Movietone roughly 30 to 60 seconds have been cut. We have been in touch with the makers of Movietone and in the light of present circumstances they agreed to their newsreel being cut by us. They realise what may be accepted by English audiences may not go down so well here.[57]

But there appeared to be little real hostility to the British per se. Research conducted in Dublin during 1972 found almost 90% agreed that 'the British are a pretty decent people'; 36% had no objection to the British people but disliked their government; 27.5% thought that 'British soldiers are generally cruel and brutal' – though 57.4% disagreed with that proposition in the year of Bloody Sunday.[58] In the protests following that massacre, British nationals in several parts of the Republic received threats and holiday homes were burnt out in Kerry.[59] But many agreed with the *Longford Leader*'s assertion that 'given the facts of our cause' the British people 'could be our greatest friends and greatest allies'.[60] In Tipperary, Sinn Féin asserted that 'we have no fight against English people. They have always been accepted (here) and we are sure they will continue to be so.'[61]

Many distinguished between the British military and the rest of that society, particularly the working class. A *Kerryman* correspondent asserted in 1973 that 'there is no better man than the British working man – when led by (trade unionist) Vic Feather, rather than Brigadier Kitson'.[62] In the midst of an angry denunciation of collaboration with Britain, one republican could still assert that 'the ordinary English people are decent kindly people and (I) have often been treated kindly by them'.[63]

But visceral anti-Britishness remained a factor for those who saw Britain as culturally as well as politically alien. Right-wing activist Úna Mhic Mhathuna responded to Pauline Carmody's condemnation of the London bombs by suggesting that 'perhaps she will write again on the same subject from her experience as a nurse in London, and tell us of the systematic and State-sponsored murder of thousands of babies which goes on, year in, year out, in the hospitals where she earns her bread'.[64] Fr. Denis Faul, a high-profile campaigner against internment (though not an IRA supporter), would contend in 1974 that the aim of Britain's 'gross anti-Catholic, anti-Irish policy' was to 'force the South of Ireland to abandon its Gaelic and Catholic characteristics and moral values and become a State acceptable, culturally and socially, to the British neo-pagan way of life'.[65] Noting the centuries of 'Bloody Sundays and regular pogroms', a Portarlington man added 'the number of Irish women who are going to England to have their unborn children murdered and we get a grand total of killings, but no screaming headlines … there is no howl unless an Irishman kills an invader'.[66]

'As nationally minded as anyone else'

And what of Irishmen who wore the uniform of the invader? When Dublin car assembly workers marched after Bloody Sunday, their ranks included 'many ex-British servicemen who are sickened by the actions of this uniformed body of killers'.[67] Waterford CIE tractor driver Bill Collins, an ex-Sherwood Forester and veteran of Anzio, went to 10 Downing St. and returned his war medals, one of a number of Irish veterans who did so.[68] Service in the British military had not been unusual for men from southern Ireland, and did not neccesarily imply support for British policy.[69] After the firebombing of the British Legion club in Cork in 1970, an ex-soldier claimed that 'It makes no sense at all to me … I may have joined the British Army, but I'm as nationally minded as anyone else.'[70]

But by 1971, Irish-born soldiers, such as 25-year-old Private Robert Benner, were being killed. Though Benner had left Dundalk in his teenage years, joining the British Army in 1964, his death caused much local disquiet. *Hibernia* noted that in the early 1960s, 'many from the area were enlisting, including some who now hold high office in the local Republican movement'. Benner had been visiting his fiancée when he was abducted.[71] In the aftermath of his death, Mairin Lynch (wife of Taoiseach Jack Lynch) wrote to the press to ask 'what right have these so-called arbiters of justice to wreck the lives of young people'?[72] When Private Thomas McCann from Drimnagh in Dublin (who also had a brother in the Royal Air Force) was murdered in February 1972, his family asked that there be no representative of the British Embassy or the British Army at his funeral.[73] In contrast, after Martin Rooney, a soldier in the Royal Anglian Regiment, was killed in Belfast in July that year, hundreds attended his funeral in Carrick-on-Shannon and Leitrim County Council passed a motion of sympathy. Rooney had been a member of the FCA and his brother was serving in the Irish Army.[74]

'Under the heel of the British'

Ex-British soldiers were also represented in the leadership of some of the state's trade unions. In 1970, there were 386,800 trade union members in the Republic of Ireland, around 52% of the workforce.[75] Strikes and industrial relations were a feature of everyday life and union leaders had high media profiles. The largest union, the 150,000 strong ITGWU, was organized in Northern Ireland, where it had 6,400 members. The Irish National Teachers Organisation also had 3,500 members in the North.[76] Both it and the ITGWU's northern membership were overwhelmingly Catholic in composition. But almost 20 trade unions in the Republic, with 54,800 members, had their headquarters in Britain and organized both north and south of the border.[77] The most important of these was the ATGWU, which had 20,000 members in the Republic. In Northern Ireland, however, the ATGWU organized over 70,000, both Catholic and Protestant.[78] Rivalry (with deep historical roots) between these bodies influenced their reactions.[79] A factor in attitudes was also the opportunity to settle scores over other grievances. In August 1969, the ITGWU's *Liberty* asserted that

> once more, Irish men and women are suffering hardship and anguish resulting from (the) economic and political power and sway which Britain continues to exercise over part of our motherland. That this power is in the control of a British socialist government and local Tory hardliners makes it no less palatable to Irishmen then it ever has been down the past six hundred years or so.

Liberty criticized the president of the Irish Congress of Trade Unions James Morrow, a member of the 'British-based ... AEFU' (Amalgamated Union of

Engineering and Foundry Workers) for not denouncing the 'killing, the maiming
and the abuse of Irish Catholic workers by the bigoted sectarian para-military
B Specials and their anti-Christ supporters led by a specimen of the male
species who claims to be a priest of sorts'. Morrow was Irish secretary of the
AEFU and a former Belfast shipyard worker. *Liberty*'s hostility may have been
partly related to the role his union played in the bitter maintenance dispute
of early 1969, in which the ITGWU and the craft unions had clashed.[80]
    As well as involvement in various relief efforts, during 1970 the ITGWU
began campaigning for the release of Belfast docker Joe McBrinn, a member
of its Executive, who was being held in England on arms charges. An indication
of the politics of some of its leadership came when Michael Mullen organized
a function for Fianna Fáil's Charles Haughey at Liberty Hall on the eve of the
Arms Trial. Mullen was also close to people in both factions of the IRA.[81]
After the introduction of internment, *Liberty* could not resist pointing out that

> it must surely be an extraordinary experience for any Irishman who is a member
> of a British trade union, to know that Irish workers in the Six Counties are being
> ground under the heel of the British jackboot. So much so, that all Irish workers
> in British trade unions in Ireland should demand that their unions condemn in
> the most forthright terms internment without trial (and) should demand that these
> same unions bring pressure on the British Government to atone for their six-county
> sins and make immediate reparation. It is the least we expect of them.[82]

However, many British-based unions in the Republic had been playing a part
in the protests. Bloody Sunday again brought these tensions to the surface.
The Navan Northern Aid Committee was among those calling on Irish workers
to leave British-based unions.[83] There was considerable pressure put on ATGWU
members to leave their union, despite the fact that three of Derry dead had
been members of it and the union's leader Matt Merrigan was prominent on
the republican left.[84]

'Never murdered a man in his life!'

A different tone was struck by the 31,000 strong WUI, which organized
exclusively in the South. The 1970 WUI conference voted to condemn gunrun-
ning, and its secretary Denis Larkin warned of the danger of 'civil war'.[85] In
general, the WUI's rhetoric was less nationalist than that of the ITGWU. At
the grave of the union's founder, James Larkin, in 1972, WUI president John
Foster asserted that 'it was not with bombs and bullets that Larkin first brought
together Catholic and Protestant'.[86]
    Clashes over the union's position on special powers arose at its May 1972
conference. When a delegate claimed that Jim Larkin had 'favoured violence',
Denis Larkin interjected that his father 'never murdered a man in his life!'
Instead he claimed that Larkin and Connolly 'taught Irishmen to fight for

Ireland, but they did not teach them to use guns or to plant bombs that would blow innocent passers-by into kingdom come'. A motion condemning the Special Criminal Court was defeated by 94 votes to 62.[87] While Michael Mullen and a number of other ITGWU activists had been members of the IRA, the WUI included among its senior leadership Paddy Cardiff and Jack Harte, both ex-British soldiers and Second World War veterans.[88] But some of the most vociferous opposition to 'assassination, terror and intimidation' came from the union's leader Denis Larkin and Frank Cluskey, a Labour TD and Dublin butcher.[89] On the 'national question', the British-based ATGWU took a more militant line than the Irish WUI. ATGWU activists in Waterford were to the fore in supporting the demands of hunger-strikers in Portlaoise and opposing emergency legislation.[90]

'All the good nationalists are dead'

There was also opposition to republican activity expressed by trade unionists. In 1977, members of the National Graphical Association at the *Galway Advertiser* refused to set or print an advert for a 'Brits Out' rally in Tuam as a 'peaceful protest against what is being done in the Six Counties'.[91] Frank Callaghan, the Irish leader of the militant and powerful engineering union, the (British-based) Amalgamated Union of Engineering Workers (AUEW), claimed in 1978 that

> nationalism creates problems. Most of it is pseudo – all the good nationalists are dead. Some unions use it as a way of attracting members. They forget that the trade union movement talks about internationalism, about working-class people getting together for better conditions.[92]

Union conferences were battlegrounds for issues connected to the conflict throughout the 1970s. It was not abstract for those who organized on either side of the border. At least six ITGWU members were killed in Belfast during 1972, and most of the workmen shot dead by the IRA at Kingsmills were in the ATGWU.[93] Though by definition representing the opinions of activists rather than all union members, many of the views that divided southerners in other spheres were expressed in the labour movement. They reflected what one activist referred to as 'the split in working class consciousness between the social and national questions – or even the lack of any interest in the national question'.[94]

'A quiet ban on our some of our finer ballads'

In August 1971, the Wolfe Tones withdrew £200 worth of advertising from RTE because the station decided that their radio ad for the LP 'Up The Rebels' was 'inflammatory'. The advert contained two 15-second excerpts of the songs 'Tricoloured Ribbon' and 'Song Of The Backwoods'.[95] It was apparent by late 1971 that RTE Radio had placed an unofficial ban on 'rebel' songs, despite there being no government instruction to do so. This became evident when the Barleycorn's 'The Men Behind The Wire' was such a huge hit, selling over 100,000 copies and topping the charts for five weeks. Though RTE claimed that they did not ban songs, and that 'traditional patriotic ballads were freely and regularly broadcast', the song was not played on RTE's 'Top Ten Show', because the station claimed it was not suitable for a pop music programme.[96] Tony Meade in the *Kerryman* noted how 'the shameless wretches in RTE' had 'placed a quiet ban on some of our finer ballads. And no come-back from anyone of note in the station decrying this action for the piece of nonsense it is.'[97] In April 1972, 'Over The Wall' by the Wolfhounds (a song about an IRA prison escape) reached No. 8 in the charts.[98] On RTE Radio's pop show, 'Discs a Gogan', DJ Larry Gogan mentioned the song, but did not play it.[99]

'Reflecting the feelings of the Nationalist people in the North'

Though there was no formal ban, 'rebel' songs were not played on RTE radio after 1972.[100] Nevertheless, they continued to be extremely popular. During the spring of 1972, two versions of 'Four Green Fields' made the top ten, while two songs about Bloody Sunday were hits – the Paddywagon's 'Sunday Bloody Sunday' going to No.1 in April. Sean Dunphy and the Hoedowners 'Michael Collins' was a No. 2 hit the same month, while the Wolfe Tone's 'On The One Road' reached No. 20.[101] Despite the lack of radio play, 'rebel' songs remained part of many bands' repertoires and the stock and trade of groups such as the Wolfe Tones.

More dramatically, songs which celebrated the escape of prisoners from southern Irish prisons were huge hits. In November 1973, the Wolfe Tones 'Up And Away' went straight in at No. 1 and spent four weeks there.[102] The song hailed the successful escape of three IRA leaders by helicopter from Mountjoy. After the Portlaoise escape in August 1974, Dermot Hegarty released '19 Men' – the tale of the republican jailbreakers who didn't use the door, 'just blew a little hole where there wasn't one before'. Despite receiving no airplay, it went to No. 1 – much to the chagrin of Minister for Justice Paddy Cooney, who wondered how 'a gramophone record exalting the Portlaoise escape has become a chart-topper'.[103] Earlier in 1974, the Barleycorn's 'Bring Them Home' in support of the Price sisters' campaign had reached No. 4. A song by the Wolfhounds remembering the hunger-striker 'Michael Gaughan' charted at No. 18 in October the same year. [104] Groups who recorded explicitly political songs could expect to be banned from radio – as The Freemen's album 'Sean South' was in 1975.[105]

Given that there was just one national radio channel and that it only played a few hours of music every day, recording such songs was obviously risky in career terms. In the North overtly pro-IRA music groups emerged, but they were largely unknown to those outside the movement. However, a number of more mainstream groups performed at republican functions, including the Barleycorn, the Dublin City Ramblers, Jim McCann and Paddy Reilly.[106] Many others recorded no political material but were happy to perform 'rebel' songs at concerts.

By far the most successful exponents of the genre were the Wolfe Tones, who had been performing since the 1960s. By the mid 1970s they were hugely successful, touring the United States and performing for the All Black's rugby team and the Manchester United squad among others. In 1978, the *Sunday Independent* noted how 'RTE may have banned most of their songs but the sobering fact remains that they are one of the biggest album sellers in Ireland after ABBA. "Let the People Sing" sold a staggering 150,000 copies-an incredible feat for the Irish market.' RTE's Liam Ó Murchú provided sleeve notes for the group's 'Belt Of The Celts', describing how 'recent years saw much new thinking in the cultural life of Ireland, some of it questioning the very basis of what Irishness means. The Wolfe Tones, I am happy to see, were never in any doubt about that.'[107] Band member Derek Warfield described their music as 'reflecting the feelings of the Nationalist people in the North'.[108] When questioned about the relationship between their music and politics, Warfield asserted that

> eleven years ago we had everyone following us and everyone loved our songs because they were Irish songs. But then when the trouble starts, all of a sudden the songs that we always sang and which were formerly perfectly acceptable, suddenly become treated as violence-orientated.

In his view, 'Irish history is full of violence, our folk songs deal with the history of the nation, therefore genuine folk songs must be about those violent times'.[109] Nevertheless, the Wolfe Tones did not explicitly identify with republican organizations, and their music was popular with a cross-section of the public. In 1975, the *Sunday World* cynically noted that 'for such a staunch republican group they don't venture North much'.[110] In contrast, Dermot O'Brien, whose 1966 bestseller 'The Merry Ploughboy' had summed up the celebratory nature of that year's commemorations of the Easter Rising, reflected that 'at that time there was no trouble in the North and the record was a great hit. I am still asked to sing it, although I am completely against violence and don't think that sort of song goes well at the present moment.'[111] By the late 1970s, more consciously political music inspired by the conflict emerged. Christy's Moore's song about the Belfast Official IRA man 'Joe McCann' featured on his 'Iron Behind The Velvet' album during 1978. In the same year, Moore produced an album featuring music and poetry in support of the prisoners in H-Block.[112]

At that stage, however, the singer was still far more associated with protest over the proposed Carnsore nuclear plant than with the North.[113]

'Excessive attention on the North'

As the national channel, RTE had to devote coverage to the North, which featured in documentaries and dramas as well as current affairs. One 1978 episode of 'The Riordans' soap opera examined attitudes towards the IRA. An old friend of one of the main characters, Benjy Riordan, arrived at his home on the run. While Benjy's wife Maggie was absolutely opposed to republican violence, Benjy himself was torn.[114] The station also broadcast Sam Thompson's play *Over the Bridge* dealing with sectarianism in Belfast and Eugene McCabe's *Victims* trilogy, about violence along the border.[115] In 1977, Olivia O'Leary presented a documentary about the Catholic community of Cooke Street in south Belfast, examining how loyalist violence and republican feuding had impacted on their lives. When asked what they thought of the Republic, one of those interviewed told O'Leary that he 'couldn't care less ... because I'm sure they're not thinking about us'.[116]

Apart from the censoring of republican activists through Section 31, many critics also accused RTE of promoting an anti-national agenda. This was personified by the popular TV and radio host Gay Byrne. In 1974, *An Phoblacht* argued that 'no man has done more' than Byrne to destroy Irish culture.[117] Byrne made no secret of his opposition to the IRA, after the Mountbatten assassination asserting 'not for the first time ... I was overwhelmed with the shame of being Irish'.[118] More than hostility, however, Byrne often suggested that he was 'fed up hearing' about the North, despite hosting several 'Late Late Show' specials on the issue.[119] As Gene Kerrigan noted, Byrne delivered 'verdicts rather than opinions ... publicly espousing for most of the past decade that the question of the North is "boring"'. Byrne's opinions were 'coloured by an infatuation with the intellectual abilities of Conor Cruise O'Brien, and he has vouched publicly that O'Brien's book, *States of Ireland*, coincided with his own views on the issue'.[120]

However, also evident from an early stage was a feeling that many RTE viewers thought coverage of the North had reached 'saturation point'.[121] During 1970, 58% of those polled in an audience research survey claimed that there was 'too much' attention given to events across the border.[122] Desmond Fisher, RTE's Deputy Head of News in the early 1970s, claimed that 'it was not long before complaints began to come in from listeners and viewers about what was categorised as excessive attention on the North ... It is not so much that they were positively antagonistic to regarding Northern Ireland as part of the country; rather it was that they did not consider events there as of interest and concern.'[123] Others worried about the impact that 'the violence they see daily from the Six Counties on our T.V. screens' was having on children, one

Dublin woman noting that her 4-year old son had been 'playing tarring and feathering' with his friends.[124]

'Some beauties, to be sure'

Regardless of the issue, the North was useful as a political football. There was constant reiteration of what the IRA campaign, in particular, was costing the state. During the 1977 election campaign, Minister for Defence Oliver J. Flanagan asserted that 'one out of every five persons unemployed today must realise that this is because of the Northern troubles'. He claimed that fear of the violence had prevented 'foreign industrialists coming to this country'.[125] Conor Cruise O'Brien talked of the 'severe drop in our standard of living' that would be caused by an influx of refugees in 1974.[126] When bank staff threatened strike action in 1976, the *Southern Star* opined that

> our economy is going through a pretty desperate period but nobody seems to care and certainly not the greedy ones with well-paid jobs like our bank officials. Looked at in terms of the Northern tragedy, whether political or economic, what a scandalous example they represent of the Irish nation ... Up North, their counterparts have mostly no jobs, no decent housing and no future of any kind, or so it seems, and yet our privileged classes, safe from bomb and bullet and protected in so many ways, thank the nation that feeds them by throwing their well-paid jobs in its face. What nationalism, what patriotism and what thanks for the men who went out in 1916 to ensure the birth of that 'terrible beauty.' Some beauties, to be sure.[127]

'Extremely serious repercussions'

But the conflict's cost was a real factor. A government report during 1978 estimated that at least £200 million had been lost due to increased security, damage to property and 'economic losses from lower tourism etc.'.[128] The impact on tourism was apparent from an early stage. In 1972, it was estimated that because of the decrease in 'British, North American and Northern Ireland' visitors, tourism, 'which last year earned £104-m, will be fortunate to reach £84-m'.[129] In 1975, David Kane of the Irish Hotels Federation explained that 'between 1968 and 1972, tourist numbers fell from a peak of 1.9 million to 1.4 million – a drop of more than 25%. The effect on the hotel industry was traumatic – those hotels, particularly the smaller and medium-sized hotels, who had built their trade around British tourists, were particularly hard hit.'[130] Even the UDA's relatively minor hotel bombs in the summer of 1976 had 'extremely serious repercussions', because 'hoteliers and other interests – led by Bord Failte – have consistently preached abroad that the Republic was a safe place for holidays'.[131] Cosgrave claimed in 1976 that tourist numbers from 'our nearest neighbour' were down by 300,000 compared to the mid 1960s.[132] The desire to attract such visitors influenced a motion that condemned violence committed in 'our name' at the Irish Hotel's Federation conference in 1974. The motion, which was to be conveyed to the Federation's counterparts in Britain and Northern Ireland, received loud applause from the conference. But when a delegate added an amendment that also condemned internment, the conference split – with many objecting to the introduction of 'politics' – and both motions were dropped.[133]

'I would kick his arse for it'

In 1977, Sinn Féin began a 'Brits Out' campaign with extensive slogan painting that provoked heated discussions on councils across the Republic. A recurring theme was the 'untold damage' this could do to tourism from Britain.[134] At Donegal County Council, Senator Bernard McGlinchey claimed 'I want to see tourists coming to this country. If we went to England and saw signs saying "Irish out" what would we think?' Fellow Fianna Fáil councillor Clement Coughlan noted that 'these slogans were done at night and I would love to see one of these fellows doing it in daylight. If I got one of the fellows writing on my property I would kick his arse for it.' [135]

After the Mountbatten killings, there 'was general agreement among officials that the impact of these atrocities will be more damaging and longer lasting than any other "incidents" in past ten years'. They were considered to be 'especially' damaging for tourism because – (i) it happened in Ireland; (ii) he (Mountbatten) was frequent visitor, a 'holidaymaker' and because it called 'into question concepts projected by Bord Failte and tourism identity in Britain for past number of years – WELCOME and SAFETY.' Civil servants also noted the widespread 'offensive "Brits Out" signs', were 'more than ever before, upsetting British visitors'.[136]

'Raw, naked tribalism'

In October 1978, the Republic of Ireland played England in qualifiers for the European Championships. Though at the beginning of the game in Dublin a 'fairly large section of the crowd booed God Save the Queen', there was no crowd trouble.[137] In contrast, when Northern Ireland had visited Dublin the previous month there had been several arrests and bouts of stone throwing between fans of the rival Irish teams. Lansdowne Road had resounded to chants of 'UVF' and 'come and have a go at the Ulster aggro', while the majority of the southern fans had looked on with a mixture of 'curiosity, distaste, fear (and) horror'.[138] Those clashes were minor compared to when Belfast's Linfield came to Dundalk a year later. There were running battles between rival fans and Gardai, dressing rooms had to be used to treat the injured and shops and houses outside the ground were attacked. The *Irish Times* bemoaned how 'the concept of All-Ireland club football was killed stone dead' because of 'two hours of raw, naked tribalism on the terraces' which convinced 'even the most reformist among us that the dark gospel of the paramilitaries has permeated Irish sport to the point where all attempts at reconciliation are futile'.[139]

'Bigoted, Bible-spouting ... Orangemen'

Whatever about attitudes towards Britain, opinions about Northern Ireland's Unionists remained largely hostile throughout the decade. This was despite substantial rethinking on the subject among sections of the political and academic elite. One prevailing stereotype of the 'Black North' prior to 1969 was that it was a 'grim industrial place of little amusement and high unemployment run by bigoted, Bible-spouting Protestant Orangemen in bowler hats who slander the Pope'.[140] The view that northern Protestants were essentially bigots remained widespread. The 1979 ESRI survey, while causing consternation with its claims of support for the IRA, also revealed strong levels of antagonism to Unionists. The report's authors stated that what was 'quite clear' was that 'the prevailing attitude towards Northern Protestants is one of opposition'. Almost 75% of respondants expressed varying degrees of hostility to Unionists, while only 7.1% were sympathetic. [141] Perhaps significantly this aspect of the survey caused no controversy. Dervla Murphy thought while had many had 'outgrown' what she called the anti-Partition cult, some had 'outgrown it merely because the North has become too hot to hold; not because they see the Unionists have a point of view which is valid'.[142]

During the early stages of the conflict, some asserted that if the south wanted a united Ireland it would have to make concessions on 'liberal' issues. This suggestion often provoked angry responses. Shortly after Bloody Sunday, the Dáil voted against (by 75 votes to 44) an attempt by Noel Browne to allow greater access to information on contraception. While Browne spoke, he was heckled about the injustices suffered by Catholics in the North. TDs chanted 'Bogside' and

> when Dr. Browne asked whether the vote might not confirm Northern Protestants in their suspicion that a united Ireland would be a Catholic Ireland, Fianna Fáil deputy Paddy Burke responded: 'Up the Bogside!' To which Gerry L'Estrange of Fine Gael replied: 'Up the backside!' and the Dáil exploded with laughter.[143]

The British considered that the result reflected 'the genuine wishes of the great majority in the Republic, who fear liberalisation of their laws' and that southerners placed this aspect of their beliefs above that of a united Ireland.[144] Nevertheless, when opinion was surveyed during 1972 for the proposition that the 'position and influence of the Roman Catholic Church in the Republic has been a real obstacle to Irish unity', while 53.3% said no, a large minority of 40.8% agreed.[145]

'We don't owe them anything'

There were some who maintained that concessions were unnecessary. As Caitlin Ní Murcu from Waterford told the 1972 Fianna Fáil Ard Fheis, the Constitution 'suits the Irish people and let the six county Protestants take it or leave it ... why should we make concessions for the Unionists? We don't owe them anything.'[146] Aodogan O'Rahilly explained in a letter to the *Irish Times* five years later that 'the only concession which could help us is the one we cannot give them: which is quite simply to confirm them in and perpetuate their status as the "Herrenvolk", the "Master-Race"... they have enjoyed since the Battle of the Boyne'. O Rahilly asserted that 'history abounds with records of privileged groups who have been deprived of their privileges; but it has never happened without a bitter struggle and usually much bloodshed'.[147]

'Go back to Britain'

As early as 1971, it had become a truism to assert that the Unionists could not be forced into a united Ireland. While Cardinal William Conway may have been the first to argue that you could not 'bomb one million Protestants into a united Ireland', the phrase soon became commonplace.[148] But in the heated atmosphere after Bloody Sunday there were many who disputed this. Meath councillor Sean Conway stated that 'if the Unionist element in the North wished to continue their allegiance to the Queen when national re-unification was achieved, their best plan would be to pack up and go back to Britain'.[149] On Sligo council, Fianna Fáil's Ray McSharry stated that if northern Unionists 'do not want to be part of the South, they should make up their minds. We do not want to bomb them into submission, but if we have to bomb them out, we will do so.'[150]

Warnings of loyalist resistance were often dismissed, Cavan councillor T. O'Connor asserting that 'this thing about the Protestant backlash is a lot of hooey and sheer bluff'.[151] In July 1972, Mayo TD Joseph Leneghan would suggest that 'one solution to the present problems would be to transfer all the Scots people in the North back to Scotland and replace them in the North by Irish people who had been forced to live in Scotland'.[152] There was a tendency to see Unionist opposition as based solely on Britain's willingness to support partition. Neil Blaney asserted that once 'the hard-headed Unionist businessmen of the North found that the British financial support was gone they would very quickly come on terms with Dublin'.[153] Even some of those who agreed that 'you can't force a man at the point of a gun to love his neighbour', such as General Michael J. Costello, felt that the solution was 'not to be found through appeasement. The Unionist has more respect for the Southern man who stands up for his own sentiments, his own religion, than for the man of no principle.'[154] One Fine Gael supporter advised TD Richie

Ryan in 1973 that it 'would be, a catastrophic mistake, to appear to be in any way doing anything that will favour the Unionists because, deep down, 90% of the Irish people, including, 90% of our own supporters, are, Irish and proud of it, and have great contempt for the Unionists of the North'.[155]

'Pied-Oranges'?

Appeals to Irish republican history were not convincing for some critics of Unionism. Corkman Finbar Dowdall argued that there had been a 'disproportionate emphasis on the part some of their number played in the United Irishmen', when in fact many nationalists 'desire co-citizenship with these self-styled "loyalists" as little as they desire it with us'.[156] At Macroom Council, Sean Twomey argued that 'these people were not Irish and were in the wrong country. They should be repatriated the same as happened the French in Algeria. France was a bigger and stronger country to-day for doing this.'[157] A correspondent in the Irish language magazine *Pobal* argued that 'the Northern Unionists, regardless of the length of time they have been in the country, are colonists, of Irish, Scottish and English ancestry, for one's nationalism or independence exists in the mind'.[158] Others wondered whether 'the time is approaching … when the Algerian solution will have to be thought about, to send the "pied-oranges" back to the mainland'.[159]

The comparison between northern loyalists and the Algerian 'colons' became a common one on sections of the far-left, influencing debates within the Provisionals. Seeing the loyalists as colonists moving in the direction of fascism contributed to justfying violence against them.[160] In 1976, the editor of People's Democracy's *Unfree Citizen* would argue that the Kingsmill's massacre was 'inevitable and neccesary'.[161] Others, unsympathetic to republicanism, would nevertheless see loyalists as little more than gangsters. Writing after the Dublin bombings, Desmond Rushe of the *Irish Independent* noted Sammy Smyth of the UDA's support for the atrocity. Rushe argued that 'the demonic violence which has engulfed the North has brutalized (Smyth) to the extent that he is much more animal than human being. He is a thug and a savage, so dehumanised and desensitised that he is happy with the slaughter of innocent people.' Yet Rushe reserved even harsher condemnation for republicans, perhaps because little else was expected of loyalists.[162] There was little southern understanding, let alone affection, for the 'the obnoxious Orange Order'.[163] One writer thought a TV documentary on northern Unionists in 1973 showed how 'these people were so bigoted that they were incapable of objective thinking. They were unable to rise above their inherited prejudices.'[164]

'We are not looking for a unitary nation state'

But among republicans there were more diverse views. The activist cleric Austin Flannery argued in 1972 that the south 'would benefit from the creative tension which would exist in a 32-county State between the sturdy Presbyterian tradition, and the tradition, also sturdy, of our own Catholic population'. In Flannery's view, class politics might emerge more easily in a united Ireland and 'the lines of demarcation between the haves and have-less and the have-nots would in time, become more clearly drawn between them. At present the lines are blurred.'[165]

While the Official republicans would increasingly stress reaching out to Protestants as a central part of their politics, these debates were heard in the Provisionals also.[166] By 1976, Ruairí Ó Brádaigh would explain that republicans no longer used the term 'united Ireland … because of what it has come to mean for the Loyalist in the North – being submerged in a Catholic-type state of the South … we are not looking for a unitary nation state. So to avoid misunderstanding we don't use that phrase any more.' The Sinn Féin leader contended that

> the Protestant working class were exploited the same way as the Catholic working class. They both suffered the same wretched housing conditions. But in the matter of employment, whatever was going, the Protestants got it first … In other words the Protestant were more of (sic) less analogous to the poor whites of the southern states of America while the Catholics are the negroes.[167]

During a loyalist strike in 1977, *An Phoblacht* informed readers that 'it is no harm to remember a prophecy by the 1916 leader, so heavily under attack by the revisionists of Dublin at present … the time would come when Orangemen would be engaged militarily against the Crown. When that day dawned, according to Mac Piarais, the place of Republicans would be alongside their "Orange" brothers.'[168] Some were not convinced. 'Disgusted student' wrote to complain that 'most people will agree that these "fellow Irishmen" who so vigorously celebrated their queen's jubilee on the Shankill and Sandy Row, waving their Union Jacks and shouting "f… the taigs and f… the Pope" are *definitely* not Irish.'[169] Another correspondent complained that *An Phoblacht* 'does seem to be going like the (Official) *United Irishman*'. He stressed that 'in a new Irish Republic, I do not want an Orangeman on my right as a next door neighbour … an Orangeman is British'.[170] Disagreements about the nature of loyalism and how to relate to Ulster Protestants would be part of an internal division within the Provisionals, expressed openly at their 1978 Ard Fheis.[171] Most people outside their ranks had no knowledge of of those arguments, but they had little sympathy for Unionists and none for what a *Sunday Indepependent* writer called 'genuinely evil men like William Craig, Ian Paisley and the organisers of the so-called Ulster Workers Council'.[172] As a Fine Gael supporter wrote to Liam Cosgrave during 1974, 'it puzzles me … that not one politician has the courage to say that Orange Bigotry is the cause of all the trouble here'.[173] Many southerners disliked the IRA, but for most this did not imply any understanding of, or sympathy with, Unionism. Indeed, by the mid 1970s there were those who increasingly asked (if at times sotto voce) 'why don't the Brits get out and let them all slaughter each other if that's how they feel? There's nothing to choose between them. Why did we ever long for a united Ireland?'[174]

Even for those who professed little interest in it, the northern conflict formed a backdrop to almost all aspects of life throughout the 1970s. There was no corner of southern society that remained unaffected. The economy, the state's relationship with Britain, popular culture and debates about social change were all linked at some stage to the 'Troubles'.

Notes

1 D. Connery, *The Irish* (London, 1968) p. 208.
2 Coogan, *Ireland*, p. 284.
3 Connery, *Irish*, p. 208.
4 *New Statesman*, 11 Feb. 1972.
5 *Irish Press*, 26 April 1968.
6 Noonan, *What*, p. 29.
7 McVeigh, *Taking a Stand,* pp. 81–82.
8 Travers and Fetherstone, *The Miami*, p. 58.
9 *Irish Press*, 26 April 1968.
10 Irish Marketing Surveys, *A Survey of Prevailing Attitudes*, Q.12.
11 R. Rose, I. McAllister and P. Mair, P, 'Is there a concurring majority about Northern Ireland?', *Studies in Public Policy* No. 22 (Glasgow, 1978) p. 37.
12 *Magill*, Oct. 1977.
13 *Irish Press*, 28 March 1974.
14 *Irish Times*, 2 April 1974.
15 Murphy, *Place*, p. 21.
16 Coogan, *Ireland*, p. 284. It would be interesting to discern if there was a communal aspect to this and whether northern Protestants became less likely to travel.
17 Harvey *et al.*, *Emerald Curtain*, pp. 59 and 89.
18 Boran, *Invisible Prison*, p. 4.
19 Ibid., p. 137.
20 *Magill*, Sept. 1979.
21 Republic of Ireland Annual Review, 18 Feb. 1975, FCO 87/416 NAUK.
22 *Irish Press*, 30 Nov. 1974.
23 *Irish Independent*, 22 Jan. 1974.
24 *The Kerryman*, 14 Sept. 1979.
25 Outline Report on Tourism Impact of Mountbatten and Warrenpoint Incidents, N/D (Sept. 1979) DFA 2009/120/1955 NAI.
26 E. Delaney, *Demography, State and Society: Irish Migration to Britain, 1921–1971* (Liverpool, 2000) p. 264.
27 J. Moran, *Irish Birmingham: A History* (Liverpool, 2010) p. 197.
28 *Irish Independent*, 19 Dec. 1974.
29 *Anglo-Celt*, 28 May 1976.
30 *Irish Press*, 10 June 1974.
31 *The Kerryman*, 26 Feb. 1972.
32 K. Fennessey to R. Ryan, 20 Aug. 1971, in R. Ryan Papers, P272/170 UCDA.
33 *This Week*, 5 March 1971.
34 K. Conway, *Southside*, p. 1.
35 *Irish Independent*, 26 Jan. 1971.

36 Gogan, *Pop*, pp. 31 and 51.
37 *Irish Times*, 13 March 1971 and 17 Sept. 1976.
38 Boran, *Invisible Prison*, pp. 153–154. B. Hanley, 'Charlie Bourne, Jack Ford and the Green Fields of France' in J. Horne and E. Madigan (Eds) *Towards Commemoration: Ireland in War and Revolution, 1912–1923* (Dublin, 2013) pp. 105–114.
39 Mac Gréil, *Prejudice*, p. 380.
40 Ivory, 'RTE', p. 32.
41 *Southern Star*, 1 July 1972.
42 *Fortnight*, 22 Feb. 1974. *Irish Times*, 26 Feb. 1973.
43 F. Tobin, *The Best of Decades: Ireland in the 1960s* (Dublin, 1984) p. 235.
44 G. Kerrigan, *Another Country: Growing up in 50's Ireland* (Dublin, 1998) p. 36.
45 J.T. White, *Irish Devils: The Official Story of Manchester United and the Irish* (London, 2012) p. 129.
46 *Irish Independent*, 13 Nov. 1973.
47 *Irish Press*, 20 Nov. 1973.
48 Ibid., 30 Sept. 1971.
49 *An Phoblacht*, 15 Feb. 1978.
50 *Irish Press*, 1 Nov. 1975.
51 Ibid., 27 Sept. 1975.
52 Enda Delaney, 'Facing up the Auld Enemy', *Irish Times*, 9 Aug. 2014.
53 E. Dunphy, *The Rocky Road* (Dublin, 2013) p. 41.
54 Ibid., p. 177, and *Irish Times*, 1 Feb. 1974.
55 S. O'Callaghan, *The Informer* (London, 1999) p. 32.
56 D. Whelan, *Who Stole Our Game? The Fall and Fall of Irish Soccer* (Dublin, 2006) p. 106.
57 *Sunday Press*, 9 Jan. 1972.
58 Mac Gréil, *Prejudice*, p. 363.
59 *The Kerryman*, 26 Feb. 1972.
60 *Longford Leader*, Feb. 1972.
61 *Nenagh Guardian*, 12 Feb. 1972.
62 *The Kerryman*, 16 Nov. 1973.
63 *Irish Press*, 27 June 1974.
64 *The Kerryman*, 15 Feb. 1974.
65 *Irish Times*, 23 Nov. 1974.
66 *Southern Star*, 12 August 1972.
67 *Irish Times*, 1 Feb. 1972.
68 *Munster Express*, 11 Feb. 1972.
69 E. Sheridan, *Me Father was a Hero and me Mother is a Saint* (Durham, CT, 2011) pp. vi and 21. Kerrigan, *Another*, pp. 74–75.
70 *Irish Times*, 30 June 1970.
71 *Hibernia*, 17 Dec. 1971.
72 *Irish Press*, 3 Dec. 1971.
73 *Irish Times*, 18 Feb. 1972.
74 *Leitrim Observer*, 22 July 1972.
75 C. McCarthy, *The Decade of Upheaval*, p. 252. There were 263,000 trade unionists in Northern Ireland.
76 Figures from INTO Executive reports, courtesy Niamh Puirséil.
77 C. McCarthy, *The Decade of Upheaval*, p. 252.
78 *Irish Times*, 18 Jan. 1979.
79 E. O'Connor, *A Labour History of Ireland 1824–2000* (Dublin, 2011) pp. 149–150, 163–169.
80 C. McCarthy, *The Decade of Upheaval*, pp. 150–183.

81 Ibid., Jan. 1972. Puirséil, *Labour*, p. 291. Hanley and Millar, *Revolution*, p. 133 and 170. See also M. Mullen, *Why Britain Should Leave Ireland* (Dublin, 1979).
82 *Liberty*, Sept. 1971.
83 *Meath Chronicle*, 12 Feb. 1972.
84 M. Merrigan, *Eagle or Cuckoo: The Story of the ATGWU in Ireland* (Dublin, 1989) pp. 236–238. *Irish Times*, 29 Jan. 1976.
85 *Irish Press*, 12 May 1970.
86 Ibid., 31 Jan. 1972.
87 Ibid., 29 May 1972.
88 C. Callan and B. Desmond, *Irish Labour Lives: A Biographical Dictionary of Irish Labour Party Deputies, Senators, MPs and MEPs* (Dublin, 2010) pp. 188–189. F. Devine, '*Understanding Social Justice*': *Paddy Cardiff and the Discipline of Trade Unionism* (Dublin, 2002).
89 Callan and Desmond, *Lives*, pp. 41–43.
90 E. O'Connor, *A Labour History of Waterford* (Waterford, 1989) pp. 360–361.
91 *Connacht Tribune*, 18 March 1977.
92 *Irish Times*, 25 May 1978.
93 *Liberty*, May 1973. *The Worker*, Feb/March 1976.
94 SWM *Bulletin*, No. 19, Nov. 1974.
95 *Irish Press*, 20 Aug. 1971.
96 Ibid., 8 Jan. 1972. Gogan, *Pop*, p. 167.
97 *The Kerryman*, 8 Jan. 1972.
98 Gogan, *Pop*, p. 156.
99 *Irish Times*, 8 April 1972.
100 *Irish Independent*, 8 April 1972.
101 Gogan, *Pop*, pp. 107 and 155.
102 Ibid., p. 156.
103 *Irish Times*, 20 Sept. 1974. *Hibernia*, 27 Sept. 1974.
104 Gogan, *Pop*, pp. 12 and 156.
105 *Donegal News*, 9 Aug. 1975.
106 *An Phoblacht*, 26 April 1974, 22 Nov. 1974 and 7 May 1976.
107 *Sunday Independent*, 28 May 1978.
108 Ibid., 14 March 1976.
109 Ibid., 17 Nov. 1974.
110 *Sunday World*, 9 March 1975.
111 Ibid., 6 July 1975.
112 *Rebel*, Dec. 1978.
113 *Irish Press*, 20 Jan. 1979. *Hot Press*, 8–22 Feb. 1979.
114 Sheehan, *Irish Television Drama*, pp. 174–175.
115 Ibid., pp. 184–199.
116 'Cooke Street', RTE, 1977. *Irish Press*, 8 Oct. 1977.
117 *An Phoblacht*, 16 Nov. 1973.
118 *Sunday World*, 2 Sept. 1979.
119 *An Phoblacht*, 5 July 1974.
120 *Magill*, Feb. 1979.
121 Ivory, 'RTE', p. 46.
122 Horgan, *Broadcasting*, p. 75.
123 D. Fisher, 'Getting tough with RTE' in Corcoran and O'Brien (Eds), *Political Censorship*, p. 63.
124 *Woman's Way*, 21 Jan. 1972.
125 *Irish Times*, 10 June 1977.
126 *Hibernia*, 27 Sept. 1974.

127 *Southern Star*, 21 Aug. 1976.
128 Report, 27 Nov. 1978, in D/T 2008/148/709 NAI.
129 *Irish Press*, 15 July 1972.
130 *Irish Times*, 16 May 1975.
131 *Sunday Independent*, 4 July 1976.
132 Ibid.
133 *Irish Times*, 27 Nov. 1974.
134 *Irish Press*, 4 April 1977. *Meath Chronicle*, 19 March 1977. *Connaught Telegraph*, 6 April 1977.
135 *An Phoblacht*, 12 April 1977.
136 Outline Report on Tourism Impact of Mountbatten and Warrenpoint Incidents, N/D (Sept. 1979) DFA 2009/120/1955 NAI. 'Ireland' in this case was clearly the Republic.
137 *Irish Times*, 26 Oct. 1978.
138 *Irish Press*, 22 Sept. 1978 and *Magill*, Oct. 1978.
139 *Irish Times*, 30 Aug. 1979.
140 Connery, *Irish*, p. 209.
141 Davis and Sinnott, *Attitudes*, p. 101.
142 Murphy, *Place*, pp. 20–21
143 McCann, *Bloody Sunday in Derry*, p. 174.
144 J. Peck, 18 September 1972, FCO 87/11 NAUK.
145 Mac Gréil, *Prejudice*, p. 379.
146 *Irish Times*, 21 Feb. 1972.
147 Ibid., 7 April 1978.
148 *Irish Times*, 15 July 1972. Ó Corrain, *Rendering to God*, p. 162.
149 *Drogheda Independent*, 11 Feb. 1972.
150 *Sligo Champion*, 4 Feb. 1972.
151 *Anglo-Celt*, 4 Feb. 1972.
152 *Irish Times*, 14 July 1972.
153 *The Kerryman*, 26 Feb. 1972.
154 *Nenagh Guardian*, 1 Jan. 1977.
155 T.F. Roe to R. Ryan, 4 March 1973, in R. Ryan Papers, P272/172 UCDA.
156 *Irish Press*, 31 Jan. 1972.
157 *Southern Star*, 20 Nov. 1971.
158 *Pobal,* July 1970.
159 Ibid.
160 SWM *Bulletin*, Vol. 2. No. 1, Jan. 1976.
161 *Unfree Citizen*, Vol. 5, No. 9, 1976.
162 *Irish Independent*, 22 May 1974.
163 *Word*, Dec. 1971.
164 *Irish Press*, 5 Sept. 1973.
165 *Irish Independent*, 23 March 1972.
166 Hanley and Millar, *Revolution*, p. 223.
167 *An Phoblacht*, 16 July 1976.
168 Ibid., 11 May 1977.
169 Ibid., 13 July 1977.
170 Ibid., 10 Aug. 1977.
171 Ibid., 28 Oct. 1978.
172 *Sunday Independent*, 26 May 1974.
173 Hannah O'Donnell to L. Cosgrave, 9 July 1974, in D/T 2005/7/585 NAI.
174 Murphy, *Place*, p. 11.

Conclusion

On 22 January 1980, in what the *Irish Times* called the 'biggest demonstration of organised labour in the history of the state', an estimated 700,000 people participated in trade union marches across the Republic. They were demanding reform of the state's tax regime.[1] Later that year, Tim Pat Coogan lamented that 'more people marched to get the PAYE system changed in a few days than the North brought onto the streets in ten years'.[2] Indeed, the previous year 150,000 people in Dublin had taken part in one of the first tax marches. Then 'Homer' in the *Andersonstown News* had written about

> another march in Dublin a few years ago. It was 1972 and busloads of us went down to Dublin to arouse the Dubliners to the evils of internment. I remember standing on O'Connell Street giving out leaflets. I remember the indifference and even the hostility of the passers by. I remember the march up O'Connell Street ... very few Dubliners joined in. And now, apparently they have discovered a cause worth marching for. A cause in which justice coincides with self interest. It's not an altogether bad cause ... but at the end of the day, its money they're marching for and not idealism. The marchers could have marched for many better causes, but they chose to march for money. Their manifest priorities tell us something about the twenty-six county state and its ethos.[3]

'Not their people at all'

The perception of southern self-interest being far more powerful than solidarity with nationalists was a strong one. In early 1972, republican Rita O'Hare had complained of Dublin that 'it's just unbelievable the apathy down here ... people just don't seem to care here. Their whole outlook is unbelievable. It's as though we were not their people at all.'[4] But that year actually saw unprecedented mobilization in support of northern nationalists. It was true that the atmosphere after Bloody Sunday, which the British Ambassador described as unleashing 'a wave of fury and exasperation the like of which I had never encountered in my life', was never replicated.[5] Then the academic and broadcaster Brian Farrell had warned of real danger to 'political and social stability in the Republic' and feared that 'the centre cannot hold'.[6]

'We could have taken over the country'

In contrast, republicans and radicals came to rue what they saw as the missed opportunities of that period. IRA leader Joe Cahill later reflected that if after Bloody Sunday 'we had been in a strong position politically, then we could have taken over the country'.[7] In 1984, *An Phoblacht/Republican News* described how the aftermath of Derry's massacre had seen 'a re-awakening of national consciousness amongst Southerners which for a week afterwards had the potential to unite all Irish nationalists in the struggle for Irish unity'. The far-left also spent much time in later years bemoaning how 'the leadership of the massive upsurge in the North slipp(ed) through its fingers'.[8]

For republicans, it was the southern establishment which was to blame. *An Phoblacht* claimed that the momentum of 1972 was 'cynically defused by the Dublin government'.[9] There was no explanation as to how a government could simply 'cynically defuse' such a movement and no sense that the IRA themselves might have contributed to this demobilization. It is clear that active southern sympathy declined in tandem with the IRA's car-bombing campaign. But some radicals recognized that while events such as Bloody Sunday provoked 'a massive emotional reaction', that reaction was 'quickly and easily contained … because it (was) purely emotional'.[10] And while it was true that the northern crisis invigorated many, it alienated others. Tony Gregory, during 1969 a republican activist in Dublin, recalled how there was a 'huge radicalism among young people and probably all of that was diverted or destroyed by the North. The North blew up and it dissipated.'[11] Campaigners for social change were to remain divided personally and politically over the importance of the 'national question'.[12]

'A deep abiding sense of sorrow'

If people reacted emotionally to August 1969, internment and Bloody Sunday, they reacted in a similar fashion to Aldershot and Bloody Friday. A cynic might ask why Aldershot had such an impact, when 15 people had been killed at McGurk's bar in Belfast just two months before. It is a good question. But more people died at McGurk's than on Bloody Sunday, which produced more public rage than any event of the 1970s, including far greater slaughter in Dublin. From the outset of the conflict, killings by loyalists (with the exception

of the Miami massacre) provoked much less interest in the south than those
carried out by the IRA or the British Army.

The reaction to the carnage of Dublin and Monaghan is most perplexing
of all. The slaughter, for which British agents were immediately blamed, did
not provoke a ferocious backlash but resignation. At the time, Tim Pat Coogan
found 'no public outrage, just a deep abiding sense of sorrow, shame and shock
that it should all come to this'.[13] In part this was because both government
and opposition largely blamed the IRA for provoking the attacks. Unlike after
Bloody Sunday, there was no National Day of Mourning and public displays
of sorrow were minimal; flags at half-mast on government buildings in Dublin
and Monaghan.[14] As Hugh Munro pointed out in the *Irish Press*, it seemed
that 'responsibility for the deaths lay with all sorts of people but no responsibility
at all is specifically imputed to those who actually planted the bombs'.[15] But
it was not only officialdom that expressed such views. Several correspondents
echoed the Dublin man who wrote to praise Liam Cosgrave for pointing out
that 'everybody who practiced or preached violence must bear responsibility'.[16]
Denis Barror, injured by the Talbot Street bomb, remembered that

> there was almost a feeling that the Republic had paid its due for the havoc released
> by the IRA in the North ... and that the politicians, in common with an awful
> lot of people in this country, almost felt personally responsible for the depredations
> of the organisation that carried out bombings in the North in the name of the
> Irish Republican Army.[17]

Neil Jordan, whose wife's aunt was killed in the bombings, returned to Dublin
on board a ferry on which

> every passenger was an Irish emigrant coming back to bury an aunt, sister, mother
> or father. I can still remember a huge, strawhaired Dublin woman cursing the
> country that had sent her jobless to England twenty years before only to draw her
> back to identify the bunch of remains that had once been her father ... the fact
> that nobody knew who had placed the bomb seemed irrelevant at the time. It
> was part of the depressing pall of violence that had smothered the North and was
> now threatening to spread down South. And the present masters of this violence
> were, it seemed, the Provisional IRA.[18]

Within a year, relatives of the dead struggled to explain why the events were
already almost forgotten. Those who tried to campaign on the issue would
face official disinterest, Garda harassment and public responses that included
pleas that they 'let bygones be bygones' and assumptions that the IRA had
actually been responsible.[19] Contemporary reports also contain detail that has
vanished from popular memory. A Parnell Street butcher, who was injured
along with his son, remembered how his 'shop was looted and £170 in cash

was taken'. John Molloy was hurt in the bombings himself, but while helping others who were injured observed 'several skinheads making for shattered shops along the street and getting away with suits and other items'. The *Irish Press* described how as 'rescue workers were fighting desperately to save the lives of their fellow citizens, there were others who stooped so low as to take advantage of the tragedy to line their own pockets'.[20] Campaigners have managed to push the bombings back onto the contemporary political agenda. But even if involvement of British intelligence agencies was proven, it would not explain the popular response in Dublin and elsewhere.

'The mainstream political establishment'

Republicans have sometimes asserted that without censorship the south would have risen in their support. The mirror image of that belief is that without Section 31 the public would have blindly followed the IRA. The reality was more complex and more confusing. Most southern nationalists believed that the 'old' IRA had waged a noble struggle, avoiding both atrocities and civilian casualties. This view may have been naïve and historically incorrect, but it was sincerely held. And it meant that the modern IRA would always be judged harshly and held to a far higher standard than loyalists, for whom almost nobody had any illusions or affection. Even sympathetic observers could assert that the IRA included the 'small-minded bigot, the petty intriguer, the low-sized and the low intellect trying to make themselves large with a gun'.[21] Republicans are right to identify that censorship circumscribed discussion of the North. But to presume that the nationalist voice was completely silenced is to ignore the considerable influence of the *Sunday World* and the *Irish Press*, as well as critical media such as *Hibernia* and *Magill*. Indeed, there was arguably more diversity on the question of the North in the mainstream media during the 1970s then there was regarding economic policy during the recent recession. And censorship was not simply the work of a few zealots at RTE. Colum Kenny has correctly identified that it was

> the mainstream political establishment ... not merely mavericks ... that piloted and maintained Section 31. Any demonisation of such individuals by opponents of Section 31 allows quieter, cuter or more cowardly members of Fianna Fáil, Fine Gael (and) Labour ... off the hook of responsibility for the measure ... the political censorship of Section 31 was effectively supported by all of the major parties.[22]

RTE's overall treatment of the North, in both news and drama, deserves a study of its own. But censorship was maintained in part because there was relatively little popular opposition to it. Indeed, the fact that a significant number of people could access British TV channels, from which republicans were not banned, probably blunted anger over the issue.

'It would still turn people off'[23]

In the early 1970s, Michael Farrell was one of those activists who saw the northern question as providing the spark for an Irish revolution. His comments 20 years later, on the divergence between north and south, were prescient. Farrell noted that

> Northern nationalists tend not to understand the South … their attitude is sometimes very much a moralistic sort of one – 'We are oppressed, why don't you come to our aid?' (but) It's now a very long time since the military struggle in this part of the country … Northern republicans don't see it like that. They make a quite legitimate point that a lot of the activities of the IRA are not very different from those of the IRA in the War of Independence. But that's out of the direct memory of most people here now. And as things have got worse, and as there have been more atrocities, completely indefensible actions and killings of civilians, a lot of people here have got very alienated by them and they have a sort of defence mechanism which is to turn off …[24]

Tommy McKearney, a leading Tyrone republican, remembered how in the 1970s the IRA had 'a large degree of sympathy and solidarity from the South'. But by 1990, he believed that 'most people in the Republic wouldn't lose an hours sleep for a united Ireland let alone die for it'. 'Surely,' he asked 'that's an indictment of the IRA's inability to win any kind of national support for their cause?'[25]

The one issue on which republicans could draw wider sympathy was around prison protests. But many of those who supported the hunger-strikers' demands in 1975 and 1977 were also very anxious to distance themselves from the IRA. While some, particularly in the early years, believed that violence might have some justification in the North, republican activity in the south was usually a different matter. During 1972, for example, the *Kilkenny People* could argue that while the IRA were 'the only security many Nationalists have against UDA terror', the organization had 'no valid role to play here in the Republic'.[26]

The constant reiteration by media and government that republicans were responsible for the conflict undoubtedly had an effect. But, as Farrell put it, 'some aspects of the violence you could explain till the cows come home and it would still turn people off'.[27]

'Deliberate pleasure in repression'

Given the charged nature of discussion about the North, it is understandable how strongly people feel about these events. But it is a mistake to judge them through the lens of 2018. The *Sunday Independent* and the *Sunday World* of the 1970s were very different newspapers to their counterparts today. There is no contemporary version of the *Irish Press*. In the early 1970s, politicians regularly claimed that RTE was *too* sympathetic to the IRA. There remains a far greater popular memory of coercion under Fine Gael and Labour than under Fianna Fáil. But the key legislation aimed at combatting the IRA was drawn up between 1970–72, before Cosgrave's Coalition. Perhaps more recall the Coalition because, as Joe Lee suggests, Cosgrave's government appeared to take 'deliberate pleasure in repression for its own sake rather than treating it, like (Jack) Lynch, as disagreeable neccesity'.[28] It is also true that while what were once the Provisional and Official republicans hold considerably different political positions today, their partisans still continue to contest the ideological ground, sometimes indulging in self-serving rewriting of events.[29]

'Shudder at the thought'

Revisionism must also be critically examined rather than assumed to have been omnipotent. In the 1970s, most government ministers, civil servants, Gardai, soldiers and journalists were products of a largely nationalist (and Catholic) education system, the same schools that allegedly produced 'little IRA men'.[30] Yet when the state faced a challenge, the majority of them rallied to its defence. Perhaps the British Ambassador was correct when he suggested, in 1972, that the southern establishment 'shudder at the thought of an IRA leading a Northern minority set on unification as its only guarantee of civil justice'.[31] This was not because of historical re-writing, but because a broad section of society saw the southern state as theirs. Despite years of anti-partitionist rhetoric, the North now seemed to represent an external threat. It is perhaps ironic that one of the historians associated with the revisionist trend, Theo Moody, was a member of the RTE Authority sacked for defying the government in 1972. At the time, he argued that 'a democratic society needs to face disagreeable truths, and the best service the communications media can render at a time of grave crisis may well be to help it do so'.[32] Moody was more opposed to censorship at this point than many in Fianna Fáil and sections of the press who considered themselves republicans.

But even after almost a decade of revisionist 're-writing' of Irish history, most people still identified strongly with the idea of a united Ireland, though they did not want it to come about through violence. Like censorship, the influence of revisionism can be used as a get out clause for those who wish to ignore the multitude of reasons why people made the choices they did.

'Bewildered and bored by it all'

Labels are useful for the purpose of polemic: 'Provos', 'revisionists', 'Stickies', 'west Brits', 'Free Staters', 'sneaking regarders' and so on. But they do not do justice to the complexities of Irish life, to the attitudes forged in the context of class, religion, experience and age. Labels tell us little about why people sang 'The Men Behind The Wire' and put money in republican collection tins in 1972, but recoiled from any involvement with the North a few years later. Denouncing governments for their policies does not explain why much of the time people accept them. Attempting to unravel the views of 'real people ... in a real context' is a difficult task.[33] For most people, most of the time, making a living and providing for their loved ones takes precedence over politics. Some contemporary leftists did recognize that people in the south 'were born and bred in a partitioned country. Their problems they see as directly related to the state in which they live. Cork workers will be hard put to tie up their housing problems with the sectarian murders in Belfast.'[34] Moral appeals could only convince relatively small numbers of people to take an active interest in the issue.

People could and did hold very contradictory views about the North. When it came to the conflict, some no doubt were 'bewildered and bored by it all'.[35] Others were simply afraid. In 1972, a south Dublin housewife reflected that she had been proud a few years earlier of how 'prosperous and peaceful the country was and how far we had progressed'. But after Bloody Sunday all that was threatened.[36] Some reacted by resenting those from the North itself, by seeing them (in Liam Cosgrave's words) as a people 'deeply imbued with violence'.[37] But many others marched, collected money, housed refugees or took northern children on holidays. People changed their minds; it is likely that some of those who took part in the demonstrations after Bloody Sunday joined peace marches a few years later. The war did 'boil over', if not as violently as Cardinal Conway feared in 1971, and the lives of substantial numbers of people were changed forever. While most were not as dramatically affected as the families of those killed or injured, the conflict remained a constant backdrop to their lives. We cannot understand either Ireland in the 1970s, or how the North is discussed today, without acknowledging that.

Notes

1 *Irish Times*, 23 Jan. 1980.
2 *Hibernia*, 16 Oct. 1980.
3 *Andersonstown News*, 31 March 1979.
4 *Sunday Press*, 30 Jan. 1972.
5 Peck, *Dublin*, pp. 3–4.
6 *Sunday Press*, 6 Feb. 1972.
7 Anderson, *Cahill*, p. 239–241
8 *Magill*, Dec. 1977.
9 *An Phoblacht/Republican News*, 26 Jan. 1984.
10 People's Democracy – Revolutionary Struggle, *Fascism: The Threat in the North of Ireland* (Dublin, 1975).
11 *In Dublin*, 5 Aug. 1992.
12 On feminism, for example, see N. McCafferty, *Nell* (London, 2004) pp. 293–294.
13 Coogan, *The Irish*, p. 225

14 Govt. Information Service, 21 May 1974, in D/T 2005/660 NAI. Among those seeking a day of mourning were the National Engineering and Electrical Trade Union.

15 *Irish Press*, 27 May 1974.

16 J.D. O'Sullivan to L. Cosgrave, 19 May 1974, in D/T 2005/660 NAI.

17 D. Mullan, *The Dublin and Monaghan Bombings* (Dublin, 2000) p. 60.

18 N. Jordan, *Michael Collins: Film Diary & Screenplay* (London, 1996) p. 2.

19 E. O'Neill and B.J. Whyte, *Two Little Boys: An Account of the Dublin & Monaghan Bombings and their Aftermath* (Dublin, 2004) p. 110.

20 *Irish Press*, 16 May 1975.

21 Coogan, *The Irish*, p. 197.

22 C. Kenny, 'Censorship, not "self-censorship"' in Corcoran and O'Brien (Eds) *Political Censorship*, pp. 73–85.

23 F. O'Connor, *In Search of a State: Catholics in Northern Ireland* (Belfast, 1993) pp. 260–261.

24 Ibid.

25 *Hot Press*, 31 May 1990.

26 *Kilkenny People*, 10 Nov. 1972.

27 F. O'Connor, *Search*, p. 261.

28 Lee, *Ireland*, p. 483.

29 For a notable example, see E. Harris, 'Beginning to Talk to "Billy": Revising Southern Stereotypes of Unionism' in T.P. Burgess and G. Mulvenna (Eds) *The Contested Identities of Ulster Protestants* (London, 2015) pp. 9–23.

30 *Irish Times*, 26 May 1972.

31 J. Peck, 27 June 1972, FCO 87/11 NAUK.

32 *Irish Times*, 27 Nov. 1972.

33 E.P. Thompson, *The Making of the English Working Class* (London, 1963) pp. 9–14.

34 Independent Socialist Party, *The Independent Socialist Party: An Introduction* (Dublin, 1977) p. 5.

35 Murphy, *Place*, p. 9.

36 A. Howlett to G. FitzGerald, 3 Feb. 1972, in FitzGerald Papers, P215/4 UCDA. See also Tobin, *Best*, p. 206 and T. Brown, *Ireland: A Social and Cultural History 1922–2002* (London, 2004) pp. 246–249.

37 *Irish Press*, 14 June 1974.

Bibliography

Newspapers and Journals

Andersonstown News
Anglo-Celt
An Phoblacht
An Phoblacht/Republican News
Belfast Bulletin
Bottom Dog
Business and Finance
Church of Ireland Gazette
Clare Champion
Comment
Connacht Tribune
Cork Examiner
Derry Journal
Donegal Democrat
Donegal News
Drogheda Independent
Dublin Review of Books
Dundalk Democrat
Echo and South Leinster Advertiser
Evening Herald
Evening Press
Garda Review
Herald and Western Advertiser
Hibernia
Hot Press
In Dublin
International Socialism
Ireland's Own
Irish Independent
Irish People

Irish Press
Irish Reporter
Irish Socialist
Irish Times
The Kerryman
Kilkenny People
Leinster Leader
Leitrim Observer
Liberty
Limerick Leader
Limerick Socialist
London Review of Books
Longford Leader
Magill
Mayo News
Meath Chronicle
Munster Express
Nationalist (Clonmel)
Nationalist and Leinster Times
Nenagh Guardian
New Ross Standard
New Statesman
Northern Standard
Nusight
Pobal
Profile
Rebel
Roscommon Herald
Sligo Champion
Socialist Republic
Southern Star
Starry Plough
Sunday Independent
Sunday Press
Sunday Tribune
Sunday World
The Word
The Worker
This Week
Time Out
Tipperary Star
Trade Union Information
Tuam Herald
TUCCAR Newsletter
Unfree Citizen
United Irishman
Vanguard
Village
Western People
Westmeath Examiner
Westmeath-Offaly Independent
Wexford People

248 *Bibliography*

Wicklow People
Woman's Way
Workers' Weekly

Books

Adair, L. and Murphy, C., *Untold Stories: Protestants in the Republic of Ireland 1922–2002* (Dublin, 2002).

Ahern, B., *The Autobiography* (London, 2009).

Allen, G., *The Garda Síochána: Policing Independent Ireland 1922–82* (Dublin, 1999).

Anderson, B., *Joe Cahill: A Life in the IRA* (Dublin, 2002).

Arnold, B., *What Kind of Country; Modern Irish Politics 1968–1983* (London, 1984).

Barrett, J.J., *Martin Ferris: Man of Kerry* (Dingle, 2005).

Bean, K., *The New Politics of Sinn Féin* (Liverpool, 2007).

Boland, K., *Up Dev!* (Dublin, 1977).

— *"We Won't Stand (Idly) By"* (Dublin, 1972).

Boran, P., *The Invisible Prison: Scenes from an Irish Childhood* (Dublin, 2009).

Bourke, R., 'Languages of conflict and the Northern Ireland Troubles', *The Journal of Modern History* 83 (September, 2011).

Bowen, K., *Protestants in a Catholic State: Ireland's Privileged Minority* (Dublin, 1983).

Bowman, J., *Window and Mirror: RTÉ Television: 1961–2011* (Cork, 2011).

Bowyer Bell, J., *The Secret Army: A History of the IRA 1915–1970* (London, 1970).

— *The Secret Army: The IRA* (Dublin, 1979).

— *In Dubious Battle: The Dublin Bombings, 1972–74* (Dublin, 1996).

Brady, C., *The Guarding of Ireland: The Garda Síochána and the Irish State 1960–2014* (Dublin, 2014).

Bray, P., *Inside Man: Life as an Irish Prison Officer* (Dublin, 2008).

Brewer, J.D., Lockhart, B. and Rodgers, P., 'Crime in Ireland 1945–95' in A.F. Heath, R. Breen and C.T. Whelan (Eds), *Ireland North and South: Perspectives from Social Science* (Oxford, 1999).

British & Irish Communist Organisation, *Aspects of Nationalism* (Belfast, 1971).

— *The Economics of Partition* (Belfast, 1972).

— *The Rise of Papal Power in Ireland* (Belfast, 1979).

— *Stalin and the Irish Working Class* (Belfast, 1979).

Browne, N.C., *Against the Tide* (Dublin, 1986).

Browne, T., *Ireland: A Social and Cultural History 1922–2002* (London, 2004).

Browne, V. and Farrell, M., *The Magill Book of Irish Politics* (Dublin, 1981).

Burgess, T.P. and Mulvenna, G. (Eds) *The Contested Identities of Ulster Protestants* (London, 2015).

Bury, R., *Buried Lives: The Protestants of Southern Ireland* (Dublin, 2017).

Busteed, M.A., *Voting Behaviour in the Republic of Ireland: A Geographical Persepctive* (Oxford, 1990).

Busteed, M.A. and Mason, H., 'The 1973 General Election in the Republic of Ireland', *Irish Geography* 7 (1974).

Busteed, M.A., Neal, F. and Tonge, J. (Eds) *Irish Protestant Identities* (Manchester, 2008).

Byrne, G., *The Time of My Life: An Autobiography* (Dublin, 1989).

— *To Whom it Concerns* (Dublin, 1972).

Cadwallader, A., *Lethal Allies: British Collusion in Ireland* (Cork, 2013).

Callan, C. and Desmond, B., *Irish Labour Lives: A Biographical Dictionary of Irish Labour Party Deputies, Senators, MPs and MEPs* (Dublin, 2010).

Callanan, F., *The Literary and Historical Society, 1955–2005* (Dublin, 2005).

Cathcart, R. and Muldoon, M., 'The Mass Media in Twentieth-century Ireland' in *New History of Ireland* Vol. VII, J. Hill (Ed.) *Ireland 1921–1984* (Oxford, 2004).

Chubb, B. 'Society and the Political System' in H. Penniman (Ed.) *Ireland at the Polls: The 1977 Dáil Elections* (Washington DC, 1978) pp. 1–20.

Clann na hÉireann, *Spies in Ireland* (London, 1974).

Cody, S., O'Dowd, J. and Rigney, P., *The Parliament of Labour: 100 Years of the Dublin Council of Trade Unions* (Dublin, 1986).

Connery, D., *The Irish* (London, 1968).

Connolly, L. and O'Toole, T., *Documenting Irish Feminisms: The Second Wave* (Dublin, 2005).

Conlon, E. (Ed.) *Later On: The Monaghan Bombing Memorial Anthology* (Dingle, 2004).

Convery, D. (Ed.) *'Locked Out': A Century of Irish Working Class Life* (Dublin, 2013).

Conway, K., *Southside Provisional: From Freedom Fighter to Four Courts* (Dublin, 2014).

Conway, V., *Policing Twentieth-Century Ireland: A History of An Garda Síochána* (London, 2014).

Coogan, T.P., *Ireland Since the Rising* (London, 1966).

— *The IRA* (London, 1970).

— *The Irish: A Personal View* (London, 1975).

— *A Memoir* (London, 2008).

Corcoran, M.P. and O'Brien, M. (Eds) *Political Censorship and the Democratic State: The Irish Broadcasting Ban* (Dublin, 2005).

Courtney, J., *It Was Murder!* (Dublin, 1996).

Craig, A., *Crisis of Confidence: Anglo-Irish Relations in the Early Troubles, 1966–1974* (Dublin, 2010).

Crawford, H., *Outside the Glow: Protestants and Irishness in Independent Ireland* (Dublin, 2010).

Cunningham, M., *Monaghan: County of Intrigue* (Donegal, 1979).

D'Alton, I., "A Vestigal Population"? Perspectives on Southern Irish Protestants in the twentieth century', *Éire – Ireland* 44 (Fall/Winter 2009).

Daly, C., *Violence in Ireland and Christian Conscience* (Dublin, 1973).

Daly, M., *Sixties Ireland: Reshaping the Economy, State and Society, 1957–1973* (Cambridge, 2016).

Daly, P., O'Brien, R. and Rouse, P., *Making the Difference: The Irish Labour Party, 1912–2012* (Cork, 2012).

Davis, E.E. and Sinnott, R., *Attitudes In The Republic of Ireland Relevant To The Northern Ireland Problem: Vol 1*, Dublin Economic and Social Research Institute Paper No. 97 (September, 1979).

— 'The controversy concerning attitudes to the Northern Ireland problem', *Studies* 69 (Autumn/Winter 1980).

Delaney, E., *Demography, State and Society: Irish Migration to Britain, 1921–1971* (Liverpool, 2000).

— *The Irish in Post-War Britain* (Oxford, 2007).

de Paor, L., *Divided Ulster* (London, 1980).

— *Unfinished Business: Ireland Today and Tomorrow* (London, 1990).

— 'UCD and the Pattern of Revolt' in P. Pettit (Ed.) *The Gentle Revolution: Crisis in the Universities* (Dublin, 1969) pp. 60–66.

Derwin, D., 'The ITGWU', *International Socialism* 92 (Oct. 1976) pp. 34–36.

Desmond, B., *Finally and in Conclusion* (Dublin, 2000).

Devine, F., *Understanding Social Justice: Paddy Cardiff and the Discipline of Trade Unionism* (Dublin, 2002).

— *Organising History: A Centenary of SIPTU, 1909–2009* (Dublin, 2009).

— 'Mattie O'Neill', *Saothar* 17 (1992).

Drogheda Community Forum, *Dispelling the Myths* (Drogheda, 2004).

Duggan, J.P., *A History of the Irish Army* (Dublin, 1991).

Dunlop, F., *Yes Taoiseach: Irish Politics from Behind Closed Doors* (Dublin, 2004).

Dunne, D. and Kerrigan, G., *Round Up the Usual Suspects: Nicky Kelly and the Cosgrave Coalition* (Dublin, 1984).

Dunne, T., *Rebellions: Memoir, Memory and 1798* (Dublin, 2004).

Dunne, T. and Geary, L., *History and the Public Sphere: Essays in Honour of John A. Murphy* (Cork, 2005).

Dunphy, E., *The Rocky Road* (Dublin, 2013).

Fanning, R., *Independent Ireland* (Dublin, 1983).

Farrell, B. and Manning, M., 'The Election' in H. Penniman (Ed.) *Ireland at the Polls: The Dáil Elections of 1977* (Washington D.C., 1978).

Farset Community, *Separated by Partition: An Encounter between Protestants from East Donegal and East Belfast* (Belfast, 2000).

Faulkner, P., *As I Saw It: Reviewing Over 30 Years of Fianna Fáil & Irish Politics* (Dublin, 2005).

Feeney, T., *Seán MacEntee: A Political Life* (Dublin, 2008).

Fennell, D., *Build the Third Republic* (Galway, 1972).

— *A New Nationalism for a New Ireland* (Monaghan, 1972).

— *Nice People and Rednecks: Ireland in the 1980s* (Dublin, 1986).

— *The Revision of Irish Nationalism* (Dublin, 1989).

— *About Being Normal: My Life in Abnormal Circumstances* (Cork, 2017).

Ferris, M., *Prison Struggle: Portlaoise Gaol 1917–1985* (Dublin, 1994).

Ferriter, D., *Ambiguous Republic: Ireland in the 1970s* (London, 2012).

FitzGerald, G., *Towards a New Ireland* (London, 1972).

— *All in a Life: An Autobiography* (London, 1992).

— 'The 1974–75 threat of a British withdrawal from Northern Ireland', *Irish Studies in International Affairs* 17 (2006).

Fitzpatrick, D., *Descendancy: Irish Protestant Histories since 1795* (Cambridge, 2014).

Foley, F., 'North-South relations and the outbreak of the Troubles: the response of the *Irish Press*', *Irish Studies in International Affairs* 14 (2003).

Foster, R.F., *Luck and the Irish: A Brief History of Change 1970–2000* (London, 2007).

Gallagher, M. (Ed.) *Irish Elections, 1948–77: Results and Analysis* (Oxford, 2009).

Geraghty, T. and Whitehead, T., *The Dublin Fire Brigade* (Dublin, 2004).

Gibson, B., *The Birmingham Bombs* (Chichester, 1976).

Gillfillan, K. (Ed.) *Trinity Tales: Trinity College Dublin in the Seventies* (Dublin, 2011).

Gogan, L., *Larry Gogan's Pop File* (Dublin, 1979).

Hachey, T. (Ed.) *Turning Points in Twentieth-Century Irish History* (Dublin, 2011).

Hanley, B., 'Charlie Bourne, Jack Ford and the Green Fields of France' in J. Horne and E. Madigan (Eds) *Towards Commemoration: Ireland in War and Revolution, 1912–1923* (Dublin, 2013).

— 'But then they started all this killing': attitudes to the IRA in the Irish Republic since 1969', *Irish Historical Studies* 38 (May 2013).

— 'I ran away'? The IRA and 1969: the evolution of a myth', *Irish Historical Studies* 38 (Nov. 2013).

— 'We mourn our brothers ...' Workers respond to Bloody Sunday and the Northern Ireland conflict, 1968–72', *Saothar* 42 (2017).

Hanley, B. and Millar, S., *The Lost Revolution: The Story of the Official IRA and the Workers Party* (Dublin, 2010).

Harte, P., *Young Tigers and Mongrel Foxes* (Dublin, 2005).

Harvey, B., *Cosgrave's Coalition* (London, 1978).

Harvey, B., Kelly, A., McGearty, S. and Murray, S., *The Emerald Curtain: The Social Impact of the Irish Border* (Monaghan, 2005).

Hennessey, T., *Northern Ireland: The Origins of the Troubles* (Dublin, 2005).

Higgins, R., *Transforming 1916: Meaning, Memory and the Fiftieth Anniversary of the Easter Rising* (Cork, 2012).

Holland, J. and McDonald, H., *INLA: Deadly Divisions* (Dublin, 1994).

Holohan, C., 'Challenges to social order and Irish identity? youth culture in the sixties', *Irish Historical Studies* 151 (May 2013).

Hopkinson, M., *Green against Green: The Irish Civil War* (Dublin, 1988).

Horgan, J., *Noel Browne: Passionate Outsider* (Dublin, 1997).

— *Broadcasting and Public Life: RTE News and Current Affairs, 1926–1997* (Dublin, 2004).

— 'Irish television and newspapers, 1962–72: an armed truce?', *Éire–Ireland* 50, No. 1 and 2 (Spring/Summer 2015).

Howard, P., *Hostage: Notorious Irish Kidnappings* (Dublin, 2004).

Hussey, B. and Kealy, A. (Ed.) *Nothing is Written in Stone: The Notebook of Justin Keating* (Dublin, 2017).

Independent Socialist Party, *The Independent Socialist Party: An Introduction* (Dublin, 1977).

Irish Council for Civil Liberties, *The Emergency Powers Act, 1976: A Critique* (Dublin, 1977).

Irish Marketing Surveys, *Northern Ireland: A Survey of Prevailing Attitudes in the Republic of Ireland* (Dublin, 1978).

Irish Republican Socialist Party, *Framed Through The Special Criminal Court, The 'Great Train Robbery' Trial* (Dublin, 1979).

Ivory, G., 'Fianna Fáil, Northern Ireland and the limits of conciliation, 1969–1973', *Irish Political Studies* 29 (Jan. 2013).

— 'RTÉ and the Coverage of Northern Ireland on television news bulletins in the early years of the Troubles', *Irish Communications Review* 13 (2013).

Jordan, N., *Michael Collins: Film Diary & Screenplay* (London, 1996).

Kee, R., *Ireland: A History* (London, 1980).

Kelly, S., *'A Failed Political Entity': Charles Haughey and the Northern Ireland Question, 1945–1992* (Dublin, 2013).

— *Fianna Fail, Partition and Northern Ireland, 1926–1971* (Dublin, 2016).

Kennedy, M., 'This Tragic and Most Intractable Problem': the reaction of the Department of External Affairs to the outbreak of the Troubles in Northern Ireland', *Irish Studies in International Affairs* 12 (2001).

Kenny, B., *Tony Heffernan, From Merrion Square to Merrion St* (Dublin, 2013).

Kenny, I., *Talking to Ourselves: Conversations with Editors of the Irish News Media* (Galway, 1994).

Keogh, D., *Jack Lynch: A Biography* (Dublin, 2008).

Kerrigan, G., *Hard Cases: True Stories of Irish Crime* (Dublin, 1996).

— *Another Country: Growing Up in 1950's Ireland* (Dublin, 1998).

— 'The confession of Christy Lynch', *Magill*, 1 Feb. 1984.

Knatchbull, T., *From a Clear Blue Sky: Surviving the Mountbatten Bomb* (London, 2010).

Knight, J. and Baxter-Moore, N., *Republic of Ireland: The General Elections of 1969 and 1973* (London, 1973).

Lee, J.J., (Ed.) *Ireland, 1945–70* (Dublin, 1979).

— *Modern Ireland, 1912–1985: Politics and Society* (Cambridge, 1989).

Logue, P., *Them and Us: A Socialist Response to 'Work is the Key'* (Dublin, 1994).

Mac Gréil, M., *Prejudice and Tolerance in Ireland: Based on a Survey of Intergroup Attitudes of Dublin Adults and Other Sources* (Dublin, 1977).

Mac Mánais, R., *The Road From Ardoyne: The Making of a President* (Dingle, 2005).

Mac Stiofáin, S., *Memoirs of a Revolutionary* (London, 1975).

Madden, A., *Fear and Loathing in Dublin* (Dublin, 2009).

Madden, G., 'Responses in the west of Ireland to civil rights protest in Northern Ireland, 1968–72', *Irish Historical Studies* 41 (May, 2017).

Magee, J., 'The teaching of Irish history in Irish schools', *The Northern Teacher* 10, No. 1 (Winter 1970).

Maguire, C., *Roddy Connolly and the Struggle for Socialism in Ireland* (Cork, 2008).

— 'Defenders of the State: the Irish Labour Party, coalitionism and revisionism, 1969–77', *Irish Studies Review* 23 (2015).

Maguire, M., *To Take Arms: My Year with the IRA Provisionals* (London, 1973).

Maye, B., *Fine Gael 1923–1987* (Dublin, 1993).

McBride, I., 'The shadow of the gunman: Irish historians and the IRA', *Journal of Contemporary History* 46, No. 3 (2011).

McCafferty, N., *Nell* (London, 2004).

McCann, E., *War and an Irish Town* (London, 1974).

— *Bloody Sunday in Derry: What Really Happened* (Dingle, 1992).

McCarthy, C., *The Decade of Upheaval: Irish Trade Unions in the Nineteen Sixties* (Dublin, 1973).

McCarthy, Conor, *Modernisation, Crisis and Culture in Ireland, 1969–1992* (Dublin, 2000).

McCarthy, K., *Republican Cobh and the East Cork Volunteers since 1913* (Dublin, 2008).

McCarthy, M., *Ireland's 1916 Rising: Explorations of Historial Memory, Commemoration and Heritage in Modern Times* (Surrey, 2012).

McCreary, A., *Profiles of Hope* (Belfast, 1981).

McDaid, S., 'The David Thornley Affair: Republicanism and the Irish Labour Party' in C. Nic Dháibhéid and C. Reid (Eds) *From Parnell to Paisley* (Dublin, 2010).

McDowell, R.B., *Crisis and Decline: The Fate of the Southern Unionists* (Dublin, 1997).

— *McDowell on McDowell: A Memoir* (Dublin, 2008).

McGinley, J. (Ed.) *Frank Cluskey: The Conscience of Labour* (Dublin, 2015).

McGladdery, G., *The Provisional IRA in England: The Bombing Campaign, 1973–1997* (Dublin, 2006).

McGrain, D., 'From Peking to Aubane', www.Indymedia.ie/article/80451.

McGuire, C., 'Defenders of the State: The Irish Labour Party, coalitionism and revisionism, 1969–77', *Irish Studies Review* 23 (2015) pp. 1–20.

McKay, S., *Bear in Mind these Dead* (London, 2008).

McKearney, T., *The Provisional IRA: From Insurrection to Parliament* (London, 2011).

McKeown, K., 'A critical examination of some findings of the Davis and Sinnott Report', *Studies* 69 (Summer, 1980).

McKittrick, D., Kelter, S., Feeney, B. and Thornton, C., *Lost Lives: The Stories of the Men, Women and Children Who Died as a Result of the Northern Ireland Troubles* (Edinburgh, 1999).

McNulty, T.A., *Exiled: 40 Years an Exile* (Monaghan, 2013).

McVeigh, J., *Taking a Stand: Memoir of an Irish Parish Priest* (Dublin, 2008).

Manseragh, M., *The Legacy of History: For Making Peace in Ireland: Letters and Commemorative Addresses* (Cork, 2003).

Meehan, C., *A Just Society for Ireland? 1964–1987* (Hampshire, 2013).

Meehan, N., 'Eoghan Harris fed the hand that bit him', *Village*, Sept. 2009.

Meehan, N. and Murphy, B.P., *The Embers of Revisionism: Essays Critiquing Creationist Irish History* (Cork, 2017).

Merrigan, M., *Eagle or Cuckoo? The Story of the ATGWU in Ireland* (Dublin, 1989).

— *Eggs and Rashers: Irish Socialist Memories* (Dublin, 2014).

Mills, M., *Hurler on the Ditch: Memoir of a Journalist who Became Ireland's First Ombundsman* (Dublin, 2005).

Millward, S., *Fast Forward: Music and Politics in 1974* (Leicester, 2016).

Moore, C., *The Christy Moore Songbook* (Dingle, 1984).

Moran, J., *Irish Birmingham: A History* (Liverpool, 2010).

Morash, C., *A History of the Media in Ireland* (Cambridge, 2010).

Mullan, D., *The Dublin and Monaghan Bombings* (Dublin, 2000).

Mullen, M., *Why Britain Should Leave Ireland* (London, 1979).

Mullin, C., *Error of Judgement: The Truth about the Birmingham Bombings* (Dublin, 1997).

Mulroe, P., *Bombs, Bullets and the Border: Policing Ireland's Frontier, Irish Security Policy, 1969–1978* (Dublin, 2017).

Murphy, C. and Adair, L., *Untold Stories: Protestants in the Republic of Ireland 1922–2002* (Dublin, 2002).

Murphy, D., *A Place Apart* (London, 1978).

Murphy, J.A., *Ireland in the Twentieth Century* (Dublin, 1975).

— 'Further Reflections on Irish Nationalism', *The Crane Bag 2*, No. 1/2 (1978).

Murray Defence Campaign, *No Hanging Here* (Dublin, 1976).

Myers, K., *Watching the Door: A Memoir, 1971–1978* (Dublin, 2006).

National Commemoration Committee, *Tírghrá: Ireland's Patriot Dead* (Dublin, 2002).

Noonan, J., *What Do I Do Now?* (Dublin, 2005).

Ó Beacháin, D., *Destiny of the Soldiers: Fianna Fáil, Irish Republicanism and the IRA, 1926–1973* (Dublin, 2010).

O'Brien, C., *Protecting Civil Liberties, Promoting Human Rights: 30 Years of the ICCL* (Dublin, 2006).

O'Brien, C.C., *States of Ireland* (London, 1972).

— *Herod: Reflections on Political Violence* (London, 1978).

— *Memoir: My life and themes* (Dublin, 1998).

O'Brien, J., *The Arms Trial* (Dublin, 2000).

O'Brien, M., *De Valera, Fianna Fáil and the Irish Press: The Truth in the News* (Dublin, 2001).

— *The Fourth Estate: Journalism in Twentieth Century Ireland* (Manchester, 2017).

O'Brien, M. and Rafter, K. (Eds) *Independent Newspapers: A History* (Dublin, 2012).

O'Brien, M.C., *The Same Age as the State: The Autobiography of Máire Cruise O'Brien* (Dublin, 2003).

O'Callaghan, J., *Teaching Irish Independence: History in Irish Schools, 1922–72* (Cambridge, 2009).

O'Callaghan, M., 'The Past Never Stands Still: Commemorating the Easter Rising in 1966 and 1976' in J. Smyth (Ed.) *Remembering the Troubles* (Notre Dame, 2017).

O'Callaghan, S. *The Informer* (London, 1999).

O'Connor, E., *A Labour History of Waterford* (Waterford, 1989).

— *A Labour History of Ireland 1824–2000* (Dublin, 2011).

O'Connor, F., *In Search of a State: Catholics in Northern Ireland* (Belfast, 1993).

O'Connor Lysaght, R., *End of a Liberal: the Literary Politics of Conor Cruise O'Brien* (Dublin, 1976).

— (Ed.) *100 Years of Liberty Hall* (Dublin, 2013).

Ó Corráin, D., *Rendering to God and Caesar: The Irish Churches and the Two States in Ireland, 1949–73* (Manchester University Press, 2006).

O'Donnell, C., *Fianna Fáil, Irish Republicanism and the Northern Ireland Troubles 1968–2005* (Dublin, 2007).

O'Donnell, R., *Special Category: The IRA in English Prisons* Vol.1: 1968–1978 (Dublin, 2012).

Ó Dúlaing, D., *Donncha's World: The Roads, the Stories and the Wireless* (Wexford, 2014).

Ó Faoleán, G., 'Ireland's Ho Chi Minh trail? The Republic of Ireland's role in the Provisional IRA's bombing campaign, 1970–1976', *Small Wars & Insurgencies* 25 (October, 2014).

O'Halloran, C., *Partition and the Limits of Irish Nationalism* (Dublin, 1987).

O'Halpin, E., *Defending Ireland: The Irish State and its Enemies since 1922* (Oxford, 1999).

— 'A Greek Authoritarian Phase'? The Irish Army and the Irish Crisis, 1969–70', *Irish Political Studies* 23 (2008).

O'Hanlon, T.J., *The Irish: Portrait of a People* (London, 1975).

O'Leary, C., *Irish Elections 1918–1977* (Dublin, 1979).

O'Leary, J., *On the Doorsteps: Memoirs of a Long-serving TD* (Kerry, 2015).

O'Leary, O., www.ewartbiggsprize.org.uk2013–2/olivia-olearys.

O'Mahony, A., *Creating Space: The Education of a Broadcaster* (Dublin, 2016).

O'Malley, D., *Conduct Unbecoming* (Dublin, 2014).

O Mally, P., *The Uncivil Wars: Ireland Today* (Boston, 1990).

O'Neill E. and Whyte, B.J., *Two Little Boys: An Account of the Dublin & Monaghan Bombings and their Aftermath* (Dublin, 2004).

O'Neill. G., *Where Were You? Dublin Youth Culture and Style 1950–2000* (Dublin, 2011).

Ó Riain, S., *Provos: Patriots or Terrorists* (Dublin, 1974).

O'Sullivan, M., *Mary Robinson: The Life and Times of an Irish Liberal* (Dublin, 1993).

O'Sullivan, P.M., *Patriot Graves: Reistance in Ireland* (Westchester, 1972).

Patterson, H., *Ireland since 1939: The Persistance of Conflict* (Dublin, 2007).

— *Ireland's Violent Frontier: The Border and Anglo-Irish Relations During the Troubles* (London, 2013).

— 'Unionism, 1921–1972' in A. Jackson (Ed.) *The Oxford Handbook of Modern Irish History* (Oxford, 2014).

Peck, J., *Dublin From Downing Street* (Dublin, 1978).

Penniman, H. (Ed.) *Ireland at the Polls: The Dáil Elections of 1977* (Washington DC, 1978).

People's Democracy – Revolutionary Struggle, *Fascism: The Threat in the North of Ireland* (Dublin, 1975).

Perry, R., *Revisionist Scholarship and Modern Irish Politics* (Surrey, 2013).

Petit, P. (Ed.) *The Gentle Revolution: The Crisis in Irish Universities* (Dublin, 1969).

Pierse, M., *Writing Dublin's working class: Dublin after O'Casey* (London, 2011).

Pringle, P., *About Time: Surviving Ireland's Death Row* (Dublin, 2012).

Provisional IRA, *Freedom Struggle* (Dublin, 1973).

Puirséil, N., *The Irish Labour Party, 1922–73* (Dublin, 2007).

Purcell, B., *Inside RTE: A Memoir* (Dublin, 2014).

Quinn, T. (Ed.) *Desmond Fennell: His Life and Work* (Dublin, 2002).

Rahaleen Ltd, *All Over the Place: People Displaced to and from the Southern Border Counties as a Result of the Conflict 1969–1994* (Dublin, 2005).

Raven, J., Whelan, C.T., Pfretzschner, P.A. and Borock, D.M., *Political Culture in Ireland: The Views of Two Generations* (Dublin, 1976).

Regan, J.M., *Myth and the Irish State* (Dublin, 2013).

Revolutionary Struggle, *Ireland: The Class War and Our Tasks* (Dublin, 1977).

Reynolds, M., 'The Gaelic Athletic Association and the 1981 H-Block hunger strike', *International Journal of the History of Sport* 34 (June, 2017).

Rice, B., '"Hawks turn to Doves": the response of the post-revolutionary generation to the "new troubles" in Ireland, 1969–71', *Irish Political Studies* 30, No. 32 (2015).

Robinson, M., *The Special Criminal Court* (Dublin, 1974).

Ross, F.S., *Smashing H-Block* (Liverpool, 2011).

Rose, R., McAllister, I. and Mair, P., 'Is there a concurring majority about Northern Ireland?', *Studies in Public Policy*, No. 22 (Glasgow, 1978).

Sacks, P.M., *The Donegal Mafia* (Yale, 1976).

Savage, R., *A Loss of Innocence: Television and Irish Society 1960–72* (Manchester, 2010).

Shaw, F., 'The canon of Irish history – a challenge', *Studies* 61 (Summer, 1972).

Sheehan, H., *Irish Television Drama: a Society and its Stories* (Dublin, 1987).

Sheils-Makowski, B., *Daughter of Derry: The Story of Brigid Sheils Makowski* (London, 1989).
Sheridan, E., *Me Father was a Hero and me Mother is a Saint* (Durham, 2011).
Sinn Féin the Workers Party, *The Irish Industrial Revolution* (Dublin, 1977).
Smith, R., *Garret: The Enigma* (Dublin, 1985).
Socialist Workers Movement, *The Working Class and the National Question* (Dublin, 1974).
Sorohan, S., *Irish London during the Troubles* (Dublin, 2012).
Sweeney, E., *Down, Down, Deeper and Down: Ireland in the 70s and 80s* (Dublin, 2010).
Sweetman, R., *On Our Knees: Ireland, 1972* (London, 1972).
— *On Our Backs: Sexual Attitudes in a Changing Ireland* (London, 1979).
Thompson, E.P., *The Making of the English Working Class* (London, 1963).
Thornley, U., *Unquiet Spirit: Essays in Memory of David Thornley* (Dublin, 2008).
Tiernan, J., *The Dublin and Monaghan Bombings* (Dublin, 2004).
Tierney M. and MacCurtain, M., *The Birth of Modern Ireland* (Dublin, 1969).
Tobin, F., *The Best of Decades: Ireland in the 1960s* (Dublin, 1984).
Tóibín, C., *Walking along the Border* (London, 1987).
— 'New ways of killing your father', *London Review of Books*, 18 Nov. 1993.
Townshend, C. (Ed.) *Consensus in Ireland: Approaches and Recessions* (Oxford, 1988).
Travers, S. and Fetherstone, N., *The Miami Showband Massacre: A Survivor's Search for Truth* (Frontline Noir, 2017).
Uris, L. and Uris, J., *Ireland: A Terrible Beauty: The Story of Ireland Today* (New York, 1975).
Urwin, M., *A State in Denial: British Collaboration with Loyalist Paramilitaries* (Cork, 2016).
Vaughan, W.E. and Fitzpatrick, A.J., *Irish Historical Statistics: Population, 1821–1971* (Dublin, 1978).
Viney, M., *The Five Percent: A Survey of Protestants in the Irish Republic* (Dublin, 1966).
Walsh, J., *Patrick Hillery: The Official Biography* (Dublin, 2008).
Walsh, L., *The Final Beat: Gardaí Killed in the Line of Duty* (Dublin, 2001).
Walshe, E., *Cissie's Abattoir* (Cork, 2009).
Waters, J., *Jiving at the Crossroads* (Belfast, 1991).
Whelan, D., *Who Stole Our Game? The Fall and Fall of Irish Soccer* (Dublin, 2006).
Whitaker, A. (Ed.) *Bright, Brilliant Days, Douglas Gageby and the Irish Times* (Dublin, 2006).
White, J., *Minority Report: The Protestants in the Republic of Ireland* (Dublin, 1975).
White, J.T., *Irish Devils: The Official Story of Manchester United and the Irish* (London, 2012).
White, R.W., *Ruairí Ó Brádaigh: The Life and Politics of an Irish Revolutionary* (Indiana, 2006).
— *Out of the Ashes: An Oral History of the Provisional Irish Republican Movement* (Dublin, 2017).
Williamson, D.C., *Anglo-Irish Relations in the Early Troubles: 1969–1972* (London, 2016).
Woods, P., 'Rumours from Monaghan: a radio documentary', *The Irish Review* (Spring, 2008).

Official reports

Dáil Debates

Houses of the Oireachtas, *Interim Report on the Report of the Independent Commission of Inquiry into the Dublin and Monaaghan Bombings* (Dublin, 2003).
Houses of the Oireachtas, *Interim Report on the Report of the Independent Commission of Inquiry into the Dublin Bombings of 1972 and 1973* (Dublin, 2004).
Houses of the Oireachtas, *Interim Report on the Report of the Independent Commission of Inquiry into the Bombing of Kay's Tavern, Dundalk* (Dublin, 2006).
Irish Congress of Trade Unions, *Annual Reports* (Dublin, 1969–79).

Visual and audio sources

Battle Station (RTE, 2011).
A Bloody Friday: the Dublin/Monaghan Bombings (TV3, 2010).
Bombings: Miami Showband (RTE, 2011).
Seven Ages (RTE, 2001).
Ireland: a Television History (BBC, 1980).
Cooke Street (RTE, 1977).
RTE Radio 1: 'We Couldn't Understand the Peace' (2016).
RTE Radio 1: Rumours from Monaghan RTE (2008).
Green-and-blue.org.

Theses and unpublished papers

Finn, D., *'Challengers to Provisional Republicanism: The Official Republican Movement, People's Democracy and the Irish Republican Socialist Party, 1968–1998'* (Phd: UCC, 2013).
Long, O., *'The Land that Made them Refugees: North-South Population Movements at the Outset of the Political Troubles, 1969–72'* (MA: UCC, 2008).
Madden, G., *'Political Change in Northern Ireland and its Impact on the West of Ireland, 1968–1982'* (MA: NUI Galway, 2013).
McGuill, P., *'Political Violence in the Republic of Ireland 1969–1997'* (MA, UCD, 1998).
Mulroe, P., *The Gardai, Violence and the Border: Irish Border Security policy 1969–1978* (PhD: UU, 2015).
Ní Bheachain, C., *'A Brief Examination/Analysis of the Intellectual Response to the Dublin-Monaghan Bombings of 1974'* (Unpublished, N/D) Sean O'Mahony Papers, NLI.

Index

EU authorised representative for GPSR:
Easy Access System Europe, Mustamäe tee 50,
10621 Tallinn, Estonia
gpsr.requests@easproject.com

www.ingramcontent.com/pod-product-compliance
Lightning Source LLC
Chambersburg PA
CBHW071849270326
41929CB00013B/2155